Date Due

D1165964

NATIONAL WOMEN'S HISTORY PROJECT
7738 Bell Road
Windsor, CA 95492

The Power of Femininity in the New South

The Power of Femininity in the New South

Women's Organizations and Politics in North Carolina, 1880–1930

Anastatia Sims

UNIVERSITY OF SOUTH CAROLINA PRESS

Published in Columbia, South Carolina, by the
University of South Carolina Press

Manufactured in the United States of America

01 00 99 98 97   5 4 3 2 1

Library of Congress Cataloging-in-Publication Data

An earlier version of chapter 2 and portions of chapter 1 appeared as "'The
Sword of the Spirit: The WCTU and Moral Reform in North Carolina, 1883–
1933" in *North Carolina Historical Review* 64 (October 1987): 394–415.

Sims, Anastatia
    The power of femininity in the new south : women's organizations
and politics in North Carolina, 1880–1930 / Anastatia Sims.
        p.   cm.
    Includes bibliographical references and index.
    ISBN 1–57003–178–9 (cloth)
    1. Women—North Carolina—Societies and clubs—History. 2. Women
in politics—North Carolina—History. 3. Women social reformers—
North Carolina—History. I. Title
HQ1905.N8S56 1997
305.4'06'0756—DC21   97–4862

For my family

Contents

Illustrations

Acknowledgments

The seeds for this book were sown at the family dinner table when I was a child. The dinner hour was sacrosanct at our house. My parents insisted that the family eat together, even though that meant they had to mop up gallons of spilled milk and mediate countless childish and adolescent squabbles among my brothers and me. Television and radio were banned at mealtime, so we talked. Our discussions covered a range of subjects, but one of the most frequent topics was history. My parents recalled their experiences as children during the Great Depression and as young adults during World War II. They also passed along to us the stories they had heard when they were growing up, many of which had to do with the experiences of white southerners before, during, and after the Civil War. In our household, both World War II and the Civil War were referred to simply as "the war"; only the context of a particular conversation clarified which war was being discussed at the time. I owe my fascination with history and my awareness of the ways in which the past shapes the present and influences all of our lives to those hours at the dinner table with my family.

My upbringing led directly to my interest in southern women's history. My mother constantly admonished me to "act like a lady" and made clear to me that while all ladies were women, not all women were ladies. I grew up thinking of the lady as a model of graciousness, gentility, benevolence, and fortitude. Only later did I begin to recognize the negative connotations the image also carried. My attempt to understand the ideal in all its complexity and to examine its lasting impact on southern women sparked the research that led to this book.

Like many manuscripts, this one has evolved over time. I received a great deal of help and support every step of the way. I was fortunate to work with an exceptional faculty at the University of North Carolina at Chapel Hill. Peter Filene, George Brown Tindall, and Joel Williamson provided excellent guidance as the work passed through its earlier incarnations. I am particularly indebted to Donald G. Mathews and to Jacquelyn Dowd Hall. Don encouraged me at a crucial time in my graduate career.

Jacquelyn helped me find my voice as a historian and by example taught me never to settle for less than my best. Both of them have read the manuscript in all of its versions and have offered invaluable criticism and suggestions at every stage.

The Triangle area of North Carolina—Raleigh, Durham, and Chapel Hill—boasts an array of sources for southern historians and is home to an exceptional group of librarians and archivists. Past and present staff members in the Special Collections Library of Duke University and the North Carolina Division of Archives and History have been unfailingly courteous, helpful, and efficient. In Chapel Hill, the Southern Historical Collection continues to be a wonderful place to work. I wish to thank Susan Ballinger, Brenda Eagles, Richard Shrader, and John White for all of the assistance they have given me. The North Carolina Collection has at times seemed like my home away from home, and I am very grateful to its staff—especially Bob Anthony, Alice Cotten, Jerry Cotten, Jeff Hicks, and Harry McKown—for their help and for their friendship.

It has been a pleasure to work with editors Warren Slesinger and Joyce Harrison at the University of South Carolina Press. I am especially grateful to Warren, whose faith in this project never wavered. I also wish to thank copy editor Jean Ross for the skill and sensitivity she applied to the manuscript.

There are two things that are always in short supply for any scholar. One is money; the other is time. I was fortunate to receive both when I needed them. An Archie K. Davis fellowship from the North Caroliniana Society and a faculty research grant from the Georgia Southern Foundation subsidized research trips to Chapel Hill. At a critical juncture I had the opportunity to leave survey classes and faculty committees behind and move into a different environment that enabled me to do research and to think. In 1990–91 I received a Rockefeller Humanist-in-Residence fellowship from the Duke Unviersity— University of North Carolina Center for Research on Women. Christina Greene, the Center's director, made that year pleasant as well as productive.

At the Center I benefited from the labors of a superb research assistant, Alisa Johnson, who enthusiastically embraced this project even though it was out of her primary research area. Since returning to Statesboro I have also received assistance from Jennifer Darby, Lisa Fore, Rwanda Gates, Rod Lee, and Wanda Scott.

I have been blessed with a number of friends and colleagues who have contributed in various ways to the completion of this book. Anne Bailey, Judi Downs, Don Doyle, Meg Geddy, Peggy Hargis, Walter Jackson, Jeanette Keith, Carolyn Malone, Dale Martin, Don Miller, Anne Swenson, and Ruth Thompson have never read a line of it, but they have generously given their good humor and moral support. Anne Firor Scott shared her manuscript on voluntary associations with me before its publication; she has always encouraged me in my work. Glenda Elizabeth Gilmore offered advice on locating sources on African American women. Mary Jo Klingeman, who introduced me to primary sources when I was in high school, has been both teacher and friend. Dianne and Jim Leloudis have been gracious hosts on numerous occasions, and I have frequently tapped Jim's vast knowledge of North Carolina and the New South. Louise Vrande and Cheryl Walker opened their home to me during a research trip to Boston. Jay Fraser, former chair of the history department at Georgia Southern University, not only introduced me to Warren Slesinger at the University of South Carolina Press but also pushed me along by asking repeatedly, "When are you going to get that book done?" Students in my Women and Public Policy class at Vanderbilt University helped me frame the questions that guided subsequent research. Colleagues in the history departments of Virginia Tech and Georgia Southern made helpful suggestions in departmental colloquia and also demonstrated the good sense to know when I wanted to talk about the book and when I didn't.

Gaines Foster, Harold Livesay, and Peter Wallenstein gave thorough critiques of an early version of this manuscript that helped me to identify its strengths and its weaknesses. In addition, Gaines read the penultimate draft of chapter 2, and Harold read the entire manuscript as it neared completion. Alan Downs, Jay Fraser, Charlton Moseley, George Shriver, and Elizabeth Hayes Turner each read portions of the manuscript and offered trenchant criticism. Marcia Synnott and Marjorie Spruill Wheeler provided thoughtful, careful readings of the almost completed manuscript and suggested revisions that substantially strengthened the final version. Marjorie has always been enthusiastic about this project; I am grateful for her generosity in sharing her expertise on southern women's history and for her friendship.

Lu Ann Jones and Mary Murphy have read everything I've ever written and have been instrumental in helping me shape my ideas. Our conversations began in graduate school and have continued ever since by telephone, letter, and e-mail. (Indeed, at this juncture I should probably also thank AT&T, MCI, the United States Postal Service, and the Internet.) Lu and Mary have served as cheerleaders, counselors, and critics. Each of them has been generous with her time, her knowledge of history, her editorial skills, and her excellent sense of humor. They have known when to encourage, when to console, and when to admonish. In short, Lu and Mary have been true friends.

I complete this book with considerable relief but also with great sadness, for several of the people who were anxious to hold it in their hands did not live to see its completion. My aunts—Margaret Hodgens, Bobbie Sims Leduc, Nolan Meroney, and Quintilla Meroney Sullivan—and my uncles—Charles Thornton Meroney and Walter Lee Sims—were not familiar with the book's topic but believed that if I wrote about it, it must be important. I miss them, but their influence on my life endures.

Those family dinners that were such significant rituals in my youth are rare these days. Like many other families, ours has scattered and expanded. My brothers, Jim and John, live on the West Coast with their families: my sister-in-law Lynne, my nieces Cory Shay and DeShana, and my nephew Revel. My parents, Mamie Meroney Sims and James M. Sims Sr., remain in San Antonio. I hope that soon we will arrange to be in the same place at the same time and that once again we will sit down to enjoy a good meal and good conversation. And this time, I promise, I won't spill my milk.

Middleground, Georgia
August 14, 1996

*The Power of Femininity
in the New South*

Introduction

Women's history is about relationships. This book is about the relationship of women to a complex, and sometimes contradictory, feminine ideal; the relationship between racial and gender ideologies in the New South; and women's changing relationship to government and politics.

The setting is North Carolina, a state that many people regarded as a shining star in the New South constellation: a leader in economic development, a model of southern Progressivism. The protagonists were members of voluntary associations. Women's organizations proliferated between 1880 and 1930. Groups such as the Woman's Christian Temperance Union, the Colonial Dames, the Daughters of the American Revolution and its lesser known counterpart the Daughters of the Revolution, the United Daughters of the Confederacy, the King's Daughters, the Equal Suffrage Association and its successor the League of Women Voters, and the two state federations of women's clubs—one for whites, the other for African Americans—opened the gates to public life for thousands of North Carolina women. Women who joined voluntary associations proudly described themselves as trailblazers, exploring new frontiers for women and articulating altered definitions of woman's place. Simultaneously, as they frequently reminded skeptical men who worried about where these changes in women's behavior might lead, they cherished the southern lady as the most sacred ideal of womanhood.

The lady cast a powerful and enduring image in southern culture. Men extolled her many virtues; women tried to practice those virtues in their own lives. She exemplified the attributes nineteenth-century Americans found most desirable in "true women": she was modest, pious, nurturing, self-sacrificing, gentle, gracious, kind, loyal, and extraordinarily tolerant of masculine shortcomings. Her physical frailty belied her moral fortitude. She also proved to be remarkably resilient. Born in the years before the Civil War, she survived well into the twentieth century.[1]

She endured because she changed with the times. Southerners, especially women, reinterpreted and updated the ideal, emphasizing different aspects of her character to suit different circumstances. In the late nineteenth and early twentieth centuries, white southern women revised the lady's image. Drawing on their foremothers' experiences during the Civil War and Reconstruction, they demonstrated that the lady could be brave, resourceful, and quick-witted. White southerners, male and female alike, delighted in tales of Confederate women who outsmarted Yankee soldiers during the war or who resisted Republican rule afterward. These stories highlighted a different dimension of the feminine ideal. In addition to being sweet, gentle, and selfless, the lady was also resolute, self-reliant, and, on occasion, outspoken. Reconciling these apparently contradictory characteristics might have posed an insurmountable challenge, but one of the lady's hallmarks was her instinct for doing the right thing at the right time. A woman who defied masculine authority imposed from *outside* the South merited praise; a woman who rebelled against white male hegemony *within* the South fell from grace and emerged a pariah.

The lady was more than a role model for southern women; she also served as a potent political symbol. At the turn of the century, white supremacists invoked her name to justify segregation, disfranchisement, and lynching. "Protection of white womanhood" became a rallying cry for whites seeking to eliminate African American men from politics. They argued that emancipation and political power had unleashed in black men an uncontrollable lust for white women. Sexual assault was rampant, they claimed, and white southern women—ladies all in this scenario—must be protected. Their solution to the alleged epidemic of rape was to take the ballot away from black men. Anointing themselves the gallant guardians of the lady's purity, white supremacists ruthlessly relegated African Americans to second-class citizenship.[2]

White supremacist thought intertwined race and gender, sexuality and politics. Nowhere was this more evident than in North Carolina in 1898 and 1900. During fiercely fought election campaigns, white Democrats seeking to oust Republican and Populist officeholders exploited racist fears of black violence and sexuality in order to destroy the political alliance between African Americans and poor whites. The rhetoric that bound race and gender together profoundly influenced political discourse in years to come and had a lasting impact on relations between whites and African Americans and between men and women.[3]

While white supremacists used the lady to uphold the Jim Crow system, African American women employed the image to subvert it. Black women activists engaged in what Evelyn Brooks Higginbotham has described as "the politics of respectability." They conformed to the highest standards of ladylike behavior and fought to overcome racist stereotypes that portrayed black women as immoral. They struggled to demonstrate to whites that African American women were just as virtuous, just as nurturing, just as genteel as white women—and that they too deserved respect and protection from insult and assault. When African American women demanded recognition as southern ladies, they struck a blow for racial equality and lashed out against the ideological foundations of white supremacy.[4]

In the late nineteenth and early twentieth centuries, white and African American women shared a desire to expand their influence in their communities and in their state. Denied the right to vote or hold office, they found their voice in voluntary associations. Organized women, as they called themselves, developed agendas for reform and strategies to improve the quality of life for themselves, their families, and their neighbors. They described their public projects as extensions of their domestic responsibilities and called themselves "public housekeepers."

Public housekeeping encompassed a wide range of activities. African American and white women crusaded for prohibition and against sexual misconduct to protect their families from vice. They established public libraries, sponsored art exhibits, and staged concerts and plays to promote "Culture." They built monuments and presented historical pageants to instill patriotism. They extended women's traditional responsibility for childrearing and early childhood education from the home to the school, lobbying for better school buildings, curriculum reform, longer school terms, compulsory education laws, and higher salaries for teachers. They expanded their concern for health and cleanliness into their communities, sponsoring cleanup and beautification campaigns and pressuring city officials to institute regular trash collection, pass sanitation ordinances, and enact pure food laws. When government could not or would not act, they filled needs themselves, establishing parks and playgrounds, hiring public health nurses, and raising money to build reformatories for juvenile offenders. They collected food, money, and clothing for the poor, as women had done for generations. At the same time, however, they pleaded with state and local governments to increase their services to the indigent.

When North Carolina women translated private domesticity into public housekeeping they contributed to a redefinition of the proper role of government. In part because of their efforts, state and local governments expanded their responsibility for the welfare of their citizens. Responding to the demands of organized women and their male allies, city councils, county commissions, and the state legislature initiated new programs to benefit children, the elderly, and the poor; increased appropriations for education; enacted legislation to protect public health; and revamped the prison system to emphasize rehabilitation. Using the power of indirect influence, organized women accomplished a great deal years before they got the vote. Key players in Progressive reform, they helped North Carolina earn its reputation as the most Progressive state in the New South.

The Power of Femininity in the New South has a dual meaning and a dual focus. First it refers to the persistence of the traditional feminine ideal in the face of significant changes in the realities of women's lives. Organized women in North Carolina created new roles for themselves, but they remained loyal to the image of the southern lady. *The Power of Femininity* speaks to the tenacious hold the lady and the code of feminine behavior she represented had on southern minds. It also refers to the power *in* the ideal, the power of indirect influence and moral authority vested in the southern lady. In its second focus, *The Power of Femininity in the New South* describes the ways in which North Carolina women in voluntary associations worked within accepted gender conventions to shape public policy and bring about social reform.

Discussions of women's efforts to expand feminine power lead almost inevitably to the question, Were they feminists? That question drove much of the early research in women's history and still has relevance to analyses of women and politics; however, historians disagree about the characteristics and beliefs that define a feminist. Thus for North Carolina's organized women in the late nineteenth and early twentieth centuries, the answer can be either yes or no, depending on which definition of feminism one accepts. They displayed many of the characteristics of the women that some scholars call "social feminists" and others describe as "maternalist." Organized women themselves rejected the feminist label. Committed to an ethos of service, they sought to expand their own rights in order to enhance their ability to help others. They wanted a voice in politics because they advocated political solutions to social problems. White women saw themselves as the heirs of a feminine tradition of caring for the weak and the less fortunate. African American women recognized that any progress they made contributed to the advancement of their race.[5]

North Carolina's organized women resembled "difference feminists" of the late twentieth century in some respects. They celebrated the traits that distinguished women from men, and they basked in the popular adage that woman was "man's superior, not his equal." They believed that women possessed unique talents and skills that could be put to good use in the public interest, and they urged men to give them the opportunity to apply their expertise to public policy. Their belief in profound gender differences was at the heart of the power of femininity.

Organized women's reliance on the ideology of difference reaped mixed results. Sometimes it served them well. Their insistence that they were merely carrying out traditional feminine obligations and their adherence to standards of ladylike decorum made powerful men more receptive to their message. After all, men too abided by gender conventions and a code of chivalry that required gentlemen to treat ladies with respect. Women understood that a polite request from a soft-spoken southern lady was more effective than a strident demand from a virago. They won authority in "feminine" areas of public policy such as education and social welfare, and many of the men who were concerned with these issues came to regard organized women as partners in reform.

Nevertheless, their emphasis on gender difference and a unique feminine perspective also imposed limitations. Because organized women established a gendered division of labor in the public arena, some areas remained out of bounds for women. Moreover, indirect influence and moral suasion proved to be unreliable leverage in politics. When the time came to make law and policy, the courtly politicians who pledged to grant every feminine wish and whim paid more attention to the conventional tools of political power—money and votes—than to the decorous entreaties of disfranchised ladies. Although women persuaded legislators to enact many of the items on their agenda, the power of femininity was no match for entrenched economic and political forces such as the textile and tobacco industries and the Democratic Party machine. Over time, more and more women decided that they needed to supplement indirect influence with the more tangible power of the ballot.

This book tells the story of North Carolina's organized women, a story of reformers acting through a variety of organizations to realize their vision of a better society. It describes the causes they adopted, the successes they achieved, the failures they suffered, the compromises they made.

It also tells the story of women coming to terms with an image of feminine nature and an ideal of feminine behavior—exploring its possibilities, discovering its limitations, and ultimately transforming it by their own actions. In voluntary associations North Carolina women created a nondomestic role based on domesticity, gained power for themselves without directly challenging men's authority, and ushered the lady into the New South.

I

"The Foundation for a Sisterhood"
Origins of Women's Activism

The lady was the most sacred cultural icon of the antebellum South. She represented the best of southern civilization, and her goodness offset its imperfections. She was gracious and gentle in a society founded on the premise that one race could hold another in bondage. She was pure in a region where miscegenation and illegitimacy were widespread. She was genteel and pious in a culture that condoned violence, heavy drinking, and gambling. White southern men revered her, although they praised most in her the virtues they themselves practiced least.[1]

More than a symbol, the lady set the standard of behavior for generations of white southern women. Throughout the nineteenth century, daughters of the white South learned that they were expected to couple moral strength with physical frailty, intuition with irrationality, piety with impracticality. Weakness and dependence, liabilities in men, were in women the source of an "irresistible power," the power to conquer masculine strength and intellect with feminine charm.[2]

While all white southern girls might aspire to be ladies, before the Civil War only those of the upper class could achieve that status. Poor and middling white women might act like ladies and share common traits of womanhood with their elite counterparts, but they could not be recognized as ladies. And white minds consigned African American women to another world entirely. The image of the black woman was the opposite of the southern feminine ideal. Whites praised ladies for their purity but assumed that black women were lustful and licentious. Whites extolled the sacred love that bound a mother to her offspring, and entrusted their young to black mammies, but denied that African American women had any maternal feelings, and separated slave mothers from their children with few apparent qualms. Whites declared that women were delicate and fragile, but they assigned slave women to the fields or to heavy household labor. Definitions of femininity might in some instances transcend class, but they never transcended race.[3]

Antebellum preachers, educators, and authors ignored the true circumstances of slave women's lives—and the lives of many free women of

both races—and declared that domesticity was the only proper vocation
for women because "feminine nature" left them ill equipped to survive on
their own. Incapable of coping with the practical affairs of daily life, women
must pledge obedience to men in exchange for sustenance and protection. Economic reality reinforced this particular tenet of femininity. There
were few jobs for free women in the antebellum South, a situation that
sometimes drew protest from women who had to support themselves. In
1851 "A Sewing Girl" wrote to a North Carolina newspaper complaining
of low wages and pleading for wider employment opportunities. Seam-
stresses, she concluded, earned only misery as they plied their trade

> In poverty, hunger and dirt
> Sewing at once with a double thread
> A *shroud* as well as a shirt.[4]

To avoid this fate, most white girls made marriage their goal. When a
woman married, she not only risked her heart and her happiness; she
gambled on her future economic status as well. The choice of a husband
was the most momentous decision a woman would make. Courtship was
serious business, one made more complicated by the fact that some men
thought of it as a sport. One young man warned his sister, "Flirtation is
not courtship. All men are villains." He advised her to approach romance
like a military campaign: "Keep very shady as to your own feelings. Always
try to draw the enemy out first. Mention casually that your grown up
brothers are all crack shots, and *single* men." Parents kept a watchful eye
over prospective suitors and tried to protect their daughters from undesir-
able matches.[5]

Marriage could guarantee a woman financial security, or it could reduce her to poverty. A single woman's property rights began to erode when
she became engaged. North Carolina courts ruled that a bride-to-be who
conveyed property without her fiancé's knowledge defrauded him. After
marriage, the husband's dominance was absolute. A married woman could
not sue or be sued, and, under common law, all the property she brought
to the marriage, except for her clothing, belonged to her spouse. Any income that she or her property might earn also fell under her husband's
control. Equity law permitted the creation of a "separate estate" for a
married woman. While that legal maneuver gave her some economic security independent of her husband's fortunes or misfortunes, it still did
not give her full rights over her own property.[6]

The antebellum South was a white man's world in which elite white
women occupied a paradoxical position. Law and custom denied them the
rights and liberties that their menfolk enjoyed. Nevertheless, ladies were

persons of privilege in the region's racial and class hierarchy. They could not go to college, but at a time when nearly 17 percent of North Carolina's adult white women could neither read nor write, most did attend female academies. They could not vote or hold office, but many of them knew or were related to influential politicians and thus had indirect access to government and policy making. Ladies could not practice medicine or law, but they never worked in the fields, as many African American women and white women of nonslaveholding families did. They bore the burdens of running large households, but they supervised slaves who did most of the cooking, cleaning, canning, sewing, and other chores. Ladies had authority over slaves and, because of their family connections, influence over lower-class whites as well. White yeomen, with political and economic independence, deferred to ladies because of their social status. Bound by the legal and economic restrictions that governed all women and by a rigid code of feminine conduct, ladies were nevertheless part of the ruling elite and had more power than other women and some men. They were at one and the same time powerful and powerless.[7]

Codes of law and codes of conduct regulated women's behavior. Social position and legal status (slave or free; single or married) determined their autonomy and power. One other force cut across racial and class boundaries to shape southern women's lives: religion. Evangelical churches dominated North Carolina and the rest of the South, and their expectations and teachings had a profound impact on women. Preachers held women to a higher standard than men and praised them for piety, humility, and service to others. Religion reinforced popular assumptions about women's physical weakness and instructed women to obey their husbands and fathers.[8]

Clergymen might demand more of women than of men, but they also thought that women were capable of giving more because, they believed, women by nature more closely approximated the Christian ideal. Obituaries of real women as well as prescriptive articles in religious journals described women who met pain, suffering, and betrayal with forbearance, love, and forgiveness, just as Christ had done. Intermingled with calls to sacrifice and subordination in evangelical teachings, then, were reminders of feminine strength and spiritual superiority. Emotion and intuition overshadowed rationality, logic, and intellect in the dominant evangelical religion of the South, and emotion and intuition were defined as inherently feminine characteristics. If such traits had little worth in the temporal world of the cotton and tobacco merchants, they were highly valued in the spiritual realm of the ministers, who were creating a value system that offered women earthly esteem as well as eternal salvation. It is not surprising that during the nineteenth century women came to outnumber men as church members.[9]

In church, antebellum North Carolina women encountered a world beyond family and neighborhood. Particularly in rural communities, the church was an important gathering place, where women met and got to know each other and where, in mission programs, they learned about women whose lives were very different from their own. Churches upheld traditional feminine roles and, at the same time, created new opportunities for women. North Carolina women first organized voluntary associations under church auspices. "Mite" or "cent" societies began appearing among white Baptist women in North Carolina as early as 1810; white women in other denominations soon followed the Baptist example. The societies distributed religious leaflets and raised money to support foreign missionaries. Local groups acted independently of each other, and all answered to male church leaders. White women also united to dispense charity at home. Guion Griffis Johnson, historian of antebellum North Carolina, found that, after 1810, "almost every village church in the State had a female benevolent society."[10]

Town women organized independent charitable groups. White women in New Bern incorporated a Female Charitable Society in 1812. In 1813 Fayetteville women received a charter for a female orphan asylum. The orphanage survived for a while but had folded by 1830, so the women tried again. They founded the Female Society of Industry, which sponsored a school for "the relief and education of distressed and indigent children." Women in Elizabeth City, Raleigh, Warrenton, and Wilmington supported similar institutions.[11]

White women also took a limited part in reform and politics. In the mid-1820s, women in Jamestown, Springfield, Kennet, Center, and New Salem formed auxiliaries to the North Carolina Manumission Society, an antislavery group that Quaker men had organized in 1816. Women attended the society's semiannual meetings as spectators, and men welcomed them. In 1826 the society recorded its approval of women's work for manumission as beneficial to the antislavery cause and to women themselves: "An enlarged participation in these works of *Justice, Benevolence,* and *humanity* . . . will enlarge the circle which custom has improperly prescribed to their *action* and *usefulness* and elivate [sic] them to the sphere in which nature intended them to move." The Manumission Society met for the last time in 1834; its demise marked the end of North Carolina women's organized involvement in the antislavery movement.[12]

Some North Carolina men also encouraged women to join in the temperance crusade. In 1842 the North Carolina Temperance Union suggested that women could help the cause by attending temperance meetings, refusing to serve liquor in their homes, and spurning the company of men who drank. Six years later, North Carolina women formed a state branch of the Daughters of Temperance, auxiliary to the Sons of Temperance. By

1852 the organization had twenty-nine chapters. Members pledged to refrain from consumption of alcohol and to spread the temperance message. The association also functioned as a mutual aid society, maintaining a fund to assist the ill and needy among its members and contribute to funeral costs of "sisters" who died.[13]

Some North Carolina women attended political rallies during the 1840 presidential campaign, and in 1844 Whig women in Raleigh openly demonstrated their support for Henry Clay.[14] Tar Heel women also participated in the first national women's patriotic society. In December 1853 "A Southern Matron" appealed to the "Ladies of the South" to raise money for the purchase and restoration of George Washington's home, Mount Vernon. The Southern Matron was, in fact, Ann Pamela Cunningham, a thirty-seven-year-old spinster from Laurens County, South Carolina. The *Charleston Mercury* published her letter, and other southern newspapers reprinted it. Early in 1854 women began organizing to save Mount Vernon.

Although Cunningham originally intended it to be an exclusively southern effort, northern newspapers publicized the movement, and northern women requested that it be expanded to include women of all regions. By 1859 the Mount Vernon Ladies Association of the Union had chapters in thirty states and the District of Columbia. Under Cunningham's leadership, the Association raised the two hundred thousand dollars necessary to purchase the estate from the Washington family and took possession in the summer of 1860. Having "rescued" Mount Vernon, the women then campaigned for funds to restore and maintain it.[15]

The Mount Vernon Ladies Association differed from most women's organizations in antebellum America. Its members did not help the poor, spread the gospel, or espouse social reform. Instead they envisioned a distinct political role for women. Unlike feminists, who thought that women should share equally with men the responsibilities and privileges of citizenship, Ann Pamela Cunningham and her colleagues believed that women performed a special function, different from men's but of equal or greater importance. Women must set standards for political behavior, just as they set standards for moral behavior. Men, bogged down in the mire of day-to-day political intrigue, might lose sight of the high ideals that should guide political discourse. Women, aloof from electioneering and lawmaking, could remind adult males of the principles that should govern their actions. At the same time, women could instill these values in their sons, the leaders of the future. American women "should never forget," wrote the vice president of the Illinois chapter of the Mount Vernon Ladies Association in 1859, "that they are, and are to become, the mothers and educators of our rulers and statesmen." They had, she continued, "a special, a peculiar, and an undeniable mission." The success or failure of "the great experi-

ment of the Republic" depended on women's success or failure as preceptors of democracy and virtue.[16]

In the tense political atmosphere of the 1850s, the future of "the
great experiment of the Republic" seemed precarious. No wonder, then,
that women seeking to fulfill their obligation to their country seized on
Mount Vernon as a potent symbol of American ideals. Women in both
North and South hoped that by restoring Washington's home they could
restore a national political consensus based on the principles of the Founding Fathers. Although Mount Vernon failed to become the unifying symbol they sought, the women established an important precedent: they
denied that politics was an exclusively male domain, and they held that
women played an essential, if indirect, part in politics and government.
Their assumption that it was the special mission of their sex to preserve
and interpret the national heritage would serve as the foundation for the
hereditary and patriotic societies to be formed in the 1890s.[17]

Although the work of the Mount Vernon Ladies Association was out
of the ordinary for antebellum women, the group approached its task in a
ladylike manner. Its members adhered to the most rigid standards of feminine decorum. They shunned publicity and relied on men to make public
appeals in behalf of their cause. During the Association's early years,
Cunningham was careful to maintain her anonymity. When, in 1861, her
name was published in connection with the work, she was so appalled
that, as she later recalled, "I felt as if I should faint." The ladies of the
North Carolina branch were particularly successful in avoiding publicity.
Although they raised several thousand dollars, their contemporaries knew
little of their activities. In February 1860 the organization's national newspaper reported: "We have before remarked on the efforts made in the
commencement of the enterprise, to combine the work of collecting for
the Mount Vernon fund with strict privacy; in no state was this as marked
or as successful as in North Carolina. Less publicity was given to the
work, and less was known at the time of what was really going on, than in
any other state."[18]

Perhaps North Carolina women's discretion grew out of their awareness of widespread hostility toward women who openly defied convention. Feminism, an offspring of the abolition movement, was as unpopular
in North Carolina as it was in the rest of the South. Responding to a
women's rights convention in Massachusetts in 1850, the *North Carolina
Standard* ridiculed northern feminists for demanding the right to "be men."
Eight years later the *Oxford Leisure Hour* called the feminist movement
"the most ridiculous escapade of this century." Although women might
recognize that they had an equal stake in politics and government, most
men wanted women to stay out of public debates.[19]

Still, North Carolina's women, like the state's men, could not ignore the political turmoil of the 1850s. Most North Carolinians remained loyal to the United States even as, one by one, other southern states followed South Carolina out of the Union in the winter of 1861. They grieved over the outbreak of war in April and reluctantly seceded on May 20; North Carolina was the last state to join the Confederacy. In the next four years North Carolinians were to shoulder more than their share of the burden in a war that few had wanted. Nearly all of the state's white males of military age—approximately 125,000—served in the Confederate army, and more than 40,000 of them died. North Carolina lost more men than any other Confederate state.[20]

When the government called men to arms, women were left to fend for themselves and their children. Despite the *North Carolina Standard's* admonition a decade earlier, during the war white southern women were expected to "be men." Planters' wives managed plantations and attempted to control a restive slave population. Women of nonslaveholding families did men's chores as well as their own and prayed that they would survive the hard work and scant rations. The absence of men, combined with the Confederate government's ever increasing demands for food, money, and supplies, left thousands of North Carolina families destitute.[21]

At the beginning of the war, white women rallied to the Confederate cause. Wilmington women, for example, formed a Soldiers' Aid Society in May 1861. Similar groups throughout the state raised money, rolled bandages, and sewed for the troops. When federal forces invaded, African American women in New Bern organized a society to assist black soldiers in the Union army.[22]

African American women could look forward to the promise of freedom, but for many white women the war brought only suffering and grief. The fighting dragged on, conditions worsened at home, and state and national governments ignored pleas for relief. So some women took matters into their own hands. In March 1863 a group of women in Salisbury called on local merchants, demanding flour at a fair price. They threatened to take it by force if the shopkeepers refused to cooperate, and the store owners capitulated. High Point women staged a similar demonstration that same year. In 1864 and 1865 women in Yadkin and Yancey counties seized corn from government warehouses.[23]

The women who led the food riots most likely came from nonslaveholding families, who had the least to gain from a war for slavery and states' rights. If it was "a rich man's war and a poor man's fight," it was a poor woman's fight as well. Women struggled to keep body and soul together, staving off attacks from Yankee invaders and from an insatiable Confederate government that robbed their hearts of the men they loved

and their stomachs of the food they needed. As the war continued, shortages of food, clothing, and other necessities affected the lives of almost all
white southern women, regardless of class. Many became disillusioned
with the Confederate cause. Still they struggled, and they survived.[24]

The icon of the lady survived too. Postwar novelists lamenting the
demise of the Old South used her to symbolize a beneficent plantation
economy and a benign system of slavery in which the planter and his
mistress served as kindly parents to their childlike slaves. However, the
wartime experiences of real women added a new dimension to the southern feminine ideal. During the war, many white southern women demonstrated courage and strength that went beyond the lady's fabled moral and
spiritual superiority. They proved that they were neither weak nor irratio-
nal, and they learned that they were capable, resilient, and self-reliant.
But war is a harsh teacher, and white southern women no doubt would
have preferred to discover their strengths under more favorable circumstances. In the years immediately following the war, most refused to explore the implications of the war's lessons about feminine intelligence,
ingenuity, and fortitude. The lessons were there nonetheless. After the
war, white southerners increasingly portrayed the lady as brave and resourceful as well as kind, gracious, pious, and gentle.[25]

In the aftermath of war, the image also lost some of its class connotations. So many of the South's elite found themselves in financial straits
that wealth was no longer an accurate measure of social status. Moreover,
racist ideologues warned that the end of slavery left all white women equally
vulnerable to attacks by African American men. In the post–Civil War
South, white southerners came to acknowledge that middle-class white
women, and even some poor white women, might be ladies—if they behaved as ladies should.

And most white southern women did. White southern men lost on
the battlefield, then lost their political power at home. White women rallied to soothe the physical and psychological wounds of defeat. They honored the veterans and glorified the dead. North Carolina women, like
women throughout the South, began organizing memorial associations
soon after the war's end. On May 23, 1866, Raleigh women formed a
society to establish a Confederate cemetery and care for the graves. "We
may be poor," the women wrote in the preamble to their constitution, "but
enough is left to prove our hearts to be still rich in the treasures of grati-
tude and affection." Poverty hampered their efforts until businessman
Henry Mordecai donated land for a Confederate cemetery. The women
began locating the remains of Confederate soldiers in the Raleigh area
and planned to move them to new graves in the spring of 1867. They
accelerated their schedule after the federal government took over the Rock

Quarry Cemetery, where soldiers of both sides were buried. In February 1867, rumors circulated that Union troops were threatening to dig up Confederate remains and leave them in the road. The Ladies Memorial Association mobilized a brigade of male volunteers, who quickly removed the southern dead from Rock Quarry and interred them in the new grave-yard.[26]

Historians of memorial associations portrayed women's early efforts to honor the Confederate dead as courageous acts of civil disobedience in an occupied land. According to an account published in 1938, Raleigh women defied a federal order against observance of Confederate Memo-rial Day on May 10, 1867. Ignoring officers' threats to fire on memorial processions, women gathered in small groups and went to the Confeder-ate cemetery to place wreaths on soldiers' graves. Union troops stood by and watched. A founding member of the memorial association in Wilmington recalled that when the society was formed in July of 1866 "word was carried to Washington City that the rebel women of Wilmington were plotting treason." When government officials instructed the military commander to investigate, he allegedly replied, "The ladies of Wilmington are quietly at their homes doing nothing." Chronicles of postwar memo-rial associations implied that southern women succeeded where southern men had failed; even the victorious United States army surrendered to the power of femininity.[27]

The Ladies Memorial Associations commemorated Confederate Me-morial Day, cared for and marked the graves of Confederate dead, and cooperated with veterans in raising money for memorials to the heroes of the Lost Cause. In June 1870 the Raleigh group voted to bring the re-mains of more than a hundred North Carolina soldiers back from Gettysburg. Fifteen years later they did the same for North Carolinians buried in Arlington, Virginia. Women in Warren County bought a tomb-stone for the grave of Robert E. Lee's daughter; Anne Carter Lee had died there in 1862, a refugee from war-torn Virginia. Fayetteville women placed a monument in the old Cross Creek Cemetery in 1867; they claimed it was the first Confederate monument in North Carolina. Wilmington un-veiled its Confederate monument in 1872, and in 1875 local veterans asked women to cosponsor a "variety entertainment" to benefit the Robert E. Lee monument fund.[28]

When North Carolina men decided to build a Confederate monu-ment on the state capitol grounds more than twenty-five years after the war's end, they enlisted women to help. Samuel A. Ashe, Democratic poli-tician and editor of the *Raleigh News and Observer,* convened a meeting of women in the Supreme Court chambers in 1892 to organize the Ladies Monumental Association. Nancy Branch Jones was chosen president. The

General Assembly incorporated the association in 1893 and appropriated ten thousand dollars for the monument. Two years later the legislature granted an additional ten thousand dollars. On both occasions women of the monumental association were present, and men credited them with persuading lawmakers to support the project. In addition to securing state money for the memorial, the ladies raised five thousand dollars on their own. The monument was unveiled in May 1895.[29]

The Ladies Monumental Association (LMA) drew its members from North Carolina's white elite. Nancy Jones, for example, was married to Armistead Jones, attorney for Wake County and chairman of the Wake County Democratic Committee. Many of the other officers and board members of the Monumental Association were equally prominent. Mary Woodson Jarvis was the wife of former governor Thomas Jarvis. Susan Graham Clark was married to Supreme Court justice Walter Clark. Sallie Caldwell Kluttz's husband, Theodore, was a merchant, lawyer, and textile executive in Salisbury. Fanny deBerniere Hooper Whitaker was the wife of a former chairman of the state Democratic Committee. Fifty-six-year-old Elvira Evelyna Moffitt was the daughter of Jonathan Worth, who had served as governor of North Carolina from 1865 until 1868. Three years before she joined the Monumental Association she had been widowed for the third time. For Moffitt participation in the LMA marked the beginning of a long career in patriotic societies and women's clubs. No one would question the respectability or propriety of these southern ladies, and when they banded together to praise white southern men they won an exemption from the proscription on female participation in public life.

Indeed, southerners applied the taboo against public activity for women selectively. Even before the Civil War white southern men tolerated, and sometimes encouraged, white women's organized efforts in the interest of benevolence, reform, and patriotism. As long as women worked for others rather than themselves, they remained within the boundaries of proper feminine behavior. After the war some men, like Ashe, recognized the potential of harnessing women's energies and talents. Beginning in the 1870s and 1880s, leaders of the major Protestant denominations established state or regional auxiliaries for women.

The General Conference of the white Methodist Episcopal Church, South, created the Woman's Foreign Missionary Society in 1878 and the Woman's Home Missionary Society in 1886. The two merged in 1910, becoming the Woman's Missionary Society. White Baptist men were less enthusiastic about female associations than their Methodist counterparts. In 1877 the Foreign Mission Board of the Southern Baptist Convention appointed a Woman's Central Committee for Missions in North Carolina, but the state Baptist convention ordered it dissolved. It was reorganized in

Mary Jarvis
Wife of Governor Thomas Jarvis, Mary Jarvis led women's campaign for statewide prohibition in 1881 and served as president of the Ladies Monumental Association in the 1890s.

1886. In 1888 Southern Baptist women met in Richmond to form the Woman's Missionary Union, auxiliary to the Southern Baptist Convention. Again North Carolina Baptist leaders opposed it, and North Carolina Baptist women did not affiliate with it until 1891.[30]

White Episcopalians in the North Carolina diocese organized the Woman's Auxiliary to the Board of Missions in 1881 at the request of the bishop, the Right Reverend Theodore Lyman. The Auxiliary confined itself to foreign mission work, although some local societies undertook social service projects in their communities. The bishop appointed diocesan officers, and rectors of local churches appointed parish officers. White Presbyterian women formed local missionary and aid societies but waited until 1912 to establish the Woman's Synodical Auxiliary of the Presbyterian Synod of North Carolina.[31]

Women's religious associations labored to further the churches' mission programs both abroad and within the United States. Members collected money and supplies for foreign missions and studied the traditions, geography, and history of the countries where these outposts were located. In an era of American territorial and economic expansion, the drive to spread Christianity to Asia and Africa captured the imaginations of thousands of American women.[32]

Male leaders viewed women's work for home and foreign missions as part of a comprehensive church program. The women disagreed. From the beginning, women in missionary societies resisted a structure that gave men control of the money women raised. As women's groups grew, they initiated their own projects, directed toward women and children. The Woman's Missionary Council of the Methodist Episcopal Church, South, for example, funded women's hospitals, various kinds of schools for girls and women (ranging from high schools to a medical college), and coeducational orphanages and primary schools, but only one academy exclusively for boys. Churchwomen summed up their philosophy in the slogan "Woman's work for woman." They wanted to minister to members of their own sex, within the United States and overseas. They believed their mission was particularly important in non-Christian lands, where "pagan" practices degraded women. They thought that Christianity would improve the lives of women on earth at the same time it saved their souls for eternity.[33]

White women in church societies identified strongly with female missionaries. They corresponded with the wives of clergymen and teachers overseas and demanded that single women be allowed to serve in foreign fields. They recruited young women for missionary work and established colleges to train them for the Lord's service. They argued that American women in non-Christian countries could minister where men could not, for they alone could preach to native women who could then, in turn, spread the message to their families.[34]

At home, women of the South's white churches established schools and colleges for girls, boardinghouses for working women, settlement houses, and homes for unwed mothers and female criminals. They also attempted to spread the gospel in their own communities and impose Christian values. Members of local missionary societies raised money to build parsonages, distributed food and clothing to the poor, visited the sick, conducted religious services in jails, and circulated religious leaflets. State and regional organizations endorsed Sabbath observance and temperance and tried to eliminate the double standard of sexual morality. Home mission programs addressed local, regional, and national problems that directly affected the lives of white southern women. Yet home mission work was never as popular among white women as support for foreign missions. Many white southern churchwomen seemed eager to transform alien cultures but unwilling to confront the flaws in their own.[35]

African American churches also established missionary societies for women. In 1880 the General Conference of the African Methodist Episcopal Zion (AMEZ) Church created the Ladies' Home and Foreign Mission Society. Eight years later the name was changed to the Woman's Home and Foreign Mission Society. Men of the Conference selected wives and daughters of bishops as general officers and appointed a vice president, usually a minister's wife, for each state. The vice presidents were supposed to encourage women to form local auxiliaries, a task that turned out to be more difficult than they expected. Four years after the organization's founding, the women reported little progress. Men resisted their efforts to organize chapters in local churches, they said, and they had raised only $486.64. North Carolina's contribution was $7.65, and the state's vice president, Katie McCoy Hood of Fayetteville, complained that preachers were not interested in the society.[36]

Despite male opposition, the society grew, won acceptance, and eventually took the lead in the church's mission program. In 1899 the Reverend J. Harvey Anderson commented, "The men of the Church contribute, but it is left entirely to women to formulate plans, arrange and superintend the details of carrying on the work of benevolence in the church and community." A year later, a report on the women's missionary society in the *Star of Zion,* the denomination's official newspaper, asserted, "Missionary work has come to be looked upon almost distinctively as women's work."[37]

North Carolina women played major roles in the development of the Woman's Home and Foreign Mission Society. Katie Hood, for example, was elected General Conference secretary in 1892. When the president died in 1895, the bishop asked Hood to replace her. She won election to the presidency in 1896 and served until 1912, when she lost her bid for another four-year term. Meriah Elizabeth Harris of Salisbury served as recording secretary from 1884 until 1892 and treasurer from 1896 to 1912. Victoria Richardson formed the first Young Woman's Home and Foreign Missionary Society at her home in Salisbury in 1909 and directed young women's work until her death in 1928. Marie Clay Clinton of Charlotte headed the children's division from 1904 until 1932. Several other North Carolina women also held national office.[38]

African American Baptist women formed the Home Mission Convention of North Carolina in 1884 with Lizzie Neely of Salisbury as president. From the beginning, Baptist women acted independently of the men's convention and resisted male attempts to make the group an auxiliary to the men's missionary society. They cooperated with the men but set their own agenda and even conducted meetings differently. "Instead of their sessions being devoted to discussions of business, often useless," the Reverend A. H. Whitted observed, "they were given to papers and addresses on useful topics and to songs and devotions." By 1908 the North Carolina society claimed eight thousand members.[39]

Unlike white churchwomen, African American women found home missions more appealing than foreign ventures. Baptist women decided at the outset that theirs was a home mission society. They donated food and clothing to the poor, ministered to the sick, and raised money for their churches. They also supported the black orphanage at Oxford (which had been founded by Baptists), promoted Bible study and Sunday schools, and visited neighboring families to teach "proper regulations and practices within the home circle." While they made an annual donation to the church's foreign mission board, and in 1907 voted to support a single woman missionary in Africa, they made clear that they wanted to tend to problems at home before they saved souls abroad.[40]

Other denominations also concentrated on local benevolent work and paid special attention to education. When Methodist Episcopal women formed their Woman's Home Mission Society in 1905, they immediately voted to support Bennett College for women in Greensboro and the Allen High School, a girls' boarding school in Asheville. African American churchwomen living in the Jim Crow South faced problems on their own doorsteps that were much more compelling than the needs of people thousands of miles away.[41]

One of the problems that confronted black and white women alike was alcohol abuse. Private drinking became a public matter in the 1870s and 1880s, and women of both races joined the fight against "demon rum." The women's temperance crusade began in Hillsboro, Ohio, in

December 1873. Inspired by professional lecturer Dr. Diocletian Lewis, Hillsboro women set out to close the village's saloons shortly before Christmas. Within a few weeks, nine of the town's thirteen liquor dealers had gone out of business. Throughout the winter Lewis took his message to other Ohio towns, with similar results. Newspapers reported on the women's success, and the movement spread throughout the Midwest and into Pennsylvania and New Jersey. By the fall of 1874, women were ready to do battle nationwide. Nearly three hundred women assembled in the lecture room of the Second Presbyterian Church of Cleveland, Ohio, to form the Woman's Christian Temperance Union (WCTU).[42]

In its early days, the WCTU concentrated on direct action to convert individuals. Members—called "white ribboners" because of the badges of white ribbon they wore—signed the total abstinence pledge and encouraged others to do likewise. They distributed pamphlets and leaflets on the evils of alcohol, and they resorted to militant tactics to stop the liquor trade. Brigades of white ribboners marched boldly into saloons. They sang hymns and prayed for the souls of the proprietor and his customers. Such behavior discouraged patronage and usually convinced the saloonkeeper to close his establishment or at least suspend liquor sales.[43]

After the election of Frances Willard as president in 1879, the WCTU altered its strategy and enlarged its scope. The union officially adopted legal prohibition as its goal, although it continued to endorse individual abstinence. It also got involved in a wide range of issues that had nothing to do with temperance reform. Willard exhorted her followers to "Do Everything," and they tried to obey. In the 1880s and the 1890s white ribboners incorporated woman suffrage, equal pay for women workers, and elimination of the double standard of sexual morality into the national platform. Annual conventions called for prison reform, praised the kindergarten movement, condemned military training in schools, investigated industrial working conditions, and even pleaded with the czar of Russia to treat Siberian exiles with more kindness. Willard shaped the union program to reflect her own far-reaching interests. While most of the rank and file preferred to concentrate on temperance, the union under Willard's leadership introduced women to a range of issues many would otherwise have ignored.[44]

The WCTU developed more slowly in the South than in the North. When the movement was getting underway in the Midwest, southerners were still coping with the effects of the Civil War and Reconstruction, and southern women were preoccupied with matters other than the liquor question. But when prohibition became a major political issue in the South, southern women, like their northern counterparts, formed independent organizations to fight the liquor traffic.[45]

North Carolina women organized temperance societies in 1881, a year after the "drys," led by the North Carolina Conference of the Methodist Episcopal Church, South, and the Baptist state convention, initiated a campaign for statewide prohibition. More then a hundred thousand North Carolinians signed petitions to the legislature demanding that liquor be outlawed. In response, the 1881 General Assembly passed a bill forbidding the manufacture of "spirituous and malt liquors" and prohibiting the sale of alcohol except for medical, chemical, or mechanical purposes. The law was to go into effect October 1 if voters approved it at a special election on August 4.[46]

From the beginning, male prohibition leaders sought women's support. In April a prohibition convention in Raleigh resolved that "the ladies should be organized into prohibitory societies." Prohibition committee chairman H. A. Gudger outlined the role he anticipated for women in the campaign in an open letter "to the Ladies of North Carolina." "It is not to be expected that the ladies take an active part publicly," he wrote, "but in quiet ways they can do much good." The "quiet ways" included raising money and distributing temperance literature.[47]

Some women were eager to participate. On April 29 a group of white women met in Raleigh's Temperance Hall and formed state and local branches of the WCTU. They chose Mary Jarvis state president. They hoped to start auxiliaries among white women throughout the state. They succeeded in five towns: Asheville, Charlotte, Greensboro, Tarboro, and Wilmington. In Charlotte, African American women also joined the crusade, in a separate organization. A "large and enthusiastic meeting of the colored women of Charlotte" established the Ladies' Prohibition Association in July.[48]

Despite the efforts of "drys" of both sexes and races, North Carolina voters defeated the referendum by a vote of 166,325 to 48,370. Soon thereafter the state and local women's temperance societies disbanded. In 1883 the national union listed North Carolina as one of two states without a state WCTU, and there was only one local auxiliary, formed in Greensboro in April of that year. The situation worried Frances Willard. She had made up her mind that every state in the United States should have a statewide WCTU before the national organization celebrated its tenth anniversary in 1884. In November 1883 she came to Greensboro and established the Woman's Christian Temperance Union of North Carolina. By the time it held its second convention in 1884, the North Carolina WCTU claimed 458 members in twelve chapters. Three years later the corresponding secretary reported 600 members enrolled in twenty local branches.[49]

In its early years the WCTU was strongest in the piedmont and drew

AN APPEAL.

—

Albright Township, Chatham Co., N. C., July 20, 1881.

Dear Sisters: Constrained by the love we bear to our children, brothers, lovers, husbands, and for whose sake we wish to unite our influence, to save them from the terrible evils of Intemperance, we invite you to come out to the election at Flint Ridge, on the first Thursday in August, so that, by our presence, we may encourage those we love to deal a death blow to King Alcohol, and free us from the misery, woe, wretchedness and ruin, caused by this demon, that " biteth like a serpent and stingeth like an adder."

Mrs. Patsy Johnson,
" Flora A. Dixon,
" Mary Henley,
" Ellen Dixon,
" M. K. Lineberry,
" Martha Johnson,
" B. P. Duncan,
" Bettie Vestal,
" Catharine Thomas,
" Ruth D. Pike,

Mrs. A. B. Chapin,
" Sally Hornaday,
Miss Florence Dixon.
" Etta Jones,
" S. D. Albright,
" Roxie Dixon,
" Flora Dixon,
" Emily F. Johnson,
" Mary A. Thompson.

RECORD PRINT, PITTSBORO, N. C.

"An Appeal"

This broadside invited women to appear at polling places on August 4, 1881, when a prohibition referendum was on the ballot. Although women could not vote, temperance advocates urged them to exercise their moral authority in favor of prohibition.

(Courtesy of North Carolina Division of Archives and History)

many of its leaders from the Quaker community surrounding New Garden Boarding School and Guilford College. The Quaker meeting founded New Garden Boarding School for boys and girls in 1838; the boarding school became Guilford College fifty years later. Quaker tradition encouraged education for girls and activism among women. Between 1883 and 1908 at least a dozen women associated with the boarding school or college held statewide offices in the WCTU. Three Quaker women—Mary Mendenhall Hobbs, Laura Annie Winston, and Mary Chawner Woody—were particularly important to the union during its early years.

Mary Mendenhall Hobbs was born in 1852 into a prominent North Carolina Quaker family. Her father, Nereus Mendenhall, was the principal of New Garden Boarding School. She attended New Garden, then went on to Miss Howland's School on Lake Cayuga in Union Springs, New York. She taught for a year at Miss Howland's, then joined the New Garden faculty as a teacher of Latin and history in 1878. Two years later she married Lewis Lyndon Hobbs. The couple had known each other since both were students at New Garden. At the time of their marriage, he was New Garden's principal; he went on to become the first president of Guilford College. Mary Hobbs worked alongside her husband at New Garden and Guilford, reared their five children, and became an active reformer. She fought for better education for girls and women, supported woman suffrage, and was active in the state WCTU for twenty-five years. She held at least one statewide office every year from 1885 through 1911.[50]

Hobbs's contemporary Laura Annie Ballinger Winston was born in Guilford County in 1850. Like Hobbs, she attended New Garden Boarding School, and she too became a teacher. She taught at the state school for the blind and deaf in Raleigh until her marriage to Alonzo Hinton Winston in 1872. Laura Winston's personal life was filled with tragedy. Her husband died in 1873, leaving her with an infant daughter. A few years later the child also died. After her daughter's death, Laura Winston reportedly vowed to "try to live for someone else's daughter." She went to work at the state's new school for the deaf when it opened in Morganton in 1894 and was active in the WCTU from its founding. She was its first recording secretary and continued to hold various state offices for the next thirty-nine years. She chaired the Department of Legislation and Petition from 1889 to 1894 and served as vice president from 1894 to 1903, as president for five months in 1905, and as assistant superintendent of Evangelism from 1906 to 1916. She was the superintendent of Moral Education, Race Betterment, and Rescue Work from 1918 to 1920 and at the time of her death in 1922 was assistant superintendent for Social Morality and Purity in Art and Literature.[51]

Mary Chawner Woody, the most influential of the Quaker leaders in the WCTU, was born in Indiana in 1846. She moved to North Carolina in 1880, when she and her husband, John Warren Woody, joined the faculty at New Garden. The New Garden Meeting recognized her as a minister in 1884, and she played an important role in the local meeting and in the North Carolina Yearly Meeting. She was active in the revival movement of the 1880s, presided over the founding of the state's first Quaker women's missionary society in 1885, and represented North Carolina at the first national meeting of Quakers, held in Richmond, Indiana, in 1887. She was elected president of the North Carolina WCTU in 1884 and held that post until 1894, when she and her husband moved to California. The union named her honorary president in 1896. The Woodys returned to North Carolina in 1899, when John Woody became president of the Slater Industrial and Normal School, a school for African Americans that evolved into Winston-Salem State University, and Mary Woody once again became active in the WCTU. She was superintendent of Evangelical Work from 1899 to 1917.[52]

African American women organized their own local branches of the WCTU, sometimes with the assistance of white women, sometimes independently. In 1885 Rosa B. Steele, superintendent of Colored Work for the state WCTU, reported one chapter for black women in Greensboro and seventeen societies for black youth throughout the state. A year later African American temperance societies in Greensboro and Charlotte sent delegates to the state convention. Because Steele was absent from the meeting, the convention invited one of the black women to describe the progress of "colored work." Florence A. Garrett, president of Greensboro's African American WCTU, delivered an extemporaneous speech; she was probably the first African American woman to address an audience of white women in North Carolina.[53]

African American women also attended the 1887 state convention, at which Steele reported five new societies for adult women and thirty-two juvenile societies. They were present again in 1888, when the WCTU claimed fourteen branches of black women. According to Steele, two of the fourteen had been organized in the past year—implying that nine had existed previously, even though white women had known of only seven the year before. Clearly, African American women were undertaking temperance work on their own initiative. Indeed, some whites complained that blacks were suspicious of white attempts to organize them for temperance.[54]

African American women had complaints too. Their delegates to the 1888 state convention reported that white union members treated them with a "lack of courtesy and due recognition." Their experience prompted African American temperance workers to withdraw from the white-dominated state union and to make plans to form their own organization. On July 15, 1890, black temperance advocates held an organizational meeting at St. Matthew's church in Greensboro, with Florence Garrett presiding. Frances Willard, Mary Woody, and several ministers spoke, and the women elected Mrs. M. J. O'Connell, a preacher's wife, president of the new union.[55]

The new state organization called itself W.C.T.U. Number 2. "We cautiously avoided using the word *colored*," O'Connell told readers of the WCTU's national newspaper, the *Union Signal,* because "that would exclude any white sisters who might wish to work with us; in other words, we wanted it distinctly understood that we had no race prejudice, for *we* believe *all* men are equal." Black Christian women, she continued, "have come to join our hearts and prayers with yours." The state's white WCTU officially welcomed the union and promised its help and cooperation. W.C.T.U. Number 2 of North Carolina was the first state temperance organization for African American women in the nation. By December 1891 it had approximately four hundred members in nineteen local unions.[56]

With the formation of W.C.T.U. Number 2, North Carolina women of both races seemed well on their way to establishing networks of voluntary associations comparable to those formed by women in other states. Then came the 1890s. It was a turbulent decade in North Carolina politics, a decade in which fierce political battles pitted Democrats against Republicans and Populists, New South apostles against agrarian reformers, and whites against blacks. Debates over economic policy gave way to vicious campaigns of racial hatred. The political turmoil affected women as well as men and had a lasting impact on the growth and development of independent women's organizations.

North Carolinians in the 1890s reacted to changes that had been under way since Reconstruction. Entrepreneurs had begun building factories in the 1870s and 1880s. Eager to transform the "Rip Van Winkle" state into a leader of the New South, merchants, educators, and politicians welcomed the new enterprises and prescribed industrialization to cure North Carolina's economic ills. The prescription appeared to work. North Carolina, Mary Woody announced in 1890, "is on a boom. Mines are being opened, manufactories are being built, cotton and woolen factories line our rivers." Woody's description was exaggerated, but the process was real.[57]

Tobacco, textiles, and furniture provided the basis for the Tar Heel State's industrial expansion. W. T. Blackwell and Company began selling Bull Durham smoking tobacco in the 1860s. The tobacco industry burgeoned in the 1870s under the leadership of the Dukes in Durham and Richard J. Reynolds in Winston. Using aggressive business strategies, North

Carolina manufacturers came to dominate the national market for cigarettes and smoking tobacco by the early 1900s. The cotton mill building boom began in 1880; an average of six new factories opened each year for the next twenty years. By 1900 North Carolina ranked third in the nation in the production of cotton goods, and textile manufacture was the state's leading industry. Around the turn of the century furniture mills began expanding, rounding out the triumvirate of North Carolina industries.[58]

Despite industrial expansion, agriculture remained the backbone of the economy. But the nature of farming was changing. Fewer farmers were growing food for their families; more and more were raising cash crops—especially cotton—for the market. Moreover, farmers increasingly tilled soil that belonged to others. By 1900 tenants operated 41 percent of North Carolina farms. Debt and dependency were replacing self-sufficiency as the lot of many who lived on the land. Independent yeomen became tenants when they could not meet the mortgage. Tenants became mill hands when they failed to pay off the liens on their crops or simply got tired of the endless cycle of debt. "The farms are being deserted," a Rockingham woman warned in 1902, "and the people are swarming to the mills where ready money can be earned for their labor."[59]

While debt forced some farmers off the land, it propelled others into politics. The Southern Farmers' Alliance, founded in Texas in the 1870s, arrived in North Carolina in 1887 and grew rapidly. By 1890 the Alliance's ninety thousand members were ready to use their votes to elect a government more responsive to farmers' problems. Working through the Democratic Party, Alliancemen won a majority in the General Assembly that convened in 1891, replacing entrenched leaders committed to industrial growth and probusiness policies with men who promised to use government power to solve farmers' economic problems and institute reform. A year later, however, Alliancemen running on an independent, third-party ticket lost the ground they had gained. Democrats defeated both Populist and Republican candidates to reclaim a legislative majority and hold on to the governorship. But Populists and Republicans together outpolled the victorious Democrats, and the defeated parties were quick to understand the meaning of the election results. A majority of North Carolina voters were dissatisfied with the incumbent regime, and if the Democrats' opponents united (or "fused") they could oust the conservatives. The Populist-Republican fusion ticket won control of the legislature in 1894 and captured the governorship in 1896.[60]

The campaigns of 1894 and 1896 were bitter and hard-fought. Unlike some political races, they were not friendly competitions for political power between men who basically agreed on most issues. They were instead contests between men with fundamentally different visions of North

Carolina's future and opposing formulas for bringing lasting prosperity to the state. The Democratic Party represented the interests of the men of the New South: factory owners, businessmen, merchants, and railroad executives who championed industrialization and economic growth. These men believed that government should do what it could to nurture commerce, business, and industry even if that meant defying the popular will. Some Republicans shared this view. Populists, however, had a different vision. Concerned with the plight of the rural majority, they wanted government to curb the excesses of powerful businesses and railroads and to increase and improve the services it provided for its citizens. Moreover, they wanted to do away with electoral rules that restricted the influence of voters on government. Politicians on both sides had both selfish and altruistic motives. They wanted political power for themselves, but they also believed they acted in the best interests of North Carolina.[61]

The liquor question was subordinate to other issues in state politics in the 1890s, but it did not completely disappear. Fusion legislators were more sympathetic to the prohibitionist cause than their Democratic predecessors had been, and the Southern Farmers' Alliance and Populist Party were more receptive than other political organizations to women's participation in politics. That may explain why the WCTU began growing rapidly in 1896. Membership in the white union had fluctuated between 400 and 600 since 1884, but in 1896 the WCTU increased its enrollment from 600 to 948. By 1898 the WCTU boasted 1,500 active members in fifty-seven local auxiliaries. One year later almost 2,000 white North Carolina women had joined the temperance crusade.[62]

The African American WCTU also grew. Although the union was dormant for a time after 1892, it revived in 1896. The state convention met in Salisbury that year and elected Mary A. Lynch state president. Lynch, "a learned, cultured, and pious woman," was born in Charlotte and attended Scotia Seminary, a Presbyterian school for African American girls in Concord. After graduation she taught in the Charlotte public schools. In 1891 she joined the faculty at Livingstone College, a coeducational school for African Americans that was supported by the AMEZ Church. She remained at Livingstone as a librarian and teacher of English grammar and composition until her death in 1928. One of her first actions at Livingstone was to organize a Young Woman's Christian Temperance Union. Described by one observer as "perhaps the most enthusiastic advocate of temperance in the state," Lynch led the WCTU for more than twenty-five years.[63]

While the WCTU prospered in the 1890s, North Carolina's first woman suffrage society fared less well. In November 1894 Helen Morris Lewis convened a meeting of forty-five men and women at the home of Asheville mayor Thomas W. Patton and formed an equal suffrage association. Lewis, a native of Charleston, South Carolina, had moved to Asheville a few years earlier with her younger sister. She taught music, ran a boarding-house, and traveled throughout the state trying to win support for suffrage. Under her leadership the equal suffrage association brought some of the nation's most prominent suffragists to North Carolina, including Belle Kearney of Mississippi, Laura Clay of Kentucky, and the WCTU's Frances Willard. Perhaps Lewis and other early suffragists thought that the insurgent victories in the 1890s foreshadowed a more open political system, one in which disfranchised groups might be given a voice in government. If this was their assumption, it was soon proven wrong. Suffragists found few sympathizers, and by 1900 the equal suffrage association had ceased to exist. In 1906 Lewis returned to Charleston.[64]

The only new statewide women's organizations to develop successfully in North Carolina during the 1890s were patriotic and hereditary societies, similar in purpose to the Ladies Monumental Association that Samuel Ashe organized in 1892. Founded by the wives and daughters of the state's Democratic elite, these organizations existed to glorify white men. (Some of their members had a different agenda, but they kept it to themselves until after 1900.) Unlike church groups and the WCTU, which actively sought new members, the patriotic associations prided themselves on their exclusivity. In order to join, an applicant was required to document her relationship to some worthy individual, usually male, in the past: a colonial official, a Revolutionary patriot, a Confederate soldier. As class and racial conflict intensified in North Carolina in the 1890s, white women joined hereditary organizations to preserve class and racial hierarchies and to inculcate their version of history and their definition of patriotism into all North Carolinians.

All of the major women's patriotic societies—the Colonial Dames, the United Daughters of the Confederacy, the Daughters of the American Revolution, and its rival, the Daughters of the Revolution—established chapters in North Carolina in the 1890s. The Colonial Dames led the way. The National Society of Colonial Dames grew out of an organization of Pennsylvania women formed in 1891. Three years later, as the society's national council prepared to meet in Washington, D.C., the secretary discovered that North Carolina was the only one of the former British colonies that did not have a branch. She contacted Florence Kidder of Wilmington and urged her to form a chapter in time for North Carolina to send a delegate to the national meeting. On March 24, 1894, twenty-four ladies of colonial ancestry assembled in Kidder's parlor to organize the North Carolina Society of Colonial Dames. The Society was incorporated June 29, 1894, with Florence Kidder as its first president.[65]

United Daughters of the Confederacy Convention, Durham, 1906
In the early 1900s, the United Daughters of the Confederacy was one of the largest organizations for white women in North Carolina.

(Courtesy of North Carolina Collection, University of North Carolina Library at Chapel Hill)

The Colonial Dames adopted membership requirements similar to those of other patriotic societies. Any woman over the age of twenty-one was eligible to join if she could trace lineal descent from someone who had settled in America prior to 1750 and had achieved prominence in some way. Applicants were required to submit "pedigree papers" to document their claims. Each application had to be endorsed by two members of the society, neither of whom could be a member of the applicant's immediate family. An admissions committee reviewed each application, then the Board of Managers, governing body of the organization, voted to accept or reject the applicant. Despite, or perhaps because of, the restrictive membership requirements, the society attracted much interest. In 1897 Kidder reported a rapid increase in membership and urged revision of the bylaws to reduce the workload of the admissions committee. The society showed steady, if not spectacular, growth: from 95 members in 1897 to 265 ten years later.[66]

Wilmington women dominated the state association. The "running spirit" of the North Carolina Society of Colonial Dames in its early years was Florence Kidder, who served as president from 1894 until 1900. Kidder had been one of North Carolina's "lady managers" at the Columbian Exposition, the fair held in Chicago in 1893 to commemorate Christopher Columbus's first voyage to America 401 years earlier. That experience brought her into contact with prominent women from all over the nation and established her as a leader of North Carolina's white women. Kidder's successor as Colonial Dames president was Catherine deRosset Meares, daughter of a prominent Wilmington family and widow of a Confederate officer. Kate Meares was active in the society from the time of its founding and spent six years as president. Meares's niece, Gabrielle deRosset Waddell, also played a significant role. The third wife of Democratic politician Alfred Moore Waddell, she had no children and devoted her life to voluntary organizations, especially the Colonial Dames. She was recording secretary of the state branch from 1896 to 1908, vice president from 1908 to 1916, and president from 1916 to 1935.[67]

Leaders of the Colonial Dames were determined to prove that the society was more than what Kidder called "a social fad," and from the beginning they set the Dames to work on various historical projects. They raised money for a memorial to Revolutionary patriot Cornelius Harnett, worked to preserve the yard and ruins of St. Philip's, a church constructed in New Bern in 1725, and made typescripts of historical documents. During the Spanish-American War they collected supplies for soldiers.[68]

Not all of the organization's members shared their leaders' zeal for historical and patriotic projects; some seemed more interested in the society's social functions than its stated purposes. So few women attended meetings of the Wilmington chapter that often meetings had to be adjourned for lack of a quorum. When members did show up, they talked to each other instead of paying attention to the business at hand. The chapter solved both problems by levying fines for absences and for whispering during meetings. Local branches of other patriotic societies would experience similar problems and adopt similar solutions in their early years.[69]

If the Colonial Dames had trouble maintaining discipline, at least they had enough members to hold meetings. Societies for descendants of Revolutionary heroes were not so fortunate in the 1890s. They had a hard time enrolling women in North Carolina, and they hurt their own cause by competing with each other. The Daughters of the American Revolution (DAR) and the Daughters of the Revolution (DR) were, and are, distinct organizations and were bitter rivals. The DAR, always the larger and more famous of the two, was founded in Washington, D.C., in 1890 as a female counterpart to the Sons of the American Revolution. By 1897 the society boasted 397 chapters in thirty-eight states.[70]

The national board of the DAR appointed a regent for North Carolina in 1892, but no chapters were established in the state until 1898, when the board named Hattie Nisbet Latta of Charlotte state executive. Latta was the wife of Charlotte real estate developer and industrialist Edward Dilworth Latta and the mother of two sons. Under her leadership, fourteen Charlotte women organized the Mecklenburg Chapter of the DAR in September. The society grew slowly. The Daughters did not hold their first statewide meeting until 1901, and then only four towns had DAR organizations. Ten years later the association had 533 members in nineteen chapters.[71]

Flora Adams Darling, a disgruntled cofounder and former vice president of the DAR, organized the General Society of the Daughters of the Revolution largely out of spite. Repeated disputes over policy and administration between Darling and other members of the DAR's board of managers led the board to remove Mrs. Darling from office in July 1891. In retaliation she resigned from the organization and formed her own hereditary group, the DR, in August. The Darling society never approached the numerical strength of the DAR—a fact, DR members claimed, that proved their society's superiority: "It must be remembered that it is the chosen few who bear the burden and heat of the day. From time immemorial quality, not quantity, has held the power of the world in the balance." By 1895 the DR had recruited "quality" members in seventeen states.[72]

The national board appointed Fanny deBerniere Hooper Whitaker state regent in September 1894. She founded the North Carolina Society of the Daughters of the Revolution two years later, on October 19, 1896. The daughter of a University of North Carolina professor and valedictorian of her graduating class at Chowan Female Institute, Fanny Hooper married Spier Whitaker in 1866. Mr. Whitaker was a Confederate veteran who went on to become a lawyer, judge, and chairman of the state Democratic Party. Mrs. Whitaker became the mother of five children, an amateur historian, and a devotee of patriotic societies. In addition to being DR regent from 1896 to 1902, she was a state officer of the Colonial Dames and a member of the United Daughters of the Confederacy. She was a charter member of the North Carolina Literary and Historical Association and wrote articles and biographical sketches for the DR's historical quarterly the *North Carolina Booklet,* the *Cyclopedia of American Biographies,* and Samuel Ashe's *Biographical History of North Carolina.* Ashe, who worked with Whitaker when she served on the board of the Ladies Monumental Association, described her as "a woman of rare intellectual gifts."[73]

During her term as DR regent Whitaker was zealous, but selective, in her efforts to attract new members. Elvira Moffitt, her friend and co-worker in organized patriotism, recalled that, for Whitaker, the society's exclusivity was part of its appeal. That was no doubt true for other Daughters as well. The organization expanded very slowly and never included more than a few hundred women. As one account of the society's early years reported, it "grew in strength of purpose, more than numerically."[74]

National leaders of the Colonial Dames, DAR, and DR complained of recruitment difficulties in the South because of competition with the United Daughters of the Confederacy (UDC). This association was open to the wives, mothers, sisters, and descendants of Confederate soldiers and officeholders and to women who had themselves served the Confederacy. It was by far the most popular patriotic group among white southern women. The UDC grew out of the local memorial societies and relief associations that had sprung up all over the South after the Civil War. In September 1894, under the guidance of Anna Davenport Raines of Savannah and Caroline Meriweather Goodlett of Nashville, representatives from some of these societies met in Nashville to form a regional organization.[75]

That same autumn, the Ladies Memorial Association of Wilmington, seeking a more formal organizational structure, appointed a committee to write a constitution. The chair of the committee was Eliza Nutt Parsley, a Civil War bride and a Confederate widow. She married Captain William Murdock Parsley in 1862, when she was twenty. He was killed just three days before Lee's surrender, leaving her with two infant daughters. She supported herself and her children by teaching and kept her husband's memory alive in the Ladies Memorial Association. When Parsley read about the organization of the UDC, she immediately wrote to Anna Raines to find out how Wilmington women could affiliate with the new association.[76]

On December 24, 1894, the Cape Fear Chapter of the UDC received its charter. It was the third chapter in the South, following Savannah and Nashville. The state division of the UDC was organized in 1897, with Eliza Parsley as president. Nancy Jones and Mary Jarvis of the Ladies Monumental Association also served as officers during the first two years. By 1901 the UDC had more than a thousand members in thirty-three affiliates and was the second-largest white women's voluntary association in the state. Although North Carolina's white women were slow to join other voluntary associations, they flocked to the UDC.[77]

At first glance, the popularity of the UDC seems inconsistent with the state's history. After all, North Carolinians had been reluctant Confederates, whose interests had been ill served by a long and bloody war for slavery. They suffered much, gained little, and endured the war's consequences long after Appomattox. Ironically, that made the UDC's mission even more compelling. Many of the women who joined the UDC in the 1890s had lived through the war; the rest had lived all their lives in its shadow. The worst fate of all would be the knowledge that all the sacrifices had been in vain. Descendants, relatives, and survivors of a defeated people, the Daughters believed they were engaged in a holy task. "This rises above all other work, to a true Southern woman, except her duty to her God," Mrs. Frontis Burbank told the 1899 convention. With religious fervor the Daughters set out to prove—perhaps to themselves as well as to others—that the Lost Cause had been a just cause.[78]

The political situation in North Carolina in the 1890s enhanced the meaning of the UDC's work. Republicans and Populists, including some turncoat Democrats, were in power; African American men held office, and the white Democrats who had grown accustomed to ruling found themselves shut out of state government. It was Reconstruction all over again—at least that was how Democratic rhetoric portrayed it. Reconstruction itself had come about because white southern men had failed to win military victory and protect their homes and families from the Yankee invasion. Would they be more successful this time, or would they once again lose control of their state?

In the uncertain political climate, Democrats must have found white women's continued loyalty very reassuring. Most white North Carolina women refrained from openly challenging male authority, and some of the women most closely associated with the ousted Democrats intensified their efforts to praise the men who had been defeated thirty years earlier. As Democratic politicians compared current events to those of the 1860s and 1870s and prepared to wage political war to win back their power, the

UDC rewrote history and turned military defeat into moral victory.

The year after the founding of the state division of the UDC, North Carolina faced one of the most important elections in its history. The significance of the issues at stake and the depth of political divisions created in the elections of the early 1890s guaranteed that the 1898 campaign would be ugly. Despite some disagreements among themselves, Republicans and Populists—collectively called "fusionists"—believed their coalition could survive if they continued to focus on the political and economic questions that had swept them into office in 1894 and 1896. Democrats, however, were determined to regain control of state government, and they seized on the one issue certain to unite a majority of the state's white voters: race.

Racist rhetoric had been a part of North Carolina's political vocabulary for a long time, but it became a major theme in the campaign of 1898. Citing the increase in the number of African American officeholders since 1894, the Democrats cried "Negro domination" and charged that under fusion rule the racial hierarchy had been overturned. Democratic newspapers, such as the *Raleigh News and Observer*, played on racial antagonisms with editorial cartoons, pictures, and headlines such as "Negro Control in Wilmington" and "Negroes Have Social Equality." Meanwhile, Democratic speakers and pamphlets delivered the message of white supremacy to the voters. In the eastern part of the state, Democrats formed White Government Unions, where men met to discuss the superiority of the white race and the corruption of fusion rule.[79]

Democrats made white women the symbolic centerpiece of the campaign. Democratic propaganda relentlessly reminded North Carolina's white men that "Negro domination" meant not only that African American men possessed political power but that they might also presume to possess white women. Some black political appointees—postmasters, for instance—had jobs that brought them into contact with white women. African American men who conducted business with white women, Democrats warned, might want to mingle with them socially as well.[80]

In a few cases, African American men held positions that gave them authority over white women. Broadsides cited instances of white women being arrested by African American policemen and tried by African American magistrates. A black legislator and member of the board of the state school for the blind and deaf, James H. Young, became a favorite Democratic target. Editorial cartoons in the *Raleigh News and Observer* showed him visiting a class of blind white girls and inspecting the living quarters of a white female teacher. Although there was no evidence that the incidents actually took place, the Democratic handbook described the situation as "white slavery to a negro master." Young's resignation from the board to accept an army commission was not enough to silence his Democratic critics.[81]

The Democrats' vehement response to Young was mild compared to their reaction to Alex Manly, editor of the *Wilmington Record*. In August 1898 Manly published an editorial on lynching, rape, and miscegenation. He pointed out that, contrary to the impression white newspapers conveyed, African American men were not brutal savages. He challenged white men to look more closely at relationships between African American men and white women and blamed white men for neglecting their women. "We suggest that the whites guard their women more closely, . . . thus giving no opportunity for the human fiend, be he white or black. You leave your goods out of doors, and then complain because they are taken away."[82]

Despite the rhetoric, Manly recognized that white women were more than chattel. Indeed, he continued, some white women voluntarily entered relationships with African American men and charged rape only when their clandestine affairs were discovered. "Every negro lynched is called a 'big burley black brute,'" he wrote, "when, in fact, many of those who have thus been dealt with had white men for their fathers, and were not only not 'black' and 'burley,' but were sufficiently attractive for white girls of culture and refinement to fall in love with them." When white women chose African American men as sexual partners, they were following the example of men of their own race who had never let racial barriers thwart their desire for black women. Manly accused white men of being "carping hypocrites . . . you cry aloud for the virtue of your women while you seek to destroy the morality of ours." White men, he concluded, were now reaping the harvest of centuries of sexual exploitation of black women.[83]

Manly ripped apart the elaborate tapestry of sexual mores in which race and gender were interwoven. In the South, the "double standard" was a double entendre; it prescribed sexual conduct on the basis of race as well as gender. White women were expected to be pure and virtuous; black women, lewd and licentious. White men could flout taboos against miscegenation; black men could not. Guarding the purity of white women was the measure of honor and manliness for white southern men. Black men were powerless to protect their mothers, wives, sisters, and daughters. The South's multidimensional double standard elevated white men, degraded black men, and treated all women as objects—those on one side of the color line to be cherished, those on the other to be used.[84]

The lady was, in the words of Jacquelyn Dowd Hall, "the ultimate symbol" of white male dominance, the prize that black men might covet but could never claim. The "goddess" of southern civilization, she pledged her loyalty and her obedience to white men in exchange for protection from the savagery of the "black beast." But in that hot North Carolina

August, Alex Manly exposed the truth that belied the South's racial ortho-
doxy. Some white women rejected "protection" and fell in love with black
men.[85] Manly taunted white men with the possibility that black men could
be equal competitors in the contest for white women and with the fact
that some white women preferred "burley black brutes" to their white
lords and masters. Alex Manly's editorial shattered the myths that
undergirded white male supremacy. By revealing black men and white
women to be autonomous beings who could, and did, defy the will of
white men, it challenged white men's authority in both gender and race
relations. It insulted the pride of men who staked their honor on their
ability to control absolutely African American men and all women.

When Ida B. Wells published a similar editorial in the *Memphis Free
Speech* six years earlier, an angry mob destroyed the newspaper's offices
and warned Wells, who was visiting Philadelphia and New York, not to
return. Although Manly and his newspaper escaped immediate harm, his
editorial enraged many white North Carolinians; they refused to acknowledge the existence of the liaisons he described. Instead, they accused the
newspaper editor of assailing the purity of white womanhood and condemned his insolence for suggesting that white women might voluntarily
consort with men of a supposedly inferior race. This interpretation lent
credence to what the Democrats had been saying all summer: that African
American men, made impudent by their growing political power under
fusion rule, now believed they had a right to white women.

Democrats were quick to exploit the situation. The *Raleigh News and
Observer* ran the article under the headline "Vile and Villainous." Other
newspapers reprinted it, and Democratic speakers read it aloud at political rallies. Democrats alleged that white women were no longer safe in
North Carolina. One broadside included a section entitled "The Menace
to Womanhood" that warned farmers of the dangers of leaving their wives
and daughters alone in the house while they worked in the fields, and it
predicted "an epidemic of assaults" if fusionists won the election in November. Newspapers published numerous accounts of African American
attacks on white women. The incidents—a few real, some exaggerated,
many fabricated—ranged from insult to attempted rape; Democrats held
the fusion regime responsible for all of them. The Populist-Republican
coalition had courted black voters and appointed African American men
to office. As a result, white supremacists declared, "bad government had
followed, homes had been invaded and the sanctity of woman endan-
gered."[86]

In the name of defending the honor of white women, North Carolina
Democrats rallied to reassert their dominance. "Every white man who
could talk was on the stump; every white man who could write was writ-

ing, and every white man who could ride and could influence a vote was enthusiastically at work," recalled *News and Observer* editor Josephus Daniels. "Business was forgotten, and the one business of the white people of the state was to redeem it." Eight thousand men met at a white supremacy convention held in Goldsboro in October and pledged "to free ourselves of this negro domination." Late in the campaign "Red Shirt" clubs appeared in some counties along the South Carolina border. Clad in bright red shirts, riding horseback and carrying guns, the Red Shirts disrupted Republican rallies and rode through black communities. Their avowed goal was intimidation, but they also resorted to violence on occasion. According to Daniels, "They created terror."[87]

When Democrats deliberately magnified real and imagined assaults on white women, they painted a bleak picture in which every African American male was a potential rapist, every white woman a potential victim, and Democratic politicians were the valiant knights who offered women their only hope for protection. A cartoon on the front page of the *Wilmington Morning Star* three weeks before the election showed a white woman clinging to a white man who was standing tall against an approaching black cyclone labeled "Negro Domination." The caption read, "North Carolina's Womanhood Appeals to White Men For Protection."[88]

White women responded in various ways. Some saw the Democratic rhetoric for exactly what it was—a political ploy intended to divert attention from other issues. Sarah Mitchell of Bertie County called "negro supremacy" and "going back into slavery" the "two horrific hobgoblins" raised by "the money power" to divide black and white farmers who had common economic interests. Others believed what they heard. "*Where are* the white men and their shotguns?" Rebecca Cameron demanded of her cousin, Alfred Moore Waddell, in October 1898. The time had come, Cameron wrote, to use violence to end fusion rule: "It has reached the point where blood letting is needed for the hearts of the commonwealth, and when the depletion commences *let it be thorough.*" Should all efforts fail, Cameron implored "the white men to get out their shotguns and empty them into the hearts of all the decent white women in the state. If the white men can stand Negro supremacy, we neither can nor will."[89]

White men, claiming to fear violence at the polls, had their shotguns ready on election day November 8; however, the day passed quietly. When it was over, Democrats had won a majority in the General Assembly as well as five of the state's nine Congressional seats. But the racial antagonism the campaign had aroused could not be easily put to rest. On November 10 a race riot erupted in Wilmington. White men, led by Alfred Moore Waddell, torched Alex Manly's newspaper office, then roamed through black neighborhoods firing shotguns. As many as thirty African

Americans died, and hundreds of others, including Alex Manly, fled the city. At the end of the day, the mob demanded the resignations of the town's fusionist government and named Waddell the new mayor.[90]

White leaders blamed African Americans for the riot. They repeated stories of insults to white women and circulated rumors of violent African American plots against whites. One such rumor spoke of a cook who threatened to poison her employer's food. Another alleged that children's nursemaids would harm their charges if blacks lost political power. Whites had been in danger, Democrats argued, and acted to protect themselves.[91]

Not all whites accepted their explanation. Jane Cronly, a white woman living in Wilmington, responded to the riot with "indignation and sorrow." "For the first time in my life I have been ashamed of my state and of the Democratic party," she wrote a few days after the uprising. She described the city's black population as "peaceful" and "law-abiding." There was, in her mind, "no excuse" for what had happened. Cronly hoped that other white women would join her protest, but none did. Indeed, she reported that some of Wilmington's white women laughed at the sufferings of their African American neighbors. Cronly expressed her indignation in an account of the riot and in letters to newspaper editors, but she asked that her letters not be published or acknowledged in any way. Apparently she feared retribution if she publicly denounced the white supremacists.[92]

In 1900 Democrats repeated the formula that had brought them victory two years before. Historian Joseph F. Steelman described the campaign as "a sustained emotional orgy." Gubernatorial nominee Charles Brantley Aycock, running on a platform of white supremacy and educational reform, repeatedly reminded North Carolina's white men that protection of the state's white women was a divine obligation, the "first duty which God . . . laid upon us for all time." Aycock rallies featured young white women, wearing white dresses, sitting silent on floats drawn by white horses. In at least two parades—at Roxboro and Concord—above the women's heads was a banner that read "Protect Us." Democratic newspapers published an appeal from a group of white women: "As you honor your mother, as you love your wife, as you cherish your daughter, cast your vote for white supremacy." The authors insisted that their plea was authentic and "no campaign letter," but they remained anonymous.[93]

The strategy worked. Aycock soundly defeated his Republican opponent for the governorship. That same year, voters approved a constitutional amendment instituting a poll tax and a literacy requirement for voting. The amendment accomplished its purpose: it effectively disfranchised most African Americans. White Democracy reigned once again in North Carolina.[94]

Thus Democrats successfully used race to obscure other issues. They established white supremacy, and they secured their hold on state government. But their tactics had far-reaching, and unanticipated, consequences.

During the campaigns of 1898 and 1900, Democrats reduced control of the state to the lowest common denominator of power: men's control over women. They reinforced the connection between gender and racial ideologies, and they equated political power with sexual dominance. When men's access to women became the measure of political power, women's powerlessness itself became part of the political equation. African American men must never be strong enough to threaten white women; white women must never be strong enough to protect themselves.[95]

White supremacists asserted not only that suffrage was a *white* prerogative, but that it was a white *male* prerogative. Locke Craig—Democratic politician, lawyer, and coauthor of the state's "grandfather clause," which enfranchised illiterate whites while disqualifying illiterate blacks—declared that "manhood" was "the highest test of the right to vote." According to Craig and his colleagues, African American men were doomed to fail that test because of their history. White supremacists argued that centuries of slavery had bred habits of dependence in blacks and prevented them from becoming "real men." Illiterate white men, they said, were capable of voting responsibly because they had something African American men lacked: a heritage of liberty and autonomy. The link between masculinity and the right to vote in campaigns to disfranchise African Americans emasculated black men and cast them, along with women and children, as subjects of the white patriarchy.[96]

Democrats aimed their messages at other men to galvanize whites and intimidate blacks. They gave little thought to the effect of their propaganda on women; yet Democratic rhetoric had a profound impact on women of both races. For months North Carolina women could not pick up a newspaper or listen to conversations on the street without hearing tales of rape and assault. Each newspaper account, each whispered rumor reverberated with the same refrain: no *white* woman is safe. The absence of black women from the Democratic scenario underscored their exclusion from the conventions of gender. African American women knew that they too could be victims of rape. They also knew that when a black woman was sexually abused, no one protested, and no one rose up to avenge the crime. Whites vociferously condemned black assaults on white women but remained silent when white men attacked black women. They denied the dignity of African American women as individuals, and they denied the dignity of black womanhood. In the face of degradation, African American women fought for the respect they knew they deserved. They became even more determined to claim for themselves the veneration automatically accorded white women.[97]

While Democrats loudly proclaimed their respect and adoration for white women throughout the campaigns, they did so in a way that was more likely to make white women feel insecure than exalted. The rhetoric of rape aroused genuine fear. Some women, like Sarah Mitchell, might dismiss the stories as exaggerated; others, like Rebecca Cameron, might look to Democratic men to protect them. Still, the fear lingered—fear of rape and fear of the wrath of white men if women violated the code of the lady and challenged male authority.[98]

When Democrats repeated lurid tales of African American men assaulting white women, they reinforced the lesson white southern women were taught from childhood: that they were weak, fragile, and vulnerable. But Democrats also delivered another message to white women. When they invoked the Lost Cause—and they often did—they conjured up a very different portrait of womanhood. Stories of Civil War heroines celebrated the courage, self-reliance, and independence of white southern women. Politicians routinely used images of feminine strength together with images of feminine weakness without ever acknowledging the contrast. Charles Brantley Aycock, for example, in one breath praised North Carolina's "noble and true-hearted women" who "took upon themselves to run the farm and the forge, the shop and the factory" during the Civil War, and in the next breath condemned the fusion-inspired "lawlessness" that permitted "insults to white ladies by negro brutes." Apparently it never occurred to him that if white women could withstand economic hardship and enemy invasion while their men were away at war, they could probably withstand insults and threats of violence when their men were at home.[99]

The juxtaposition of feminine strength and feminine frailty was nothing new; it had been a staple of southern thought since the antebellum era. Aycock and others merely highlighted two sides of the multifaceted image of the southern lady. But their timing was crucial. Just as women's opportunities in education, employment, and public life were expanding, white supremacist rhetoric emphasized an ideal that simultaneously enhanced and subverted white women's self-esteem. White women in turn-of-the-century North Carolina took both messages to heart. Images of feminine competence and courage inspired them to widen their horizons; racial fears ensured that they did not venture too far. Fear and flattery kept them in their place, even as that place expanded into the public realm.[100]

The white supremacy campaigns influenced the development of women's voluntary associations. The growth of the WCTU in the 1890s coincided with the Populist ascendancy. Both groups endorsed prohibition, and both encouraged African Americans to get involved in politics

and reform. But the fragile alliance of black and white temperance advocates, already weakened by white hostility toward African American delegates to state conventions in the 1880s, could not withstand the racist
politics of the 1890s. Reports of "colored work" disappeared from the
minutes of the white organization after 1895. A year later African American union members voted to change the name of their state organization
from W.C.T.U. Number 2 to the Woman's Christian Temperance Union
of North Carolina, the name usually reserved for the white organization.
With the name change, African American women reaffirmed the belief in
racial equality that Mrs. M. J. O'Connell had articulated at the time of the
union's founding. Perhaps they hoped that white women in the state's
other WCTU would be able to follow the example of Populist and Republican men and work with their African American counterparts in the interest of a common cause. But racism undermined women's efforts to
cooperate for reform, just as it destroyed the fusion coalition. The two
state unions continued to function independently of each other.[101]

Patriotic societies took hold in the 1890s, and the UDC flourished—
perhaps it was a beneficiary of the white supremacist glorification of the
Lost Cause. Despite the vast differences in constituencies and platforms,
the various "daughters" shared one characteristic with their WCTU contemporaries: they were engaged in public work that men sanctioned.

The groups that failed in the 1890s, on the other hand, were organizations that in some way asserted women's independence. Helen Lewis's
equal suffrage association is an obvious example. Women who asked for
the right to vote threatened white male authority. Women's clubs posed a
more subtle threat. In literary societies women met for self-improvement,
not service, and in civic associations they drew up their own plans for
reform and social betterment, plans that sometimes were at odds with
men's goals. Women's clubs were conspicuously absent from North Carolina in the 1890s.

By 1890 the club movement was well under way in the United States.
Clubs had existed in the Northeast, Midwest, and West since the 1860s.
They had begun developing in southern cities in the 1880s and spread
through the South in the 1890s. In 1889 white clubwomen formed the
General Federation of Women's Clubs, and in the 1890s most states, in-
cluding eight southern states, formed their own federations. But not North
Carolina. In 1899 Sallie Southall Cotten of Pitt County wrote a letter "To
The Women of North Carolina" proposing the organization of a North
Carolina federation. "The Women of North Carolina" responded without
enthusiasm. As Cotten later recalled, "Clubs were few and *unpopular*—
were considered unwomanly and existed solely for mental culture."[102]

Cotten, however, was not the sort of woman who gave up easily. Born

To the Women of North Carolina:

I am making an effort to form a State Federation, composed of all the organizations of women in North Carolina. This will bring the women of this State in touch with each other and with the women of other States, thereby securing the increased benefits which come from enlarged acquaintance, exchange of thought, and unity of action with definite aim. *All* organizations of women, and all Women's Departments of mixed organizations (such as Daughters of Rebekah, Rathbone Sisters, etc,) are invited to join in this movement, which is non-sectarian, non-political, and only designed for mutual helpfulness.

If this effort meets with general approval, a convention of women will be called at an early day to organize this Federation, adopt a constitution, and outline future action for the same.

This body of women, representing the organizations in the State, will decide whether this State Federation shall affiliate with the National Federation of Women's Clubs, and all other action proposed to the convention. Each delegate representing an organization will be entitled to vote on all questions discussed by the convention.

An effort will be made to secure reduced railroad rates for the delegates, and the fact duly published.

All organizations of women are requested to communicate with me on this subject.

All State papers are requested to copy this letter.

Any information desired on the subject of the proposed Federation will be cheerfully and promptly given. Address,

MRS. ROBERT R. COTTEN,
425 Blount Street, Raleigh, N. C.

"To the Women of North Carolina"

In 1899 Sallie Southall Cotten sent this letter to women throughout North Carolina in an attempt to form a state federation of women's clubs. Although this initial effort failed, white clubwomen formed the North Carolina Federation of Women's Clubs three years later.

(Cotten Family Papers, Southern Historical Collection,
University of North Carolina at Chapel Hill)

in Virginia in 1846, Sallie Swepson Sims Southall went to live with her uncle in Murfreesboro, North Carolina, as a child. She graduated from Greensboro Female College in 1863, then taught until 1866, when she married Robert Randolph Cotten, an ambitious Confederate veteran. Over the next twenty years he became a successful planter and merchant, and she devoted her energies to running a growing household; the Cottens had nine children, seven of whom survived infancy. Cotten's public career began in the 1890s. She, along with Florence Kidder, was one of North Carolina's "lady managers" at the Columbian Exposition. For Cotten, as for Kidder, that experience created new opportunities. She became an enthusiastic supporter of women's clubs and devoted the rest of her life to promoting them in North Carolina. In 1900 the General Federation of Women's Clubs chose her to chair the state's Committee of Correspondence, a group of three women who were to encourage local women's clubs to affiliate with the national organization.[103]

Aycock's victory in 1900 made the committee's job easier. It silenced the rhetoric of rape, subdued fears of assault, and gave white women more latitude to experiment with new roles. The women likely to join women's clubs were middle-class town women. Their fathers, brothers, and husbands were the "new men" of the New South: merchants, industrialists, educators, and professionals who championed economic development and voted the Democratic ticket. Having secured their dominance over their political opponents in the white supremacy campaigns, these men were more likely to tolerate women's attempts to move beyond domesticity. They recognized too that women could help them promote their agenda. The Democratic triumph was a triumph of sorts for white clubwomen as well. It gave them the opportunity to move into public life and to establish their place in the new order. At the same time, however, it bound their interests to white supremacy and the Democratic Party.[104]

In May 1902 representatives of seven clubs met at Salem College to found the North Carolina Federation of Women's Clubs (NCFWC). They elected Sallie Cotten vice president and chose Lucy Bramlette Patterson president. Married to attorney and industrialist J. Lindsay Patterson, the federation's first president was a Salem alumna, a freelance journalist, and founder of the Embroidery Club of Winston-Salem. Like Cotten, she was well known among Tar Heel women.[105]

The list of Patterson's successors reads like a who's who of North Carolina women. It includes Laura Holmes Reilley, cofounder of North Carolina's second equal suffrage league, trustee of Charlotte's Mint Museum, and chair of the Woman's Committee of the Council of National Defense during World War I; Cotten; Clara Souther Lingle, wife of Davidson college professor and Presbyterian minister Thomas Wilson

Sallie Southall Cotten
Known as "Mother Cotten," Sallie Southall Cotten was a leader among white clubwomen and one of the best known and most beloved women in early twentieth-century North Carolina.

(Charles Van Noppen Papers, Special Collections Library, Duke University)

Lingle; Kate Burr Johnson, who in the 1920s would become the first woman in the United States to be appointed a state commissioner of public welfare; and Gertrude Dills McKee, who became the first woman to serve in the North Carolina state senate. From the beginning, the NCFWC drew its leaders from among the best educated and most talented white women in the state.

The federation became the most influential of the white women's organizations. By 1905 it included twenty-nine clubs with 550 members. Six years later it represented seventy-nine clubs with 2,300 members. The biggest increase in membership came in 1923, when the home demonstration clubs for rural women merged with the NCFWC. By 1924 the federation claimed to represent more than 50,000 North Carolina women.[106]

Other white women's organizations also grew after 1900. The Colonial Dames reported approximately 600 members in 1915 and more than 1,000 in 1929. The DAR went from 850 in 1915 to 1,330 in 1920. After 1920 the society expanded more rapidly; by 1930 the North Carolina DAR claimed 2,576 members in thirty-six chapters. The UDC remained the most popular of the patriotic societies. It more than doubled in size between 1901 and 1905 and continued to attract new members. The North Carolina division reported 3,541 members in 1910, 5,018 in 1915, 11,454 in 1925, and 13,716 in 1930.[107]

Democratic endorsement of prohibition triggered a brief expansion in the white WCTU at the turn of the century. In 1903 state officers boasted of "nearly 3,000" members in sixty-five affiliates. The union "held its own" until 1906, but after that participation declined. In 1908, the year North Carolina adopted statewide prohibition, the white WCTU claimed approximately 1,000 supporters in fifty chapters. The association continued to report a constituency of between 800 and 1,000 until 1930, but there were fewer local unions. By 1930 only thirty-six towns had white WCTU chapters.[108]

Some organizations that had local chapters in the 1880s and 1890s formed statewide associations after 1900. The DAR was one such group; the King's Daughters was another. The International Order of the King's Daughters and Sons originated in 1886 in New York City. Its founder, Margaret Bottome, intended it to be a "Sisterhood of Silent Service." It was a nondenominational Christian charitable society with the slogan "Not to be ministered unto, but to minister." White women in Wilmington, Greensboro, Salisbury, Greenville, and Raleigh formed circles in the 1880s. Several of these started in particular churches and later expanded to include women of other congregations or denominations. The Daughters maintained a loosely structured state organization in the 1890s but first adopted a statewide program in 1902. By 1904 there were twenty-nine circles in North Carolina, and "about 600" members.[109]

The Order of King's Daughters was open to all women, regardless of wealth or race. Following the prevailing custom, however, circles and state societies were segregated. In North Carolina many of its white leaders and members came from elite families. Sallie Cotten, Mary Jarvis, and Elvira Moffitt were all active members. Margaret Dunlop Burgwyn, who served as state president from 1901 to 1924, was born in Richmond, Virginia, in 1848. She was married to William Hyslop Sumner Burgwyn, a Harvard law school graduate and Confederate officer who became a prominent North Carolina banker. Other state officers included Florence Davis Cooper, wife of Henderson cotton manufacturer and railroad executive David Young Cooper; Kate Olds, whose husband Fred was a journalist and curator of the North Carolina Hall of History; and Flora Keith Overman, wife of Salisbury merchant William H. Overman and sister-in-law of Senator Lee Slater Overman. Olds and Overman each served a term as president of the state division of the UDC, and Cooper became treasurer of the North Carolina Federation of Women's Clubs in 1915. The white King's Daughters were few in number compared to other women's organizations, but they wielded a great deal of influence because of their social and economic clout.[110]

African American women formed their own branches of the King's Daughters, just as they organized independent chapters of the WCTU. They also founded their own civic and literary clubs. Frustrated in their attempts to affiliate with the General Federation of Women's Clubs and excluded from participation in the woman's exhibit at the Columbian Exposition, black women organized two national associations in the early 1890s: the National Colored Women's League and the National Federation of Afro-American Women. In 1896 these groups merged into the National Association of Colored Women (NACW), with Mary Church Terrell as president.[111]

North Carolina's African American clubwomen formed the North Carolina Federation of Colored Women's Clubs (NCFCWC) in Charlotte in 1909. Like their white counterparts, the founders of the state federation of black women's clubs came from the elite. Maud Brooks Cotton was married to John Adams Cotton, president of the Henderson Normal and Industrial School. Marie Clay Clinton was the third wife of George Wylie Clinton, a bishop in the AMEZ Church. Born in Alabama in 1871, she graduated from Clark University with high honors. She was vice principal of a school in Huntsville, Alabama, when she married George Clinton in 1901. A gifted singer, she was also "a good speaker, a talented writer, and a woman of queenly dignity and cordial disposition." In addition to being first president of the NCFCWC, she was an officer in the Woman's Home and Foreign Mission Society of the AMEZ Church.[112]

Marie Clinton's successor, Charlotte Hawkins Brown, held office until 1935. Brown, who was principal of Palmer Memorial Institute in Sedalia, near Greensboro, became a nationally known leader of African American women. Born in Henderson in 1883, the granddaughter of a slave, she moved with her family to Cambridge, Massachusetts, when she was a child. She attended Cambridge public schools and was considered a gifted student. A chance meeting with Alice Freeman Palmer, president of Wellesley College, enabled her to go to college. Palmer paid her expenses at Salem Normal College in Massachusetts and was an important influence on Brown for the rest of her life. In 1901 a field secretary of the American Missionary Association persuaded Brown to return to North Carolina to teach. When she arrived, she found a primitive school. The missionary association closed it early in 1902, and Brown decided to open her own liberal arts and industrial school. With the help of Charles Duncan McIver, president of North Carolina's normal college for white women in Greensboro, and Harvard's Charles W. Eliot, she raised enough money to establish the new school. After Alice Freeman Palmer's death in December 1902, she named it Palmer Memorial Institute in honor of her mentor and benefactor.[113]

The NCFCWC served as a focal point for black women's reform, much as the NCFWC did for white women. Unlike the white federation, however, the state association of African American women had an avowedly political purpose from the beginning: it aimed at securing equal rights for blacks.

Although white women denied any interest in politics or the vote, the interests of women's voluntary associations, especially women's clubs, led them inevitably into politics, and woman suffrage sentiment began to grow in the first decade of the twentieth century. In 1913 white women in Morganton and Greenville formed local suffrage societies. In December of that year, a group of women including Laura Holmes Reilley, Anna Forbes Liddell, and Suzanne Bynum organized the Equal Suffrage Association of North Carolina (ESA). Within a year the association claimed chapters in fifteen towns, with members-at-large all over the state.[114]

Woman suffrage was unpopular in North Carolina, and suffragists needed leaders who lent respectability to the cause. Barbara Bynum Henderson, president of the ESA from 1913 to 1916, filled the bill. She was the daughter of Episcopal minister William Shipp Bynum, the wife of

University of North Carolina professor Archibald Henderson, and the mother of five children. She was a gracious hostess, and her hobbies included painting, embroidery, and other "ladylike accomplishments." She was also a Phi Beta Kappa graduate of the University of North Carolina, a scholar, and a poet. Her poems were published in periodicals throughout the nation, and her translation of Hans Ernst Lissauer's "Hassgesangegen England" ("Hymn of Hate Against England") from German to English won her international renown. Better educated and more intelligent than many men, with all the charm of the southern lady, Barbara Henderson was a living refutation of many of the arguments against woman suffrage.[115]

The ESA's work came to an end in 1920, when the Nineteenth Amendment enfranchised American women. North Carolina suffragists, like those in the rest of the nation, turned their attention to teaching women how to use their newly won rights. In October 1920 they organized the North Carolina League of Women Voters (LWV). The league considered itself an educational agency, instructing men as well as women in the mechanics of citizenship and encouraging voters to become familiar with political candidates and political issues, but it also developed its own agenda for reform. In 1926 journalist Nell Battle Lewis called it "the most radical women's organization in the State," although, she conceded, it "indulges only in conservative radicalism."[116]

Gertrude Weil of Goldsboro served as the last president of the ESA and became the first president of the state League of Women Voters. Although she was a native North Carolinian, her background set her apart from her colleagues in female voluntary associations. Her father, Henry Weil, was a Jewish immigrant who had come to the United States from Germany in 1860. Fifteen years later, Henry married sixteen-year-old Mina Rosenthal. By the time Gertrude was born in 1879, Henry and his two brothers, Herman and Sol, were prosperous merchants. Gertrude spent much of her adolescence away from North Carolina; she attended Horace Mann High School in New York and Smith College in Northampton, Massachusetts. While at Smith, she became interested in social reform and in "home culture clubs" for working-class women in particular. She vowed to find useful work, as a volunteer if not as a paid professional. After she graduated from Smith in 1901, she returned to Goldsboro and became active in the Goldsboro Woman's Club and in the NCFWC. A courageous woman, Weil never shied away from controversy throughout her long life.[117]

North Carolina's women reformers hoped that the ballot would increase their influence in state government. Just two months after the ratification of the Nineteenth Amendment, representatives of some of the major white women's organizations—the NCFWC, the WCTU, the LWV, and the Federation of Business and Professional Women's Clubs—met to

Barbara Bynum Henderson
A poet and an internationally known scholar of German literature,
Barbara Bynum Henderson served as president of the North Carolina
Equal Suffrage Association from 1913 to 1916. She is shown here with
two of her five children.

**Gertrude Weil, at the time of her graduation
from Smith College, 1901**
Gertrude Weil became interested in women's clubs while she was in
college. She went on to become a leader in the North Carolina Federation of Women's Clubs, the Equal Suffrage Association, and the League
of Women Voters.

discuss the formation of a women's lobby. The result was the Legislative Council of North Carolina Women. The council focused on legislation of particular interest to women. It worked only for bills that all of its member organizations supported and that were not being pushed by other organizations. During the 1920s the council endorsed a wide range of reforms.[118]

The council benefited from the administrative talents of its first president, Cornelia Petty Jerman, who held office until 1933. Born in Moore County in 1874, Cornelia Petty moved to Carthage, the county seat, as a child. She had a beautiful voice and studied at the New England Conservatory of Music, where her teachers encouraged her to become a professional opera singer. When her father objected, she abandoned that idea and taught for a year at LaGrange College for Women. While visiting friends in Raleigh she met T. Palmer Jerman, a businessman. She married him in 1898 and lived the rest of her life in Raleigh. Jerman participated in a number of voluntary associations. She was a charter member of the Raleigh Woman's Club and the Raleigh Equal Suffrage Association and served terms as president of the North Carolina ESA and the NCFWC. Her extensive experience with these organizations made her the ideal candidate to lead the council. She earned the respect of men and women alike; Josephus Daniels called her "The State's First Woman."[119]

Jerman was typical of the women who led North Carolina's voluntary associations in the late nineteenth and early twentieth centuries. They were well-educated, talented women who created their own opportunities when society denied them access to politics and the professions on an equal basis with men. They were women who were proud of their sex and who believed in the power of femininity—the power of women to accomplish good through united effort.

White women in voluntary associations drew much of their inspiration from the feminine ideal that white southerners had begun developing before the Civil War. The lady was a compelling image and an empowering one. Women in the New South found in the ideal of the lady imperatives for action that would move them beyond domesticity. Over the years, white southern women had deemphasized the lady's weaknesses—her frailty, passivity, and irrationality—and instead had focused on her strengths—her moral superiority, domestic management skills, nurturing qualities, fortitude, and courage. Building on a heritage of feminine strength that had been most dramatically demonstrated during the war that destroyed the Old South, white southern women wanted to exert their "irresistible power" in shaping the New South. They wanted to enter the public realm and redefine it to include roles for themselves. They believed that they were uniquely qualified to address issues of particular concern to women: health, charity, morality, and human welfare.

The lady also influenced the lives and thought of African American organized women. While white women used their status as ladies to justify their public activities, African American women attempted to convince whites—men and women alike—that they *were* ladies, entitled to the same respect and privileges automatically granted to white women. In her memoirs Charlotte Hawkins Brown recalled the words of a white woman to her mother: "Caroline, if there be anything like a colored lady I want you to be one." Those words impelled Brown throughout her life. "What a challenge to Negro womanhood!" she wrote. "That story—that challenge burnt its way into my very soul, and I now suspect my first real knowledge of difference in races was born when I heard it." Brown and other African American clubwomen wanted to win for themselves the right to exercise the power of femininity and to use that power to improve the status of their race. Assumptions about gender—about black men, black women, white men, white women—formed the ideological foundation of white supremacy. When African American women demanded that gender take precedence over race, when they insisted that generalizations about women applied to all women, not just those with light skin, they struck at the very heart of the South's system of race relations.[120]

African American and white women in voluntary associations had much in common, a fact that most black women recognized, while most white women did not. They undertook similar projects, they worked for similar goals, and they adhered to the same model of womanhood, although it affected them in different ways. North Carolina's ladies shared a common rhetoric, a common code of conduct, a common definition of femininity and feminine responsibility. Ladies believed that they had special obligations to uphold moral standards, to oversee their families' well-being, to care for the less fortunate, to preserve their heritage and to transmit it to the next generation. Ladies found that voluntary associations enabled them to perform their duties more effectively. Women's leaders of both races worked to establish networks of women's voluntary associations, networks that would, in the words of Sallie Cotten, be "the foundation for a sisterhood of women in the future."[121]

Cotten's "sisterhood" was an exclusive sorority, bound by the constraints of race and class. When she and other white female reformers spoke of "women," they most often meant women like themselves: white and privileged. Most of them assumed that African American women were incapable of behaving like ladies. They acknowledged in theory that working-class and poor white women could be ladies; in practice, however, they often viewed these women as their wards, to be protected and enlightened. While white organized women frequently initiated projects to assist other women, their attitude toward those they helped was more like that of a kindly aunt toward an ignorant and sometimes misguided niece than that of one sister helping another. Class distinctions divided African American women as well, as middle- and upper-class women struggled to uplift other members of their race at the same time they separated themselves from the black masses. Organized women considered women of their own class and race to be kindred spirits, but they distinguished themselves from women who failed to conform to the lady's code of conduct. The southern feminine ideal that was, to borrow Cotten's phrase, the "foundation for a sisterhood" created powerful bonds among women; it also created sharp divisions between them.

The "sisterhood" of organized women in North Carolina included rural temperance advocates, urban clubwomen, patriotic Daughters, and suffragists. Despite differences among them, they shared a faith in the power of femininity and a desire to exercise that power in the world outside their homes—a world that, they believed, desperately needed women's unique skills to solve its problems.

Between 1880 and 1930 they championed a number of causes and sponsored many different projects at local and state levels. For many women, however, the most pressing concerns were problems resulting from alcohol abuse and sexual misconduct, behavior that destroyed individuals, disrupted families, and caused immense suffering and heartache among innocent women and children. Steeped in a rhetoric that proclaimed feminine moral superiority and determined to exercise the lady's moral authority, organized women made their first impact on public life in crusades for prohibition and moral reform.

II

"The Sword of the Spirit"
CRUSADES FOR TEMPERANCE AND MORAL REFORM

"*I* believe God is calling us by name to take the 'Sword of the Spirit' and go forth as brave soldiers battling for Him, our homes and our native State."[1]

The year was 1884; the speaker, Laura Annie Winston. Addressing the second convention of the North Carolina WCTU, Winston blended the rhetoric of religion and revolution to enlist recruits in a war to protect their homes, their families, and their communities. The enemy included drinking, illicit sex, divorce, suggestive literature, and popular music. The weapon women would use to vanquish the foe was their own righteousness. Winston and her sisters in arms believed that women were morally superior to men and that they were obliged to uphold and enforce moral standards at home and in public. Violations of conventional morality devastated families and disrupted community life; they also represented a challenge to women's moral authority. "Our homes are in jeopardy," cried the WCTU president in 1886. "The children of our people are in danger." Women fought back to protect their families and to assert their power. In the late nineteenth and early twentieth centuries, thousands of women took up the "Sword of the Spirit" and set out to champion virtue in a sinful world.[2]

They joined with men who agreed that drinking was the source of a variety of social and economic ills. Liquor, a Davie County man wrote in 1885, "destroys all moral principle, all sentiments of honor, all feelings of humanity; it changes good nature to churlishness, a kind husband to an unfeeling monster, an industrious and thriving man to an idle vagabond."[3] Intoxication could lead a man to commit violent and criminal acts; habitual inebriation could leave his family destitute, dependent on relatives or public charity for support.

Crime and poverty were just two of the problems that temperance advocates attributed to alcohol abuse. They also believed that the "liquor traffic" discouraged economic growth. Money invested in saloons, breweries, and distilleries was money diverted from businesses that reformers considered more worthwhile. Intoxication and its aftereffects hampered the efficiency and reliability of industrial and agricultural workers and increased the risk of on-the-job accidents. Liquor contributed little to the common good, reformers argued; instead, it debilitated men and discouraged productive labor. The WCTU and its allies saw alcohol as the cause of a myriad of social ills and offered temperance—defined as "the moderate use of all things helpful and the total abstinence from all things harmful"—as the cure.[4]

In the 1880s and early 1890s, campaigns against "demon rum" united middle-class whites and African Americans. African American prohibitionists thought that liquor was especially harmful for blacks. "We are affected by its presence as is no other race in the country," a Winston correspondent wrote in the *Star of Zion* in 1886. Nearly two decades later, a prominent clubwoman declared that "intemperance is one of the greatest foes to the progress and development of the Negro." Moreover, black leaders hoped that interracial cooperation in the temperance movement would help to dispel prejudice. "As we have said before, it is the one issue which is to go farther toward settling the race problem in the South than all other issues combined," the *Star of Zion* editorialized. "White people of the South have learned more of the ability of the Negro through the Prohibition agitation than from any other question which has been discussed since the war. We gladly welcome it." For African American reformers, temperance was a major milestone on the road to "uplifting" blacks and achieving equality.[5]

Although whites and African Americans joined together in the fight for prohibition, it was an unequal partnership. Blacks complained when whites invited them to attend temperance rallies and then sent them to sit in the galleries. Some African Americans believed prohibition to be an "obstruction to the moral, social, political and material progress of our people," yet another attempt by whites to restrict the liberty of the race the Civil War had supposedly set free. Writing in 1929, in the waning years of national prohibition, the editor of the *Norwich (New York) Union* argued that white southerners outlawed liquor solely to ensure a docile black labor force: "Sober, the southern negro was industrious and civil; drunk, he was worthless as a laborer and dangerous as a citizen. To keep liquor away from the negro was the object of the prohibition movement in the south." White reformers, the editor concluded, never intended to restrict drinking among members of their own race.[6]

The *Union*'s writer must have been familiar with temperance propaganda. In the late 1800s and early 1900s white prohibitionists appealed to white racism even as they attempted to win African American support. They recognized that they needed black votes; according to Mary Woody, North Carolina blacks were "a great lever to be adjusted and applied against the liquor traffic." But at the same time that whites sought to manipulate the "lever" of African American political power, they also used the race card to trump their white opponents. Southern prohibition literature was replete with references to violent, drunken black men who threatened white women. When local option referenda failed, white temperance advocates blamed African Americans who, they charged, sold their votes to the "wets." In 1900 white supremacists included this allegation among their justifications for disfranchisement.[7]

As Glenda Gilmore has argued, the temperance movement began as "a novel experiment in interracial cooperation" but became instead an example of missed opportunities, especially among women. Women of both races signed the total abstinence pledge, donned the badge of white ribbon, and marched onto the public stage. WCTU leaders developed what Barbara Leslie Epstein has called a "politics of domesticity," a politics that grew out of popular assumptions about inherent feminine traits and that promoted gender solidarity. They emphasized commonalities among women and urged women to help each other. Temperance tracts focused on the havoc liquor wreaked in the lives of women and their offspring. They portrayed battered wives and abused children—victims of alcohol-induced violence—and told tragic tales of families reduced to poverty when male breadwinners squandered money on drink or lost their jobs because of alcohol addiction. Orators and pamphlets warned women that intoxication weakened a man's ability to resist other temptations. A husband's sexual indiscretions not only threatened marital harmony; they might also endanger his wife's health if he infected her with a sexually transmitted disease. The lurid stories reiterated the same theme: innocent women suffered when men they loved and relied on drank to excess, and all women should empathize because someday they might be forced to endure similar hardships. The underlying message in WCTU propaganda was that all women were equal in their dependence and vulnerability.[8] Female temperance reformers understood that some women in both races and all classes bore the consequences of alcohol abuse, and they professed a belief that women shared a set of universal feminine values and characteristics. But they had trouble converting these abstractions into concrete practices when they confronted differences among themselves in the WCTU.

White and African American women in North Carolina were unable to surmount the barriers race imposed. Part of the problem stemmed from white women's reluctance to relinquish control over temperance work among blacks to African American women. As Gilmore explains, "white women refused to acknowledge black women leaders and consistently tried to subordinate black temperance activities to white authority." African

American women responded by forming their own state union.[9]

Although white racism was the immediate cause of friction between blacks and whites in the state WCTU, other factors also coalesced to create obstacles to interracial cooperation. Participation in the temperance movement held fundamentally different meanings for white and African American women because of the immense dissimilarities in the contexts of their lives. White women were accustomed to operating in a society that extolled their virtue and praised them for their purity, piety, and moral superiority. They were members of the ruling race who, because of their status as white southern women, had at least nominal authority in some areas. When they entered public life as arbiters of morality, they were acting within a long-standing tradition and could use gender conventions to expand their influence. For white women, as Ruth Bordin and Barbara Leslie Epstein have argued, the temperance movement represented an assertion of the power of femininity, an attempt to enshrine domestic values in the public realm. "Home is the central power of the world," a WCTU leader proclaimed. "The nation is only the door yard in which the bigger boys play." In 1888 Mary Woody predicted: "The future shall be fashioned in the interest of the home. Though now the air rings with the anthem of 'Home, sweet home,' then the whole country will be filled with its atmosphere. The homes of this nation are to be established. Woman is to be the priestess in fact as well as in name." White women in the WCTU wanted to invest the institution of the home—woman's domain—with the authority of the established church of the colonial era and to claim for themselves the power previously accorded ministers and male lay leaders. They imagined a world in which feminine moral influence was a real force, and they found in the temperance movement a forum for the assertion of feminine sovereignty over all issues relating to morality.[10]

White women were able to use feminine stereotypes to their advantage. African Americans, on the other hand, had to fight against prevailing assumptions about black women. White society granted African American women no authority, moral or otherwise; indeed, whites frequently portrayed African American women as immoral or, at best, amoral. These images, deeply embedded in popular culture, doubtless influenced even the most well-meaning white WCTU members in their efforts to cooperate with blacks and added an extra chore to the work of African American women for temperance: they had to demonstrate that they too were qualified for the position of "priestess." For African American women, temperance was part of a larger crusade to win white respect for black womanhood and to improve the status of African Americans. They insisted that *all* women possessed the characteristic virtues that gender conventions ascribed to ladies, and thereby they asserted their equality with whites. In addition, they worked to eliminate liquor because they believed that alcohol abuse held blacks down. While white temperance advocates attempted to reorder the world according to "feminine" values, African Americans endeavored to promote the progress of their race and to turn their ideal of racial equality into reality.[11]

Both white and African American temperance advocates relied on the rhetoric of domesticity to win support for their work. "Our homes are the grand centres of the nation, citadels of power, purity and every good influence," the white president of the Texas WCTU declared in 1886. Several years later an African American minister in North Carolina praised the WCTU for building "happy homes," while an article on "Woman's Work" among blacks called the home "the centre of civilization." In temperance parlance, home was synonymous with family, and the institution of the family was the cornerstone of the social structure. Stable families and secure homes nurtured the self-discipline and morality that individuals needed to become productive members of society.[12]

Although blacks and whites used similar language, their agendas were quite different. According to many African American reformers in the late nineteenth century, blacks had been deprived of a heritage of domestic stability. An 1899 editorial in Hampton Institute's *Southern Workman* decried "the greatest curse of slavery, the extinction of home life." So while white WCTU members talked of *defending* the family and the sanctity of the home, African Americans spoke of *creating* a domestic sanctuary and of preparing black women to assume the mantle of moral authority. "The race calls for mothers," the vice president of an African American women's college told the WCTU convention in 1901, "women whose duty it will be to train mothers who shall know how to educate children." Union president Mary Lynch responded by boasting that because of the WCTU, "homes are purer, womankind more conscientious, and childhood safer than five years ago. Young ladies who have been temperance advocates are now mothers of homes." White WCTU leaders sought to "establish" the institution of the home and increase women's influence in public life; their African American counterparts concentrated on strengthening families and nurturing domestic values in the black community as part of their overall program of racial uplift.[13]

The patterns African American and white women set in the WCTU would be replicated in other female voluntary associations. White and black women formed identical organizations, enunciated many of the same goals, frequently undertook similar projects, and shared a common rhetoric. But the many similarities did not erase fundamental differences. Race and gender interacted to shape the public lives of North Carolina's organized women. The results of that interaction became evident when women took up the "Sword of the Spirit" and launched their first sustained foray into the public arena.

For African American and white women—first in the WCTU, later in other associations—liquor was the most visible of numerous threats to the moral well-being of their families. Activists feared that the forces of industrialization and urbanization that were transforming North Carolina economically and socially were eating away at the moral fiber of the state's population. Annie Blackwell, corresponding secretary of the African American WCTU and editor of its newspaper, the *Tidings*, decried the materialism and greed of modern life and condemned "saturnalian revelries" such as "the song and dance of the young lady and the gambling of the young man, and the greatest of the great, rum." Several years earlier Mary Woody had warned the white WCTU that "all this improvement means . . . the increase of saloons, the growth of sin." Blackwell, Woody, and other reformers worried that North Carolinians had bartered their souls for economic prosperity.[14]

Vice was the enemy, and the saloon was the enemy's lair, a "sinful cess-pool for the souls of men." It lured men away from the family hearth and offered an array of temptations antithetical to the values the home symbolized. The home created an atmosphere of stability; the saloon catered to a transient clientele. The home protected purity and the sanctity of marriage; the saloon harbored prostitution. The home instilled republican principles in children; the saloon was the scene of vote buying and shady political deals. The WCTU summed up the contrast in a resolution adopted in 1888: "Home is to women and children their most sacred heritage, and the saloon its blighting curse." The home epitomized goodness and the virtues women of the WCTU cherished; the saloon represented all the evils they wanted to eradicate. "The doors of the saloon," a white WCTU member announced, "open towards hell."[15]

Both African American and white temperance activists wanted to prevent children from walking down that deadly path. An African American woman called for prohibition "to save the boys and girls," while Mary Woody advised, "The first work to be mentioned after the organization of a Union is work among the children." WCTU leaders of both races and at all levels—national, state, and local—emphasized the importance of juvenile auxiliaries, called Bands of Hope or Loyal Temperance Legions. "A Union without an L.T.L.," decreed the white state president in 1896, "is like a home without children." At the first state convention in 1883, the Greensboro union reported organizing one Band of Hope for white children and donating "Band of Hope lesson books" to four black Sunday schools. Other branches followed suit. Most white locals formed auxiliaries for white children, and some also worked with blacks. African American unions established Bands of Hope or Loyal Temperance Legions in their communities. Whites sometimes found that starting children's groups was easier than sustaining them; African Americans may have encountered the same difficulty. In 1893 the superintendent of the white WCTU's Juvenile Department attributed the decline in young people's affiliates to the increased emphasis on temperance in Sunday schools, the lack of dedicated leaders for children at the local level, and the inability of the state association to hire an organizer for children.[16]

In addition to the juvenile societies, the union sponsored competitions in writing and public speaking; women adopted the slogan "From contest to conquest" and awarded gold and silver medals to the winners. Speech contests were particularly popular in the years before North Carolina enacted prohibition because they accomplished several purposes: they introduced participants to the arguments against alcohol consumption, raised money for local unions, and provided publicity for the temperance cause. In 1893 the white state superintendent of contest work reported 189 contests in the previous year, with "at least" 1136 speakers. A year later 317 competitions were held. Interest in the program declined among whites later in the decade, after the state organization stopped furnishing the medals free of charge, but a few chapters continued to sponsor the contests, and the white state association continued to endorse the tactic. The competitions remained popular among African American temperance unions.[17]

State leaders also reminded women of their obligations to their own children. In 1885, for example, an officer in the white organization advised women to avoid serving items like peppers, pepper sauces, and pickles to their sons. "They cultivate a taste for firey [sic] things in the growing boy," she declared. "Ought not every mother to know that if her boys fill themselves up on such things at her table not all the prayers of all the saints can save him from the wine cup and the brothel?" Temperance work, she concluded, began in the kitchen.[18]

And it led to the statehouse. Adopting a view of government similar to that of twentieth-century Progressives, the white WCTU believed the state should intervene to save children from the temptations of "the wine cup and the brothel." For nearly fifty years, North Carolina's white WCTU lobbied for enactment and enforcement of a scientific temperance instruction law, a law that would require public schools to incorporate lessons about the harmful effects of alcohol into their curricula. The national WCTU first proposed a plan for temperance education in 1879. The plan required members to visit physiology classes and ask school boards to adopt Julia Colman's *Alcohol and Hygiene* as a required textbook. Within three years the union was demanding state laws that would make temperance education compulsory.[19]

The North Carolina WCTU took up the cause at the time of its founding in 1883. Although the women endorsed a state law, at first they concentrated on persuading individual teachers to include temperance in the curriculum because, as the superintendent of scientific temperance instruction explained in 1884, the public might not be ready for the state to require it. The state union purchased "about four hundred copies" of Colman's book and distributed them to schools. The union also advertised the book at county normal institutes for white and African American teachers and initiated a petition drive for a scientific temperance instruction law. During 1885 the women collected signatures, appealed to teachers and school officials for support, and sent material to every member of the General Assembly. The 1885 legislature failed to enact the WCTU's proposed law but instituted a mandatory examination on physiology and hygiene for all teachers and adopted a textbook the union recommended. "Thus we have the substance without the name of that which we desire," the superintendent of scientific temperance instruction concluded.[20]

Still, the union continued to work for "the name" as well. In 1887 local chapters renewed the petition drive; more than seventeen thousand North Carolinians signed. Lydia Blair, the superintendent of the Department of Scientific Temperance Instruction, wrote every legislator and encouraged each WCTU member to write to the representatives from her district. Blair and the superintendent of Legislation and Petition appeared before the General Assembly's committee on education to plead for the bill, but no one agreed to sponsor it. At the annual convention in October, Blair glumly reported, "The superintendent of this department has no account of victories won or flattering hopes to place before her hearers, but simply a plain statement of facts concerning a failure."[21]

The WCTU persisted. The women continued their petition drive and asked teachers and principals to introduce the subject voluntarily until a law was enacted. In the fall of 1890 Blair distributed a hundred petitions but secured only eight hundred signatures. The disappointing return caused her to reconsider her plan to submit the scientific temperance instruction proposal to the upcoming legislature, scheduled to convene in January, but state president Mary Woody persuaded her to persevere. Blair sent additional petitions to locals, along with a letter explaining the urgency of the matter. A Democratic lawyer, who remained anonymous in WCTU records, agreed to draft the bill. In 1891 the General Assembly, composed "largely of home-loving, [Southern Farmers'] Alliance men," unanimously passed the measure. The women were jubilant, and the *Union Signal* called it one of the best laws of its kind in the nation.[22]

Passage of the scientific temperance instruction law was the first major legislative victory for North Carolina's organized women, and it foreshadowed things to come. Women's voluntary associations would continue to lobby for legislation they believed would benefit North Carolinians, and, in the process, they would participate in a redefinition of government and its responsibilities. When Mary Woody asked in 1884, "Why should not the State hold the teachers responsible for drunkenness?" she posed a specific question that was part of a larger discussion on the proper role of government. Woody and other temperance advocates envisioned a government that actively promoted the welfare of its citizens, a government that acted to protect individuals from their own frailties. When Woody argued that the state should "hold the teachers responsible for drunkenness," she was conceding to government greater authority over individual behavior than it had had in the recent past. In the early twentieth century, Progressive reformers would extend that authority even further, in areas ranging from education to prison reform. Increasingly, state government would assume responsibility for the moral, physical, intellectual, and cultural development of its people.[23]

For the WCTU, legislative victory was just the beginning. Union leaders were determined that, once passed, the law would be enforced. "The most important duty before our Union for the coming year is to see that the Scientific Instruction law does not become a dead letter by being neglected in the schools," began the "Plan of Work" for 1891–92. The state organization told local affiliates to appoint representatives to visit schools, talk to teachers and administrators about the harmful effects of alcohol, and distribute literature. If they discovered teachers who refused to teach temperance lessons, the women were to report them to the county superintendent of schools. "Use all sweet and gentle influence to rectify matters," the state "Plan of Work" instructed; then it added, "if these fail, report to the State Superintendent of Public Instruction and appeal to the strong arm of the law." In 1896 the union asked newspapers to publish the text of the law; women hoped that if people understood what it meant they would demand its enforcement. Two years later twelve unions reported that the law was being observed in their towns, and nine found some compliance. Sixteen unions complained that schools ignored the mandate in their communities; eight of those blamed the indifference of local officials for the lack of enforcement. The WCTU continued to demand that scientific temperance instruction be incorporated into the curriculum. Some local unions provided textbooks, and the state organization monitored the activities of the General Assembly to halt attempts to weaken or repeal the law.[24]

While the white state WCTU focused much of its attention on the scientific temperance instruction law in the 1880s and 1890s, women of both races found other ways to fight "the Hydra-Headed fiend—Alcohol." Since women could not vote, they knew that achieving their ultimate goal—prohibition—depended on their ability to convert men to the temperance cause; therefore, unions waged relentless publicity campaigns. Members signed the "total abstinence" pledge and encouraged others to do likewise. They urged ministers to preach temperance sermons and asked congregations to substitute grape juice for wine at communion; often they supplied the juice themselves. Where they found sympathetic editors, they wrote regular temperance columns for local newspapers. They operated booths at both the white and the African American state fairs and asked fair officials to prohibit the sale of alcoholic beverages and abolish prizes for homemade wines. Each state union also published its own periodical—the *Tidings* for African Americans and the *North Carolina White Ribbon* for whites. Unions distributed pamphlets and leaflets "to create a temperance sentiment among all classes of people." They believed that their efforts reaped results. In 1896 the white WCTU president reported, "A recent Liquor Dealers' Association in its annual meeting declared that 'it had no enemy to fear but the W.C.T.U.'"[25]

They also held numerous mass meetings. State officers believed these meetings could exert a powerful influence on public opinion, and they offered detailed instructions for local unions that were conducting them. "The mass meeting should be thoroughly announced for days and planned for as carefully as you would plan for a wedding," white state president Mary Cartland told the 1892 convention, comparing temperance rallies to the ritual that marked one of the most significant events in a woman's life. White and African American leaders insisted that children should have a part in the program, "for they are the fortress of the future." Meetings featured speeches, prayers, hymn singing, and recitations and sometimes provoked an emotional response from the audience. In 1890, for example, African American temperance organizer Maggie Stevens reported that after hearing children read and recite at one meeting, "Great strong men came forward with tears in their eyes, saying it was what had long been needed."[26]

Moving men to tears was not enough; they must be moved to the ballot box as well. Local unions stepped up their activities when towns held local option elections. In Charlotte, for example, women started conducting daily prayer meetings a week before an election scheduled for 7 June 1886. Some women observed a day of prayer and fasting at the Tryon Street Methodist Church on election day. Other women showed up at the polls to pray, and organized bands of children marched by "carrying flowers and bearing aloft banners inscribed with mottos." Despite the women's efforts, the referendum failed. The *Charlotte Daily Observer* blamed the defeat on a heavy turnout by African Americans "who voted almost solidly for license"; the paper neglected to note that whites also overwhelmingly endorsed the saloon. According to historian Janette Greenwood, "Only the Fourth Ward, the city's most prosperous white neighborhood, supported the dry cause, and then by only thirteen votes."[27]

Unions in other towns employed tactics similar to those used in Charlotte. They sponsored rallies, circulated pamphlets and tracts prior to elections, and held prayer vigils on election day. In some places antiprohibitionists accused their opponents of manipulating women in order to intimidate voters. A reporter for the *New York World*, for example, claimed that during a local option election in Salisbury "preachers and prohibitionists" stationed "hundreds of women and children" at polling places, where they "clutched at the coats of the voters" and begged them, "Mister, for God's sake don't vote for whiskey." The reporter, who demonstrated more sympathy for the "wets" than the "drys," condemned such tactics because, he said, men who opposed prohibition stayed home rather than face the heartrending pleas of women and children. Female temperance advocates, on the other hand, complained that it was their supporters who shied away from the polls during local option referenda.[28]

Win or lose, women's work did not end when the votes were counted. State union leaders warned chapters in dry towns to remain vigilant to ensure that the law was enforced and advised them to hire private detectives if necessary to "ferret the matter out." Women in wet areas continued their campaigns to close the saloons. The white state organization, along with leading male prohibitionists, recommended that every application for a license to sell liquor be countered by a petition requesting that the license be denied. "No license" proved to be a successful strategy; some towns that had voted to remain wet in fact became dry. In 1893 liquor lobbyists convinced the legislature to pass a law removing the discretionary power of county commissioners, but the 1897 legislature restored the power. The white WCTU, meanwhile, began advocating "revised local option," a plan that would require voter approval before saloons could open at all. The plan's architects maintained that this would shift the burden of proof from the prohibitionists to the liquor dealers. The proposal never gained widespread support.[29]

Despite some setbacks, the WCTU was gaining ground. In 1902 the union acquired an influential ally when male representatives of the major white Protestant denominations met in Raleigh and formed the North Carolina Anti-Saloon League. From then on, the nonpartisan league led the fight against liquor in the state, while the WCTU kept up its publicity campaigns. The white union continued to remind teachers and school administrators to obey the scientific temperance instruction law and to admonish public officials to enforce it. African American unions maintained their efforts to eradicate alcohol abuse among blacks. "The gospel of temperance is being faithfully spread throughout the length and breadth of the State," the *Star of Zion* reported in 1903, "and the harvest will surely come."[30]

Temperance advocates had already begun to reap the harvest earlier that year. In January two antiliquor bills were introduced in the General Assembly: the Watts Bill, which prohibited the manufacture and sale of alcohol in rural areas, and the London Bill, which extended the ban to include small towns. The Anti-Saloon League and the white WCTU endorsed the London proposal, and the union circulated petitions in its behalf. According to historian Daniel Jay Whitener, "more than 100,000 voters and many women" signed. Antiprohibitionists also mobilized, and debate over both bills raged in the legislature and in the press for nearly two months. When it became apparent that the London Bill did not have enough votes to pass both houses, prohibitionists shifted their support to the Watts measure. Both houses approved it in late February. WCTU members were pleased but not ecstatic; the president of the white state union called it "a stepping stone to something higher."[31]

The something higher the WCTU aspired to was, of course, statewide prohibition. Although the Watts Law effectively eliminated liquor from much of North Carolina, union members would not be satisfied with anything less than the absolute exclusion of the "liquor traffic." The major white Protestant denominations agreed, and in 1907 the Anti-Saloon League went on record in favor of statewide prohibition. Governor Robert B. Glenn also sympathized. "One of the very first things I did after I became Governor," he boasted, "was to make a pledge to the Woman's Christian Temperance Union that I would devote every energy of my intellect and body to banish the drink demon forever from the borders of the State." In January 1908 he made good his promise; he asked a special session of the General Assembly to outlaw the manufacture and sale of "intoxicating liquors" throughout North Carolina. The legislature complied but added one amendment: the bill would take effect only if a majority of voters approved it in a special election to be held on May 26, 1908.[32]

Both sides immediately mobilized. The WCTU, applying skills perfected during twenty-five years of campaigning, worked to sway public opinion to the dry point of view. Women who were not affiliated with the union also participated. They organized "Ladies' Prohibition Committees" whose purpose was "to get up Prohibition Rallies, scatter literature, songs &c, influence voters and in every way possible may advance the Cause." In the town of Washington in eastern North Carolina, the women's committee sponsored a parade of "about six hundred school children and a large number of ladies in carriages." They sang songs and carried white flags and banners, some of which bore slogans reminiscent of the white supremacy campaigns. "Vote for Prohibition and Protect Us," one read. "You Protect Your Horses and Dogs by Law, Why Not Protect Us?" another asked. On May 26, women and children kept watch at polling places, appealing to voters just as they had done in earlier local option elections.[33]

This time they won. The referendum carried by a margin of more than forty-four thousand votes. Prohibitionists rejoiced, and the WCTU resolved to "co-operate with other Christian women in the State" to purchase a gift for Governor Glenn to thank him for his "brave stand" in support of prohibition.[34]

The enactment of statewide prohibition was a major victory for the WCTU. The union called for effective enforcement and, beginning in 1912, endorsed a prohibition amendment to the federal Constitution. But prohibition represented only one item on women's agenda for moral reform. From the time of the WCTU's founding in 1883, organized women of both races had been concerned with issues relating to sexual morality. They wanted to protect young girls from sexual abuse, to eliminate prostitution, to preserve the sanctity of marriage, and to replace the infamous double standard with a single standard of chastity that would be applied equally to both sexes.

Since before the Civil War, white southern women had complained— usually in diaries, occasionally in letters to women's magazines—about the prevailing mores that required absolute purity from women while overlooking men's sexual transgressions. Men were alleged to be too weak to resist temptations of the flesh; women, therefore, must demonstrate their superiority by forgiving men for their indiscretions. Some women wondered why men, who were supposed to be such paragons of strength and discipline, could not restrain their sexual appetites, and they called for a uniform code of sexual conduct.[35]

In the 1880s and the 1890s the white WCTU led the attack on the double standard; union president Mary Cartland labeled it a "legacy from the dark ages." At its fifth convention the North Carolina WCTU proclaimed, "We believe . . . that there should be but one standard of morality for men and women." Later conventions ratified similar resolutions, and the women searched for ways to change deeply entrenched attitudes. In 1895 one white union member blamed women themselves for perpetuating the double standard: "When will mothers recognize their responsibility in training their sons to be *protectors,* instead of *betrayers* of women, and when shall we all believe that God requires men to be just as pure as women?" Women must exercise feminine moral authority if they expected to reform masculine behavior.[36]

As we have seen, in the South the double standard in fact represented multiple codes of sexual conduct, codes that varied according to race as well as gender. The ideal of innate feminine purity applied only to white women, and from the nineteenth century onward African Americans decried stereotypes that portrayed promiscuity as the norm among black women. "A man or woman is very corrupt in their morals who entertains the idea that there are no virtuous females," the Reverend George W. Clinton declared in 1885. "None but low people think such a thing. Among our race, as well as among the white race, we have females with unspotted character." African American leaders repeatedly exhorted black men to treat African American women with the same deference white men accorded white women. "If there is any one quality of the white man for which we honor him, it is his delicate respect for, and undying devotion to, woman," the *Goldsboro Appeal* editorialized in 1886. Five years later the *Star of Zion* reminded readers that "the young man who respects himself will respect our womanhood, and will do his best to maintain its purity, and will risk his own life in defending it against the encroachments of the wretches bent on its destruction."[37]

While male ministers and writers called on black men to venerate and protect the women of their race, African American women worked to overcome negative images and to fight against sexual exploitation. Stereotypes of black female promiscuity were rooted in myth and fantasy, but sexual harassment and assault were all too real. Women who worked as domestic servants found themselves in a particularly precarious position. In 1904 educator Nannie Helen Burroughs advised black women to spurn the sexual advances of white men and implored them "to rise in the pride of their womanhood and vindicate themselves . . . by teaching all men that black womanhood is as sacred as white womanhood." Women in the WCTU and women's clubs vociferously and repeatedly defended themselves and other African American women against allegations of immorality.[38]

The sexual dimensions of white supremacy gave their crusade a political meaning. In their campaigns to disfranchise African American men white supremacists built on the premise that only white women were vulnerable to sexual assault and only white men were "men enough" to protect them. They excluded blacks from prevailing gender conventions and denied the humanity of African Americans by arguing that black women were not "real women" and black men were not "real men." If whites conceded the sanctity of African American womanhood, they must also recognize the manhood of African American men and acknowledge black men's right to protect black women in the same way white men were entitled to protect white women. African American women understood that when they asserted the sanctity of African American womanhood, they were also asserting racial equality.[39]

That was a concept most white southerners refused to accept. White women—self-proclaimed champions of feminine purity and moral righteousness—remained silent about the plight of African American women. They too were caught in a tightly woven web of white supremacy and gender conventions. Defending the virtue of black women would have required some white women to confront men in their own households; perhaps some wives found it easier to accept racist stereotypes that portrayed black women as inherently promiscuous than to blame their husbands for infidelity. Although miscegenation caused heartache for white women, they kept their grievances within their homes and launched no public crusade in behalf of their abused sisters.

Instead, white reformers concentrated on promoting "social purity" among women and men of their own race. Although they found that they could not eliminate the double standard, they attempted to assist the "fallen women" who, they believed, were its victims. In 1886 state WCTU president Mary Woody declared that "to the Christian woman's heart her sister's soul should be a precious jewel even though it be lost in the mire of filth and sin." Three years later the WCTU committed itself to retrieving those "precious jewels"; the convention resolved "that we as women will use our utmost efforts to encourage and strengthen our sisters of every name and profession—that their sorrows shall be our sorrows. If they have strayed we will try to reclaim them; if they are oppressed we will seek redress, and whenever we find the law of the State unjust towards any, we will by petition and agitation endeavor to change the same."[40]

White women in the WCTU held a sentimental view of prostitutes. They assumed that no woman entered the profession voluntarily and that, given the opportunity, prostitutes would give up their trade. Beginning in the 1880s, members of the WCTU, along with the King's Daughters, set out to "rescue and save" their deviant sisters. In 1887 delegates to the state WCTU convention pledged to "strive by our efforts at an early day to provide a home for those poor unfortunates who would turn from a life of sin to one of truth and purity." Although the state union never established such a home, some local unions offered refuge for prostitutes and assisted those who wished to change their way of life. In 1888 the Charlotte union operated two shelters for "friendless women" where women could live until they found employment. Three years later the superintendent of Social Purity in Raleigh described prayer meetings for prostitutes in a Baptist mission. Attendance was good, she reported, and many of the women responded to the religious message: "Some have asked for prayers, and one has joined our W.C.T.U." The woman, she continued, had placed her children in foster homes and found a new occupation. In addition, the Raleigh union was working with the King's Daughters to open a rescue home. Durham women cooperated with the King's Daughters in similar work. In 1891 the WCTU asked the legislature to provide for "fallen women" and to save those who might be vulnerable. Bewailing "the helpless and almost hopeless condition of girls thrown upon the world to provide for themselves without a knowledge of any occupation whereby they may earn an honest living," the state union petitioned the General Assembly to appropriate twenty thousand dollars for the establishment of an industrial school for white girls. Lawmakers failed to fulfill their request.[41]

Women in some towns visited brothels and prayed with the inmates; the visits proved to be eye-opening experiences. "We have witnessed many sad sights," one woman told the WCTU's state convention in 1895, "and been shocked at the depravity to which our poor sisters have fallen." Local circles of King's Daughters offered medical care, food, clothing, and other assistance—including "good advice"—to prostitutes and their children. "They are her [North Carolina's] daughters and our sisters," Kate Olds explained in 1902, "and it seems to remain with the women to provide and care for those who have become what they are through these 'Lords of Creation' who make a plaything of them and tiring, cast them adrift." Her contemporaries agreed that men were usually to blame when women violated standards of sexual propriety.[42]

Asheville women, led by Mrs. A. E. Pease, launched the most extensive effort to reform prostitutes in North Carolina. Pease, superintendent of Social Purity for the local WCTU, visited "women whose lives are notoriously immoral" and tried to persuade them to forsake their "evil ways." In the early 1890s she and other members of the local WCTU investigated the possibility of establishing a halfway house for prostitutes. Although the union decided to abandon the plan when women learned that similar homes elsewhere had been unsuccessful, one woman—perhaps Pease herself—refused to give up and continued to raise money. In 1893 Pease reported that women of Asheville, acting independently of the WCTU, had accumulated enough money to start an industrial school for prostitutes where they could prepare for jobs as domestic servants; however, they still needed money to pay for furnishings and operating expenses. The Lindley Training School opened in 1897. Seven members of its board of managers were also affiliated with the WCTU; Pease was the board's vice president. The school housed between fifteen and twenty women and their children. In 1900 the board of managers reported that in the preceding year a total of thirty-nine women had lived at Lindley. Of these, six had returned to their homes, nine had found jobs as domestic servants, one had married, and two had been sent away to school. Eighteen women and eight children were currently in residence. By 1912 the school had expanded to accommodate fifty-one women and their offspring.[43]

From the beginning, leaders found that North Carolina's white organized women were reluctant to undertake "rescue work." "The Department of Social Purity has received but little attention in the Local Unions," Mary Woody lamented in 1887. "I sometimes fear that this subject is misunderstood. It is on the positive side of the question—Purity—not the negative—Impurity." Despite attempts by Woody and others to convince women that this was an important part of women's special mission as society's moral guardians, efforts to reach out to prostitutes remained unpopular. Women who did get involved often found it to be a frustrating experience. Although they achieved some successes, they also suffered many failures. Some prostitutes were temporarily "rescued," only to return to their former way of life a short time later. Many of those who were "older and hardened in vice" displayed no inclination to be saved at all.[44]

In their work for moral reform, as in their campaigns against alcohol, white women focused much of their attention on children. Beginning in 1885, the state WCTU advocated teaching young people about physiology and reproduction. Mary Mendenhall Hobbs, superintendent of the union's Department of Health and Heredity, thought it especially important to educate girls and young women; she urged local branches to conduct classes for girls "where they may learn about their own bodies and how to take care of them." In 1887 Alice R. King, superintendent of the Department of Social Purity, decreed: "It has been truly said 'Ignorance is not innocence.' Let us instruct our children in things concerning their being which it is right they should know, and teach them to keep their bodies pure. . . . it is only when we have a pure childhood that we will have a pure youth, and pure youth is essential to pure manhood and pure womanhood." Although women of the WCTU might have agreed in principle, state leaders found it difficult to recruit women to teach the classes the union recommended. Proper southern ladies were not supposed to think about sex, much less discuss it. Despite the reticence of its members, the white WCTU continued to call for sex education; after the turn of the century, women's clubs and the League of Women Voters echoed the recommendation.[45]

From the 1880s onward the WCTU and other women's organizations demanded that the legislature raise the "age of consent"—the age at which a girl could legally agree to sexual relations. When the WCTU was founded in 1883, the age of consent in North Carolina, and in most other states, was ten, a holdover from English common law. Only four states had a higher age of consent—Kentucky, Louisiana, Mississippi, and West Virginia set it at twelve—and one state, Delaware, set the age at seven. Temperance unions throughout the nation lobbied diligently for changes in state statutes, and by the mid-1890s North Carolina was one of only six states in which the age of consent was ten or younger. "Every woman's soul should burn with indignation against this outrageous law," Laura Winston, the WCTU's chair of Legislation and Petition cried in 1892, because it made every ten-year-old girl "the lawful prey of any villain who might entrap her." The union, along with some "good men," appealed to the General Assembly to raise the age of consent to eighteen. Lawmakers refused to comply. Three years later, however, they extended limited protection to girls up to the age of fourteen. The 1895 law called for the death penalty for anyone convicted of molesting a child under ten who "has been previously chaste" and made sexual relations with a girl between the ages of ten and fourteen a misdemeanor. The legislature's action failed to appease the women of the WCTU. The state president labeled the new law "a blot on our statute books" and pointed out that the age of consent was below the age at which a woman could marry or dispose of her property. The union continued to regard the low age of consent as "a disgrace" and kept up its agitation to raise it.[46]

White organized women's crusade for a higher age of consent was part of their larger effort to codify a single standard of morality that required as much of men as it did of women. In their campaigns to protect young girls, female reformers vented their anger at profligate men and at laws and customs that, they believed, benefited men at the expense of women. A woman writing in the *North Carolina White Ribbon* in 1903, for example, expanded her case for a higher age of consent into an indictment of masculine promiscuity. She recounted the story of three young men who assaulted a girl just over fourteen as she was walking home from church one Sunday night. Attempts to prosecute the youths for rape failed because the girl allegedly agreed to sexual intercourse. The author of the article was enraged. She assumed that the boys were sexual predators who made the girl their helpless prey, and she called for an age of consent of eighteen or twenty. Then she used the age of consent issue as a springboard to lash out against male lust. "Is not licentiousness the greatest enemy of the home?" she demanded.[47]

Male licentiousness was a menace to women's health and happiness, and all too often women, such as the girl the article described, endured the consequences while men suffered no hardship at all. If men could not control themselves, then women would seek legal restrictions to curb men's sexual freedom.

Women's underlying agenda was evident to the men who sat in the statehouse, and it disturbed many of them. White women were seeking to protect white girls from assaults by men of their own race, not from black rapists. They were suggesting that white men were capable of committing sexual crimes just as heinous as those of which black men were frequently accused. White women's attempts to regulate male sexual conduct took on added meaning because, thanks to the white supremacists, political and sexual prerogatives had become hopelessly entangled. White men who had used the charge of unrestrained sexuality to justify the disfranchisement of African American men did not take kindly to white women's attempts to restrict their own sexual freedom.

In 1898 and 1900 white supremacists had employed a political rhetoric that equated access to ballots with access to women's bodies. White men had absolute control over both. African American men were excluded from politics; they were also denied contact with white women and deprived of the right to defend women of their own race from molestation by whites. Black men who violated the rules faced violent retribution; white men flaunted their sexual freedom as evidence of their superiority to, and domination over, African Americans. Women themselves were almost irrelevant; they were treated as the sexual property of men, not autonomous beings. When white women asked for a higher age of consent they challenged some of the basic premises of white male supremacy. They asserted their own autonomy, and they attempted to control the sexual behavior of men who used sexual license to establish their political dominance over other men. Within that framework, age of consent legislation involved more than the protection of young girls from sexual abuse. It represented an attack on white male hegemony.

In 1913 a proposal to raise the age of consent to sixteen sparked heated debate in North Carolina's lower house. Although the Democratic majority were members of the same party that had made protection of white womanhood a campaign battle cry at the turn of the century, many of them raised vigorous objections to a bill with the stated goal of protecting young girls. Opponents recognized that this law could be used to restrict the sexual freedom of white men—that is, that it would infringe upon the prerogatives that separated white men from African Americans. One of the bill's enemies urged his colleagues to think carefully before voting because "this is a very important matter, dealing with human liberty." Another legislator branded the proposal "dangerous" and expressed concern about its effect on the young men of North Carolina. "What are you going to do with our boys?" he asked the bill's sponsor. "Put them on the chain gang," the gentleman replied. Other lawmakers offered amendments to cripple the measure. One stipulated that a girl's testimony alone should be insufficient to convict an accused seducer. Another made the law applicable only to males under twenty-one. A third decreed that marriage between the two parties would prevent any further legal action. Opponents rallied to defend the unlimited sexual freedom of white men—freedom that in the Jim Crow South was a cornerstone of white male supremacy. In the end, the House defeated the bill, and the age of consent remained at fourteen.[48]

During the same session, the General Assembly considered two revisions to divorce laws that would have made it easier for women to dissolve marriages. One would have enabled wives to divorce husbands who committed a single act of adultery; the current law permitted husbands to obtain a divorce on those grounds but required a wife to prove that her husband had repeatedly consorted with another woman. The other would have granted a divorce on grounds of abandonment after a couple had been separated five years; existing law mandated a ten-year separation.

Like the proposal to raise the age of consent, divorce reform would have granted women greater autonomy while curtailing the liberty of men. This time, however, organized women were not seeking change. In fact, they opposed "loose" divorce laws. Guardians of the home, women viewed divorce as a threat to the very institution they were trying to protect. In 1913, however, they kept quiet during the public debate on the proposed revisions to divorce laws. The General Assembly was considering several issues of concern to women that session, and organized women understood that they must choose their battles carefully.[49]

The proposals for divorce reform provoked a hostile response throughout North Carolina. The *Raleigh News and Observer* condemned both bills, predicted that less stringent divorce laws would lead to the dissolution of the family, and warned that "the adoption of such loose divorce laws will be a long step backward for this State." Many lawmakers agreed. Opponents were particularly vocal in their criticism of the bill that would expand what they euphemistically called the "Biblical grounds for divorce." While several lamented the unfairness of the double standard, they insisted that women had an obligation to enforce moral codes and protect the sanctity of the family. One legislator argued that while law could not change men's behavior, women could, if they required men to abide by higher standards. Apparently he was unaware of the WCTU's long-standing effort to do just that. Others asserted that "if one act of marital infidelity were made a ground for divorce, . . . there would be many a man to take advantage of such provision in order to goad his wife into divorce proceedings."[50]

The author of the proposal—the same representative who had sponsored the age of consent legislation—defended himself and his bill by saying that he "was for the moral side of the question." When asked, "Which moral side?" he replied, "The side that prevents a husband from going to houses of ill fame." Once again he had introduced a measure to limit the sexual prerogatives of white men, and once again his bill, along with the other proposal, failed. The *News and Observer* praised the gentlemen of the General Assembly for expressing "their belief in the superiority of women by demanding that they be better than men could be if they would or would be if they could." In the debate over divorce reform, men paid lip service to feminine moral authority while maintaining their own privileges.[51]

Women accepted the General Assembly's action without comment. Some watched debate over the bills from the galleries; however, they said little. The *News and Observer* reported that "the sentiment of women was overwhelmingly against lowering the period of abandonment from ten to five years." But women remained silent about the other proposal. The newspaper attributed their reticence to "the nature of things" and added that female spectators "spontaneously" left the galleries when discussion of the "Biblical grounds" bill began. Certainly women had a stake in preserving the sanctity of marriage—most women depended on their husbands for financial security and social status, and many believed that even a bad marriage was better than none at all. Still, given reformers' repeated complaints about masculine promiscuity, perhaps some women wished that they could invoke the law to end spousal infidelity.[52]

Men who opposed divorce reform and women who favored a higher age of consent used women's alleged moral superiority to bolster their arguments. By 1913, however, many female reformers had concluded that some of their sisters were neither moral nor superior to men. Not only had the WCTU and other women's organizations abandoned most of their attempts to rehabilitate prostitutes; they also looked to government to take action to stop prostitution. When the King's Daughters and the Florence Crittenten League renewed the drive for a reformatory for "fallen women and erring girls," they omitted the sentimental references to innocent women led astray that had permeated discussions of "rescue work" in the 1880s and 1890s. Instead they talked of "that class of women known as prostitutes" and the need for "a central reformatory where they will be forcibly detained from breaking the moral law and have also an opportunity of reforming under moral conditions." It was clear, however, that the women held out little hope for reform. Their petition to the General Assembly described the career of a fourteen-year-old girl who was so "morally debased" that the Salvation Army, the Catholic Church, and even her mother refused to offer her further assistance. "Unless a reformatory is arranged so that she and her kind can be forcibly detained," the petition warned, "they must be turned loose in society." If the state took no action, this girl "and her kind" would continue to "spread moral and physical decay among men and girls." Rescue work took on a new meaning as the

King's Daughters and the Crittenten League begged legislators "to come to the rescue of the women who are fighting for the protection of their sons and daughters from this class of women who would destroy body and soul." Now it was the virtuous women and men of North Carolina who needed to be saved from the evil influences of women who were beyond redemption.[53]

The petition expressed the disillusionment of white female reformers who had come to realize that many prostitutes could not or would not be reformed. After 1900 white organized women increasingly distinguished between "young girls who have taken the first wrong step" and "old offenders." They continued their efforts to help the former while advocating harsh legal action against the latter. As early as 1897 the white WCTU began pressing for more stringent laws against brothels, and in 1908 the union's executive committee endorsed a resolution requesting public officials to levy the maximum fine on "female vagrants." The Florence Crittenten Home, established in Charlotte in 1905, accepted only "girls who have left the right path and truly want to return to it." By 1916 the Lindley Training School had been transformed from a halfway house for prostitutes into a home for unwed mothers. Eight years later the school closed its doors, and the city of Asheville bought the property to use as a correctional facility for delinquent girls.[54]

As the change in their attitudes toward prostitutes indicates, white organized women increasingly adopted a coercive approach toward moral reform. They became more interested in enforcing their moral code than in reclaiming lost souls who strayed from the straight and narrow, and they stepped up their efforts to impose their standards of propriety on their communities. Early on the white WCTU established the Department for the Suppression of Impure Literature. In 1888 its superintendent criticized newspapers for striving to be "pleasing rather than elevating" and called on editors to eliminate gruesome stories of murders and violent crimes. In the 1890s the union concentrated on other issues, but after 1900 the organization renewed its efforts to regulate public behavior and popular entertainment. The state convention denounced the immodest trend in feminine fashion and in 1913 proclaimed "indecency in dress" to be an "obstacle to moral progress" that equalled alcohol abuse or drug use in the threat it posed to social order. The WCTU and women's clubs attempted to ban plays and motion pictures their members found objectionable. In 1914 protests from the Greensboro Woman's Club forced notorious actress Evelyn Nesbit Thaw to cancel a scheduled performance. During World War I, North Carolina women joined with the Mother's Circle of the Child Conservation League of America to pressure owners of movie theaters to designate Friday and Saturday as children's days "when only instructive and wholesomely amusing pictures" would be shown. During the 1920s the white temperance union and the white state federation of women's clubs advocated the establishment of a state censorship board to regulate movies, "with a majority of women" as members.[55]

During the first two decades of the twentieth century, white women attempting to act out the role of "priestess" that Mary Woody had outlined in the 1880s encountered failure and frustration more often than success. Men in the legislature steadfastly refused to raise the age of consent, most prostitutes stubbornly resisted reformation, and the fashion and movie industries ignored protests against revealing designs and passionate love scenes. White organized women were more successful in their efforts to preserve the sanctity of marriage by blocking divorce reform, but only because lawmakers were reluctant to enact legislation that would give wives the same rights husbands already enjoyed. Although the air still rang "with the anthem of 'Home, sweet home,'" society had not been reordered according to domestic values, and white women's moral authority in the public realm remained more nominal than real.

African Americans, meanwhile, kept up their struggle against racial stereotypes that labeled all black women immoral. In the second decade of the twentieth century, educators, ministers, and journalists echoed earlier pleas to men of both races to revere African American womanhood and criticized the southern system of chivalry that applied to white women only. They argued that black women were entitled to the same veneration, and they spoke out against a criminal justice system that failed to protect black women from sexual assault and penalized those who tried to protect themselves. A 1916 editorial in the AMEZ's newspaper, the *Star of Zion*, for example, demanded that age of consent laws be applied to black girls as well as white. Three years later North Carolina educator Charles N. Hunter responded to a newspaper article written by a white minister, "The Race Question in the United States," with an angry account of two criminal cases involving black women and white men. In the first, an African American woman shot and killed a white man who was trying to break into her home. Despite a deathbed statement from the victim exonerating her of wrongdoing, she was convicted of manslaughter and served three years on a chain gang. In the second, a white man who confessed to raping a black woman in the presence of her children pled guilty to simple assault and paid a $25 fine; the state then dropped all other charges against him. "Our women—our mothers, sisters, wives and daughters—have little or no protection from insult and outrage when the offender is white," Hunter declared. "The law does not shield them and prevailing sentiment is against them." Crimes against black women provoked little outrage, a fact that some whites began to acknowledge after 1920. "No mob, howling rampantly in its boasted defense of white womanhood, has stood guard ready with hemp and fagot in hand, to defend the sanctity of NEGRO womanhood," a white Methodist newspaper, the *Southwestern Christian Advocate,* observed in 1922.[56]

Black organized women continued to link moral reform with racial progress and racial justice. "No family and no race rises higher than its womanhood," the North Carolina Federation of Colored Women's Clubs insisted. "Hence, the intelligence of women must be cultivated and the purity and dignity of women must be protected by the maintenance of a single standard of morals *for both races* [emphasis added]." African American women called for a code of sexual behavior that crossed the boundaries of race as well as gender and that would force whites of both sexes to acknowledge the sanctity of black womanhood. They agreed with their white counterparts that white men were the greatest beneficiaries of the prevailing system, but unlike most white women, they also recognized that black women were its greatest victims. "The average white man in the South feels that the Negro woman has no rights that he is bound to respect, and no one of us is free from his insults," Charlotte Hawkins Brown wrote in 1926. Brown and other clubwomen not only attempted to change attitudes among whites; they also established rescue missions and homes for unwed mothers.[57]

While African American and white women championed a wide range of causes related to moral reform, they never abandoned the crusade against alcohol. During World War I the WCTU advocated prohibition in order to conserve grain for the war effort. In 1918 women rejoiced when Congress passed the Eighteenth Amendment to the federal Constitution, which banned the manufacture, sale, and transportation of liquor within the United States. The enactment of national prohibition, along with the enfranchisement of women in 1920, energized moral reformers, and throughout the 1920s organized women revisited old issues and adopted new ones.[58]

Promoting sexual morality and protecting the sanctity of the home continued to rank high on these women's list of concerns. In 1923 the General Assembly raised the age of consent to sixteen; forty years of agitation by the WCTU and other women's groups had finally reaped results, although the law still fell short of the age of eighteen or twenty-one, which women preferred. White women's organizations reiterated their calls for harsh penalties for women convicted of prostitution, and they used the need to rid communities of the corrupting influence of prostitutes to bolster their arguments in favor of state-run prisons for women and girls. The League of Women Voters recommended that male and female sex offenders should "be held equally responsible and punished equally," and it also endorsed programs for the prevention and treatment of venereal disease.[59]

Alarmed by the rising divorce rate, the Legislative Council of North Carolina Women lobbied for a marriage banns law that would require couples to publish a notice of their intent to marry at least two weeks before the wedding. Women believed that this measure would reduce the number of "hasty, unwise marriages" and lower the divorce rate. The House voted to table the bill in 1925, and it died in committee during the 1927 session. In 1929, according to one report, "it went back and forth from House to Senate and from Senate to House till one was almost dizzy watching it." Both houses eventually passed the bill, but it was considerably weaker than the council wanted. It decreased the amount of time required to five days, exempted couples who had announced their engagement in a newspaper, gave the clerk of the county's superior court the power to suspend the requirement in individual cases, and applied only to couples under twenty-one.[60]

Organized women still regarded liquor as a primary threat to home and family, and during the 1920s they worked for the expansion and enforcement of prohibition. Once the United States went dry, the WCTU vowed to secure worldwide prohibition. The union, along with the North Carolina Federation of Women's Clubs, the League of Women Voters, church women's missionary societies, and other women's groups, demanded strict enforcement of laws against liquor. As criticism of prohibition mounted, many organized women defended it and argued that the ban on alcohol was a success and a great benefit to society. A member of the League of Women Voters linked prohibition with a reported decrease in cases of venereal disease, and in mid-October 1929 the president of the white WCTU attributed the economic prosperity of the 1920s to prohibition. Money formerly spent on liquor, she declared, was now being spent on other commodities, thus stimulating production of consumer goods. After the onset of the Great Depression, the WCTU fought repeal of the Eighteenth Amendment. In 1930 union members affirmed that "continued prohibition in our state and nation is the hope and salvation of our children."[61]

In 1930, as in 1880, women wanted to protect children from the ravages of alcohol abuse. After prohibition was enacted, however, they also looked to children to preserve their achievement. "Temperance work in its early stages relied mainly on the work done in the schools," a white WCTU leader reminded delegates to the state convention in 1929, "and the star-of-hope for this cause still hangs over the school house." Shortly after Congress passed the Eighteenth Amendment, the white North Carolina WCTU renewed its commitment to compulsory temperance education. Although the 1891 scientific temperance instruction law remained on the books, it was largely ignored. In 1919 the union began calling for a

Temperance Day in the public schools. Nine years later the executive board voted to hire two organizers—one African American, the other white—to work with schools in establishing a temperance curriculum and to form juvenile auxiliaries among schoolchildren. Throughout the 1920s the white WCTU, with support from the Legislative Council of North Carolina Women and Governor Oliver Max Gardner, demanded that the scientific temperance instruction law be revised and strengthened. The General Assembly complied, passing the Spence Bill in 1929. The law required public schools to provide "adequate and scientific instruction" on alcoholism and drug addiction.[62]

Despite the WCTU's efforts, opposition to prohibition continued to grow. Even some organized women began to doubt the effectiveness of the national ban on liquor. In 1930 NCFWC president Marie Long Land called for "wise settlement" of the prohibition issue instead of the strict enforcement her predecessors had demanded. Still, the WCTU clung to its principles. At its annual convention in the fall of 1932, North Carolina's white union vowed to fight on, "with trust in God and firmness in the right." The following year, national prohibition ended. North Carolinians, however, defeated the repeal referendum in a landslide, a defeat some observers attributed "in part to the steady efforts of these faithful temperance women."[63]

Since 1880 these "faithful temperance women" had used the "Sword of the Spirit" to battle a variety of evils. The war against sin had forced women out of the sanctuary of the home and into the political arena. But by 1933 the notion of women's moral authority was less compelling than it had been when women had burst on the public scene fifty years earlier. Female reformers of both races had become politically sophisticated and had expanded their attention to issues that stretched far beyond their attempts to regulate public and private morality. In the early 1900s growing numbers of North Carolina women joined voluntary associations and took up the chores of public housekeeping.

III

"A Power for Good"
THE PROGRESSIVE IMPULSE

*I*n March 1899 Mina Rosenthal Weil became a clubwoman. "Very much love is all I have time to send to-day," she wrote her daughter Gertrude, who was a student at Smith College in Massachusetts. "I have just joined a Woman's Club, so I am too busy to write letters to my children, or go and tend to dinner." Weil was a charter member of the white woman's club in her hometown of Goldsboro, a thriving community in eastern North Carolina. Since 1870 Goldsboro had grown from a quiet, rural village of a thousand souls into a commercial and industrial town of the New South, with three railroad lines, forty-six factories, and six thousand residents. As the nineteenth century drew to a close, townspeople struggled to adjust to the changes that had taken place. Population growth and the opening of new businesses increased demands on public services and facilities. Moreover, the town had to accommodate a more diversified social structure: entrepreneurs and mill hands, longtime residents and newcomers, whites and blacks all had a stake in Goldsboro's future. The Goldsboro Woman's Club was one of several institutions that emerged to cope with Goldsboro's new status as a center of trade, transportation, and manufacturing. While merchants and factory owners planned for further expansion, their wives, mothers, sisters, and daughters addressed the social consequences of economic development.[1]

Goldsboro women were not alone. White and African American women were organizing similar associations throughout the United States. The objects of the Goldsboro Woman's Club—"to form a recognized centre for social and mental culture; to further the education of women for the responsibilities of life; to encourage movements for the betterment of society; to aid by its organized effort such worthy causes as may secure its sympathy; and to foster a generous public spirit in the community"—incorporated the goals of self-improvement and social reform espoused by clubwomen all over the nation. It was an ambitious agenda, and Mina Weil recognized that the new organization would have to tackle one item at a time. "I approve starting out with an attempt to do just one rather easy thing that will be for the betterment of the town and the people in it, and

Gertrude Weil with her mother, Mina Rosenthal Weil
Mina Rosenthal Weil was a charter member of the Goldsboro Woman's
Club. Gertrude joined the club after her graduation from Smith College.
(Courtesy of North Carolina Division of Archives and History)

then let success be the incentive to undertake other things gradually," she told Gertrude when she first heard of plans to form a woman's club in Goldsboro. "I don't like to hear women talk about doing so much & then have nothing that can really be seen for all their meetings." No doubt Weil was aware of skeptics who charged that women's clubs were nothing but forums for gossip and idle chatter, and she understood that Goldsboro women needed to demonstrate their competence and seriousness early on.[2]

The Weils believed that a woman's club could be of real benefit to a town. "I had already thought on the possibilities of instituting a Home Culture Club in Goldsboro," Gertrude wrote in reply to her mother's description of the proposed club. "It would be a splendid thing if it once got to going—if the people know what it means." Mina and Gertrude Weil hoped that the people of Goldsboro would understand what a club could do and that the new organization would play a positive role in the community. "May be we'll be a power for good some day—we feel almost sure of doing no harm," Mina confided to Gertrude soon after the club's founding.[3]

A power for good. For the next three decades that phrase and variations of it were used again and again to describe women's clubs. By 1913 it had become so commonplace that the *Raleigh News and Observer* editorialized: "It is a trite thing to talk of the influence of women being for the good, as that fact denies negation, and so it is also being learned that where women organize into clubs they become a force for civic betterment along many lines of life." Ten years later, state commissioner of public welfare Kate Burr Johnson praised the NCFWC for making social service "its principal activity." African American clubwomen also earned applause for their work. "By banding themselves together in the interest of education and morality and by adopting what seemed to them the most practical and useful means to this end, during the last forty or fifty years colored women have been a tremendous power for good," Mary Church Terrell, founder of the National Association of Colored Women, observed in 1928. Voluntary associations gave women a voice in public policy even before they won the ballot, and they spoke out in favor of programs they believed would benefit others.[4]

Women of both races were able to become a power because they agreed with men about what was good for their communities. When women in Wilson formed a woman's club in 1915, a newspaper reported that men welcomed the new organization because the women intended "to co-operate with the men in making Wilson a cleaner, better city." White clubwomen attempted to alleviate the problems economic growth created, but most of them did not challenge the fundamental premises of the New South creed or question the inequities of the new order. African American clubwomen promoted the philosophy of self-help and racial uplift that male leaders endorsed. But clubwomen wanted to be more than helpmates. While they worked alongside male reformers, they also felt that as women they could make unique contributions to social betterment.[5]

Women who aspired to make their voluntary associations "a power for good" believed that women and men were fundamentally different and that women could offer a distinctively feminine perspective on public policy. They also recognized that the boundary between public and private spheres was more permeable than conventional wisdom decreed. Women's clubs like the one established in Goldsboro in 1899 emerged at a time when both male and female reformers were rethinking the role of government. Increasingly, local and state governments assumed responsibility in areas that previously had been relegated to the family, the church, or voluntary associations—cultural enrichment, health and sanitation, landscaping and beautification, recreation, assistance for the poor, care for the aged and the infirm. Governments also began paying more attention to education and the needs of children. Women's associations were instrumental in translating private concerns into public issues, and organized women sought to establish their place in a civil universe that, as Paula Baker has written, was becoming "domesticated."[6]

The creation of a public role for women resulted from the convergence of two trends: the emergence of a class of educated women of both races who wanted to put their knowledge to use for the public good (as they defined it), and reformers' insistence that government's mission included serving and taking care of its people. The prevailing feminine ideal, which postulated women's capacity for nurturing and service, dovetailed with new ideas about government's responsibility for the physical and moral welfare of its citizens to enable women to step out of the domestic circle and into the public arena—or at least into part of it.[7]

In North Carolina, Jim Crow played a hand as well. The elimination of black men from politics after 1900 not only allowed white women's clubs to flourish; it also enhanced the importance of African American women's organizations. Black female reformers often found ways to provide the services that government denied their race. After African American men were disfranchised, African American clubwomen served as emissaries to local governments controlled by whites.[8]

As Anne Scott and Glenda Gilmore have explained, the activities of African American women were "virtually invisible" to their white contemporaries. But white clubwomen were highly visible and found it necessary to justify their new public roles. Clubwomen argued that their involvement in civic affairs represented an attempt to apply their domestic skills

to the chores of public housekeeping. "Has not woman's training for generations fitted her in a remarkable way to advise in some branches of
municipal reform?" asked Elvira Moffitt, cofounder of the Raleigh Woman's
Club, in 1902. "As the City is the next thing to the home it is but natural
that she should feel a vital interest in its progress." Clubwomen frequently
pointed out that the causes they championed in civic life could be seen as
extensions of tasks individual women performed in their own households.
"The organized woman's club is to the community what the individual
woman is to the home circle," NCFWC president Clara Lingle told white
clubwomen in 1915. "One woman alone can keep her own home spotless,
a hundred women acting together can make civic and moral righteousness not only a possibility but an actuality."[9]

Clubwomen emphasized that they were concerned with matters that
men neglected. "It was not through lack of confidence in the masculine
mind and heart that brought the Woman's Club into existence, but to
cultivate a virgin soil rich in possibilities," declared clubwoman and journalist Mamie Fairbrother. Clubwomen throughout the United States made
similar assertions, but statements such as Fairbrother's took on added
significance in the South, where gender conventions undergirded racial
hierarchy. North Carolina's white organized women repeatedly denied any
interest in electoral politics; that was masculine territory where women
dared not tread. But partisan politics was only one part of an expanding
public terrain, and women in voluntary associations frequently expressed
their desire to "cultivate a virgin soil" of government-sponsored social service and public welfare programs. In Goldsboro and throughout North
Carolina, organized women indicated that they did not want "to invade
men's kingdom" but to subdivide the public sphere into masculine and
feminine realms.[10]

Goldsboro's white woman's club was committed to the development
of "mental culture," and soon after the club's founding its members set
out to provide a library for their town. Clubwomen operated a library on
their own until 1908, when they turned their holdings over to the city.
Many other white women's organizations also made a public library their
first civic project. The Lend-A-Hand circle of King's Daughters in Southern Pines used the front room of its building as a library and reading
room. In Wilmington the King's Daughters loaned books for a small fee in
order to raise money, while the local woman's club, the North Carolina
Sorosis, maintained a reading room and library that by 1905 was circulating approximately twelve hundred books. The following year the club donated its collection to the new municipal library.[11]

White women's clubs in other North Carolina communities also opened libraries and then persuaded town governments to support them. After they relinquished control, clubwomen continued to contribute to public libraries in various ways. They collected books and magazines; they raised money to pay for new acquisitions, new buildings, and to hire librarians; they campaigned for library bond issues. In 1923 one observer estimated that women's clubs had "originated or kept alive" 80 percent of the state's libraries. Louis Round Wilson, librarian of the University of North Carolina and a zealous advocate of public libraries, praised clubwomen for "constantly taking the initial step in many communities in establishing library sentiment."[12]

White women's work for municipal libraries exemplified the connection between an appropriately feminine public role for women in the New South and Progressive ideas. The feminine ideal attributed to women an inherent affinity for literature and the fine arts and designated them the agents of high culture. Men would produce literary, musical, and artistic masterpieces; women would publicize and preserve men's achievements. Many women's clubs originated for "self-culture," and clubwomen hoped to spread their knowledge and appreciation of literature and the arts to other townspeople. As Gertrude Weil explained in 1912, the woman's club should "form a sort of cultural centre effecting [*sic*] by its radiating influence the whole community." The public library represented a tangible expression of clubwomen's "radiating influence" because, as Dee Garrison has written, "libraries held books, and books denoted Culture with a capital 'C.'"[13]

Books, libraries, and "Culture with a capital 'C'" were important components of Progressives' plans for a New South. Clubwomen and other reformers wanted to rescue their region from provincialism and inculcate modern values of efficiency, rationality, and self-discipline. Education was the linchpin in the machinery of reform, and the library ranked with the public school as an educational institution. According to one clubwoman, "After the school, the library is the most effective influence for good in America." Another called the library "a dominant factor in civic efficiency and the greatest educational factor that we have" and claimed that it helped to "make intelligent citizens [and] build up good morals." Reformers considered the library a necessary auxiliary to the public school. "To have compulsory education without the free public library," declared the North Carolina Library Commission in 1928, "is to write an insurance policy and leave off the signature that makes it protect; it is to build a house without a roof; it is to raise the crop and neglect the harvest; it is unthinkable."[14]

The library extended Progressives' influence to those outside the reach of the school system—in particular, working men, women, and children—

and gave people the resources to teach themselves. Like the school, the library was a source of both practical information and intellectual stimulation. Reformers believed that southerners needed both if they wanted their region to prosper. The public library, wrote Louis Round Wilson in 1911, "is the agency specialty [sic] organized and maintained by a community to serve as an aid to the material progress of the individual and to promote the culture of a community through the individual. . . . it must aid the mechanic in his daily task if he is to have a larger income and more leisure time by means of which his life may be opened to the influence of culture." In the library, Wilson's "mechanic" could learn the utilitarian skills that would enable him to earn more money and have more free time—so that he could spend more time in the library, absorbing the benefits of high culture. He would help himself, and he would contribute to the progress of his region as part of the educated workforce and the enlightened, forward-thinking citizenry the New South required. Wilson's conception of the role of the library reflected the assumptions of women and men who dreamed of a New South: "material progress" and cultural advancement were mutually dependent and reinforced each other, for individuals, their communities, and the region as a whole.[15]

The public library symbolized a community's commitment to "Culture with a capital 'C'" and the values of modern civilization. "A public library is a necessity—not a luxury," Mary Ragan told the 1917 NCFWC convention. "Every community which realizes this, and establishes a library, proclaims itself an intelligent, progressive town and one worth living in." Just as factories signified a town's economic prosperity, a public library indicated its intellectual enrichment and was a good investment in the future.[16]

Public libraries and the women who worked in them succeeded in transforming the lives of some North Carolinians, just as clubwomen and reformers intended. In his memoirs journalist David Brinkley recalled that Wilmington's public library, housed on the third floor of the city hall, offered refuge from an unhappy home life when he was growing up in the 1920s and 1930s. The librarian took him under her wing, concluded that the public schools could never give him the breadth of knowledge he needed, and directed his reading in literature and history; she even required him to write papers, which she critiqued during her leisure time. He asked her why she was willing to expend so much time and effort, and her reply revealed the frustration she and other librarians must have felt when they set out to bring high culture to residents of small towns. Her work with him, she said, relieved the monotony of spending day after day assisting people who preferred entertainment to enlightenment; most of the library's patrons read only cheap, escapist fiction. When Brinkley graduated from high school the librarian gave him a copy of Oswald Spengler's *Decline of the West*. The publisher had donated the book to the library, she explained, but no one in Wilmington would read it.

Wilmington's librarian met with the same problem reformers had encountered earlier: some North Carolinians stubbornly refused to be enriched. In 1909 the NCFWC's chair of Library Extension reported that most of North Carolina's towns lacked libraries and that citizens consistently voted against taxes to build them. To remedy this situation and to reach the state's rural population, white clubwomen established traveling libraries. These small collections of books and magazines were sent to villages or outlying communities, where, housed in schools or private homes, they remained for several months. The traveling library idea originated in Georgia in 1898 and quickly spread through the southern states. Frequently local women's clubs or state federations initiated the program. The Goldsboro Woman's Club sponsored North Carolina's first traveling libraries; by 1902 the club was circulating eleven sets of books. White women's clubs in Raleigh, Charlotte, and Greensboro followed Goldsboro's example, and the NCFWC's Department of Library Extension also supported traveling collections. In 1903 there were thirty-nine traveling libraries in the state; six years later the federation reported ninety-two, with a total of two thousand volumes.[17]

NCFWC members were proud of the success of the traveling libraries and believed that the program would be even more successful if state government took control. In 1909, largely through the efforts of Goldsboro clubwoman Sarah Weil (Mina's sister-in-law), the legislature appropriated fifteen hundred dollars for the newly formed state library commission, and the commission assumed responsibility for the traveling libraries. Women's clubs continued to collect books and magazines for the libraries until 1913, when the commission abruptly stopped accepting the federation's help. But the program clubwomen had started lived on. By 1928 the commission maintained nearly four hundred traveling libraries, each containing approximately forty volumes.[18]

Southern Progressives expected the traveling library to perform the same functions in the country that the public library fulfilled in town. Louis Round Wilson claimed that the presence of even a small set of books profoundly altered the tenor of life in isolated communities: "The books are not only read, but talked over again and again, and often change the whole current of neighborhood thought." Gertrude Weil called the traveling library "an instrument of the most broad spread education." It would, she continued, generate an interest in reading and demand for books that would in turn arouse support for the establishment of a permanent library. In 1911 the chair of the NCFWC's Department of Library

Extension summarized the benefits of the traveling library program: "There is no better opportunity for one to help his neighbor than by the circulating of these traveling libraries. They help to mould the characters of children, and help to educate those who have to leave school early to work in the mills, etc., and give them one last chance, that of self-education."[19]

Providing libraries "to mould the characters of children" and to give mill hands and others "one last chance" was a high priority among clubwomen. Library Extension was one of the original four departments of the NCFWC, and it continued to be an important part of the federation's program. State leaders encouraged club members to support existing libraries and to keep working for the establishment of new ones. The NCFWC advocated countywide library systems and in 1928 joined with the North Carolina Library Association, the DAR, the UDC, and home demonstration clubs in endorsing the Citizens' Library Movement.[20]

Despite clubwomen's hard work and accomplishments, much remained to be done for libraries in North Carolina. According to Wilson, in 1923 there were only sixty-seven public libraries serving a population of more than two million. Five years later North Carolina still ranked last in the United States in libraries; forty-six counties—nearly half of the entire state—had no public libraries at all.[21]

If library facilities were inadequate for whites, they were virtually nonexistent for black North Carolinians. State-supported traveling libraries usually went to white communities, and locally funded municipal libraries were for whites only. African Americans were left to fend for themselves, even before the enactment of rigidly enforced segregation laws. In 1891 the *Raleigh Gazette,* a newspaper that served African Americans in the capital city, reported that Miss Sarah P. Brigham of Grafton, Massachusetts, was in town to organize a reading room and library for blacks. The *Gazette* provided the room. Nearly three decades later, in 1918, the *Negro Year Book* listed only one public library for African Americans in North Carolina, a library established by the Carnegie Endowment in Greensboro. In 1923 Wilson claimed that three of North Carolina's sixty-seven public libraries were for blacks, and he cited research by W. C. Jackson, a professor at the North Carolina College for Women, who said there were five. Wilson did not say where the libraries were located, nor did he attempt to explain the discrepancy between his figures and those of Professor Jackson.[22]

The effort to found and sustain public libraries was the most important, but not the only, part of clubwomen's work to promote high culture. They also endeavored to stimulate interest in the fine arts. Local clubs sponsored lectures on music, art, and drama. They exhibited paintings and sculpture, including reproductions of masterpieces and original works by native artists. The NCFWC operated traveling art exhibits (similar to the traveling libraries) and joined with the North Carolina Art Society in calling for a state art museum. Music departments held concerts and organized community sings, choral societies, and civic bands and orchestras. In 1925 one club staged an opera cast entirely with local talent. During the 1920s white clubwomen became interested in "industrial music": music in stores, factories, and offices. The chair of the federation's Department of Music told the 1924 convention: "What Industrial Music has been able to do in the three years of its existence has been gratifying indeed. It is impossible to estimate the importance and value of music in industrial plants, mercantile houses, etc. It improves the health and morals of the employes [sic] and makes for better relations between them and their employers." If music's proverbial charms could soothe a savage breast, perhaps they could also tame a restless work force.[23]

"No association of women in the State is doing a larger, or more lasting work than the State Federation of Women's Clubs," journalist Edward L. Conn observed in 1910. "It is setting free the fountains of civilization, spreading culture, refinement and the joy of living everywhere it reaches."[24] Like Conn, most men accepted this feminine foray into the public sphere, even when it involved some very unfeminine activities, such as raising money, campaigning for bond issues, or appearing before city councils to request municipal support for libraries or other cultural projects. Women's work on behalf of "Culture with a capital 'C'" was consistent with popular perceptions of femininity and was also in line with the goals of Progressive reform. Although many people may have overlooked organized women's work to promote the arts and literature, in towns throughout North Carolina the public library stood as a monument to clubwomen's determination to make their mark on public policy and to the commitment they shared with other Progressives to a government that counted the aesthetic and intellectual enrichment of its people among its responsibilities.

"Education means progress."

Clubwoman Elvira Moffitt made that statement in 1903 and in those three words summed up one of the fundamental tenets of southern Progressivism. Progressives agreed that a strong system of public education was vital for the cultural and material advancement of their region. The public school could instill middle-class values in students of both races and from all social backgrounds and prepare the rising generation to participate in a modern industrial economy. Reformers cultivated grass roots support for educational innovations, spreading the messages conveyed in the schoolhouse to a wider audience. In the late nineteenth and early twentieth centuries, a new generation of educators and their supporters

Business meeting, North Carolina Federation of Women's Clubs convention, New Bern, 1913
The convention met from Tuesday evening until Friday noon. Day sessions were devoted to business, with special programs in the evening.

(Cotten Family Papers, Southern Historical Collection, University of North Carolina at Chapel Hill)

revamped curricula, updated teaching methods, and installed the graded school concept in classrooms throughout North Carolina. They transformed public education and saw education as the means to transform their society.[25]

Organized women embraced school reform early on and continued to support it through the first three decades of the twentieth century. The WCTU recognized that the lessons children learned in school could affect their behavior as adults, and from its inception the union petitioned for a scientific temperance instruction law. In 1884 Mary Woody, who was in charge of the campaign for the law, portrayed the school as the institutional symbol of righteousness and contrasted the moral instruction it offered with the evil influence of the saloon:

> The school teaches its pupils to be prompt, punctual, efficient. The saloon teaches them to dawdle and loaf, and takes all the *snap* out of them. The school urges them to be industrious. The saloon trains them to be shiftless and thriftless. The school would inspire them with reverence for the law. The saloon trains them to trample upon all law, human and divine. The school inculcates the principles of true citizenship. The saloon inculcates the lowest demagogism.

Woody and other white ribboners firmly believed that the school manufactured the hardworking, patriotic citizens the New South needed; the saloon produced lazy, irresponsible louts who would retard economic development. They endeavored to strengthen one institution at the same time they sought to destroy the other.[26]

For nineteenth-century southerners, women's special interest in schools seemed as natural as their distaste for saloons. Mothers were expected to instruct their children in manners, morals, and citizenship. When educational reformers attempted to transfer these responsibilities from the home to the school, they intruded in women's domain. Organized women, who desired a wider sphere, cheered the interlopers on. Women seeking to shape educational policy joined with men who wanted to expand the school's influence to modernize North Carolina's public school system.[27]

Women participated in the crusade as professionals and as volunteers. As James Leloudis has explained, the new pedagogy enjoined teachers to nurture young minds and spirits and to discipline with love instead of force; therefore, male administrators welcomed to the classroom those who were supposed to personify nurturance, affection, and gentleness. Pecuniary factors also disposed educational reformers to recruit women;

female teachers commanded lower salaries than their male colleagues. Still, teaching offered women career opportunities that had been unavailable to them previously, and members of female voluntary associations encouraged young women to take advantage of these options. In 1891 the white WCTU and the King's Daughters united with male educational leaders in a successful bid for the establishment of an industrial and normal college for white women. The school opened in Greensboro in October 1892, with Charles Duncan McIver as its first president.[28]

Although McIver was young—he celebrated his thirty-second birthday just days before the college enrolled its first students—he was a veteran campaigner for school reform, and his new post heightened his prestige and influence. McIver acknowledged the potential of organized womanhood but believed that too often women wasted their energy on "chimerical schemes and foolish crusades." He wanted to harness feminine power under masculine authority and put women to work to benefit North Carolina's public schools. In March 1902 McIver oversaw the founding of the Woman's Association for the Betterment of Public Schoolhouses (WABPS) in Greensboro. The organization grew rapidly; by the fall it claimed more than two thousand members. In October a representative of the WABPS attended the first convention of the NCFWC in Salem. The newly formed federation gave the WABPS a "hearty endorsement."[29]

McIver may have planned for an association composed of women and directed by men, but the women who joined had other ideas. Sue Hollowell of Goldsboro, one of the driving forces in the WABPS, assured delegates to the Ninth Conference for Education in the South that the organization was "purely feminine and has been from its origin." She went on to explain one of its "strictly feminine" features: "We allow men to pay the money to carry on this work." White women could enroll in the WABPS by volunteering their time and energy; they paid no dues. Men (and women who could not spare time or labor) could become associate members for a one-dollar fee. Only the women who were full members could vote. "The women do all the voting in this association," Hollowell declared, "and the men pay all the money." Although the WABPS cooperated with male reformers like McIver and received funding from the Southern Education Board, its leaders made clear that they intended it to be an autonomous organization.[30]

From the beginning, the "purely feminine" association had the blessing of prominent male North Carolinians. Governor Charles Brantley Aycock, who was known as the "educational governor," and state superintendent of public instruction James Yadkin Joyner, McIver's college classmate, close friend, and ally in educational reform, attended the WABPS's first public meeting in April 1902. Six years later Lula Martin McIver

(Charles McIver's wife and WABPS field secretary) recalled that "teachers and county superintendents eagerly welcomed" the new group; she quoted a "leading newspaper" that called its formation "an event of deep satisfaction." If the organization spread throughout North Carolina and met its goals, the newspaper continued, "it will revolutionize the public schools of the State. The poor schoolhouse is a lion in the path of rapid progress."[31]

Reformers knew that taming the lion would be a formidable task. In the early years of the twentieth century, North Carolina ranked at or near the bottom of all states in just about every educational category. Nearly one-third of white children and almost half of African American children between the ages of ten and fourteen did not attend school. Attendance rates were even lower for children ages five to nine: two-thirds of whites and three-quarters of African Americans were not enrolled. The school term lasted an average of eighty-five days (compared with a regional average of ninety-nine). In addition, North Carolina lagged behind the rest of the South in per capita expenditures—an average of $4.39 for each pupil, while other southern states averaged $6.95. Voters resisted efforts to impose or raise taxes to support the schools. North Carolina also had a high rate of adult illiteracy: 19.5 percent of whites and 47.6 percent of African Americans over the age of ten could not read or write. Only the states of the Deep South—Louisiana, Alabama, South Carolina, Georgia, and Mississippi—had higher rates of illiteracy among blacks. The statistic that probably most troubled white educational reformers, however, was the illiteracy rate of the state's white children. The United States census of 1900 revealed that 166.1 out of every 1,000 white children between the ages of ten and fourteen could not read or write. That placed North Carolina third from the bottom among states and territories; only New Mexico and the Indian Territory ranked lower.[32]

The sorry condition of public education in North Carolina was a major issue in the gubernatorial campaign of 1900. As the state prepared to enact a constitutional amendment that would disfranchise illiterates, Democratic nominee Charles Brantley Aycock committed himself to universal public education and to the improvement of the public schools. Although Aycock endorsed white supremacy, he believed that education was just as important for African Americans as for whites. Indeed, Aycock and educational reformers argued that the new restrictions on voter registration would be a boon for public education for both races. In an article written for the *Southern Workman*, a monthly magazine published at Hampton Institute, Charles McIver declared that the literacy requirement would create a demand for better schools for African Americans and whites alike. "At worst the amendment need not mean more than the temporary disfranchisement of a portion of the colored race," he wrote. McIver may have intended to soothe some of the anxieties of African Americans, but his next statement contained a message that was simultaneously promising and ominous: "Universal education is a necessity and a birthright; universal suffrage is neither a necessity nor a birthright." Once in office, Aycock resisted efforts to allocate school taxes on the basis of race, with revenue collected from blacks going to black schools and that from whites to white institutions. Still, North Carolina, like other southern states, maintained school systems that were separate and unequal. African Americans received less funding for schools, had shabbier school buildings, and suffered even greater shortages of equipment and textbooks than whites.[33]

Most of the state's white educational reformers showed little inclination to ease the plight of blacks. The WABPS constitution specified that it was for whites only, although some of its members ignored that provision on occasion. In 1904 Sue Hollowell invited an African American woman to address the WABPS's state convention. Charles McIver, who knew nothing of Hollowell's plans in advance, was dismayed. He worried that if word of the unorthodox event spread, the WABPS would find itself embroiled in a controversy over racial issues that would decrease its effectiveness as an agency for school improvement. He begged newspapers to squelch the story and scolded Hollowell for violating the code of white supremacy. McIver's reproof had little effect. A year later Hollowell recruited blacks along with whites for a WABPS chapter in Granville County. Again McIver reprimanded her. Twenty years earlier Hollowell had worked under the auspices of the WCTU to organize African Americans for temperance. Although the fragile interracial alliance had been a casualty of the political wars of the 1890s, when Hollowell took up school reform she once again tried to persuade whites and blacks to cooperate to solve their common problems.[34]

While Hollowell wanted to build bridges across the racial chasm, few other whites did, and the educational reform movement, like the schools themselves, remained segregated. African Americans formed their own associations. In 1904—the same year that Hollowell brought her unwelcome guest to the WABPS meeting—a group of black parents in Raleigh pleaded with the local school committee for a more equitable distribution of educational resources. They asked the committee to hire more African American teachers and pay them higher salaries and to provide adequate facilities for black schoolchildren so that "none need be turned away." Although the petitioners made clear that they did not expect their schools to receive the same amount of money allocated to whites, they requested "sufficient funds" to enable African American institutions "to do the best possible work." African American parents in other communities faced the same problems in their public schools and organized similar groups to deal with them. Black women's clubs also made educational improvement a high priority.[35]

One of the major problems confronting school reformers of both races was the physical condition of school buildings. Many districts still had log schoolhouses or none at all. In others the schools were dilapidated and dirty. A WABPS member in Mecklenburg County found some of the local schools to be "in a most dreary and cheerless condition. . . . The walls were broken, the window sashes worn, and the doors were sagging on their hinges." Schoolrooms were often sparsely furnished and lacked blackboards, maps, and other basic equipment. They were poorly lit, inadequately ventilated, and cold in winter. Schoolyards were "always muddy" and sometimes strewn with litter. Poor sanitation made schools breeding grounds for disease. Students drank from a common dipper in a water bucket and used open outdoor privies. Provisions for the disposal of trash and human waste were inadequate.[36]

Schools were ugly, uninviting, and, in some instances, unsafe. Reformers found in the dismal state of school facilities an explanation for North Carolina's high rates of illiteracy and truancy. They recognized that the drab surroundings made learning difficult. "In the present condition of the average school house it is impossible to train the youth of the State properly," Elvira Moffitt complained. She and her coworkers also understood that children did not want to spend their days in such an inhospitable environment and that parents were reluctant to compel them to go. "If we could make our school houses more attractive," Charles McIver confided to Moffitt in 1902, "we could attract or force by public opinion many children into the schools who do not now go." Improving school facilities was the first step in upgrading the educational system.[37]

And who better to supervise the cleaning, decorating, repairing, and landscaping of schools than the same people who performed those tasks for their families? As McIver explained at the organizational meeting of the WABPS, "The present hard conditions" in the state's schools "can be remedied best by women." This was work that needed to be done, work that required women's expertise, and work that men were unable or unwilling to do. "In the school, as in the home, the finer, gentler, more aesthetic and cultural side of education and the equipment required therefor must be looked after by the women," declared James Yadkin Joyner a few years later, "for the men, as a rule, fail to appreciate the value and necessity of these." North Carolina's schoolhouses were badly in need of proper upkeep; it fell to North Carolina's housekeepers to refurbish them. "It is a woman's duty to use her best effort to better the surroundings of her own home first and then extend her influence toward the improvement of the public school where the majority of the children in this land receive their education," Elvira Moffitt told a Wake County audience. McIver and Joyner invited white women to increase their involvement in their communities by insisting that the state needed their talents. Moffitt urged them in the same direction by reminding them of maternal obligations. Together, they claimed for women a share of the public arena. McIver called members of the WABPS "citizen-women," and they proudly accepted the label. It was a term that captured the spirit of women who believed that they could play a unique public role, different from men's but no less important.[38]

The state WABPS offered specific instructions as to how "citizen-women" should undertake their responsibilities. The first step was to inspect all schools in the district and prepare a written report on each one. "Now of course this takes work and time," Lucy Bramlette Patterson admitted to women attending the southern conference on education in 1907, "but if properly managed it can be done without disarranging the household machinery." She assured her listeners that they could visit several schools in a day and still be home in time "to receive, welcome, and entertain" their husbands when the men returned from their "arduous toil." Patterson recommended that women conduct their survey in October and November, "as the roads are good and the weather is pleasant."[39]

Once women were aware of the problems, they could start to work. Lula McIver instructed local WABPS branches to "do the things *first* that you would do if you were going to live in the house and make it your own home. *Clean up* the house, grounds, and out buildings." Inside the school, women—WABPS members, teachers, students, and volunteers from the community—mopped floors, scrubbed walls, washed windows, cleaned stoves, and dusted furniture. "Paint and polish as if you were expecting distinguished guests," a WABPS pamphlet urged. "*You are.*" Outdoors, men—many of them husbands of WABPS members or fathers of schoolchildren—cleared away rubbish and graded and drained the grounds. Once the initial cleaning was completed, students assumed responsibility for maintenance—girls on the inside of the schoolhouse, boys on the outside.[40]

Lula McIver reminded women to include the well in their cleanup efforts and "have it covered if it is not already." The WABPS paid particular attention to sanitation and worked to secure pure water and to ensure that human waste was disposed of properly. They urged local school committees to replace water buckets with water coolers and to construct sanitary privies. They demanded that separate toilet facilities be provided for boys and girls and recommended that outbuildings be "screened by *evergreen* shrubs and vines and *kept clean*." Schools should provide toilet paper, they insisted, and should "not allow the use of newspapers or other waste." Reformers wanted to create a healthful environment in the schools and to teach children lessons that they could apply at home.[41]

When the schoolhouse was clean, the grounds cleared, and proper sanitary measures in place, school improvement entered its next phase: "Then begin to beautify," Lula McIver commanded. Under the guidance of the WABPS, students planted grass, trees, and bushes—"not perishable flowers," Sue Hollowell warned, "because the children grow discouraged." Inside, the WABPS suggested that the schoolroom be decorated with cut flowers, potted plants, and pictures. One of the association's leaflets asked each member to "lend the school, for a season, anything you enjoy in your own home—a picture, book, piece of statuary, curio or anything you wish to share with friends." Other white women's organizations joined with the WABPS in the effort to make classrooms more attractive. The patriotic societies and the NCFWC donated pictures; for several years, federation officers asked each of the NCFWC's affiliates to give at least one picture to the poorest white school in the county. Organized women thought that portraits of America's heroes would inspire students and instill patriotism, while reproductions of masterpieces would enhance aesthetic sensibilities. They were eager to bring beauty and cheer to children from homes "into which not one ray of sunshine ever comes unless it is put there by those who are more fortunate."[42]

At a regional conference on education in 1906, Sue Hollowell recounted the story of a little girl in a rural school to illustrate the results of this work. One day the school received a bundle of books. The teacher unwrapped them and tossed the packaging aside. When she returned to the schoolroom after recess, "there, pasted on that dingy school house wall, was this bit of pink paper. The teacher asked who did it, and a little child, poor, with the blue veins showing in its [sic] hands, says, 'Please, teacher, I did it; I wanted to make a pretty spot for us to look at.' That is the key-note for all the women's associations for the betterment of the public schools and school houses of North Carolina," Hollowell concluded, "to make bright, beautiful spots in the lives of those who know not what the sunshine and brightness is."[43]

Hollowell and many other white southern reformers saw the rural South and its people—"those who know not what the sunshine and brightness is"—as fertile ground for missionary work. They looked on the southern countryside in much the same way they regarded the alien cultures of China or Africa. They thought that rural southerners, Chinese warlords, and African tribesmen were equally "backward" and "primitive," and in some cases they found their neighbors in the country to be almost as exotic as the "pagans" across the sea. "While women feel called into foreign mission fields in India, in China and Africa," Hollowell declared, "there is not to-day a woman who so nearly fills that place of missionary as the country school teacher." The school was an outpost of civilization in an uncivilized land. Through the school, reformers could reach into the homes of rural southerners and lift the South's people out of the mire of poverty, filth, and ignorance. As William A. Link has demonstrated, this missionary spirit motivated many southern Progressives, and it was a major force in the campaign to refurbish North Carolina's public school buildings. The renovated schoolhouse became an object lesson in and of itself, a model of cleanliness, comfort, and beauty that, reformers hoped, rural North Carolinians would emulate in their own homes.[44]

Because they believed that adults as well as children could benefit from the lessons offered in and by the modernized public school, the women and men who led the educational crusade endeavored to involve parents and local residents in the process of school improvement. "Get the *whole community* men, women and children interested and working," Lula McIver counseled a teacher who lived in a village called Advance. WABPS literature directed branches to hold public meetings and conduct house-to-house canvasses to enlist volunteers for the initial "working-bee" to clean up the building and its grounds. Women should write up reports of their activities, including the names of the participants, for the local newspaper. After work on the schoolhouse was completed, the WABPS should host "an entertainment . . . in which all the children take a part" to show off the remodeled facilities and to raise money for equipment and decorations. "The schoolhouse should be made the center of public interest in the community," Sue Hollowell advised; "social gatherings should be frequently held; Saturday picnics, in which parents and children join debates and spelling bees, should be encouraged." Hollowell and other reformers understood that school spirit translated into community spirit; a modern, comfortable school became a source of pride for all residents and "an index of the community ideals."[45]

Once the schoolhouse became "the center of public interest" previously parsimonious voters changed their minds and enacted school taxes. "Men say they have fallen in love with local taxation wherever there is a Betterment Association of some kind," Hollowell reported in 1906. With increased revenue, school districts were able to construct modern school buildings; within a year of its founding, the WABPS claimed credit for 676 new schoolhouses. Here was the power of femininity in action. Male reformers had pleaded and exhorted and harangued for tax increases to no avail. But when women courted community support and wooed parents and children alike into the schoolhouse, opposition to higher taxes evaporated. North Carolinians learned to think of the local educational facility as "our school" instead of "the school," a mental shift that left an enduring legacy. For the rest of the twentieth century, the public school would play a major role in the life of small towns and rural communities throughout the state and the region.[46]

Growing popular support made the WABPS's job easier. In many communities the betterment association joined with local residents and other women's organizations to furnish new and remodeled school buildings with "all the necessary equipments of a modern schoolroom." Women's groups contributed things ranging from wastepaper baskets and stovewood boxes to glass panes for windows. At the Glengarry School in Bladen County, students "sat on the floor and wrote on the bench" until "friends" of the school stepped in and raised enough money to buy desks. In other communities women pleaded with school committees to purchase comfortable desks and chairs for both teachers and pupils. Women's voluntary associations also bought maps, blackboards, globes, window shades, musical instruments, playground equipment, and phonographs. They used "methods peculiar to ladies—ice cream suppers, oyster stews, etc." to raise funds to pay for these items; they also accepted monetary contributions from individuals and encouraged schoolchildren to donate money they earned from doing chores at home. Women's voluntary associations were particularly concerned with providing a library in every white public school. Although the state legislature had inaugurated appropriations for school libraries in 1901, many schools still did not have them. Under the heading "The Library," a WABPS pamphlet said simply, "Get one. If you have one, add to it." In towns, women's clubs and patriotic societies collected books and magazines, then turned them over to the WABPS for distribution to rural schools. The state betterment association instructed local branches to make sure that every school owned some reference books, including a set of encyclopedias and an unabridged dictionary; frequently a dictionary was the prize offered in competitions among schools.[47]

Organized women maintained that the school should care for pupils' bodies as well as their minds. Following the lead of the WCTU, which had advocated health education since the 1880s, the WABPS and other women's groups wanted lessons in personal hygiene and health to be incorporated into the curriculum. A WABPS pamphlet admonished, "Have children taught how to care for their bodies; first, to clean, then use properly, exercise and nourish the body, which is the 'Temple of the Holy Ghost.'" The association suggested that local branches invite a doctor or nurse to address students and parents; it distributed literature "giving rules regarding the diet, care of eyes, teeth and general health." In rural areas the WABPS advised neighborhood parents to make arrangements among themselves to have all of the neighborhood children transported to school by wagon on rainy or cold days and to bring their offspring "wraps, overshoes, and umbrellas" if bad weather developed while school was in session. "This would prevent many bad colds, save doctors' bills, and in some cases save lives," WABPS guidelines asserted. Women advocated other preventive measures, such as physical education classes and supervised exercise to strengthen young bodies and make them more resistant to disease. In some towns, women's clubs provided pupils with milk and lunches. They also sponsored dental and medical examinations for school-children. Rural schools were on the front lines in the battle against hookworm, an intestinal parasite that was widespread in rural North Carolina. Teachers and school administrators cooperated with the Rockefeller Sanitary Commission for the Eradication of Hookworm Disease (state school superintendent Joyner sat on its board and declined an offer to be its director). The commission frequently established its dispensaries for diagnosis and treatment at public schools.[48]

As the programs to safeguard children's health and promote health education indicated, the role of the public school was changing in the early twentieth century. The school assumed responsibilities far beyond teaching "the three 'r's." Organized women clamored for expanded curricula as part of the educational revolution. They asked that courses in music and art be added and also called for classes that would give young people the practical knowledge they needed to make their way in life. In rural areas, the WABPS prepared students for the world of commercial agriculture by planting school gardens and working with the state department of agriculture to establish corn clubs for boys and tomato clubs for girls. In towns, they advocated vocational education: courses in millinery, dressmaking, typing, and stenography for girls; manual training in the industrial arts for boys. Women understood that North Carolina was developing a more diversified and complex economy; they believed that the school should prepare students to take their place in the new order.[49]

In addition to improving school facilities and broadening the curriculum, educational reformers searched for ways to boost attendance among white children. In 1907 UDC president Lucy Closs Parker suggested that individual Daughters "interest themselves in getting the many white children, especially those related to Confederate soldiers, to attend public schools." The WABPS adopted a more systematic approach. The state association instructed local branches to take a census to find out how many school-age children were not enrolled and why. If a family could not afford textbooks, the women should find a way to provide them. If children were taking care of ill parents, the WABPS should "notify church or benevolent societies" so that another attendant could be found and the child sent to school. The WABPS's goal was to "get every [white] child in school every day, unless prevented by illness." The association met with some success, and the effort attracted favorable publicity. In his 1909 novel, *The Southerner*, North Carolina native Walter Hines Page described a "Ladies Public School Club" that conducted a "rough school census"; because of its efforts, "within a few months . . . school attendance was almost doubled." While Page was skeptical about the effectiveness of other women's organizations, he was clearly impressed by the WABPS and its school census program.[50]

The WABPS relied on pressure and persuasion; although these methods might reap good results in the short run, women recognized that they were insufficient for the long term. From their perspective, too many white children still remained outside the classroom, and the only effective solution was a law requiring school attendance. "The white race should here take advantage of the opportunities offered by our free school system," Elvira Moffitt lamented, "but sad to say it is not done—hence the need of a compulsory school law." Some educational reformers disagreed. J. Y. Joyner believed mandatory attendance statutes were ineffective; Charles Aycock also denied his support while he was governor, although he changed his mind after he left office. Despite the dissension, the WABPS, the NCFWC, and the WCTU, along with other groups and individuals, persisted, and in 1913 the General Assembly passed a compulsory attendance bill for children ages eight to twelve; later the law was expanded to include children from seven to fourteen.[51]

The law fell short of its advocates' expectations. Although it committed the state to mandatory school attendance in principle, in practice it was so vague that it was virtually unenforceable. It exempted children who were from extremely poor families or whose parents needed their labor on the farm. Illness of a close relative was also a legitimate reason for missing school. In fact, almost any excuse was acceptable as long as parents consented to the child's absence. Since reformers believed that apathetic parents who saw no need to educate their children were the culprits responsible for high absenteeism, they considered a law that left school attendance to parental discretion little better than no law at all. Through the 1920s white organized women lobbied for a tougher statute with more stringent enforcement procedures.[52]

The law that women's voluntary associations favored would have raised the age for compulsory attendance and also would have added an academic requirement: in order to leave school, a student would have to be sixteen years old and have passed the sixth grade. "Such a measure," Annie O'Berry argued in the League of Women Voters' newsletter, "automatically enforces the law." Organized women believed their proposal would increase the number of students in the classroom at the same time it thinned the ranks of child workers in the mills. O'Berry blamed parents for sending children to the factory instead of the schoolhouse and insisted that if parents knew children had to complete a certain grade level before they could get jobs, "even the most ignorant" among them would keep their children in school. O'Berry plainly did not understand the economic reality that many North Carolina families faced; wages were low, and every penny counted. She and other reformers saw instead philistines who valued money more than knowledge and who were willing to exploit their children. "We can't expect anything more from ignorant or indifferent parents, who never having had an education themselves, do not see any reason why their children should have one. The only thing they *do see,* is their children must work," O'Berry wrote. Apparently she and her colleagues had some blind spots of their own. In any case, the General Assembly refused to enact the "attainment as well as age" provision.[53]

Organized women joined with other educational reformers to ask the legislature to lengthen the school year. They used the same techniques they had employed in other efforts to influence lawmakers: they wrote letters, circulated petitions, and sat in the galleries when the bills they endorsed were being considered. When the House voted to provide school districts with funds for a six-month term in 1913, the *Raleigh News and Observer* reported that "many ladies" were present, "showing great interest in the proceedings." The newspaper called the law "the biggest and most far-reaching achievement of the General Assembly of 1913." Four years later North Carolinians approved an amendment to the state constitution that required schools to remain in session for a minimum of six months. A six-month school year was good, but women soon decided that eight months would be even better, and they began lobbying for the extension. In 1928 one white woman's club considered this to be so important that it raised the money to keep the town's schools open for an additional two months. That same year, the average school term was 152.7 days for white children; for African Americans, it was 137.4 days.[54]

Women's associations also promoted the professionalization of teaching. They favored licensing to ensure that only competent individuals filled teaching positions, and they consistently pushed for higher salaries for teachers to attract and keep talented people on public school faculties. In addition, women advocated a variety of other programs to improve the school system: consolidation of rural schools, increased educational appropriations, addition of a twelfth grade, a standard state curriculum.[55]

By the 1920s most observers agreed that North Carolina had "made a great deal of progress in public education." The legislature had increased appropriations for schools, and local districts had levied school taxes. Old school buildings had been remodeled or replaced. In 1920, 87 percent of all children between the ages of seven and thirteen were enrolled in school;

ten years later that number had grown to 93 percent. At the same time school attendance increased, illiteracy declined; in 1920 approximately 90 percent of North Carolinians over ten could read and write. Although North Carolina still ranked in the lower tier of states in most educational categories, its status had risen since the turn of the century. According to one source, the state had moved from forty-fifth in 1900 to thirty-ninth in 1926. Professional educators and reformers concluded that the WABPS had outlived its usefulness; in 1919 most local branches either dissolved or combined with Parent-Teacher Associations (PTAs).[56]

While reformers and educational officials had devoted most of their attention to white schools, North Carolina also won accolades for its efforts on behalf of African Americans. In the spring of 1927 *The Crisis* claimed that the state was "more advanced" than the rest of the South in black education. A few months later Dr. Nathan C. Newbold, director of public education for African Americans, boasted that the state led the nation in black education, with good schools, good equipment, and good teachers. In 1930 sociologist Samuel Huntington Hobbs Jr. declared that North Carolina had "the best Negro schools of any southern state and the best attitude toward her Negro population." There were sixty-three high schools for blacks—Texas was the only state with more—and in 1930, 88 percent of African American children between the ages of seven and thirteen were enrolled in school.[57]

Publicists used statistics to create a rosy picture, but critics pointed out that while North Carolina's public school system for blacks might be "more advanced" than those of other states, it was not necessarily good. The article in *The Crisis* complained that schools for African Americans were "not modern yet," and Newbold called for a more equitable distribution of school funds. Journalist Lewis K. McMillan published a scathing indictment of black education in the *Baltimore Afro-American* in November 1927. "This old rebel state must laugh up her sleeves as the whole country honors her with good names and seats around the council tables," he wrote, "when her rightful place is before the bar of justice—a trembling, guilty criminal—for neglecting, starving, half-feeding or polluting thousands of bright promising Negro youth." After making an "extended inspection" of the state's African American high schools, McMillan concluded that white school officials were engaged in "a purposeful scheme to keep the Negro down." In Wilmington, for example, the school board built a $1 million high school for whites, while black students had "a limited number of dirty bottles and a table in the corner of a class room for laboratory material and equipment; a hole in a wall and a few second-hand books for a library." Whites ran all of the public schools in the state and gave preference to white institutions; African Americans had to settle for cast-offs and hand-me-downs or private contributions. "All bubbles burst, including North Carolina's unearned fame in Negro education," he concluded. "The state is not serious yet about the training of Negroes to become men and women." He demanded that resources be allocated equally and that African Americans be given a voice in educational policy.[58]

African American clubwomen were committed to improving public education for children of their race, and blacks also organized PTAs that did for black schools many of the things the WABPS accomplished in white institutions. In Cleveland County, for example, local PTAs provided a piano in one school and desks in another; in a third community the association equipped a domestic science room. PTAs cleaned up and re-modeled schoolhouses; donated books, furniture, and equipment; encour-aged parents to keep their children in school; and raised money to supplement teachers' salaries and extend the school term. By 1927 there were 770 local associations claiming more than ten thousand members. Together they raised more than sixty-five thousand dollars for African American schools.[59]

By 1930 women had established their place as valuable contributors to educational reform. They continued to affirm that "education means progress" and to see a good public school system as an essential compo-nent of a comprehensive plan for the advancement of North Carolina. They also continued to believe that as women they had a special mission to look after the state's schoolchildren. "The education of children is woman's work as well as womanly work," Lucy Bramlette Patterson pro-claimed in 1907, then added, "and the two are by no means always syn-onymous." Patterson made a significant distinction. In the early twentieth century organized women believed that "woman's work" was an expanding field that stretched the boundaries of traditional femininity. They were determined to define for themselves a place in the changing public sphere. As professional educators assumed responsibility for developing the "whole child," for socialization as well as academic instruction, women parlayed their role as child rearers and nurturers into a public role in school re-form. When public agencies undertook "womanly" duties, "woman's work" acquired a public dimension.[60]

Organized women of both races believed that women needed to pre-pare for the new responsibilities that accompanied the expanding field of "woman's work." They made education—for themselves, for girls, and for other women—a high priority. Many women's clubs originated as literary societies or reading circles. Members met in each other's homes to dis-cuss common readings or to hear one of their number present a paper. They studied history, literature, geography, and the fine arts. "Our last meeting was at the Knoxes," a white clubwoman wrote to a friend in 1899, "and we talked of Dante and Boccaccio and Petrarch and their influence on our literature." That same year, African American women in two of Charlotte's literary societies focused on the works of William Shakespeare, examining one play each time they met. Although critics dismissed clubwomen as dilettantes, the women themselves took their scholarly activities very seriously. In addition to promoting "self-culture," women's clubs and patriotic societies administered scholarships and loan funds to enable girls to attend college.[61]

Organized women's faith in the power of education was as great as their faith in the power of femininity. Their optimism about the results of combining these forces—educating women—was almost boundless. In 1913 Sallie Southall Cotten prophesied that educated, Christian clubwomen would control the future of Western civilization. "Not education alone, not Christianity alone, not woman alone," she declared, "but these three in one and organized for united effort. This trinity of forces makes a power for good which will make our civilization permanent because organized women will build it on ethical foundations." When Cotten retired as president of the NCFWC, clubwomen established a fund in her honor that loaned money to young women for college; it became one of the organization's most popular and successful programs. In 1928 the fund's administrator boasted, "The Federation has not made a better contribution of service to the State or to the womanhood of North Carolina than in sending out this large group of educated women, properly equipped to meet the problems of life, for their influence in the homes and communities to which they return cannot be estimated." Organized women worked to educate members of their sex; educated women would enlighten their families and their communities.[62]

While white clubwomen considered female education important, African American women believed it was absolutely essential to black progress in the South. In 1892 Raleigh native Anna Julia Cooper argued that "the earnest well trained Christian young woman, as a teacher, as a home-maker, as wife, mother, or silent influence even, is as potent a missionary agent among our people as the theologian; and I claim that at the present stage of our development in the South she is even more important and necessary." Sarah Dudley Pettey echoed the same theme in her column in the *Star of Zion*. In the aftermath of white supremacists' victories in 1898 and 1900, Pettey insisted that educated African American women held the keys to full emancipation and equality. "In these trying days of race caste and prejudice where upon almost every hand our people are being disfranchised and denied the rights guaranteed them," she wrote in 1901, "our only hope lies in educated mothers. One generation of educated

Picnic, North Carolina Federation of Women's Clubs convention
Sallie Southall Cotten, third from left, at a picnic at the North Carolina Federation of Women's Clubs convention, New Bern, 1913. Cotten was completing her term as NCFWC president, and convention delegates voted to establish a loan fund in her honor.

(Courtesy of North Carolina Division of Archives and History)

mothers will remove the barriers restricting the rights and privileges of the Negro and thus solve the much-agitated and long talked of Negro problem." Cooper, Pettey, and other African American reformers understood the dynamics of race and gender in the New South. Educated black women would not only serve as "missionaries" to African Americans; they would also stand as living testimony against the assumptions of racial inferiority that undergirded white supremacy.[63]

Although African American and white clubwomen favored programs that would enable women to earn their own living—they supported vocational training for girls in high school and encouraged young women in college to prepare for teaching careers—they placed their greatest emphasis on developing domestic skills. Women's groups frequently conducted cooking and sewing demonstrations and studied nutrition, home decoration, budget management, and child psychology to enhance their own housekeeping and parenting abilities; they sponsored mothers' meetings to disseminate their knowledge to other women.[64]

Organized women's fascination with topics related to domesticity grew out of the reality of their lives—most were wives and mothers who looked to voluntary associations to help them fulfill their responsibilities as homemakers—and it also reflected their attitudes toward themselves and the work they did. They regarded housekeeping not as a collection of menial chores but as a science whose practice required special skills, education, and talent. "The profession of wife-hood and mother-hood is assuming its place among the legitimate professions," editor Nina Holland Covington wrote in 1917. Covington and other organized women wanted housewives to receive the honor and prestige accorded other professionals.[65]

Clubwomen believed that homemakers, like other specialists, should be trained for their jobs, and from the 1880s on, North Carolina women's organizations participated in the movement to transform housekeeping into home economics. They begged administrators to introduce domestic science courses in the public schools, and they sometimes volunteered to teach cooking and sewing themselves. "Girls from choice and from destiny inevitably become home makers," Sallie Cotten explained, "and their education should be such as to make them successful home makers." In 1920 Mrs. C. P. Blalock, the NCFWC's chair of Home Economics, warned that "the untrained teacher is a minor defaulter when compared with the untrained homemaker and mother. Our girls need to face this truth: they have no moral right to assume such obligations without preparation." Five years later, home demonstration agent Rosalind Redfearn amplified Blalock's point: "It is absolutely essential that every possible resource should be made for training girls and women in the vocation of home-making," she told delegates to the NCFWC's annual convention.[66]

If women were by nature domestic and maternal, as women's leaders so frequently averred, why was there a need for special training? The answer to that question illuminated the attitude of the middle- and upper-class women who joined voluntary associations toward their less affluent peers. Organized women lamented that not all women were "fitted by grace or culture for the great responsibilities of motherhood." According to an 1889 WCTU report on industrial schools, in the past girls had learned housekeeping from their mothers; now many women, especially poor women, lacked these skills and could not pass them along to their daughters. The report suggested that middle- and upper-class women take girls into their homes and teach them, but cautioned that these girls should not be called servants "as for some reason it seems to be distasteful to most people."[67]

In fact, the issue of domestic education was intertwined with the so-called servant problem, an oft-discussed topic among white clubwomen. "The missing link in the chain of domestic peace and happiness is trained household help," wrote Mrs. A. E. Pease of Asheville, "and one can hardly meet a lady who is not bewailing the inefficiency of servants, and seeking the solution of the problem. . . . The introduction of household industries into the schools as a part and parcel of every day education for high and low, will soon dispel these difficulties and bring joy and comfort to waiting households." As Orra Langhorne noted in a paper presented to the American Social Sciences Association in 1901, "When a Southerner speaks of servants, Negroes are always understood"; therefore, the "servant problem" was a racial problem as well. White mistresses complained that their African American maids were lazy, careless, dishonest, and ignorant, and their calls for domestic education stemmed in part from their desire to obtain efficient, obedient help within their own households. Langhorne expressed the hope of many white housewives when she argued that black women who were trained for domestic service would take pride in their work and would become better servants.[68]

White clubwomen envisioned a two-tiered system of domestic education. All women needed to learn to cook, clean, and sew—white women would use these skills to instruct their servants if necessary; African American women who became proficient domestics would enhance their employment opportunities and would also improve the care they provided their own families. But white women's education would go beyond practical chores; they would also study nutrition, child psychology, hygiene, and health. The distinction between the administrative functions of housekeeping and the physical drudgery of housework mirrored and reinforced the South's social hierarchy. White women were supposed to be domestic managers; black women were supposed to be domestic laborers.

At least that was what white clubwomen expected. African American women held a different view. Sarah Dudley Pettey reported that the conscientious black homemaker, like her white counterpart, studied domestic science and understood the "business of housekeeping." African American clubwomen demanded home economics courses because the classes would enable black women to become better wives and mothers. Like whites, they believed that the home was "the foundation of right training and good government, the basic rock of all true culture" and, like whites, they harbored class biases. They chided impoverished blacks for slovenly housekeeping, and they considered the improvement of home life among poor African Americans to be an essential component in racial uplift. Reformers argued that under slavery black home life "was not only neglected but utterly disregarded." As Georgia educator Lucy Laney explained in 1899, "In the old institution there was no attention given to homes and to home-making. Homes were only places in which to sleep, father had neither responsibility nor authority; mother, neither cares nor duties. She wielded no gentle sway nor influence." Laney and others felt that because slavery had prevented African American women from fulfilling their domestic responsibilities, it was particularly important that young girls be taught how to care for their families; black women must rise above their history and create a stable domestic environment. Laney staked black women's claim to a share of the power of femininity; African American wives and mothers should be able to exercise moral authority just as white women did. African American clubwomen resented white attempts to educate black girls only for servitude and worked to provide in their schools the same types of courses offered to whites.[69]

African American and white organized women were proud of their mastery of the "business of housekeeping." They thought of themselves as home managers and attempted to apply the principles of scientific management within their households. They defined themselves as professionals, doing a job that required a unique combination of physical and intellectual skills, and they believed they were entitled to the same respect and recognition accorded to salaried professionals. They were also eager to apply their expertise outside their homes. They were convinced that they could make valuable contributions to local and state governments that were undertaking "housekeeping" chores of their own.

In 1911 NCFWC president Laura Holmes Reilley warned, "As the evils of the outside world penetrate to its inmost sanctuary, the obligation rests upon us to change adverse conditions and correct prevailing abuses. There never was a time when the American home was so dependent upon public methods and conditions as at present, nor when the children of our land needed a more far reaching arm of protection." For North Carolina clubwomen, the home was no longer the safe haven it was supposed to have been in earlier eras. Instead it was a fortress besieged by sinister, invisible enemies that could invade at any time. As homemakers, women recognized that the environment outside their homes largely determined the well-being of the inhabitants within. Impure food and infectious diseases could enter the cleanest homes, and even the most vigilant housekeeper could not control the circumstances surrounding her family once they left her premises. Women promoted urban cleanliness and public health, therefore, not from "a desire to neglect their homes, but to keep outside civic conditions from being harmful to their homes, wherein their chief duties lay." Women portrayed their interest in urban reform as a defensive maneuver: they were attempting to carry out their domestic responsibilities, to protect their husbands and children from the evil forces that lurked just outside their front doors. In the process, however, they increased their public influence and established themselves as experts in key areas of public policy.[70]

When housewives became "public housekeepers," they followed the same steps in their hometowns that the WABPS had adopted in rural schools: clean, sanitize, beautify. Many organized women considered cleaning up to be the prerequisite for other urban reforms. "The status of a community," one white clubwoman observed in 1917, "is largely determined by its degree of physical cleanliness, for this naturally leads to beautifying, to sanitation, to the provision of recreational facilities and the whole gamut of civic betterment." Women's associations staged parades, sponsored cleanup weeks, and canvassed individual residences and businesses to persuade citizens to tidy up their houses, yards, and neighborhoods. The success of the campaigns depended on the participation of all citizens, regardless of race or class. White and African American women's groups cooperated to coordinate the cleanup and beautification projects, then coaxed, cajoled, and, on occasion, coerced their poor and working-class neighbors to take part. Organized women believed that enlisting townspeople to join together for what they defined as the common good was one of the beneficial byproducts of municipal improvement. "The whole work . . . is calculated to break down the imprisoning walls of prejudice and narrowness," Elvira Moffitt reported to the Raleigh Woman's Club, and concluded, "It will engender civic pride." Although the "imprisoning walls of prejudice and narrowness" held firm, civic improvement campaigns forced whites to pay attention to the needs of blacks and gave African Americans some leverage in their quest for government services.[71]

Even the toughest segregation ordinances could not stop the spread of sickness from one neighborhood to another, and African American lead-

ers exploited whites' fears of contagious diseases to win support for government-sponsored sanitary improvements in black residential areas. In
1913, for example, a pamphlet circulated at the African American state
fair reminded "the white people that they are not immune from the effects
of negro life in their respective communities for diseased negroes are very
apt to cause diseased white people." Six years later, black educator Charles
N. Hunter told NCFWC president Kate Burr Johnson, "It must occur to
you, as it must to all thoughtful white women of the South, that community health is inseparably linked with Negro sanitation. It must also occur
to you that, in great measure, Negro sanitation in any high degree, is
possible only through the instrumentality of the white women of the South
in cooperation with Negro women." That was a lesson white clubwomen
in some North Carolina towns had already learned. White women's clubs
in Charlotte and Salisbury discovered that in order for their cleanup projects
to succeed, they had to enlist the support of African American women.[72]

African American and white clubwomen shared common concerns
about public health and undertook similar projects: black women working
with blacks, white women with whites. Public health campaigns, like many
other Progressive reforms, frequently started with community education.
The WCTU began conducting hygiene and nutrition classes in the 1880s.
After 1900 other female voluntary associations took up the cause. Organized women were especially concerned about the welfare of children.
They held lectures and demonstrations on nutrition and child care and
sponsored "better baby" contests to encourage mothers to practice the
most advanced principles of infant nurture. In the 1920s the League of
Women Voters supported the Sheppard-Towner Act, which established a
federally funded program for maternal and infant health.[73]

Organized women urged local government to use its authority to protect public health and safety. They called for pure food laws and for inspection of milk and meats. They demanded that town officials set standards
of cleanliness for public markets and require that foodstuffs be screened
and that perishable items be refrigerated. They asked municipalities to
exterminate flies, mosquitoes, and other disease-carrying insects. They
persuaded city governments to schedule regular garbage collection, place
trash cans in public places, and install or upgrade sewage systems. During
the first three decades of the twentieth century, white and African American clubwomen appeared before town councils and city commissions
throughout North Carolina to plead for various civic improvement measures. Although there was no place for women in politics, organized women
assumed a role in government.[74]

In addition to their efforts to prevent or curb the spread of disease,
organized women attempted to care for people who became ill. The King's

Daughters played an especially important role in aiding the sick. Local circles supplied medicine, hired private-duty nurses, loaned sheets and towels to patients, and paid for operations or lengthy hospital stays. Some circles maintained a hospital room for indigent patients; others raised money to build or improve hospitals and clinics. Some circles kept cemetery plots where the "worthy dead" could be interred. Although occasionally white Daughters offered help to African Americans, for the most part members of each race were expected to look after their own. African Americans frequently formed secret societies to provide medical and life insurance. Members of the Lady Knights Department of the Royal Knights of King David, for example, pledged "to help each other in sickness, both by personal attention and financial aid, as necessity may require." Church missionary societies, the WCTU, and the Red Cross also offered assistance to the ill and infirm in black communities.[75]

While women's organizations provided medical care for many people who otherwise would have done without, not everyone appreciated their efforts. In 1909 Mrs. M. H. Russell, secretary of a circle of white King's Daughters in Rockingham, recounted the story of circle president Easdale Shaw's chance meeting with "a tall, loose-jointed man, with unkempt clothing and forlorn aspect." "Well, I reckon you ladies mean right and do good by *some* people," the stranger told Shaw, "but *I* has shore suffered by ye. Yes ma'am I has *suffered*." Startled, Shaw asked the man how the Daughters had harmed him. He explained that they had sent his wife to a hospital, and when she returned home, she promptly took their children and left him, and he had not seen her since. The man may have felt sorry for himself, but he received little sympathy from the women he blamed for his misery. Russell concluded that his suffering was more than offset by the "health and freedom" of his wife and clearly regarded the episode as one of the circle's success stories.[76]

Inevitably, some people took advantage of women's generosity. In 1912 the white Rockingham circle loaned money to a man who needed an eye operation at Grady Hospital in Atlanta. "He went to the city," the secretary reported, "but not to the hospital." He returned to Rockingham a few weeks later, "very muchly dressed up," and began spending his days at the "Near Beer Saloon" instead of the factory where he had been employed. He made no effort to repay the money he had borrowed. "Experience is the best teacher," the secretary concluded, "so I scarcely think we will advance any more money, especially to a man."[77]

Despite occasional ingratitude and fraud, organized women continued and expanded their health care programs. In many towns, women's clubs or the King's Daughters, on their own initiative or in cooperation with other groups, hired full-time public health nurses. In 1917, for instance, the Raleigh Woman's Club proudly announced that "a new system of correlated public health nursing has been inaugurated in Raleigh directly by and through the Woman's Club that will be an example in public health nursing to the state, to the South, and perhaps over wider territory." During the influenza epidemic of 1918–19, organized women operated special kitchens, employed additional nurses, and worked as volunteers to care for the sick.[78]

Hiring public health nurses was part of a larger fight against tuberculosis. Tuberculosis was a leading cause of invalidism and death; women were especially susceptible. Clubs sold Red Cross (Christmas) seals to fund research for a cure for the disease, donated cash and supplies to sanitariums, and raised money to send infected persons to hospitals for treatment. They also provided assistance to those who remained in their homes. One white circle of King's Daughters, for example, reported supplying several tubercular patients with "milk, fresh eggs, sherry, steak, bread and butter, and medicines." Although tuberculosis affected both blacks and whites, the mortality rate was higher among African Americans, who were shut out of most sanitariums. In 1927 a group of blacks in Henderson, with the help of a "sprinkling of well-wishing white people," set out to raise five thousand dollars for the construction of a tuberculosis hospital for their community. One of the "well-wishing whites" was the county welfare superintendent, who was the only white and one of few women on the ad hoc organization's executive board.[79]

Organized women wanted their towns to be safe, healthful places to live, and they wanted them to be beautiful as well. They cleared vacant lots and planted trees, bushes, and flowers. They celebrated Arbor Day and sponsored contests to encourage townspeople to trim their lawns and weed their gardens. Like other urban reformers, North Carolina women believed that physical surroundings influenced behavior and character. "Bad physical environment means bad moral environment," one white clubwoman wrote in 1912. Another exclaimed in 1929, "Trees, shrubs and flowers are growing where they never grew before, and waste places have been reclaimed and made to bloom like the rose. As a people we are recognizing more and more the value of beautiful surroundings as an uplifting influence in our community life." For clubwomen, imposing order on the city meant imposing order on city dwellers as well.[80]

White organized women also urged state and national governments to conserve natural resources. During the 1920s they lamented that billboards were supplanting trees alongside highways and called on officials to make roadways more attractive.[81]

Finally, clubwomen established parks, playgrounds, and recreation centers. Parks, they believed, soothed and uplifted and, like libraries, indicated a community's good taste and refinement. "A clean and beautiful city means not only a healthy city, but a development of an artistic sense, and spiritual growth," the NCFWC civics chairman wrote in 1926. Clubwomen thought that playgrounds and recreation centers would deter juvenile delinquency by channeling children's energies into constructive play. These facilities, like all others, were segregated. In 1905 the executive board of the Raleigh Woman's Club considered asking town officials "to set aside a certain part of the Park for colored people" but took no action. In Salisbury, African American clubwomen petitioned for a playground for black children.[82]

In 1913 Mrs. M. L. Stover of Wilmington described to the King's Daughters the vast changes that had taken place in the life of a housewife: "Now she sees her business transcending from the four walls of her house and waiting for her everywhere. From house keeping to municipal house keeping was but a step." In the late nineteenth and early twentieth centuries, African American and white women all over North Carolina were taking that step, moving out of their homes and into public life. Participation in civic reform, like their forays into cultural and educational reform, enabled organized women to find their niche in the New South. Women were motivated by the conviction that their femininity endowed them with unique knowledge and skills that could be used in the public as well as the private sphere. In their efforts to improve their towns, they applied the domestic arts to urban problems, simultaneously expanding their own realm and the public domain. Let men be the architects of the new society; women would be its housekeepers: beautifying, cleaning, maintaining, and, when necessary, improving upon the design that men had made.[83]

Public welfare work, announced an NCFWC officer in 1927, "is ours by inalienable right and undisputed province." Since the middle of the nineteenth century, organized benevolence had been an accepted part of woman's sphere. Women channeled many of their efforts to help the poor through church missionary societies, but other women's associations also assumed responsibility for "the delinquent, the dependent, and the defective." As the Reverend J. Harvey Anderson explained in 1899, "The men of the Church contribute, but it is left entirely to the women to formulate plans, and arrange and superintend the details of carrying on the work of benevolence in the church and community." Although Anderson was referring to women in the AMEZ Church, his comments applied to women of both races in all kinds of associations. North Carolina's organized women hoped that their long-range efforts at educational and social reform would ultimately eliminate poverty, crime, substance abuse, and juvenile delinquency. In the meantime, they sought to help those who could not help themselves. In addition, they pressured government to fulfill its obligation to the poor, the elderly, and the criminal.[84]

The King's Daughters, whose motto was "Not to be ministered unto, but to minister," took the lead in philanthropy. In towns throughout North Carolina, circles distributed food, clothing, heating oil, and other necessities to those in need. According to Easdale Shaw, "For a long period of years these circles did almost the entire uplift and charitable work of the communities in which they were located, with no service too great, and none too small, for them to render." Other women's groups also undertook "uplift and charitable work." WCTU members conducted the "flower mission," taking flowers to the sick; in addition, they visited almshouses and prepared dinner for inmates on holidays. In 1901 the *Star of Zion* praised Charlotte's African American WCTU for "doing much good in this city towards helping the more unfortunate people." The UDC assisted indigent Confederate veterans and their families. The King's Daughters and women's clubs in larger towns sponsored Traveller's Aid societies to assist strangers in distress. Women's groups paid particular attention to the needs of children and the elderly; they raised money and collected supplies for orphanages and established homes for aged women.[85]

Organized women adopted a systematic approach to charity; they attempted to ensure that those who needed help got it and to root out cases of fraud. In Durham, white King's Daughters divided the city into wards; they appointed two women to supervise each one and evaluate applications for assistance. Women's groups in many towns cooperated with the Associated Charities, a clearinghouse that coordinated benevolent activities. Both African American and white women's clubs affiliated with the Associated Charities, and frequently white social workers with the organization asked African American clubwomen to monitor the cases of black clients.[86]

In addition to their work with the Associated Charities at the local level, white organized women participated in the North Carolina Conference for Social Service. Raleigh clubwoman Daisy Denson was one of the conference's founders, the only woman in a group that included some of the most prominent men in North Carolina: attorney general Thomas Walter Bickett, *Progressive Farmer* editor Clarence Poe, superintendent of public instruction James Yadkin Joyner, and well-known Asheville physician Dr. Louis Burgin McBrayer, among others. The conference hoped "to insure here and now an environment of physical, mental, and moral healthfulness that will prevent human waste and make for the full development of every individual within our borders," and it adopted methods typical of Progressive reform: "investigating conditions, awakening the people, securing the remedies." The conference focused on many of the issues that concerned organized women—public health, poverty, prison reform—and from the time of its founding in 1912 cooperated with women's groups. Sallie Cotten spoke to the conference's first annual meeting on the question, "What can our women's clubs do in social service and investigation?" and the state's major female voluntary associations endorsed the conference's work.[87]

Like other Progressives, members of the conference and organized women looked to government to provide the "remedies" for social ills. They believed that government could provide social services more efficiently and more effectively than private agencies, whose efforts tended only to perpetuate poverty. "Volunteer aid only serves to pauperize our poor and to make them social parasites," an NCFWC officer commented in 1923. The federation, the conference, the League of Women Voters, and other groups lobbied for state aid to mothers with dependent children and endorsed the work of the State Board of Charities and Public Welfare.[88]

The UDC led the fight for adequate support for the men and women who had served the Confederacy during the Civil War. The Daughters summarized their case in a petition to the General Assembly in 1900. While many veterans had "by industry, perseverance and economy" saved enough to provide for themselves or had families to care for them, others needed special assistance. The petition failed to note that Confederate veterans were not alone in their plight; other elderly North Carolinians suffered equally from economic hardship. The Daughters believed, however, that the veterans were entitled to special consideration. "We do not ask that this be done in the name of charity—far from it—" the ladies wrote, "we ask it as the fulfilling of an obligation due from our common mother, the Old North State, to her sons, who, in youth, devoted themselves to her defense." These heroes deserved better, they argued, than consignment to the almshouse in their old age.[89]

The Daughters of 1900 and subsequent years demanded an increase in veterans' pensions. In addition, they exhibited a lively interest in the state home for Confederate veterans in Raleigh. Rebecca Cameron complained about the home's dilapidated condition and insisted that lobbying for greater benefits for veterans was "the most sacred obligation" of the UDC. "Let us take care of the living who can suffer before we raise memorials to the dead who, happily, are beyond all human pain and want," she wrote in 1900. Local chapters tried in various ways to "take care of the living." They collected money for the maintenance of the soldiers' home and supplied the institution with a variety of items, from pickles and preserves to furniture. The state organization petitioned the legislature to increase appropriations for the home and called for the appointment of women to its administrative board.[90]

The Daughters wanted the state to provide for the Confederacy's surviving heroines as well as its heroes. UDC president Sallie Yates Faison initiated the drive in 1908 when she drafted a bill to establish a home for the wives of the veterans in the soldiers' home. A year later she enlarged her vision to include all Confederate wives and widows but reported that little progress had been made toward realizing that goal. The campaign continued until 1913, when the bill easily passed both houses of the General Assembly. But the fight was not over: after the land had been purchased and the construction contract awarded, the ladies discovered that the state treasury did not have enough money to complete the project. In 1915 the legislature made good its promise, and the home for Confederate women opened in Fayetteville on November 15, 1915. Although the home was governed by men, representatives of the UDC served on an advisory board of "lady managers."[91]

The Confederate women's home, like the soldiers' home, received much of its operating budget from the state legislature. The UDC supplemented this allotment with contributions of cash and supplies and frequently chided North Carolina lawmakers for being too stingy. In 1919 one irate Daughter called the current allowance of five thousand dollars a year "a disgrace to the sons of women on the Appropriation Committee, whose mothers suffered and endured to raise them up, to be a blessing to suffering humanity, who compel the home to exist by such a meager appropriation." Although her phrasing may have been ambiguous, her message was plain. The gentlemen on the committee proved themselves dutiful "sons of women" when they allocated additional funds during a special legislative session in 1920 and promised to consider a permanent increase during the next regular session.[92]

As government expanded its services to the poor, the infirm, and the elderly, organized women redefined their own responsibilities. They acted as self-appointed welfare supervisors, monitoring existing programs and institutions and agitating for the establishment of new ones. In 1896 the white WCTU unsuccessfully petitioned the General Assembly "to provide a home for habitual inebriates." Twenty-eight years later the NCFWC entered a plea, also unheeded, for the establishment of a treatment center for drug addicts. Although government increasingly assumed duties that had previously belonged to voluntary associations and churches, organized women continued to regard benevolence and care for the infirm and the elderly as part of their "undisputed province."[93]

Citing a link between mental illness and crime, the white federation of women's clubs called for the expansion of facilities to treat mentally retarded children and insane adults. In 1924 the NCFWC, conceding it unlikely that the state ever would or could make adequate provisions for psychiatric patients, resolved "that we go on record as approving a workable sterilization law." The League of Women Voters adopted the same resolution the following year.[94]

Confederate Women's Home, Fayetteville

The United Daughters of the Confederacy began lobbying for a home for the wives and widows of Confederate veterans in 1908. The home opened in 1915.

(Courtesy of North Carolina Collection, University of North Carolina Library at Chapel Hill)

The NCFWC and the LWV never again officially endorsed sterilization; nevertheless, the resolution was indicative of women's attitudes toward those they were trying to help. They did not question the right of the
state to prevent "undesirables" from having children. Indeed, they believed that such social engineering was necessary for the common good.
The resolution revealed the underside of women's benevolence. While
organized women possessed a genuine desire to alleviate the plight of the
unfortunate, they also wanted to use philanthropy as a tool to reshape
society according to their own values and ideals.

Women demanded that the state care for those who could not care for
themselves: destitute widows, orphaned children, elderly veterans and their
spouses, and the "worthy poor." In addition, North Carolina's organized
women concerned themselves with those who were institutionalized by
force. They collected magazines and books for prisoners and sometimes
gave them Bibles or religious tracts. They visited jails, not only to "make a
welcome break in the monotonous lives of inmates" but also to inspect
firsthand the condition of penal institutions. They did not always like what
they found, and they added prison reform to their agenda for North Carolina.[95]

Prison reform encompassed a wide range of recommendations—from
prohibiting the flogging of prisoners and doing away with the death penalty to abolishing the convict lease system and introducing the indeterminate sentence. Organized women focused most of their attention on women
and children who were convicted of crimes. They lobbied for reformatories for juveniles of both sexes and for adult women. They protested against
the sexual abuse of female prisoners. Above all, they worked to make prisons into rehabilitation centers where inmates could repent of past crimes
and prepare to be useful, productive citizens after their release.

The white WCTU and the King's Daughters were among the first
North Carolinians to call for a reform school for white boys. The union
endorsed the idea in 1885 and through the 1890s circulated petitions,
held mass meetings, and memorialized the legislature on behalf of the
proposal. James P. Cook, the leading male advocate for the school, launched
his campaign in 1890, and the state Board of Public Charities took up the
cause two years later. The King's Daughters joined the fight in 1902, when
president Margaret Burgwyn suggested that the organization adopt a reformatory for white boys as its first statewide project.[96]

North Carolina undoubtedly needed such a facility. In 1886 the president of the white WCTU reported that the majority of the state's prisoners were less than twenty-two years of age, and one-third were under sixteen.
In 1892 statistics of the Board of Public Charities indicated that "there
were not less than 500" prisoners under twenty. Reformers believed that

for a young boy, prison served only as a training school for a career in crime. The white WCTU urged lawmakers to establish a farm colony and industrial school for juvenile offenders or, at the very least, to put them to work. "Think of a restless, growing boy pacing his cell a year or even a month," Mary Woody enjoined in 1889. "Breaking stone on the street would be preferable both for the body and mind of the child."[97]

Beginning in 1902 the King's Daughters led the campaign for a reformatory for white boys. They acknowledged the General Assembly's reluctance to act and adopted plans to build the school themselves, in hopes that the government would eventually assume responsibility. In 1903 the Daughters asked the white WCTU to help in a fund-raising drive. Two years later they offered the state fifty acres of land plus a thousand dollars to build a carpentry shop. Legislators listened to their proposal at a special hearing and decided to charter the institution—but they refused to appropriate the funds to establish it. The Daughters were disappointed but undaunted. They continued to raise money, to court public opinion, and to lobby for a state-supported reformatory. The NCFWC and the UDC also joined the crusade.[98]

In 1906 the Daughters agreed to cooperate with a newly created men's reformatory committee. Together they appealed to the 1907 session of the General Assembly. "The duty of the State to prosecute and punish young criminals is inseparable from its obligations of guarding them and giving them a chance to reform," the Daughters argued in a petition to the Senate. The Daughters and their male allies faced strong opposition from lawmakers reluctant to commit tax revenues to another state institution; earlier sessions had rejected proposals for a reformatory for financial reasons. This time, however, the bill's sponsors decided to package the measure not only as prison reform but also as a memorial to a revered southern hero. They promised that the school would be named after Confederate general Thomas Jonathan "Stonewall" Jackson, whose widow, Mary Ann, resided in North Carolina. Once Jackson's name was attached, Confederate veterans in the Assembly unanimously supported the bill, and it passed on March 2, 1907.[99]

The founding of the Stonewall Jackson Manual Training and Industrial School in Concord was a major victory for white organized women, the culmination of a twenty-year campaign. As with prohibition, women had played a vital role in mobilizing popular support for a reformatory for white boys, and men acknowledged the significance of women's contributions. Three weeks after the legislature approved the measure, a Concord attorney and a member of the men's committee congratulated Margaret Burgwyn and the Daughters for "getting an obstreperous Legislature" to pass the bill. In 1921 E. R. Preston, who had chaired the men's commit-

Proposed cottage, Stonewall Jackson Industrial Training School, Concord

The King's Daughters led the campaign for a reformatory for white boys. After the legislature voted to establish the institution, the King's Daughters and the North Carolina Federation of Women's Clubs cooperated to build a cottage at the school.

(Courtesy of North Carolina Collection, University of North Carolina Library at Chapel Hill)

tee, declared that "the King's Daughters have done more to advance this movement than all other forces combined." A year later, a *Raleigh News and Observer* editorial praised the Daughters because "they established the Stonewall Jackson School at Concord, when everyone else was talking about it, and saying it ought to be done." The newspaper exaggerated a bit—the Daughters did not act alone in 1907—and Preston failed to mention that the "other forces" included women's associations like the WCTU, the NCFWC, and the UDC as well as his committee. Still, white organized women were among the first to start "talking about" the need for a reformatory, and they convinced many people that "it ought to be done."[100]

Women had helped bring the reformatory into being, and they participated in its governance. The law chartering the institution named four women to its board of trustees: Mary Ann Jackson and three representatives of the King's Daughters: Margaret Burgwyn, Easdale Shaw, and Sallie Yates Faison. It also required the governor to consult with these four before he chose the other board members. Governor R. B. Glenn complied. He selected four additional female trustees, giving women a majority on the fifteen-member board, and appointed James P. Cook as chair. The decision to include women on the board was a tribute to women's efforts in behalf of the reformatory. It was also indicative of a government that was expanding to include "feminine" duties of nurturance and moral instruction as well as "masculine" obligations of protection and discipline. When the state established an institution for the moral regeneration of young boys, the government looked to women for advice and leadership.[101]

White organized women continued to maintain close ties with the Stonewall Jackson School. For several years the board of trustees met in conjunction with the annual convention of the King's Daughters. The NCFWC and the King's Daughters joined together to build a cottage at the school, and women sent clothes, books, and magazines to the boys. Female voluntary associations, in particular the WCTU and both federations of women's clubs, also pushed for similar institutions for African American boys and for girls of both races. In 1908 the president of the white WCTU asserted, "We rejoice that steps have been taken to produce a reform school for white boys, but still believe that provision should be made by our State for the careful reform of juvenile offenders of both colors that they may be restored to lives of usefulness."[102]

Years passed before the legislature acted on her plea, years in which African American women conducted a relentless campaign for an institution like the Stonewall Jackson School for black youth. From the time of its founding in 1909 the NCFCWC advocated the establishment of a state-supported reformatory for African American boys. Clubwomen understood that they must win over white public opinion, so they publicized their cause in North Carolina's white newspapers. Meanwhile, some African Americans attempted to build a privately funded manual and industrial school for juvenile offenders. Legislators finally passed a bill for a state reformatory in 1921. They appropriated money for it in 1923, and the Morrison Training School opened in 1925. By 1933 the school had two hundred inmates.[103]

White organized women led the fight for the establishment of a reformatory for white girls. The WCTU launched the campaign in 1888. During the next three decades other women's associations, including the NCFWC and the DAR, joined with the union. In 1919 the General Assembly at last responded, authorizing funds for a reformatory for white girls to be called Samarcand Manor. White women's organizations also agitated for a similar institution for white adult female prisoners. In 1922 one clubwoman described the need for "a place where women may be sent under an indeterminate sentence, where they may receive the physical care needed, given wholesome occupations, taught something of household duties (of which many are woefully ignorant), taught to read and write, and given religious instruction." The Legislative Council of North Carolina Women included a reformatory for white adult female offenders in its agenda, and in 1927 the legislature appropriated sixty thousand dollars for a farm colony for white women who had committed misdemeanors. After the colony began operation, organized women lobbied for increased funds for the maintenance of this "child" of theirs and also collected clothing, books, and magazines for the inmates.[104]

Despite the construction of prisons for women, many women remained incarcerated with male inmates in county jails or the state penitentiary. Organized women took it upon themselves to look after their less fortunate sisters. They worried in particular about sexual harassment and abuse. In 1924, for example, Kate Burr Johnson asked the League of Women Voters to investigate conditions in the Forsyth County Jail because "we have every reason to believe that the jailer uses the women for immoral purposes." Johnson was state commissioner of public welfare and she planned to submit a report on the situation to county officials, but she expected them to ignore it. She hoped that pressure from women's voluntary associations would force the men in charge to act. Because of incidents such as those Johnson described, women reformers advocated hiring female guards to supervise female inmates. They also asked that men and women be housed on separate corridors in city and county jails.[105]

"Prison reform is coming," a white clubwoman prophesied in 1926; "it cannot be stopped by the conservatives in North Carolina if the big human-hearted women of the state will co-operate with that splendid group of progressive men who have studied, and talked, and urged for years."

Kate Burr Johnson

An active clubwoman, Kate Burr Johnson served as president of the Raleigh Woman's Club and the North Carolina Federation of Women's Clubs before becoming Commissioner of Public Welfare in 1921. She was the first woman in the United States to be named director of a state welfare department.

(Courtesy of North Carolina Division of Archives and History)

The "human-hearted women" and "that splendid group of progressive men" had already accomplished a great deal; more than two decades of lobbying had resulted in state-supported reformatories for white and African American boys and for white girls and women. But the state had done little for African American girls and women who violated the law. Reformers were especially concerned about young black girls. "The delinquent Negro girl is perhaps the most difficult social problem confronting North Carolina Negroes," observed Lawrence A. Oxley, director of the state's welfare programs for blacks, in 1927. African American clubwomen agreed, and under the leadership of Charlotte Hawkins Brown the NCFCWC made a reformatory for black girls its top priority. In the early 1920s clubwomen raised more than twenty thousand dollars—enough money to buy 142 acres of land near the town of Efland in Orange County and to construct "a modern frame building" that included a reception room, classrooms for cooking and sewing, and dormitory space for fifteen girls. By the spring of 1926, the Industrial Home for Delinquent Negro Girls had opened its doors.[106]

From the beginning, African American clubwomen hoped that the state would assume control and expand the reformatory. They offered to turn it over to the government if the General Assembly pledged to maintain it as a state institution. The white Legislative Council—dominated by clubwomen whose support Charlotte Hawkins Brown had carefully cultivated—endorsed the NCFCWC's plan and lobbied in its behalf. Lawmakers refused to accept the gift, insisting (as usual) that the state could not afford it; in 1927, however, they did appropriate two thousand dollars a year for the school's maintenance. The NCFCWC continued to operate the home at Efland until the 1940s, when, belatedly, the legislature authorized a state-supported home for black delinquent girls.[107]

The story of Efland recapitulates the story of organized women's work for public welfare in North Carolina; it illuminates the assumptions, goals, and strategies of African American and white women striving to make their mark on public policy. African American women saw a need, and when government refused to respond, they filled the need themselves. Ultimately, however, they wanted to relinquish the school to the state. They shared the Progressive faith in government—the belief that government could perform certain tasks more effectively and more efficiently than private agencies. They followed a path familiar to women in voluntary associations throughout the nation. Organized women initiated projects (like public libraries or parks or reformatories), then, once they were established, turned them over to government.

In order to achieve their goal, African American women formed alliances with white women—in the same way that white women had earlier enlisted black women in the temperance movement and cleanup campaigns and worked with men to revitalize public schools. In the Jim Crow South, where law separated the races and custom prescribed rigid divisions on the basis of gender, whites and blacks, women and men, found common ground on the frontiers of social reform.

The industrial school at Efland, like other reformatories and the revamped public schools, was an institution infused with hope. The facility clubwomen envisioned was not a prison where young girls would be locked away and punished; it was a sanctuary where girls could be rescued from lives of crime and "brought back to the normal Christian attitudes of right living." Because organized women viewed the home as the wellspring from which all good influences flowed, they tried to simulate the domestic environment in public institutions. They believed that in a homelike atmosphere even the most degenerate souls could be reclaimed. African American clubwomen hoped that inmates of Efland would rise above their inauspicious beginnings and join the ranks of virtuous women who were a "power for good"—uplifting their families, their communities, and their race.[108]

In the campaign for the reformatory for black girls, as in all of their work, clubwomen acted from a sense of feminine obligation. It was up to women to represent the needs of the poor, the ill, the elderly, and the young to men in power and to work with men to expand government to fulfill new responsibilities. Organized women sought to reform the mechanisms for the administration of charity and justice in order that the government might use its power to improve lives and to improve its citizens. A bulletin prepared for the NCFWC by the extension division of the University of North Carolina in 1925 explained: "Public welfare is no longer thought of in the old terms of merely charities and correction, but as a very essential service toward the development of human adequacy." No longer did government exist only to police and regulate; it should also nurture and rehabilitate. As humanitarian concerns that had formerly been relegated to the private sector became issues of public policy, women assumed new positions of authority.[109]

But the story of Efland also illustrates the limits of feminine power, especially as exercised by black women. While lawmakers acceded to some of women's requests and adopted some of their suggestions, they rejected others, and they sometimes disagreed with women about North Carolina's most pressing needs. White men still controlled the agenda of the "domesticated" government, and most of them ranked an institution like Efland—a school designed to cater to the most neglected, least powerful group in southern society—low on the list of the state's priorities.

In the late nineteenth and early twentieth centuries, white and African American women set out to become a "power for good." They wanted to "uplift" North Carolina's people morally, spiritually, economically, and intellectually, to minimize conflict among social groups (while preserving social distinctions), and to alleviate human suffering. For more than three decades they worked to enact programs and create institutions they believed would benefit their state and its inhabitants. They tackled a myriad of social problems and espoused a wide range of reforms. They found room to maneuver within the fixed boundaries of racial and gender hierarchies, forming coalitions with each other and with men to achieve their ends. They helped to redefine the powers and responsibilities of government, and they appropriated certain areas of public policy—areas relating to "Culture with a capital 'C,'" education, health, and public welfare—as their own.

North Carolina's organized women saw themselves as pioneers—exploring uncharted territory in the public domain and adding civic obligations to "woman's work"—and they felt compelled to articulate a model of femininity to fit the new society they hoped to create. The New Woman of the New South should, they believed, combine "the sweetness and gentleness that characterized our mothers, with the fire and spirit and alertness that marks the twentieth century woman." Nina Holland Covington summarized this updated vision of womanhood in 1917, when she proposed "*a toast:* To the Women of the New South—Progressive but not bold; active and vigorous, but not pushing; independent and self-sufficient, but not mannish; with sweetness of manner, gentleness of spirit and a growing desire to take part in the world's work. We look to the women of the New South for achievements that will make the whole world a better place to live in." Like the New South itself, the ideal southern woman would embrace the future while clinging to the past.[110]

Covington and others remained silent on one very significant point: What was the relationship between these New Women and politics? Should they remain aloof from political power struggles, relying on feminine influence to accomplish their ends? Or should they seek political power for themselves? These were volatile questions, and organized women disagreed with each other on the answers. As women carved out a public role and increased their involvement in government, they also struggled to come to terms with the meaning of female citizenship in the New South.

IV

"Handmaidens of History"
FEMALE PATRIOTS AND THE SEARCH FOR A USABLE PAST

Middle- and upper-class white southerners in the late 1800s and early 1900s divided civic responsibility—as they did almost everything else—along the lines of gender, race, and class. White men practiced politics; white women promoted patriotism. Together they ruled over African Americans and poor whites. White women believed that their role as citizens, while different from men's, was of equal importance. "It is woman's right as well as her privilege to see that the duties of citizenship are taught in the home and in the school," DAR regent Mary Love Stringfield declared in 1903. Six years later Mary Spratt Van Landingham, who at different times held statewide offices in both the DAR and the Colonial Dames, offered a more detailed description of the restrictions and obligations that defined the civic lives of those "who are only women": "We cannot muster nor march. We cannot fight nor win battles. We cannot make speeches and laws, cause panics and strikes, have political squabbles and big presidential elections. But we can look backward with reverence, treasure our history and our traditions, commemorate deeds that are noble and events that are great, [and] teach our sons the high duty of a patriotic service." Van Landingham implied that women working quietly in their homes and in their communities could be just as influential as the men who controlled the most momentous public events. It was an article of faith that other white organized women shared. Even after women got the vote, leaders of female patriotic societies exhorted women not to forsake their traditional mission to "mould public opinion with tongue and pen, teaching patriotism instead of politics."[1]

Women's civic responsibilities were intertwined with their domestic duties, and for most of the nineteenth century they carried out their most sacred public obligations within the private sanctuary of the home. The job of "teaching patriotism" began in the nursery and by the fireside. A mother, according to one Daughter of the American Revolution, "not only rocks the cradle of the infant, but she takes the lad in hand and points the way of honor, the road that leads to useful and noble citizenship." Another Daughter declared that "the growth of patriotism is first of all in the hands of the mothers of any nation." Within their families white women shaped the characters of the boys who would govern when they became men. "As the priestess of the home altar, as the moulder of thought, and as the mother of men," a pamphlet published in the mid-1890s decreed, the American woman must learn "to mould such thoughts, and train such sons as will promote the good of the nation." The results of her work would extend far beyond her own household. Charged with raising loyal citizens, a mother held "within her grasp the destiny of the nation." For a woman, being a good citizen meant being a good mother.[2]

The link between rocking the cradle and ruling the world had been established in the early days of the United States. As historian Linda Kerber has written, late-eighteenth-century statesmen, ministers, and philosophers agreed that the American experiment in democracy required a virtuous citizenry, and they expected mothers to instill the patriotic values and ethical standards that would guarantee the survival and success of the republic. The "ideology of Republican Motherhood" designated women the agents of civic virtue at the same time that the mechanisms of republican government barred them from direct participation in civic life. This definition of feminine citizenship and civic responsibility became firmly embedded in the popular feminine ideal prescribed for white women at the turn of the century. Charles Brantley Aycock employed it in his 1900 gubernatorial campaign when he referred to "the White Goddess of Democracy—the White Womanhood of the State." North Carolina's white "goddesses" were expected to inspire and teach and to leave the day-to-day operation of politics and government to men. Aycock's comment and the political culture it represented pointedly excluded black women from any civic role. White men never elevated African American women to goddess status and were careful to deny them even the limited privileges of female citizenship.[3]

While few white women in turn-of-the-century North Carolina openly questioned their assigned civic role, some decided that it was time for the "White Goddess of Democracy" to exert her influence more directly and in a wider arena. Women who joined patriotic societies, like those who enrolled in temperance unions and women's clubs, discovered prescriptions for collective action within the conventional model of femininity. They wanted to become preceptors of patriotism for all of society, not just their own children.[4]

Although members of the Colonial Dames, the DAR, the Daughters of the Revolution (DR), and the United Daughters of the Confederacy (UDC) insisted that they were above partisan politics, their work was laden with political implications. In the wake of the Republican and Populist challenge to Democratic hegemony in the 1890s, the Daughters and Dames celebrated tradition and the status quo, and they continued to encourage respect for established hierarchies long after Democrats regained control over state government. Their loyalty to white supremacy was implicit; they also sharply delineated class distinctions among whites. Eligibility was based on ancestry, on an applicant's ability to document a satisfactory answer to that quintessentially southern question, Who are your people? These women were unabashed representatives of a white elite that was anxious to maintain its dominance in southern society. They were certain that their illustrious pedigrees endowed them with a superior understanding of the meaning of American ideals and that it was their mission to enlighten everyone else. They pledged, in the words of one DAR officer, "to keep alive the best traditions of our country, to pass along from generation to generation the American ideals of patriotism and honor and usefulness and all that is best in our civilization." While others might disagree about which of the national traditions were "best" and argue over the meaning of American ideals, the various Daughters and Dames anointed themselves the ultimate arbiters of national values. As a regent of the DAR explained in 1923, "Ours is the heritage which means American and all that America stands for, and ours is the sacred obligation to perpetuate and defend it."[5]

Their chosen medium for preserving and transmitting their values was the discipline of history. They found in the nation's past abundant examples of American ideals-in-action, and they considered knowledge of history to be the wellspring of patriotism. "How can we teach patriotism without the teaching of history?" the DAR regent asked in 1912. "These two studies go hand in hand." She and her associates searched the historical record for stories that illustrated the virtues and principles they cherished, then spread the parables far and wide. Long before scholars and politicians launched debates over "political correctness," the Daughters and Dames understood the power of history. They recognized that interpretations of the past color perspectives on the present and hopes for the future. They knew that history was a tool that could be used to forge consensus and to define the terms of political discourse. Through numerous programs and projects, they attempted to cast their rendition of the lessons of American history in stone—sometimes literally.[6]

"Blessed are women, in that they are permitted to be the handmaidens of history!" a DAR regent exclaimed in 1911. North Carolina's "handmaidens" did their job thoroughly. They collected thousands of pages of reminiscences and records, accumulated relics and artifacts, amassed vast stores of genealogical data, staged countless pageants, reviewed history textbooks, sponsored essay contests, and placed historical markers, monuments, and plaques all over the state. As Governor Aycock initiated his campaign for public education, white women's patriotic societies undertook their own educational crusade to present "true history" to adults and schoolchildren alike. They reached into the minds and imaginations of North Carolinians and influenced perceptions of American traditions and ideals in their own time and in the decades that followed.[7]

Some historians accused the patriotic societies of perpetuating historical myth instead of preserving historical fact. The DR, the DAR, and the Colonial Dames, for example, insisted on celebrating May 20 as the anniversary of the adoption of the Mecklenburg Declaration of Independence in 1775 even though most scholars doubted the document's authenticity. Charles Van Noppen was so incensed when the Colonial Dames unveiled a tablet commemorating the bogus declaration that he published a pamphlet castigating them for commissioning the marker and the North Carolina Historical Association for failing to protest against it. Van Noppen's attack did not faze the redoubtable Dames. They, along with their compatriots, continued to cite the Mecklenburg Declaration as evidence of North Carolina's preeminent role in the American Revolution.[8]

Chapters of women's hereditary associations frequently chose to honor local heroes, living and dead, as one of their first projects. Daughters of the Confederacy sought out Confederate veterans, awarding them Crosses of Honor (medals the UDC gave to any man who had served in the Confederate army), recording their stories of wartime experiences, holding banquets for them, and assisting at veterans' reunions. The UDC, along with the DR and the DAR, also located and marked graves of soldiers who died in the American Revolution and the Civil War. At meetings, members frequently read papers about the accomplishments of some local luminary; some chapters required each new inductee to present a biography of the ancestor whose service entitled her to membership. In addition, local chapters collected relics, diaries, and documents; encouraged the elderly to record their reminiscences; and interviewed Confederate veterans, former slaves, and other survivors of the Civil War and Reconstruction. The state societies lobbied for a "fireproof hall of history" in which artifacts could be displayed and manuscripts made available for historical research. Women's civic and literary clubs sometimes endorsed these endeavors but rarely participated in them.[9]

Women in patriotic societies knew that if they wanted to raise popular awareness of the past and its meaning, they could not confine history lessons to classrooms, museums, libraries, and archives; they had to find ways to bring their message to wider audiences. To this end they sponsored public programs to mark the birthdays of famous men and the anniversaries of notable historic events. White North Carolinians celebrated the birthdays of Confederate leaders Robert E. Lee and Jefferson Davis and observed Confederate Memorial Day. They also commemorated significant moments in the Revolutionary era, such as April 12, 1776, when the colonial assembly adopted the Halifax Resolves and North Carolina became the first colony to instruct its delegates to the Continental Congress to vote for independence. White organized women hoped that public observance of these holidays would intensify citizens' pride in and loyalty to their state, region, and nation. According to one clubwoman, "Pageants in which local history and traditions are portrayed enable the community to become familiar with its past while developing patriotism and urging on to great achievement."[10]

Pageants and parades captured public attention on holidays; memorials in stone and marble stood as permanent reminders of the state's heritage. Women in hereditary associations considered the construction of monuments to be their primary mission. Planning, financing, and maintaining statues and historical markers seemed to UDC member Dora Virginia MacRae of Chapel Hill "eminently woman's work. Has not she ever nurtured in the hearts of her sons a deep love of country, and a willingness to die for it, if necessary?" A DAR regent referred to "the acquisition and marking of historic spots" as "the real work of our organization."[11]

The patriotic societies built monuments to pay tribute to famous men and women, to mark historic sites, and to commemorate important events. National organizations designed, built, and maintained many memorials, but state and local branches raised the money that paid for them. North Carolina women contributed their share to the various monument funds and sometimes gave even more. The North Carolina division of the UDC, for example, for several years led other states in contributions to the Jefferson Davis Monument Fund.[12]

Proud of North Carolina's part in American history, the DR petitioned Congress to designate certain spots—such as Roanoke Island, home of the Lost Colony, and Revolutionary battlegrounds Guilford Court House and Moore's Creek Bridge—as national historic sites. The society endorsed federal bills that included appropriations for statues of notable North Carolinians—Continental army officers Francis Nash and William Lee Davidson, for example—and for paintings depicting significant events in colonial history, such as the baptism of Virginia Dare. The Daughters placed great faith in the power of visual imagery. As Elvira Moffitt explained, "a picture impresses a great event on the mind through the eye and kindles in the imagination reverence, joy, grief, or adoration, according as the subject may be. It is necessary for this American Nation to teach through the eye what this Nation stands for."[13]

African Americans also undertook historical projects. In 1907 black women in Asheville and Winston-Salem organized a committee to sponsor a North Carolina exhibit in the "Negro Building" at the Jamestown Exposition being held to commemorate the establishment of the first permanent English settlement in North America. Several years later some black North Carolinians attempted to form a state literary and historical association for African Americans similar to the one that already existed for whites. The National Association of Colored Women cooperated with the Frederick Douglass Memorial Association to restore Cedar Hill, Douglass's home in the District of Columbia. They strove to carry out the wishes of Douglass's widow, Helen, who labored until her death in 1903 to "make Cedar Hill a sort of Mount Vernon for the Colored people of America."[14]

In North Carolina, African Americans joined with whites in the effort to build a monument to Charles Brantley Aycock after the former governor's sudden death in 1912. Blacks' willingness to participate seems incongruous at first glance. Aycock had appealed to white racism to get elected, then had presided over the systematic disfranchisement of African American men while in office. But his dedication to white supremacy was matched by his commitment to universal public education. During and after his term as governor, he championed public schools for children of both races. Calling Aycock a friend to blacks as well as whites, African American educator Charles N. Hunter solicited donations to the monument fund and turned them over to the Aycock Memorial Committee. The committee, chaired by Goldsboro businessman George W. Royall, commissioned renowned sculptor Gutzon Borglum to create a statue of Aycock for the state capitol grounds. The statue was unveiled in 1924. The committee also donated a tablet designed by Borglum to the Wayne County Memorial Building in Aycock's hometown of Goldsboro. Much of the money for the monument fund came from pennies, nickels, and dimes collected from North Carolina schoolchildren.[15]

The Aycock memorial was one of many projects early-twentieth-century North Carolinians undertook to honor the state's heroes and to preserve historic sites within its borders. White women in patriotic societies complained that such work had been "long neglected" and labored diligently to compensate for previous negligence. Occasionally they received assistance from other women's voluntary associations. They restored battlefields and birthplaces, courthouses and churches. They placed plaques on historic buildings and inscribed boulders at natural landmarks. They hung tablets to commemorate historic events. They commissioned statues and portraits of notable North Carolinians. The DAR even traced George Washington's itinerary during his 1791 tour of North Carolina and in 1925 unveiled a bronze tablet in each of the nine towns he visited. Throughout the state, North Carolina's "handmaidens of history" left their mark.[16]

The UDC surpassed all other hereditary associations in North Carolina in its zeal for monuments. Year after year almost every chapter in the state listed building a local monument as one of its goals. Statues of Confederate soldiers and memorials to Confederate dead sprouted in courthouse squares all over the state in the first two decades of the twentieth century. The state division also undertook memorial projects.[17]

Members of the UDC felt a greater sense of urgency about their work than women in other patriotic orders. The Civil War was a defining moment in the collective memory of North Carolinians, and it was recent enough that there was no popular national consensus on its meaning. While Americans agreed that the Revolution was a just and glorious war, northerners and southerners held divergent views of the conflict that had torn the Union apart in the 1860s. The Daughters charged that northern accounts of the war misrepresented the South, and they took it upon themselves to set the record straight. They argued that, contrary to what some northerners thought, the war was not about slavery. Instead, they insisted that Confederates fought to defend states' rights and constitutional liberties. Southerners in general, and North Carolinians in particular, had paid a high price for their experiment with secession: 125,000 Tar Heel men left home to serve in the Confederate army, and approximately one-third of them never returned. To hear these men called "rebels" or "traitors" was more than their wives, sisters, daughters, and granddaughters could bear. Thus the UDC joined with the United Confederate Veterans in a crusade to enshrine the southern interpretation of what they preferred to call "the war between the states" in history books and in the national consciousness.[18]

They believed that they were carrying out a unique and solemn mission. "In all history of the past there exists no movement by the women of the country to secure the records of the truth in history about a lost yet sacred cause," Sallie Yates Faison announced in 1908. For the Daughters, "truth in history" meant telling the story of the war from the South's perspective. Defeated on the battlefield, white southerners were determined to win vindication in the pages of history, and this time women were on the front lines.[19]

Again and again Confederate veterans and New South leaders emphasized the magnitude and significance of the task the Daughters had undertaken. In 1895 the *Confederate Veteran* described the recently founded UDC as "one grand whole of sisterhood, banded together with 'hooks of steel,' standing shoulder to shoulder as a bulwark of truth against the assaults of every calumny and false history, which are calculated to mislead the youth of the South into false ideas of the principles for which their fathers and grandfathers fought." A few years later Captain C. B.

Denson told the North Carolina division: "Liberty, justice to the past, hope for the future of Constitutional government is in your hands. . . . With you, mothers and daughters and granddaughters of the Confederacy, all is safe. The children who nestle about your feet, when they look upon our graves, will never call us traitors." In 1906 General Julian Shakespeare Carr assured the ladies, "You represent more than a sentiment. You represent the living, pulsing embodiment of a principle that will, no, never die." A year later a Confederate major observed that "history is ofttimes false" and praised white southern women who "determined it should not unjustly cast stain or obloquy upon the names of those who made the fight and kept the faith with them for the land they loved so well." In 1910 the mayor of Rocky Mount reminded the Daughters that the defeated and disheartened Confederate soldier had assigned them "the larger and more responsible duty of preserving the history of his own achievement for the inspiration of those to come after him." Other men at the same meeting commended the UDC for having "done so much to perpetuate Southern traditions and ideals and to preserve Southern history" and called the organization's work "glorious."[20]

One man's paean, however, was another's palaver. Walter Hines Page, a native North Carolinian who fled to the North to escape southern provincialism, detected a sinister undertone in the flowery prose. In his novel *The Southerner* he excoriated such silver-tongued orators for duping women into glorifying men who, he believed, were less than noble. "With the women organized to praise them," he wrote, "these wonderful military relics may still longer suppress free thought and free action. It is the shrewdest move they ever made." Page, along with a few other white southerners, regarded the ongoing celebration of the Lost Cause as a major impediment to the South's progress.[21]

In addition to eulogizing the "military relics" Page so detested, the UDC also immortalized the heroism of Confederate women. From the beginning the organization sought to record accounts of feminine courage and ingenuity at home along with stories of masculine valor and sacrifice at the front. Proud of their heritage as southern ladies, the Daughters set out to prove that the Civil War was the finest hour in the history of white southern women. "What tongue or pen can ever tell the true story of the noble part our women took in the four long years of conflict?" Corinne Iredell Erwin asked in 1905, before applying herself to the task. She described the patience and "heroic spirit" with which women "met the privations and hardships of those years of trial and suffering." When the war was over and exhausted and dispirited men returned home, women not only "comforted and sustained in the darkest hour" but also "with ready hand and nimble wit, met the problem of how to make a little go a long way."[22]

In the UDC's version of history the flower of southern womanhood was no clinging vine; women provided both the moral fortitude and the practical skill that enabled the South to survive its birth and death as an independent nation. As Sallie Yates Faison explained, "the women of the Confederacy, though not on the battlefields, bore their part no less heroically than the men. It has always been said that without the women of the Confederacy there never would have been achieved the glories won by it and hostilities would have ceased long before they did." Lucy London Anderson's *North Carolina Women of the Confederacy,* published in 1926, was filled with stories of women's resilience and resourcefulness. Even young girls, she asserted, "showed a spirit that couldn't be put down, showing that women's wit is greater than man's wisdom."[23]

The Daughters of the American Revolution stressed the accomplishments of an earlier generation of southern women. "We love to think of those old heroines bending gracefully over the spinning wheel," Mary Love Stringfield declared in 1904, "but we now see that while she wove homely garments for the comfort of her household, she, at the same time, wove loyalty, love, a noble endurance and a holy reverence into a silken cord that still holds the American nation about the feet of God." In 1907 Corinne Iredell Erwin, who succeeded Stringfield as DAR regent, offered a more graphic description of women's activities: "We know that many a gentle woman literally put her hand to the plow and looked not back through the furrowed way [that] was red with the blood from her bruised feet." Five years later DAR historian Laura Orr told of pioneer women who "worked, and often fought by the side of men, and reared hardy sons who knew not fear." Lida Tunstall Rodman, who served as regent from 1914 to 1916, advised the Daughters to "study the lives of the pioneer mothers of America; they bore a part in the making of this country that was quite as important and courageous as that of the Revolutionary soldier."[24]

Romanticized accounts of the tribulations and triumphs of white southern women in the Revolutionary and Civil War eras more closely resembled hagiography than biography and illustrated the reasons the Daughters studied history and the lessons they expected to learn. White organized women hoped that a documented heritage of feminine strength and achievement would inspire women and silence critics of their expanding role in public life. They were not trying to avoid repetition of past mistakes or to understand the origins of current problems. They were, instead, looking for models they and their contemporaries could emulate. They used history to transmit a set of values and a code of behavior. "It is always a delight to me to think of 'The Little Lady of the South,'" the UDC's corresponding secretary reflected in 1909, "and as I consider our modern progress as a sex, I so often wonder what its benefits are toward developing the lovely, gentle, strong, true woman that we see in the real women of the Confederacy. Oh I don't want our organization to cease to hold them as the highest type."[25]

The "Little Lady of the South" possessed virtues that white southern women continued to prize: courage, endurance, patience, resourcefulness, loyalty, self-reliance (in the absence of men), and self-sacrifice. Revolutionary and Confederate heroines were brave, intelligent, and capable; they were also gentle, loving, and nurturing. Because they made their contributions without violating gender conventions, their lives seemed to be especially appropriate examples for modern women who wanted to expand the feminine sphere without challenging the assumptions on which it rested. The achievements of women in the past testified to the power of femininity, a power that organized women wanted to harness and utilize for the public good.

The Colonial Dames, DAR, DR, and UDC emphasized that what women did at home was just as important as what men did at the front or in legislative halls, and they criticized historians for ignoring women. "There is scarcely the flutter of a skirt through the pages of history," Tennessee journalist Ida Clyde Clarke lamented in 1925. "And many of the things that men have seen fit to record about women we might wish left unsaid." North Carolina women voiced similar complaints and vowed to rescue their foremothers from historical oblivion. "From the day when Virginia Dare was so wise and obliging as to open her eyes on North Carolina soil," Laura Orr declared in 1912, "the women of North Carolina have helped to *make* history." Fourteen years later one of her successors as DAR historian complained, "You may read thousands and thousands of pages of history mentioning the different great men of the times, and not a word of a single great woman, with but few exceptions. Ladies, let not history repeat itself, lay false pride aside, consider the coming generations, and see to it that history is written." Lucy London Anderson compared her search for material on women's experiences during the Civil War to "digging in the 'undug' earth for gold, hard to find, but very precious when discovered." It was an apt analogy, as the scholarship of subsequent historians of women would demonstrate.[26]

Although nearly half a century would pass before professional historians recognized women's history as a legitimate field, hereditary associations pursued their research into the experiences of ordinary women and honored those whose names were already etched into the historical record. Virginia Dare held a particular fascination for many white North Carolina women, who were convinced that her birth at the ill-fated Roanoke colony foreordained a significant role for women in American civilization: "The first white child born in America of English parents *was a girl,* and her birth and baptism would seem to dedicate the land to Christianized womanhood." North Carolina's white organized women used the story of the little girl born three hundred years earlier to justify the expanded role they hoped to play in shaping the nation's future, and they undertook several projects to perpetuate her memory.[27]

Two of these projects grew out of the Columbian Exposition in Chicago in 1893. North Carolina's "lady managers," Sallie Southall Cotten and Florence Kidder, proposed that North Carolina women sponsor a building at the fair. The building would be named for Virginia Dare, and at the end of the exposition it would be moved to North Carolina as a permanent memorial. When Cotten and Kidder failed to raise the necessary funds, they modified their plans. They commissioned Kate Cheshire—"a young North Carolina girl, who has had no instruction in carving"—to create wood panels depicting the story of Virginia Dare and the Lost Colony for a desk. The Virginia Dare desk, as it came to be known, was made of holly wood from Roanoke Island and sat in the lady managers' meeting room during the fair. Ironically, after the exposition the desk that was intended to be a memorial to the Lost Colony was itself almost lost to posterity. Sallie Cotten presented it to the Hall of History, but in 1915 it was transferred to the Raleigh Woman's Club. Some years later the desk was discarded. State auditor George Ross Pou "rescued it from a dump heap" and moved it to his office. After his death, his widow donated it to the Department of Archives and History. By 1953 the desk occupied a place of honor in the office of the department's director, Dr. Christopher Crittenden.[28]

Sallie Cotten and Florence Kidder, the lady managers who supervised the construction of the Virginia Dare desk, harbored plans for a more ambitious memorial. They decided to apply the money they had collected for the North Carolina women's building toward a monument that would be "of lasting benefit to women," a monument that would help women of the present at the same time that it paid tribute to one of North Carolina's most famous daughters. They formed the Virginia Dare Memorial Association and began campaigning for the establishment of "a national school of industrial arts and sciences for women, where they can be systematically trained for the science of domesticity and peace, just as boys are trained for war at West Point and Annapolis." The Virginia Dare Training School would be endowed by the federal government and would be located in North Carolina "because in that State the history of America, and the history of white woman in America, begins."[29]

The women who joined the Virginia Dare Memorial Association believed that housewives needed specialized education and deserved the same respect accorded to other professionals. Their desire for a federally funded school devoted to domestic science, analogous to the all-male military academies, reflected their conviction that women's work was just as important as men's. "Is not the training of girls for practical domestic life as necessary to the future progress of the nation as the training of boys?" association officers asked in a pamphlet describing the proposed school. "The home is the stronghold of a nation's life," they continued, "and woman, the guardian of the home, should be properly trained to make this stronghold impregnable to evil." The Virginia Dare Training School would stand as a public acknowledgement of the vital contributions women citizens made to the American nation.[30]

Sallie Cotten was the driving force in the memorial association. The project appealed to her because it combined several of her interests. Throughout her life she advocated improvements in female education; if girls spent more time in classrooms and laboratories, she argued, they would perform more efficiently and effectively as wives and mothers in kitchens and nurseries. She was also captivated by the story of Virginia Dare. In 1901 she would publish a long poem entitled *The White Doe: The Fate of Virginia Dare,* which recounted the legend that Dare lived among the Indians until an evil medicine man changed her into a white doe. Finally, as a result of her experiences at the Columbian Exposition, Cotten had become a zealous clubwoman. She had a boundless faith in the power of organized womanhood and devoted much of her time and energy for the next three decades to promoting women's clubs in North Carolina. Through the memorial association she was able to pursue three of her most cherished projects simultaneously.[31]

Cotten carefully planned the association's strategy. She advised local chapters to hold monthly meetings in order to sustain interest and to levy fines on members who were absent. She encouraged new branches to "adopt a set of rules for your regular proceedings and go by them. This is a good education for our women need to study parliamentary law and how to conduct meetings. I am ignorant of such things myself," she added, "but am trying to learn." Cotten's insistence on regularly scheduled meetings run according to correct parliamentary procedure served two purposes. First, it reminded women that they were engaged in serious business. Second, it prepared them to participate in the women's clubs that Cotten hoped would soon flourish in North Carolina.[32]

In 1893 Cotten persuaded the state Teachers' Assembly to endorse the school, and in 1894 she planned to "get them to appoint a committee to present it to the *National Educational Association* and get that body to *recommend it to Congress.*" Cotten campaigned tirelessly for the memorial; as she told a friend, "I am so much enthused about it that I imagine I can enthuse others." Her enthusiasm was not enough, however. The association was unable to obtain an appropriation for the school and eventually abandoned the proposal.[33]

White organized women's efforts to honor other distinguished women in North Carolina history were more successful. In 1900 the DR, at the suggestion of Fanny deBerniere Whitaker, decided to build a monument to the women who participated in the event popularly known as the Edenton Tea Party. On October 25, 1774, approximately fifty women met at the home of Elizabeth King and, "obedient to the instinct of womanhood, ever ready to do her duty," pledged to boycott British tea and cloth; an account of their meeting subsequently appeared in a London newspaper. It was one of the first occasions when American women took a public stand on a political issue, and for the DR it signified the important, but often ignored, contributions women had made at crucial junctures throughout American history. Whitaker pointed out that "the State has *never* erected a monument to a woman or to women, though many brave deeds have been done by North Carolina women worthy to be commemorated in marble or bronze." She and others in the DR thought that recognition was long overdue. They wanted to call attention to the women who had worked alongside men to secure American independence and to convince historians that the country's foremothers deserved a place in the history books. They also saw the Tea Party as a civics lesson for contemporary women. In the eyes of the Daughters, the women of Edenton were models of feminine citizenship: they understood that women had distinctive civic obligations, they were willing to sacrifice for a noble cause, and they fulfilled their public responsibilities without neglecting their domestic duties.[34]

Like Cotten and Kidder, Whitaker envisioned a memorial that would benefit present and future generations of women. She told Elvira Moffitt that she wanted it to "take an educational form; as, for instance, a Woman's Building in some college, perhaps the Normal or even the University, which would be for the use especially of the descendants of these ladies (of whom there must be many), or the descendants of any Revolutionary patriots, or the descendants of Confederate veterans." The society, however, decided on a more conventional memorial. To raise money for the project, the Daughters began publishing the *North Carolina Booklet,* an historical and genealogical journal. They also persuaded the DAR to overlook past rivalry and cooperate in the undertaking. Both groups rejoiced when a tablet commemorating the Edenton Tea Party was unveiled in the state capitol on October 24, 1908. The DR considered it their "greatest achievement."[35]

Sketch of design for Edenton Tea Party Plaque
The Daughters of the Revolution began publishing the *North Carolina Booklet* to raise money for a plaque commemorating the Edenton Tea Party of 1774.

(Elvira Evelyna Moffitt Papers, Southern Historical Collection,
University of North Carolina at Chapel Hill)

Edenton Tea Party Plaque, state capitol, Raleigh
The plaque was unveiled on October 24, 1908.

Although women's patriotic associations were eager to ensure that colonial and Revolutionary heroines garnered their share of accolades, men initiated the campaign for a monument to Confederate women. The United Confederate Veterans (UCV) began raising money for the monument in the 1890s, although at the time their top priority was a memorial to Jefferson Davis. After they met their goal for the Davis memorial in 1906, they, along with the Sons of Confederate Veterans (SCV), stepped up their efforts for a women's monument. That same year, General Julian Shakespeare Carr told the North Carolina division of the UDC of his hope "that somewhere a shaft of most beautiful and enduring marble, flawless as nature can produce and white as the untrodden snow, shall pierce the Empyrean." The monument he dreamed of was to be "a token to the fidelity, the courage, the loyalty, the self-sacrifice and the heroism and virtue of the women of the South, 1861 to 1865, representing as they did the finest civilization that ever lived under any flag." Carr expressed the sentiments of many Veterans and Sons who were determined to recognize Confederate women for their wartime service.[36]

The Daughters agreed that Confederate women were heroines who deserved veneration, but at first they resisted men's efforts to build a monument to them. In 1899 the North Carolina division of the UDC instructed its delegates to the organization's general convention to suggest that the Veterans apply the money they had collected to the Jefferson Davis monument fund, a joint venture of the UDC and UCV. The national UDC eventually endorsed the women's memorial after the turn of the century, but women and men continued to disagree about the form it should take. A number of leading Daughters recommended that the money be used to endow an industrial school for southern women. Veterans and Sons, however, insisted on a conventional monument; the fact that many of the women they were attempting to honor preferred a different type of memorial seemed immaterial. In the end, the Daughters behaved as proper ladies should. When the SCV and UCV refused to consider alternatives to a monument, the UDC gracefully acquiesced. The 1906 national convention adopted a resolution of appreciation to the Veterans, although, as one delegate reported, "the ladies seemed to prefer the money [be] put in a school or a home for Confederate women."[37]

The Daughters' reluctant acceptance of the monument did not end the debate; controversy continued over the memorial's design. The chair of the UCV's committee on the women's monument persuaded the Veterans and Sons that identical monuments should be placed in all of the former Confederate states. The committee then chose a prototype, which the Veterans overwhelmingly rejected. Next the UCV approved a statue designed by Belle Kinney of Nashville. Kinney's sketches showed a woman comforting "a wounded and exhausted Confederate soldier" while a larger female figure—Fame—placed a crown upon her head. The Veterans loved the statue; the Daughters detested it. "Time and again have come protests against that miserable design for the monument to the Women of the Confederacy by Miss Kinney," Fannie Ransom Williams reported. "North Carolina Daughters need never fear that this piece of statuary, an outrage to our noble mothers, as well as our heroic fathers, will ever rise upon our soil." Williams and other Daughters argued that Kinney's statue portrayed southern women as weak. "Can anyone looking upon it believe that it will keep alive the proud story of Confederate womanhood and Confederate valor?" a Louisiana "Woman of the Sixties" asked indignantly. The UDC protested that the sculpture also assailed the memory of southern men; the wounded soldier in the woman's arms bore no resemblance to the upright, vigilant figures featured in most Confederate statuary; it served as a grim reminder of the South's defeat.[38]

When North Carolina veterans began considering a state monument to Confederate women, the UDC offered several alternatives: a scholarship fund, a home for Confederate widows, a dormitory at the normal college for white women in Greensboro. The women did not oppose more conventional memorials to women in principle; they had participated in the campaign for the monument to Jefferson Davis's daughter, Winnie, and they marked and carefully tended the grave of Robert E. Lee's daughter, Anne, who died in North Carolina during the Civil War. But they felt that a monument to *all* Confederate women—wives and daughters of common soldiers as well as of politicians and generals—should serve a useful function for women who were trying to make their way in the New South. All of their lives the Daughters had heard stories about the hardships women had endured in the 1860s; some had lived through the war and recalled their own experiences. They knew that for many women the war did not end at Appomattox. One out of every four slain Confederate soldiers was a North Carolinian. Many of those men left behind families who struggled to survive without a male breadwinner in a region where poverty had become the norm. Although most UDC leaders had risen above the straitened circumstances of the war and Reconstruction, they were aware that many widows and descendants had not. Unlike other hereditary associations, the UDC had a philanthropic purpose as well as a historical mission: it aimed to assist Confederate veterans and their families. The UDC believed that the most fitting memorials to Confederate women would honor the dead by helping the living. When the North Carolina legislature appropriated twenty-five thousand dollars for a dormitory dedicated to Confederate women at the normal college in 1911, Fannie Williams called it the "noblest monument of all."[39]

Some veterans, however, were not satisfied. After the General Assembly failed to set aside funds for a conventional memorial, Colonel Ashley Horne decided to pay for a monument himself. Horne, one of six sons who had served the Confederacy, wanted to honor his mother and women like her. He appointed a committee that included Fannie Williams and five men to select a design. The committee completed its work in July 1912, and the monument, crafted by sculptor Augustus Lukeman of New York, was unveiled in a public ceremony on June 10, 1914. Although some of them may have harbored misgivings, the Daughters responded graciously. They presented a portrait of Colonel Horne to the state, and the UDC's president dubbed him a "Knightly Confederate soldier and gallant friend of womanhood."[40]

The Memorial to North Carolina Women of the Confederacy on the grounds of the state capitol in Raleigh might have been renamed the Monument to Republican Motherhood. It celebrated the traditional definition of feminine citizenship: a woman seated with a book in her lap exhorts a young boy kneeling at her side "to emulate the deeds of his fathers." It also reified the bargain that was at the heart of southern chivalry, a bargain in which women exchanged loyalty for protection. The boy holds a sword, suggesting that he will fight to defend this woman, as his forefathers fought to defend white southern women of earlier generations. At a time when some white North Carolina women were seeking a more active role in politics—a state equal suffrage league had been formed the year before the unveiling—the monument enshrined a division of civil responsibility that was based on gender. Women inspired; men acted. It paid tribute to women of the past and silently reminded modern women of their place in the political universe.[41]

Although women in hereditary associations might have preferred another type of memorial, the statue in Raleigh portrayed a woman performing a task that ranked high on the Daughters' and Dames' list of important feminine obligations: transmitting tradition and patriotism to the young. Increasingly, however, they shared their job with the public schools. "In the hands of the teachers lie the character and sound Americanism of our children," Gladys Avery Tillett warned the DAR in 1923. "See to it that they know it and teach it *correctly.*" Tillett and others advised members to visit schools, observe classes, examine textbooks, and devise ways to make the study of history more appealing. The female patriotic societies intended to use their influence to ensure that the schools did their job properly.[42]

Teaching "true history" was particularly important to the UDC. The ranks of the Civil War generation were thinning rapidly, and some southerners feared that memories of the Lost Cause would die along with

Memorial to North Carolina Women of the Confederacy
Colonel Ashley Horne, one of six sons who fought for the Confederacy, donated the money for this memorial to honor his mother and women like her. The momument was unveiled on June 10, 1914.

(Courtesy of North Carolina Division of Archives and History)

them. The UDC, therefore, directed its message toward the children and grandchildren of the Confederacy. "Our work," wrote Rebecca Cameron, longtime historian of the North Carolina Division of the UDC, "is for children chiefly. We shall soon be gone and upon them will rest the burden of the patriotic duty of vindicating the action of their fathers in preserving the principles of constitutional liberty, of maintaining the little that remains to us of States' rights and State sovereignty, and we should see that they are at least trained in the manual of arms and weapons already forged to their hands."[43]

The Daughters carried out their mission of vindication within their own homes and among the members of the UDC's juvenile auxiliary, the Children of the Confederacy; they made sure that their offspring learned the history of "the war between the states" from the southern perspective. Lessons taught in public school classrooms, however, were, literally and figuratively, another story. The UDC monitored school curricula and took steps to ensure that the historical interpretations students learned in school conformed to their standards. In 1901 Mildred Rutherford of Georgia proposed to the national convention that the organization use its influence to prevent northerners from teaching history. By the 1920s North Carolina's Daughters had begun delivering their message in person, speaking before school assemblies. The division historian estimated in 1927 that they had reached more than a hundred thousand children.[44]

Members of the UDC worried particularly about textbooks written by northern authors and published by northern presses that conveyed "false and injurious impressions of the South." Some saw within the textbook industry nothing less than a conspiracy to undermine southern children's pride in their ancestors and loyalty to their region. As Lucy Closs Parker explained to Ella Brodnax in 1907,

> There is nothing more important than teaching the children the truth of history from our standpoint. The North is doing its best to get their histories taught in our Southern schools. All of the Northern histories refer to our Southern soldiers as Rebels and to the war as Rebellion and it is high time we were trying to counteract the false impression already made on the Youth of our Southland. That any school in N.C. should declare Abe Lincoln a greater man than Washington is a disgrace to their teachers and to the Board of Education of the State.

Parker and her compatriots believed that the UDC should do all it could to correct this "disgrace." Thus the Daughters launched a counteroffensive in the battle to capture the minds of schoolchildren and win control of the historical record.[45]

Throughout the first three decades of the twentieth century the UDC fought to eliminate "Northern histories" from North Carolina classrooms. They corresponded with the governor, the state superintendent of schools, and publishers in their effort to secure schoolbooks sympathetic to the Confederate cause. In 1904 the chair of the state division's textbook committee proposed that representatives from local chapters inspect all textbooks used in their county schools for bias against the South. State superintendent of public instruction James Y. Joyner promised to cooperate. From then on, UDC members carefully read history textbooks and complained loudly when the books failed to teach, in Parker's telling phrase, "the truth of history from our standpoint."[46]

One of the most controversial textbooks was a volume the Daughters referred to as "Muzzey's History of America." David Saville Muzzey's *An American History* was first published in Boston in 1911, and by 1920 North Carolina educators were considering it for use in the public schools. The UDC, however, found its interpretation of the Old South and the Civil War offensive. One statement in particular provoked the Daughters' wrath. "It is impossible for the student of history today to feel otherwise than that the cause for which the South fought the War of 1861–1865 was an unworthy cause," Muzzey wrote, "and that the victory of the South would have been a calamity for every section of our country." Labeling the Lost Cause "unworthy" was heresy in the South. Protests from the UDC and other North Carolinians prompted the superintendent of schools, Eugene Clyde Brooks, to persuade the publisher to delete the most objectionable passages before he approved the book for use in the state's public schools. The fact that the chair of the UDC's education committee was *Mrs.* Eugene Clyde Brooks may have increased the Daughters' influence with the superintendent.[47]

North Carolina's UDC was not the first group to pressure publishers to alter textbooks to conform to a particular viewpoint, nor would it be the last. It was, however, among the most successful. The Daughters and similar lobbies recognized the impact of textbooks on a child's thought. The impression of American history and values that schoolbooks create in a young mind endures long after the student leaves the classroom. By dictating the contents of textbooks, the UDC ensured that generations of North Carolinians would grow to adulthood accepting as truth the southern version of the Civil War and Reconstruction.

The UDC's zealousness in convincing publishers to accept only manuscripts that portrayed the Confederacy sympathetically affected children in other parts of the country as well, since textbooks used in North Carolina might also be adopted by school boards in other states. The Daughters effectively harnessed the power of history. In part because of their efforts, for years to come historical accounts of the Old South, the Civil War, and Reconstruction were filtered through a haze of moonlight and magnolias: all southern (white) men were brave and handsome; all southern (white) women were charming and beautiful; all (black) slaves were happy and loyal; and all (white-skinned, blackhearted) Yankee abolitionists, soldiers, and carpetbaggers were uncouth and malevolent.[48]

Although women in patriotic societies wanted to make sure that children and adults alike remembered past wars and honored those who had participated in them, they, along with women in other voluntary associations, hoped that in the future the United States would be able to avoid armed conflict. In the first fifteen years of the twentieth century, the DR, the UDC, and the white WCTU adopted resolutions calling for the "settlement of all difficulties between nations by the peaceful methods of arbitration." When war broke out in Europe in 1914, North Carolina women prayed for peace and favored American neutrality.[49]

Their prayers were to no avail. In 1917 the United States declared war on Germany, and women in North Carolina and elsewhere rallied to the nation's cause. On November 23, 1917, Katie R. Beckwith, a Greenville schoolteacher, wrote to Mattie Southgate Jones of Durham, "We women now-a-days have to forget self completely in facing the many public duties which the new order of things is placing upon our unaccustomed shoulders." The declaration of war had indeed imposed a new order of things. With their country at war, American women had the opportunity to turn patriotic ideals into active service and to explore new facets of feminine citizenship.[50]

As they had done in earlier wars, women once again rose to the occasion during World War I. They made do and did without; they cooperated with the Red Cross; they endeavored to keep up the morale of the men overseas and the folks at home.

The Woman's Committee of the Council of National Defense served as the "clearing-house for all women's war work." Its purpose was twofold. First, it was "to supply a new and direct channel of communication and co-operation between the women and the departments of the United States Government." Second, it was to coordinate the wartime activities of women's organizations.[51]

The network of female voluntary associations that had developed in North Carolina since the 1880s provided the foundation for the Woman's Committee. The national committee appointed suffragist and clubwoman Laura Holmes Reilley state chair, and she recruited other prominent Tar Heel women. Members of the committee elected Reilley as permanent chair at their first meeting in June 1917 and named Sallie Cotten and Fanny Yarborough Bickett honorary chairs. Cotten was widely known among

North Carolina's white organized women because of her longstanding involvement with voluntary associations. Bickett, the wife of Governor Thomas Walter Bickett, was active in the NCFWC and UDC. The committee
included representatives of virtually every white woman's organization in
the state: Otelia Carrington Cuningham of the Equal Suffrage Association; Gabrielle deRosset Waddell of the Colonial Dames; Jacksie Daniel
Thrash of the UDC; Lucy Robertson of the Woman's Missionary Society
of the Methodist Episcopal Church, South; Mary Hilliard Hinton of the
DR; Mary Spratt Van Landingham of the DAR; Delia Dixon-Carroll,
Cornelia Petty Jerman, Kate Burr Johnson, Jane Simpson McKimmon,
Lucy Bramlette Patterson, and Gertrude Weil of the NCFWC. The state
committee organized women's committees in each county; at least fifteen
of the county chairs had held—or would soon hold—statewide offices in
female voluntary associations.[52]

Early in its existence the women's committee broke with established
custom in one key area: race. According to Laura Holmes Reilley, "The
Executive Committee, in conference with the Chairman of the State Council of National Defense, decided it would be fatal to good policy and success of the Council plan to organize separate councils composed of
negroes." Reilley actively encouraged black women's participation in county
councils and found that African Americans worked alongside whites with
"good results." She concluded, "As the work of the two races lies together,
their organizations should be together." African American women disagreed.
As long as blacks and whites worked together, blacks would be subordinate to whites. Many black women would have preferred a separate organization independent of white authority.[53]

Under the supervision of the state and county committees, women's
organizations abandoned many of their peacetime activities in favor of
war work. Some groups virtually ceased to function, as volunteers devoted
their energies to the war effort. The president of the Equal Suffrage Association reported in 1917 that "it has been difficult to talk with one time
Suffrage workers, save at a Red Cross, Conservation, or Canning club
meeting." Other associations continued to hold meetings but focused on
activities related to the war effort. In 1918 NCFWC president Kate Burr
Johnson asked clubwomen to boycott products made in Germany and "to
allow no criticism of the government or the president to go unheeded."
Locally, women's organizations altered their programs to meet the exigen-
cies of wartime. The Fortnightly Review Club of Raleigh, for example,
replaced its scheduled literary study for 1917–18 with "Ten Lessons in
Food Conservation." Women's clubs throughout the state held classes in
food canning and preservation, exchanged hints on how to substitute for
scarce items, and planted "victory gardens." One particularly enthusiastic

group reported to the NCFWC in 1918 that it had cultivated all the vacant lots in town and planted potatoes at railroad crossings.[54]

As the programs and projects of the voluntary associations demonstrate, women in North Carolina and throughout the United States eagerly responded to food commissioner Herbert Hoover's appeals for conservation. The outbreak of war lent new meaning to mundane household tasks; planning menus, buying groceries, cooking, and even eating leftovers became acts of patriotism. As the president of the national DAR explained, "This is practical work which need not disturb the routine of daily life, yet is of extreme value." Like the Edenton women who turned domestic consumption to political ends when they vowed to boycott British tea and cloth, women in the era of the Great War proved that they could serve their country without leaving their kitchens.[55]

Although organized women voluntarily suspended many of their usual programs for the duration, they carefully guarded ground gained before the war. "Maintenance of Existing Social Service Agencies" was the goal of one of the twelve departments of the North Carolina Woman's Committee. Its chair, Gertrude Weil, campaigned to convince women that "their luxuries must be the first item of expense to cut down, and that their charities are not a luxury." At the same time, organized women used the wartime emergency to justify more reform. The WCTU called for national prohibition in order to conserve grain, while the Woman's Committee reasoned that the increasing numbers of women in heavy industry needed the protection of new health and safety regulations. "It is undoubtedly in the industrial and economic field that the war will mark the most far-reaching transformation," Laura Holmes Reilley wrote. She also recommended that the Woman's Committee propose a child labor law.[56]

Red Cross work, Reilley reported, "is the war work which appeals more generally than any other line of war work." Both African American and white women volunteered for the Red Cross, and women's associations often took the lead in organizing Red Cross chapters. In Durham, for example, the DAR launched the white branch of the Red Cross. In cooperation with the Red Cross and on their own initiative, women's organizations conducted first aid classes; collected money and supplies for hospitals and refugees in the war zone; and sent books, magazines, and "comfort kits" to American soldiers. Women spent hours rolling bandages, preparing surgical dressings, and "knitting, knitting, knitting." They made donations to the "chocolate fund" and sent Victrolas and records to North Carolina troops. They offered financial assistance to soldiers' families and raised money to buy ambulances to be sent overseas. Several local groups hosted entertainments for the soldiers stationed in their towns.[57]

Conserving food and providing moral and material support to the fight-

Red Cross volunteers in Salisbury during World War I

When the United States declared war in April 1917 women's organizations rallied to support the American war effort. Members of women's clubs and patriotic societies frequently formed the nucleus of local chapters of the Red Cross.

(Courtesy of North Carolina Collection, University of North Carolina Library at Chapel Hill)

ing men had always been "woman's work" in wartime. Raising money to pay for the war was another matter entirely, and white North Carolina women found that men did not welcome their meddling in financial affairs, even in the interest of patriotism. In October 1918 Mrs. Ernest Clark of Belhaven described to Lida Rodman the difficulties that women in her area had encountered when they attempted to sell war bonds:

> I am very sorry to inform you, that the women have been unable to secure any Bonds here yet, as the men had the work well in hand, when our literature came, and had been very free to express their opinions as to this work being mens [sic] work etc. etc. etc.
>
> This discouraged the women, and I had great difficulty to get any one that would serve on a committee. I finally succeeded in appointing one, after many attempts having to serve as one of the number myself. . . .
>
> I think if we could have made a beginning when the men did, we would have had much more success, however as it is all for one purpose, perhaps it will be best for the women to withdraw as *our men* seem to think, some of them, that we would interfere with their work.[58]

Rodman forwarded Clark's letter to Mamie Brown Latham, chair of the Woman's Liberty Loan Committee for North Carolina. "I really had to laugh at your and Mrs. Clark's account of these extremely narrow men," Latham replied. "I fail to see why it is less important for women to sell Liberty Bonds than it is for them to drive motor trucks, expose themselves to the danger of shell fire on the battlefield *for men,* use their hands to nail and saw in reconstructing French villages and do many other such useful things, all of which women are doing today, and American women at that." The "extremely narrow men" notwithstanding, North Carolina women continued to sell war bonds. During the second Liberty Loan drive Lida Rodman, chair of the Beaufort County Woman's Committee, reported that volunteers raised $43,000 "in barely a week." Altogether, women collected more than $2 million in the second campaign and more than $7 million in the third. In 1918 Kate Burr Johnson, a member of the state's Central Liberty Loan Committee, estimated that women had done two-thirds of the work in Liberty Loan campaigns.[59]

World War I expanded women's opportunities, at least for the duration. The war created jobs for working-class women, and it gave middle-class women the chance to apply the administrative and organizational skills they had learned in voluntary associations to a cause universally acknowledged as important. As in previous wars, women served their country well. They made sacrifices large and small, cheered and comforted their fighting men, and rallied to the support of their government—even though women in North Carolina and throughout the South had no voice in running that government.

Many women hoped that the war would hasten the day when that would change. In January 1918 President Woodrow Wilson asked Congress to enfranchise women as a reward for their wartime service, and the House of Representatives approved a woman suffrage amendment to the United States Constitution. In October, Mamie Brown Latham predicted that "these dear brothers of Beaufort County who dread suffrage are going to have a terrible bump one of these days when suffrage really comes, for it will just as surely come as some other things which our President has approved." What had long been a jealously guarded masculine prerogative was soon to become a feminine right.[60]

Two years later the "dear brothers of Beaufort County" received the "terrible bump." In August 1920 American women won the right to vote.

V

"The Many Public Duties"
WOMAN SUFFRAGE AND WHITE SUPREMACY

Twenty-three years before the ratification of the Nineteenth Amendment, James L. Hyatt, a Republican from Yancey County in western North Carolina, introduced a woman suffrage bill in the state senate. If he had been influenced by the equal suffrage association formed in neighboring Buncombe County (Asheville) three years earlier, he kept it to himself. "I wanted to do something worthy of Abraham Lincoln," he remembered. Reading Lincoln's speeches had persuaded him that Lincoln was a suffragist, so Hyatt set out to emancipate North Carolina women. Unfortunately, his fellow senators (who, perhaps, were not as well read) refused to take his proposal seriously. They referred the measure to the committee Hyatt chaired: the committee on insane asylums. Hyatt's appeals to his colleagues to send the bill elsewhere failed. "It was plain," he recalled, "that they thought the right committee had the bill."[1]

In the highly charged political atmosphere of North Carolina in 1897, Hyatt's advocacy of voting rights for women must have appeared to many to be lunacy indeed. After the victories of Populist-Republican fusion tickets in 1894 and 1896, Democrats had made suffrage—in particular, the question of who was fit to exercise the right to vote—the focal point of state politics. Determined to neutralize African American power and destroy the fusionists' political base, Democrats wanted to reduce the electorate, not expand it. In some states, white southern reformers offered restricted woman suffrage as a solution to "the Negro problem," arguing that if educated women of property-owning families (that is, elite white women) were enfranchised, their votes would offset those of black men. But North Carolinians never seriously considered this proposal. Instead, Democratic politicians undertook vicious campaigns to discredit and disfranchise African American voters and to establish white *male* supremacy.[2]

In the 1890s, North Carolina Democrats not only eliminated African American men from politics; they guaranteed the exclusion of women as well. White supremacists constructed a political universe in which woman suffrage was at best an oxymoron and at worst a menace to social and political order. Their rhetoric welded masculinity and citizenship together; "manhood" became "the highest test of the right to vote." If manhood was the test, women would automatically fail. But Democrats were not talking to women who wanted the ballot; they were addressing black men who already had it. They declared that African American men were not "real men" and therefore were unfit to exercise the franchise. Politics became the symbolic arena for sexual competition among men; women belonged on the sidelines, the spoils of the political wars that men fought.[3]

White supremacy was predicated on the premise that women were powerless. Democratic politicians used the slogan "the protection of white womanhood" to justify the oppression of African American men. But protection entails dependence. If white women became equal participants in the political process, they might choose different protectors or reject protection entirely. Within the white supremacist scheme of things, female autonomy did not, could not, exist.

In the world the white supremacists made, racial and gender ideologies were inextricably entangled. White men used their dominance over white women to institutionalize their domination over African American men. Woman suffrage threatened to turn this world upside down. Because of the links forged between masculinity and voting during the white supremacy campaigns, the enfranchisement of women portended a radical redefinition of masculine and feminine roles. And because white supremacy rested on female subordination, if gender roles were redefined, racial barriers might also be overturned. White supremacists flaunted the right to vote as evidence of their manhood, declared that women were weak and in need of male protection, and warned women that challenges to male authority were challenges to white supremacy.

North Carolina's white women got the message. Leaders of women's organizations who might have been expected to endorse the enfranchisement of their sex instead appeared to fear it. "As a part of this Commonwealth, we Daughters of the Confederacy take part not within the legislative halls nor at the ballot box God forbid!" Lucy Closs Parker announced in 1899. Four years later DAR regent Mary Love Stringfield agreed with "Mr. Dooley of literary fame, that if we should gain our so-called political rights, we would be apt to lose our privileges, and that it is much better to retain our privileges and do without our rights." That same year Elvira Moffitt, speaking on behalf of the Woman's Association for the Betterment of Public Schoolhouses, assured her listeners, "We women do not want the privilege of voting, we prefer the quietude of home where we must do our duty." In 1904 Fannie Heck, president of the Raleigh Woman's Club, asserted that only two things frightened southern women: "doing something unwomanly and getting involved in politics."[4]

Despite their disclaimers, women of both races had been getting involved in politics since the prohibition campaigns of the 1880s, when women held meetings, circulated petitions, and monitored polling places. The state's white WCTU began petitioning for a scientific temperance instruction law soon after it was organized. Before disfranchisement stifled black political participation, African American women actively assisted the Republican Party and its candidates; Anna Julia Cooper claimed that black southern women were responsible for black men's loyalty to the party.[5]

After the turn of the century, North Carolina women stepped up their search for political solutions to social problems. Statewide prohibition, increased appropriations for schools, the library commission, homes for Confederate veterans and widows, reformatories, a juvenile court system, a state archives and museum—these projects and many others required the sanction and financial support of the state legislature. Women might not want the vote, but it became increasingly apparent that they did want a voice in policy making. A year after she insisted that women preferred "the quietude of the home" to the political fray, Elvira Moffitt, writing for the Raleigh Woman's Club in the *Raleigh News and Observer,* declared, "We, as women tax-payers, feel that the right should be accorded us in making suggestions for the advancement of our city in any line of civic improvement." In an unpublished speech Moffitt acknowledged that "taxation without recognition is not right" but added that being "debarred the ballot" was "perfectly agreeable to us." Moffitt chose her words carefully. She and other early-twentieth-century clubwomen asked for recognition *by* government, not representation *in* government. They wanted officials to pay attention to them and to take their ideas seriously. They believed they could accomplish their goals by uniting in voluntary associations. "When there is an aggregation of sentiment," Moffitt wrote, "there is power." She and other female reformers hoped that "organized womanhood" would prove to be just as powerful as an army of voters.[6]

Few women stated this as bluntly as an anonymous Daughter of the American Revolution in Greensboro in 1902. During the Guilford Battle Chapter's debate over a proposal to affiliate with the General Federation of Women's Clubs, the secretary noted, "Discussion brought out the fact of this plan being the best substitute for women's *influence, legally,* 'the power behind the throne' in lieu of *votes!*" Although the Daughters might have preferred votes, in the end they backed away even from joining the national federation. They postponed a final decision "to wait for reports on 'the Color line.'" With the rhetoric of recent Democratic campaigns still ringing in their ears, the Greensboro women subordinated their desire to enhance their own power to their loyalty to white supremacy.[7]

Like the members of the Guilford Battle Chapter, white women in other organizations wanted to influence legislation and shape public policy, but, like their counterparts in Greensboro, they acted within the constraints white supremacy imposed on them. Most continued to believe that direct participation in politics was "unwomanly," so they aspired to create a public role for themselves that was nonpolitical, a role that would enable them to achieve political ends without entering the political arena. Although such a role may seem to us fraught with inherent contradictions, it was perfectly consistent with the prevailing gender conventions of its day. The code of chivalry assured white women that as long as they behaved as ladies should, they exerted a powerful, indirect influence over all areas of southern life. Their power diminished only if they stepped "outside the magic circle" and sought direct control over themselves or others. White women in voluntary associations wanted to exercise the authority they believed was their birthright. For many years they shied away from demanding the ballot and clung to their faith in feminine influence. Southern women, wrote journalist Mamie Fairbrother in 1910, "do not wish the right of suffrage, realizing that they stand on higher ground and occupy a more commanding position without it."[8]

Around the same time Fairbrother made her sweeping proclamation, other North Carolina women were beginning to recognize the limitations of their "commanding position." Their vantage point on "higher ground" might afford women an excellent overview of the political landscape, but it gave them little authority over the men who populated the world of politics. As women added more and more items to their political agenda, some began to wish for a more active role in the political process. That desire raised questions about their fundamental assumptions about women's "proper place" in public life. Could women maintain a separate feminine domain within the public sphere? Could they wield real power without the vote? How could they increase their influence in the masculine realm of politics without sacrificing their femininity? North Carolina's white organized women were forced to confront these questions in 1913, when they waged a campaign for the right to serve on school boards.

Women had begun lobbying for school board membership even before there was an organized women's movement in the state. In 1886 Mary Bayard Clark of New Bern reported, "I am now, and have been for the past two years, making an effort to have women put on our schoolboards, and a female as well as a male principal for every mixed public school." Clark's solo crusade apparently had little effect. Eight years later Helen Morris Lewis's equal suffrage association called for female representation on school boards, and, in February 1895, "as a result of the suffrage meeting held in Asheville," the General Assembly considered a bill that would grant their request. Lillie Devereaux Blake, a Raleigh native who had become a noted author and suffragist in New York, addressed the legislature on its behalf. The measure stimulated "a hot discussion" but failed to pass. After 1900 other organizations, including the WCTU, the Woman's Association for the Betterment of Public Schoolhouses, and the state Teachers' Assembly, took up the cause. The NCFWC joined them in 1911, when the federation's newly elected president, Sallie Southall Cotten, announced that establishing women's eligibility for school board membership would be one of the two major goals of her administration.[9]

At first glance the request hardly seemed revolutionary. Female reformers had long since appropriated public education as part of the feminine domain. Yet the proposal represented a new, and potentially radical, departure. For the first time since the 1890s, women were seeking political power for themselves: they wanted to become policy makers rather than advisors. Moreover, the issue raised—in the minds of the women, their supporters, and their opponents alike—the specter of woman suffrage.

In May 1912 Sallie Cotten learned from state attorney general Thomas Walter Bickett that women were excluded from school board membership because they could not vote. Positions on school boards and textbook committees were defined as offices, and, according to the North Carolina constitution, only qualified voters—that is, men—could be officeholders. "Thought much about women on school boards," Cotten wrote in her diary a few days later. "Must we all become suffragists?"[10]

Although Cotten had labored for twenty years to advance her sex, she had never taken up the suffrage banner. She was not prepared to lead clubwomen on a futile crusade for the vote or to tarnish the federation's sterling reputation by associating it with radical feminism. And in 1912 many white North Carolinians, including many clubwomen, regarded suffrage as part of the radical feminist platform; there were no suffrage organizations in the state, and few people dared to speak publicly in favor of female enfranchisement. Cotten understood her organization's members and the milieu in which they operated. The fear of "doing something unwomanly" lingered, and echoes of white supremacists' cries linking voting with manliness reverberated. Although clubwomen held views that were progressive for their time on many issues, most abided by traditional gender conventions. They and women in other voluntary associations had created a public role based on the supposition that men and women were different, with different abilities and responsibilities. The very idea of "women's rights" was anathema to many white women reared in the tradition of the southern lady. To them, "women's rights" meant "women's right to be like men." And they did not want to be like men. They saw them-

selves as distinct from (and in some ways superior to) men and believed
that their femininity—the characteristics that set them apart from men—
was the source of their power. Yet here they were, championing a cause
that seemed to point in the direction of equality, which, in their minds,
was virtually synonymous with sameness. The requirement that school
board members be eligible voters posed a difficult dilemma for Cotten
and other clubwomen. How could they fulfill what they perceived as a
feminine obligation without demanding political rights? How could they
control public education, which was recognized as part of woman's sphere,
without venturing into man's world of politics?[11]

Soon after her meeting with Bickett, Cotten reported her findings to
the federation's annual convention. Delegates were "undaunted." They
voted to enlarge the federation's Committee on the Legal Status of Women
and to "pursue the investigation." Cotten consulted Walter Clark, chief
justice of the North Carolina Supreme Court, for advice on framing a bill
that would conform to the requirements of the state constitution and withstand challenges in court. She and other clubwomen vowed to "find the
key with which to unlock this door of opportunity."[12]

By the time the General Assembly convened the following January,
they had found it. The Committee on the Legal Status of Women persuaded state senator Victor S. Bryant of Durham to introduce a bill that
designated positions on school boards and textbook committees as places
of trust or profit rather than offices. Furthermore, it stated that "women
shall be eligible with men to serve in such places."[13]

The bill was not only politically expedient; it also conformed to
clubwomen's ideas about the proper relationship of women to politics. It
gave women authority without requiring the redistribution of political power
or the revision of gender roles. Male officeholders still selected school
board members; as one of the bill's prominent male advocates pointed
out, in all probability no women would be appointed unless they were
"absolutely needed." The Bryant Bill did not challenge the belief that politics was part of man's realm; instead, it redefined school board membership to fall within the feminine domain. It enabled clubwomen to skirt the
issue of woman suffrage, and it reinforced notions of feminine service and
maternal duty.[14]

Bryant's proposal resolved the clubwomen's dilemma, but it aroused
controversy among his colleagues. The General Assembly debated the bill
for the next two months. Opponents warned that it was a short step from
the school board to the voting booth: if women became eligible for school
board membership, soon they would demand enfranchisement. The bill's
supporters, including Wake County school superintendent Zebulon Judd,
attorney general Bickett, and the *Raleigh News and Observer*, repeatedly

denied any association between clubwomen and feminism. "This is no suffragette movement," Judd wrote. The women who endorse the bill, he continued, "do not ask for the ballot, but they do ask to be allowed to care for their own children." Bickett told a Senate committee that although he opposed woman suffrage, he favored the appointment of women to offices relating to "public education, public charity, or public health." The *News and Observer* explained to its readers, "It is not to do something for women that the proposition is made to let women go on the school boards. It is a proposition to secure needed help from those most suited to aid in the proper conducting and management of our schools." Clubwomen agreed. "We are not radical," Sallie Cotten assured Walter Clark before the session opened; "we only desire to do the things we think women especially fitted to do, and to serve where our children's welfare is involved." She reiterated that point in correspondence with other clubwomen as well. "It seems so blind and stupid for men to deny woman the opportunity to serve her state and its children where she is qualified to render good service," she told Elvira Moffitt in February. That same month, the Raleigh Woman's Club, in a well publicized meeting, voted against petitioning the legislature for municipal suffrage.[15]

Throughout the session women employed only the most ladylike methods of political persuasion. Although female teachers enthusiastically supported the measure, they refused to approach legislators in its behalf in order "to avoid even 'the appearance of evil.'" Clubwomen adopted a similar strategy. "We did not 'lobby,'" Sallie Cotten explained to her son Bruce after the fight was over, "but we kept awake and moving all the time." Women "bombarded" the legislators with letters, petitions, and resolutions. Some attended legislative sessions and hearings. Women "were present in large numbers" at a joint House-Senate committee meeting on February 19. They applauded representatives who voted for the bill, and they remained silent when their opponents voted against it. When Victor Bryant asked the spectators how they felt about the proposal, "every woman present arose so as to be counted with the force favoring the bill." Although women refused to testify, Sallie Cotten reminded lawmakers that as president of the NCFWC, she represented three thousand North Carolina women.[16]

While the women took care to behave like ladies, they found the men of the General Assembly to be less than gentlemen. Cotten reported to Elvira Moffitt that the legislators "are playing havoc with the bills we have presented and endorsed and I have heard that they are tearing up our letters and saying very rude things about our 'meddling' with legislation. . . . Yet they may accede to our request so I will try to await the result with silent patience." It was evident, however, that her patience was wearing

North Carolina Federation of Women's Clubs convention, New Bern, 1913

Walter Clark, chief justice of the North Carolina Supreme Court, addressed the convention's final evening session in a speech entitled "The Legal Status of North Carolina Women." The NCFWC's campaigns to make women eligible for school board membership and for a married woman's property law earlier in the year had heightened clubwomen's awareness of legal inequities. Clark shared the dais with the committee chairs who had orchestrated the campaign. From left to right: Edith Royster, Legal Status of Women; Sarah Weil, Legislation; Walter Clark; Mary Hendren, president of New Bern Woman's Club; Sallie Southall Cotten, federation president; Mrs. M. L. Stover, Education.

(Cotten Family Papers, Southern Historical Collection, University of North Carolina at Chapel Hill) thin. On the same day that Cotten wrote to Moffitt, the *Raleigh News and Observer* described her recent address to the North Carolina Conference on Social Service on the school board issue: "Mrs. Cotten appealed to the men to co-operate with the women rather than indulge the cynicism so characteristic of them in the work of betterment now being done by women." In their effort to increase their role in public education, women were learning lessons of their own: the South's much touted feminine "influence" was no match for entrenched political power.[17]

The fight raged on throughout the legislative session. "They killed the bill *twice,* but each time, through our friends we had it put back on the calendar," Sallie Cotten told Bruce. After the Senate's committee on elections reported unfavorably on Bryant's original bill, Zebulon Judd arranged to have a substitute introduced. Meanwhile, the House defeated its version of the proposal with a roll call vote of 45 to 43. "The bill provoked the livest [*sic*] and lengthiest discussion of the two days session," the *News and Observer* reported. The measure's sponsors refused to surrender. On the eve of the General Assembly's adjournment, both houses overcame eleventh-hour resistance and approved the school board bill. The Senate passed it on March 10 after "prolonged discussion." The House followed suit the next day, although opponents offered "ludicrous amendments" in a last-ditch effort to defeat it.[18]

Clubwomen and their allies rejoiced and congratulated each other on their success. Zebulon Judd gave the NCFWC credit for the victory: "It is chiefly due to the support given the bill by the federated clubs with their membership of more than 3,000 women that the bill became law," he said. Clubwomen responded with appropriately ladylike modesty. In public they attributed the triumph to "the fair-mindedness and justice" of North Carolina men. In private they recognized that they won because their friends in the legislature outmaneuvered their foes.[19]

"We women are satisfied," Sallie Cotten concluded after the session adjourned. Although the General Assembly had not been as reform-minded as some North Carolinians would have liked, it had enacted several laws to improve the status of women. In addition to the school board bill, the legislature approved proposals to allow married women to control their own wages and to initiate personal injury lawsuits and collect damages. Clubwomen endorsed these measures but did not promote them with the same zeal they mustered to win representation on school boards. The bills generated little controversy and passed through both houses without fanfare. North Carolina "is being generous to women in correcting the old Common Law *customs,*" Cotten told her son, "though there are many more statutes which could be improved to our credit."[20]

As Cotten observed, the legislators' generosity was limited. Attempts to raise the age of consent, reform divorce laws, and eliminate the private examination of married women in property transactions failed. Lawmakers also stifled one proposal to give women the right to vote in municipal elections and another to hold a statewide referendum on woman suffrage.[21]

The mixed results of the 1913 legislative session reveal a great deal about the attitudes of the men who sat in the statehouse. They refused to act on behalf of wives with adulterous husbands or young girls who were victims of sexual abuse because men's domination over women was one of the cornerstones of white supremacy. They were willing, however, to offer women economic autonomy. Giving married women control of their wages might alter the balance of power in individual households (although it would not directly affect members of the House and Senate, since their wives were unlikely to be wage earners), but it did not seriously threaten white male hegemony. Granting women public authority—even in the "feminine" area of education—was another matter. That issue raised the question of who should govern, a question white supremacists believed had been satisfactorily answered at the turn of the century. Although in the end the General Assembly narrowly approved the school board bill, legislators summarily dismissed plans to give women the ballot. North Carolina lawmakers in 1913 agreed with their predecessors: political power and public authority belonged to white men and only to white men. They conceded to women a measure of private economic independence and a modicum of influence in one area of public policy, but they closely guarded their political prerogatives.[22]

Although most men in North Carolina were hostile to woman suffrage, the best-known suffragist in the state at the time was Chief Justice Walter Clark. He endorsed female enfranchisement in his unsuccessful bid for the United States Senate in 1912 and drafted the married women's wage bill that passed the General Assembly in 1913. Clark believed that justice demanded that women be given the ballot. "I regard the women as the equal of our sex in intelligence and legal rights," he told one antisuffragist in 1914. "Being subject to the laws, they should have a voice in making them, and being taxed I think they should have a right to their views as to the disposition of public funds." He objected to the Fifteenth Amendment because it enfranchised African American men without enfranchising women, and he argued that it should be revised: "I think that decency and justice require that the word 'sex' should be placed after the word 'race' or before it." Like many other reformers, Clark also believed that women voters would support the Progressive agenda.[23]

Clark preached the suffrage gospel throughout North Carolina and the South but won few converts. When he addressed the Raleigh Woman's Club in 1913 in support of the municipal suffrage bill, "the women heard with pleasure, gave him a vote of thanks, and voted unanimously not to take it up." Raleigh clubwomen, the *News and Observer* reported approvingly, "are interested in everything else more than they are in woman suffrage." Because the women were concerned with "mights not rights," the story continued, they were content to remain on the sidelines of the political arena until North Carolina men in their wisdom chose to bestow the privilege of voting on the female sex. Clark realized that they might have a long wait. He advised Louisiana suffragist Kate Gordon that if southern women did not demand the vote, southern men would never give it to them. Then he added, "If however a few ladies of standing and character in each state of the South will put themselves ahead of the movement, the politicians will not dare to oppose it." Southern men were unaccustomed to refusing women's requests, he insisted, although they might employ flattery and other methods to persuade women that they did not want or need the ballot.[24]

Because of Clark's endorsement of votes for women and his reputation as "woman's real friend," suffragists appealed to him for support when they decided to organize in 1913. "The Dear Ladies seem to be waking up down here and are beginning to demand the suffrage," Charlotte lawyer and suffrage advocate William M. Wilson informed Clark. They were, Wilson continued, "quite anxious" to have Clark attend the upcoming meeting to form a statewide suffrage association. Shortly thereafter, the Equal Suffrage Association of North Carolina (ESA) named Clark one of its five male advisors.[25]

The ESA affiliated with the National American Woman Suffrage Association (NAWSA) and represented the moderate wing of the suffrage movement. In 1913 Alice Paul's Congressional Union also established branches in North Carolina, to the dismay of ESA leaders. Like most southern suffragists, they opposed the activities of the more radical union and took care to dissociate themselves and their organization from Alice Paul and her group. The association disavowed "militancy" and denounced the Congressional Union because "its methods would not suit the conditions of the Southern States." The union never attracted a large following in North Carolina.[26]

Regardless of their organizational affiliation, North Carolina suffragists faced a difficult task. They met hostility in some quarters and apathy in others. Most North Carolina men opposed woman suffrage; many women did not seem to care about it. Persuading North Carolinians that women were entitled to the ballot proved to be an uphill struggle, and suffragists fought hard for every inch of ground they gained.

Antisuffragists (or "antis") argued that giving women the vote would upset the delicate balance of southern civilization. "Personally I do not believe that the ballot would be best for you or for the race," Trinity College president William Preston Few told the North Carolina DAR in 1914; "In the light of all I know about the history of mankind, I will dare to say that if you break down in the hearts of men the chivalric ideal of women, you will strike the most disastrous blow at civilization that it has ever received." Many others shared Few's opinion. Edwin Yates Webb, who represented North Carolina's Ninth District in Congress, believed that "it would be a positive calamity to womankind in our country to thrust her into politics." Mrs. E. B. Cline, a suffrage organizer in Hickory, observed, "The opposition there is largely sentimental—same old story—Woman and the home—loss of the sweet, high, femininity etc. etc.—but it is opposition good and hard—and the situation has to be handled mighty carefully." Antis feared that giving women the vote would set off a chain of events that would culminate in the destruction of gender differences.[27]

In addition to "opposition good and hard," suffragists encountered widespread apathy. ESA organizers complained that many women seemed indifferent to the issue. Discussing her work in Hickory, Cline wrote in 1914 that "the interest isn't there." A year later Lida Rodman commented to ESA president Barbara Henderson, "It is strange that so many are still unresponsive. Though many hold back on account of domestic reasons, or fear of ridicule." Years later Gertrude Weil recalled that her hometown of Goldsboro "was very un-suffrage minded. The women just weren't interested in the right to vote."[28]

Whatever its source—apathy, domestic responsibilities, fear—the reluctance of North Carolina women to get involved in the suffrage campaign proved to be a serious obstacle. During the debate over representation on school boards, historian Joseph Gregoire de Roulhac Hamilton argued that woman suffrage was an irrelevant issue because women had not demanded the ballot. "Certainly it should never be granted until there is clear evidence that a large majority of them wish it," he wrote, because there were already too many apathetic voters. The *Raleigh News and Observer* held that if women wanted suffrage, they would get it, adding, "but if they desire to vote there has been little indication of such desire. The men will await their decision." Men who supported suffrage must have understood the deeply entrenched antagonism toward granting women political rights, and they must have realized that lawmakers would not simply hand women the ballot just because they asked for it. But they also knew that women would have to lead the fight. Without a groundswell of support among women, there was no hope at all that the General Assembly would ever enact woman suffrage.[29]

Suffragists did what they could to transform the apathetic into activists. They circulated pamphlets and petitions and publicized their activities. In 1914 Jessie Vanpel Bicknell reported to ESA treasurer Mary Palmer that she contributed a weekly suffrage column to the local newspaper, the *Morganton Messenger*. "I think it is the first paper in the state to have a regular department for suffrage news," she declared. ESA organizers tried whenever possible to recruit women who were well known and respected in their communities in the hope that other women would follow their lead. They sponsored a suffrage booth at the state fair and encouraged schools to adopt the question as a debate topic. They also recognized that projects not directly related to suffrage might produce a ripple effect. The Washington league, for example, launched an effort to have two women appointed to the city school board in May 1915. "If we don't succeed we will put the people to *thinking* which may bear results later," Lida Rodman explained to ESA president Barbara Henderson. Putting "the people to *thinking*" was the ESA's major goal in its early years. Rodman, Henderson, and other suffragists agreed with Jessie Bicknell that "publicity and education are what are needed in suffrage work."[30]

In November 1914 the ESA undertook a major educational project: they began lobbying for a woman suffrage amendment to the state constitution. They wrote to every member of the General Assembly, asking his opinion on suffrage. A few ignored the request. Among those who replied, twelve favored it, fifteen "were flatly opposed," and the "majority declared themselves open to argument." Suffragists followed up the written inquiries with personal interviews. They collected information on each representative, "ranging from views on Suffrage and political affiliations to personal characteristics." They focused much of their attention on their opponents. "By the time the Legislature convened," legislative chair Mary Henderson reported, "we had a very good catalogue of enemy legislators."[31]

The poll was just the beginning. In January 1915 the ESA established an "information bureau" at the Yarborough Hotel near the capitol in downtown Raleigh. They also arranged to have the amendment introduced simultaneously in both houses on January 23. For the next two months, members of the Raleigh league packed the visitors' galleries on days when the amendment or other issues of concern to women were on the Assembly's agenda. Meanwhile, the association's press committee sent weekly articles to "fifteen of the representative papers of the state" and cultivated support among sympathetic editors.[32]

The highlight of the session came on February 2, when House and Senate committees considering the amendment met in joint session for a public hearing on the proposal. ESA officers had worked hard to win this day in the spotlight, and they used their time well. Like their predecessors in the school board fight two years earlier, they maintained the standards of ladylike decorum, but this time women spoke for themselves. Lawmakers and a capacity crowd of spectators heard addresses by some of the most prominent women in the state and the nation, among them Anna Howard Shaw, renowned orator and president of NAWSA; T. Adelaide Goodno, president of the North Carolina WCTU; Laura Holmes Reilley, cofounder and first vice president of the suffrage association; Clara Souther Lingle, clubwoman and soon-to-be president of the NCFWC; and Mamie Fairbrother, journalist, clubwoman, and former antisuffragist.[33]

The most dazzling speaker of all was ESA president Barbara Henderson, who argued the suffragists' case with logic, wit, and a keen understanding of the attitudes and prejudices of her audience. She began by quoting the promise of a government of the people, by the people, and for the people. "Possibly you do not consider women *people*," she told the legislators;

> surely those who withhold a voice in the government to their women cannot consider them so—or they must be convicted of inconsistency; and we all know that to be an impossibility for we are assured from our cradles that inconsistency is one of the exclusively feminine characteristics which make our sex so charming as to enlist the chivalry of all men—who fall adoringly at our feet, while they kiss one fair hand and snatch the ballot from the other.

Continuing her exposition, she speculated, "Perhaps you believe in a government of the men, by the men, and *for* the women. Because, of course, *Somebody* has to be governed, and 'it might as well be me.'" She compared women's political status to "the children's games where the biggest boy is the car, the little boy is the chauffeur, and the little girl running along behind has to be the 'smell.'" Women, she said, were tired of being the "smell" and wanted to be "if not the automobile or the chauffeur, at least a passenger in the automobile."[34]

As she continued, she became less caustic but no less adept at demolishing some of the most popular objections to giving women the right to vote. She pinpointed inconsistencies in antisuffrage thought and deftly used one argument against woman suffrage to refute another. Attacking the proposition that "women are represented in the government by men," Henderson asked Assemblymen to consider how they would feel if women ruled and men were disfranchised. "Would you be content to be told that you were represented by your wives? Not a bit of it," she insisted. She built her case around a premise fundamental to the thinking of suffragists and antisuffragists alike: that men and women possessed distinct but complementary talents, skills, and characteristics. "It is the very difference in the masculine and feminine natures that forms the basis of the home and *should* form the basis of all just government. . . . The difference between the sexes is the ground upon which the anti-suffragists base their opposition to our cause. And yet they claim that one human being can be represented by another of absolutely different mental attitudes." She then proceeded to justify suffrage with the same rationale that women employed when they began forming voluntary associations: that outside forces infringed upon the home, that women needed the power to protect their families, that there existed—or should exist—a separate feminine domain in the public sphere. Women voters, she promised, would usher in a new era of social and moral reform.[35]

Although Henderson and other suffragists shared with female reformers the belief that women could make unique contributions because they were inherently different from men, they parted company with many organized women on the question of feminine influence. For the suffragists, influence was not enough; they wanted power. "If you *know* many officials who pay more attention to a constituent without a vote than a constituent *with* one, I'd like to meet the gentlemen," Henderson challenged the committee.[36]

Henderson couched her arguments in appropriately feminine terms, emphasizing that women who desired suffrage were merely carrying out their duty to serve others. She assured her listeners that she harbored no personal grievances against them and appreciated their veneration for women. "I am convinced that if chivalry exists in the world, it is found in America; and that we women of the South are more fortunate than any women in the world." However, she added, "all men are not chivalrous, and the institution of chivalry, as we understand the term, is not in practice among those classes whose women stand most in need of its benefits." She asked for the ballot not for herself—"so far as my personal happiness [and] well-being is concerned, there is nothing that suffrage can do for me"—but on behalf of women who were denied the privileges and respect accorded to southern ladies. Wives trapped in marriages to abusive husbands, wage-earning women exploited by greedy bosses—these were the women for whom Henderson pleaded. She and women like herself—women of "the class I represent"—had an obligation to women who were not so lucky. Henderson spoke for them as well as for the ESA: "All women are sisters in their motherhood, and every mother is the mother of all the babies in the world. Surely it is the happy wives and mothers who must feel most urgently their duty to those less fortunate."[37]

Henderson recognized that while the bonds of womanhood could transcend class boundaries, the promises of chivalry did not. Although she did not question in her testimony the assumption that men should protect women, she added a new twist: when men failed to honor their end of the bargain, women must step in to take care of themselves and each other. Henderson blended an expanded definition of chivalry that enabled women to be protectors as well as protected with a vision of sisterhood that was colored by notions of *noblesse oblige*. Elite white women would be the "big sisters" who protected their weaker counterparts.[38]

Henderson's description of suffragists as "happy wives and mothers" countered negative images of feminists as man-hating, barren spinsters. As the hearing drew to a close, ESA legislative chair Mary Henderson reminded her listeners that suffragists represented the "good women" of North Carolina, and she called on legislators to fulfill their obligations as gentlemen. "From our cradles, North Carolina men have assured us that our lightest wish is law. We are now testing this assertion. We are appealing to your chivalry when we ask you to report the equal suffrage bill favorably."[39]

Eloquence, reason, and appeals to chivalry were to no avail. Both committees issued negative reports on the amendment, and both houses voted it down. A few days after the defeat, Walter Clark complained that antisuffragists had used "unfair" tactics to engineer the bill's demise. "It was taken up suddenly, without notice to its friends, without fair opportunity for discussion and voted on," he told the ESA's Lalyce Duffy Buford. "Had there been fair treatment and a full discussion I think it would have gotten a majority." Most suffragists accepted the outcome with equanimity. Their poll of the General Assembly had forewarned them that the measure would fail, and they decided to make the best of the situation. Mary Henderson proclaimed the campaign for the bill "a triumphant success" because it had raised public awareness of the suffrage issue. "Equal Suffrage was, by all odds, the most widely discussed subject before the General Assembly of 1915," she told ESA members at their annual convention, "and the State is now fully alive to the fact that the Equal Suffrage movement is to be seriously reckoned with." During the legislative session suffragists circulated pamphlets and leaflets throughout the state, gaining supporters for future battles. Newspapers also provided generous coverage.[40]

Over the next few years suffragists worked to capitalize on the favorable publicity they had received during the 1915 campaign. They distributed literature and invited prominent prosuffrage lecturers to North Carolina. In January 1919, for example, William Jennings Bryan spoke at an open session of the ESA's annual convention in Raleigh. "About 3,000 were present," the convention's *Proceedings* reported, "including Tank soldiers, legislators, negroes, etc." Suffragists also continued to poll political candidates and officeholders and to lobby for suffrage legislation. In 1917 the General Assembly considered a municipal suffrage bill that would give towns the option of enfranchising women and a woman suffrage amendment to the state constitution. The bill was defeated; the amendment was tabled. In 1919 the Senate passed another municipal suffrage bill (this time it was an antisuffragist who charged that it had been "stampeded through"), but the House rejected it.[41]

Lawmakers continued to assert that North Carolina women did not want the vote, and there was some evidence that they were right. In 1918 the *Raleigh News and Observer* speculated that if women were presented with a referendum on suffrage, they would probably defeat it. The voluntary associations that claimed to speak for all of North Carolina's white women were noticeably reticent about enfranchisement. The patriotic societies tended to avoid the issue entirely, perhaps because both suffragists and antis emerged from their ranks. Lida Rodman, who was active in the DAR and the UDC, became a dedicated suffragist and served for a time as ESA treasurer. Meanwhile, DR president Mary Hilliard Hinton, with assistance from Colonial Dames president Gabrielle deRosset Waddell, led women who opposed the Nineteenth Amendment in 1920. The WCTU—which had included suffrage in its platform since the 1890s and whose president, Adelaide Goodno, had spoken in favor of the municipal suffrage bill in 1915—offered lukewarm support. In 1919 only two local unions reported any work on behalf of votes for women, and Anna Williams, superintendent of the union's Department of Franchise, pleaded: "Finally, women, even if we aren't anxious enough for the ballot to fight for it, let's be intelligent and inform ourselves on the laws of our own state, especially regarding women and children; let's recognize the fact that we will soon have a duty to perform on election day, form our own opinions and be ready to be a capable citizen when the time comes." Despite the ESA's efforts, many women remained unenthusiastic about suffrage.[42]

Most damaging of all to the ESA's case was the NCFWC's silence. The federation, with approximately eight thousand members, had a reputation for promoting "sound ideas . . . as to what might be done to make women more useful to their community and to the state and nation." It had a long history of political activism and had provided a training ground for suffrage leaders. Most suffragists were clubwomen, but not all clubwomen were suffragists.[43]

NCFWC members who wanted the vote delayed bringing a suffrage resolution before a federation convention because they understood that many of their colleagues were apprehensive about asking for the ballot. Some clubwomen worried that enfranchisement would diminish women's effectiveness by blurring the distinction between masculine and feminine roles. They maintained their faith in the power of femininity. Since the

Mary Hilliard Hinton
President of the North Carolina branch of the Daughters of the Revolution, Mary Hilliard Hinton led women who opposed the Nineteenth Amendment in the summer of 1920. Antisuffragists rejoiced when the General Assembly refused to ratify.

(Courtesy of North Carolina Collection,
University of North Carolina Library at Chapel Hill)

1880s, women had honed "feminine influence" into an effective political tool. As long as women were debarred from the political process, female reformers could claim the moral high ground above the political fray. If women gained the ballot, they might lose the moral authority of nonpartisanship. Moreover, leaders of voluntary associations could speak with the voice of "united womanhood" without fear of contradiction. Some of those who were dubious about suffrage realized that enfranchised women were unlikely to vote as a bloc and that inexperienced female candidates, excluded from established networks, would be weak competitors in the political arena. It would take more than votes to break white men's monopoly on political power; therefore, some women reasoned that for the time being they were better off on the pedestal than at the polls.[44]

Suffragists disagreed. They resented disfranchisement as a badge of inferiority, and they understood that political equality would not eradicate gender differences. Like Barbara Henderson, they considered feminine distinctiveness to be among the most compelling arguments for woman suffrage and hoped to add voting to "the many public duties" women had undertaken since the 1880s. In 1918 they decided the time had come to seek an endorsement from the NCFWC. Suffragists believed that at heart most clubwomen sympathized with their cause, and they anticipated the objections NCFWC members would raise. Some might argue that a demand for votes would compromise the federation's ability to achieve other reforms. Others might contend that North Carolina was not yet ready to accept woman suffrage and that the NCFWC should avoid taking a stand until public opinion was more favorable. Suffragists carefully planned their strategy. The resolution they proposed placed woman suffrage within the context of an issue of long-standing concern to clubwomen: education. Women could not serve as school superintendents because they could not hold public office; therefore, women needed the vote in order to advance their own careers and to use their talents to benefit the state. After an "animated" discussion, the convention passed the resolution. Opposition was "astonishingly slight"; only two delegates voted against it. ESA president Otelia Cuningham deemed it "a remarkable triumph."[45]

It was remarkable in part because it indicated a significant change in clubwomen's attitudes since 1913. When the NCFWC campaigned for representation on school boards, clubwomen recoiled from asking for power for themselves. Instead, they called on the legislature to expand women's opportunities for public service. This time they were more direct. The resolution the federation adopted stated: "We deplore conditions that may deprive capable women of positions for which they are equipped and which would be to their professional and financial advantage and that at the same time deprive the teaching profession of valuable services that it might properly command." Suffragists' educational campaign had reaped results. They persuaded white clubwomen that feminism and femininity were not mutually exclusive and that women could, and should, enhance their power to help themselves as well as others.[46]

Other North Carolinians remained unconvinced. Hallett S. Ward, a senator from the eastern part of the state, explained to Walter Clark that although he was "a good genuine progressive," he opposed woman suffrage because he abhorred "the growing tendency of womanhood to mix with and become affected by the coarser things of life, thereby destroying the delicate refinement, innocence and purity that marks the line of demarcation between them and men and between the home and the marts of trade and business." Ward was not alone. Antisuffrage politicians insisted that they only wanted to "protect" women from "the coarser things of life." Still, by 1919 some men had come to recognize that female enfranchisement was inevitable. In a letter to B. G. Crisp of Manteo, sociologist Eugene Cunningham Branson admitted he was "not a rabid woman suffragist," then continued: "But I recognize that feminism is like the rising tides of the ocean, and that it cannot be swept back with a broom, Dame Partington fashion."[47]

The tides of feminism were indeed rising, and soon they would creep into North Carolina. The United States House of Representatives approved the Nineteenth Amendment (sometimes called the Susan B. Anthony Amendment) in January 1918 and again in May 1919. After the Senate passed it on June 4, 1919, the fight over woman suffrage moved into the states. The Constitution required the approval of three-fourths of the states—thirty-six of the forty-eight in the Union at the time—before the amendment could take effect. By April 1920 thirty-five had ratified, and suffragists scrambled to win one more state in time for women to vote in the fall elections.[48]

Two states scheduled special legislative sessions to meet in August to consider the Nineteenth Amendment. One was Tennessee; the other was North Carolina. Tar Heel suffragists were confident that the amendment would ultimately triumph, and they hoped that their state would contribute to the victory. Support for suffrage had been growing; in 1920 the ESA included twenty-four local affiliates. In addition, suffragists reported great interest among college students and faculty, although school trustees prohibited the organization of suffrage societies on campus. The Raleigh branch of the Southern Association of College Women, an organization of collegiate alumnae, pledged its assistance. A number of state officials—including the lieutenant governor, the secretary of state, and the speaker of the house—favored votes for women, as did most of the major newspapers. The state Republican Party seated two female del-

North Carolina Women DO Want The Vote

These Women Have Said So:

NORTH CAROLINA FEDERATION OF WOMEN'S CLUBS.

NORTH CAROLINA FEDERATION OF BUSINESS AND PROFESSIONAL WOMEN'S CLUBS.

NORTH CAROLINA BRANCH OF WOMAN'S CHRISTIAN TEMPERANCE UNION.

EQUAL SUFFRAGE ASSOCIATION OF NORTH CAROLINA.

These organizations comprise THOUSANDS of thinking, intelligent North Carolina women in all parts of the State.

SENATOR F. M. SIMMONS RECENTLY SAID: "The women seem to want it (suffrage), and it is here, whether we like it or not. . . . I thought then (when the Federal Suffrage Resolution was before Congress) that they did not want it; it seems now that they do."

EQUAL SUFFRAGE ASSOCIATION
OF NORTH CAROLINA

RALEIGH

Broadside, North Carolina Equal Suffrage Association, 1920
Opponents of the Nineteenth Amendment frequently argued that North Carolina women did not want the vote. Suffragists used broadsides like this one to refute that argument.

(Courtesy of North Carolina Collection, University of North Carolina Library at Chapel Hill)

egates at its convention in March and nominated a woman for superintendent of public instruction.[49]

These were encouraging developments, but suffragists knew they faced strong opposition, especially within the Democratic Party. Democrats dominated state and national offices in North Carolina, and the party of white supremacy had not demonstrated much sympathy for woman suffrage in the past. Even though Democratic President Woodrow Wilson favored the Nineteenth Amendment, North Carolina's congressional delegation stubbornly opposed it. Only one representative, Zebulon Weaver of Asheville, voted for it. Congressman Edwin Yates Webb, chair of the House judiciary committee, was "a powerful foe," and Senators Lee Overman and Furnifold Simmons were among the leaders of the fight against it. (Simmons had earned his Senate seat by orchestrating the white supremacy campaigns of 1898 and 1900.) Governor Thomas W. Bickett had not changed his mind on the issue since his days as attorney general; he still thought it was a bad idea.[50]

In the spring of 1920, however, North Carolina Democrats bowed to the wishes of the president. In April the party's convention seated approximately forty female delegates, and the platform committee presented a minority report endorsing the Nineteenth Amendment. Delegates reacted to the plank "with deafening applause and a few hisses," responded to a speech opposing it "with hisses and jeers," and incorporated it into the platform.[51]

Suffrage opponents grudgingly supported the party's position. Antisuffrage gubernatorial candidate Cameron Morrison chose to remain silent on the issue at the convention. (According to one observer, it was "the first known record of him having refused to speak when he had the opportunity.") Although Simmons and Bickett accepted the plank, they made clear that they were unenthusiastic about the prospect of women voting. Simmons agreed to it for the sake of "expediency." Bickett explained to Woodrow Wilson that he saw "neither the wisdom nor the necessity for woman suffrage in North Carolina" but believed that the "sensible and graceful thing to do would be to accept the inevitable and ratify the amendment." Although Bickett was a seasoned politician who understood the importance of doing the "sensible thing," he was hardly graceful in his capitulation. He told a newspaper, "While I will take my medicine, I will never swear that it tastes good, for it does not." Woman suffrage was a bitter pill for many southern Democrats; some, like Lee Overman, refused to swallow it at all.[52]

The Democratic endorsement heartened suffragists; they hoped it would guarantee a victory in the General Assembly in August. Shortly after the convention Josephus Daniels assured NAWSA president Carrie Chapman Catt that North Carolina would be the crucial thirty-sixth state.

"It's all over but the shouting," he informed her. Daniels—secretary of the navy, former *Raleigh News and Observer* editor, and lifelong Democratic activist—proved to be a poor prognosticator. By early summer it was evident that the Nineteenth Amendment was in trouble in North Carolina. Governor Bickett expressed his hope that Tennessee would approve it, thereby sparing his state the "bitterness" a fight over ratification would generate. Suffrage leaders assessed the situation and found it grim. "At this time, I do not believe there is a ghost of a chance of ratification in either Tennessee or North Carolina," Catt confided to a Tennessee suffragist on July 12.[53]

Suffragists and antis alike mobilized for the upcoming fight in the General Assembly. The ESA, now under the leadership of Gertrude Weil and Cornelia Jerman, had been building a strong grassroots organization since 1913; longtime members were veterans of several legislative battles. In the spring and summer of 1920 they marshaled their resources to wage a vigorous campaign for the federal amendment. Antis responded by hastily developing their own organizations. The North Carolina Branch of the Southern Women's League for the Rejection of the Susan B. Anthony Amendment (usually known as the Southern Women's Rejection League) formed in Raleigh in April; Mary Hilliard Hinton was its founder and president. Its male counterpart, the States' Rights Defense League, appeared in June.[54]

The two leagues, along with unaffiliated antis, flooded the state with propaganda. They continued to assert that North Carolina's women—at least, North Carolina's white women—did not want the ballot because, in the words of an ad placed in major newspapers by the States' Rights Defense League, "voting is not a mere privilege, but an onerous duty." Coining slogans such as "Woman suffrage is the influenza of politics," suffrage opponents painted pictures of a world populated with domineering women and weak men. One popular broadside circulated throughout the South predicted that the vote would "masculinize" women, "feminize" men, and result in "organized female nagging forever!" When the *Raleigh News and Observer* solicited readers' opinions on suffrage, one writer, attempting to "protect the home-loving Christian women" from something "which they do not want," argued that married women would vote the same way as their husbands. Another insisted that wives would cancel out their husbands' choices, thus creating "grist for the divorce mill." After all, he continued, "no real male man" could possibly love a "vote-killing wife" as much as one who "remained at home and attended to her woman's business." Other correspondents warned that in their eagerness to participate in politics, women would neglect their homes and children. "If women are going to and fro on campaigning trips as of course they must, who will mould the tender minds for the future generations?" asked Mrs. A. S.

Bryant. "Are you going to leave them as plants by the wayside, or alone with some uncouth negro to bring them up?" The women and men who expressed their opposition to woman suffrage in the columns of the *News and Observer* echoed the themes of the literature the antisuffrage leagues were distributing.[55]

Above all, antis insisted that woman suffrage would undermine white supremacy, destroy states' rights, and restore political power to African Americans. "We plead in the Name of Virginia Dare, that North Carolina Remain White," screamed the headline on one broadside. It displayed a map of the United States that showed in black the states where women could vote and presented in white those in which women were disfranchised. The message was clear: woman suffrage would lead to black domination. Once African American women secured their right to vote, they would open the polls to African American men. And if the federal government started tampering with voting requirements, it might intervene in the South, just as it had done after the Civil War. Mary Hilliard Hinton cautioned that it was unwise to expand the electorate in any way, especially in the South, "where we have a race which has given us trouble in the past and may give us political annoyance in the future." In an article in the *North Carolina Booklet,* a historical magazine the DR published and Hinton edited, Henry Groves Connor Jr. declared that if North Carolina became the thirty-sixth state to accept the Nineteenth Amendment, it would rob other states of their right to determine who should vote within their borders.[56]

Antisuffrage pamphlets compared the Nineteenth Amendment to the Fifteenth, which had enfranchised African American men, and predicted that its passage would lead to "another period of Reconstruction horrors." One leaflet warned white southern men: "Heed not the call of the suffrage siren. . . . Remember that woman suffrage means a reopening of the entire Negro question. . . . Do not jeopardize the present prosperity of your sovereign state, which was so dearly bought by the blood of your fathers and the tears of your mothers, by again raising an issue which has already been adjusted at so great a cost. *Nothing* can be gained by woman suffrage and much can be lost." Another broadside reprinted a letter to a Macon, Georgia, newspaper from "a distinguished southern woman" who commanded: "Barter your own souls and your manhood if you must; play your cheap political games; weaken government when its united strength is most needed, but *spare your women!*"[57]

The anguished cries of the "distinguished southern woman" in the summer of 1920 were reminiscent of the words of Rebecca Cameron, who in 1898 instructed her cousin Alfred Moore Waddell and the rest of the state's white men to "get out their shotguns" to save white women from "Negro supremacy." The campaign against the Nineteenth Amendment in North Carolina was in many ways a reprise of the white supremacy campaigns two decades earlier. As historians Glenda Gilmore and Elna Green have demonstrated, white supremacists and antisuffragists adopted similar rhetoric and themes; even the names of the leaders remained the same: Cameron Morrison, Romulus Nunn, and George Rountree had played key roles in efforts to take the ballot away from African American men in 1898 and 1900, and they vigorously resisted attempts to hand it to women in 1920. Furnifold Simmons fought the Nineteenth Amendment in Congress and reluctantly changed his position only after it became apparent that ratification was almost certain. Alfred Moore Waddell was dead, but his widow, Gabrielle deRosset Waddell, lent her name to the antisuffrage cause. Once again the political destinies of white women and African American men were locked together. In 1898 and 1900 white supremacists had called for the disfranchisement of African American men to protect white women. In 1920 they argued for the continued disfranchisement of women to preserve white supremacy. The Jim Crow system bound white women and black men together in the political universe even as it attempted to keep them apart in everyday life.[58]

Antis throughout the nation argued that woman suffrage would erode the boundaries between masculine and feminine spheres; as women marked their ballots, they would erase gender distinctions. Such rhetoric had particular resonance in areas infected with the ideology of white supremacy. White supremacists used gender conventions to justify racial oppression. They equated the right to vote with masculinity and cited the alleged weakness and vulnerability of white women as an excuse to disfranchise and emasculate black men. Although most white southern suffragists accepted white supremacy and the protocol of chivalry, their insistence that women were the political equals of men represented a declaration of independence from male protection. Woman suffrage threatened to destroy the gender-based underpinnings of the racial order. It would empower white women by enabling them to speak for themselves in political matters. At the same time, it would deprive white men of their monopoly on the franchise, thereby eliminating one of the most significant prerogatives that separated white men from white women and from African Americans. The antis' predictions that woman suffrage would "masculinize" women and "feminize" men reflected their anxieties about the implications of the Nineteenth Amendment for both gender and racial hierarchies. Gender and race were woven tightly together in the fabric of southern politics. Pulling one thread—modifying definitions of masculine and feminine roles—might unravel the whole cloth.[59]

Antis need not have worried. White supremacy was firmly entrenched as "the southern way of life" and no longer required justification. North Carolina suffragists denied charges that woman suffrage would subvert the social order and proclaimed their loyalty to both traditional femininity and white supremacy. "Contrary to certain scurrilous reports," Gertrude Weil wrote in a letter dated August 4, 1920, "the leaders of the suffrage movement, national and State, have been and are women of unimpeachable moral character, upholding the highest standards of society. We invite you to make an investigation of our views on the sanctity of the marriage relation, or the home as the basis of society, or our record of patriotic service." In the same letter, Weil countered the Southern Women's Rejection League's prediction that woman suffrage would destroy white supremacy. States would continue to regulate voting, she explained, and African American women would be permitted to vote only if they met the same standards required of African American males. ESA literature reiterated the same arguments. "Woman Suffrage Amendment Raises No Race Issue," one broadside asserted. "The qualifications that now apply to negro men will apply to negro women; those that apply to white men will apply to white women." Another leaflet cited census data to demonstrate that whites outnumbered blacks in North Carolina and reminded voters that "U.S. Senator Simmons, who waged the successful fight for White Supremacy in North Carolina in 1898, advocates ratification of the Federal Suffrage Amendment by the Legislature." If the father of disfranchisement himself supported the Nineteenth Amendment, suffragists reasoned, surely others would see that it posed no danger to white hegemony. Although white southern suffragists renounced protection, they accepted the institutions of white supremacy that had been established in the name of protecting them. They claimed political power for themselves and separated their political destiny from that of African Americans.

Suffragists accused their opponents of deliberately magnifying the race question to divert attention from other issues. In June Carrie Chapman Catt warned a Tennessee activist that the antis would saturate the state with "the most outrageous literature it has been your lot to read. . . . the 'nigger question' will be put forth in ways to arouse the greatest possible prejudice." A North Carolina suffragist told the *Raleigh News and Observer* that the antis appealed to racial fears only because "they don't have justice on their side." Throughout the summer of 1920 suffragists worked to convince other white southerners that the enfranchisement of white women would have no effect on the disfranchisement of black men.[61]

While white suffragists and antis quarreled over the implications of woman suffrage for white supremacy, African Americans conducted a similar debate. Some, like Annie Blackwell, corresponding secretary of the Woman's Home and Foreign Missionary Society of the AMEZ Church, believed that enfranchising women would only increase white power. "When we observe closely the trend of legislation as it is directed against

North Carolina suffragists, ca. 1920

Gertrude Weil (far left) led the Equal Suffrage Association's fight for the Nineteenth Amendment in the summer of 1920.

(Courtesy of North Carolina Division of Archives and History)

equal opportunities for the Negroes in this country and realize the influence that [white] women exert without the ballot—what would it be like
with the ballot?" she queried. Advocates of woman suffrage answered by
suggesting that white southern women might eventually develop some
empathy with African Americans because they had shared the experience
of disfranchisement. Many African American leaders hoped that the expansion of women's rights would lead to the restoration of rights taken
away from blacks. "Every argument for Negro suffrage is an argument for
woman's suffrage; every argument for woman's suffrage is an argument
for Negro suffrage; both are great movements in democracy," declared a
1915 editorial in *The Crisis*. Martha Gruening, writing in the same publication three years earlier, had reminded African Americans "that all the
disfranchised of the earth have a common cause."[62]

Charlotte Hawkins Brown of the NCFCWC agreed. In the spring and
summer of 1920 she threw herself into the campaign for the Nineteenth
Amendment; she told James B. Dudley, president of North Carolina Agricultural and Technical College in Greensboro, "I am in the fight up to my
neck." She implored Dudley to join her: "I hope for the sake of the emancipation of the race from this political thralldom, you will espouse Woman
Suffrage, our only hope." Although she failed to convince Dudley, Brown
persisted, speaking to North Carolinians of both races about the importance of the vote to black women. A few days after she wrote her letter to
Dudley, Brown addressed the annual convention of the white federation
of women's clubs, reminding white clubwomen of "the right of the negro
[*sic*] woman to share equally in the franchise which would soon be granted
the womanhood of the state." She continued to advocate woman suffrage
before both African American and white audiences for the next few
months.[63]

Woman suffrage was a popular topic for discussion throughout North
Carolina that summer. Both the ESA and the Southern Women's Rejection League circulated reams of leaflets, pamphlets, and broadsides to
influence public opinion, and both established offices in hotels in downtown Raleigh—antis in the Hotel Raleigh, suffragists in the Yarborough.
Anti headquarters featured a banner that declared, "Politics are bad for
women and women are bad for politics." Suffragists displayed a poster
that read, "Women bring all the voters into the world; therefore, let women
vote." Both groups also began talking to legislators in preparation for the
upcoming vote on the Nineteenth Amendment in August. ESA leaders,
still combating images of feminists as aggressive and unladylike, promised
that they would lobby "in a quiet and dignified way." They also tried to
minimize the influence of the militant Congressional Union, which maintained a small but loyal following in the state.[64]

Equal Suffrage Association Headquarters, 1920
Suffragists established headquarters in the Yarborough Hotel in downtown Raleigh. Antisuffragists had offices in the Hotel Raleigh.
(Courtesy of North Carolina Division of Archives and History)

The General Assembly was scheduled to convene on August 10. As the session neared, antis appeared to be gaining ground. On August 2 the *Greensboro Daily News* reported that the outlook was "pessimistic, from the suffrage viewpoint." Senator Simmons and Governor Bickett had "lost some of their enthusiasm" for ratification, and the state Democratic Party was "in quite a stew over the issue." In addition, the report continued, North Carolina had never been "good suffrage ground" because of its "race problem" and "antipathy to women in politics." The day before the legislature met, antis claimed to have enough votes in the lower house to defeat the amendment.[65]

House members confirmed anti projections even before the Nineteenth Amendment came to the floor. On August 11, 63 of the 120 representatives signed a "round robin" to the Tennessee legislature, which was also meeting in special session, promising the gentlemen of that body that "we will not ratify the Federal Suffrage Amendment" and asking that "this measure be not forced on the people of North Carolina." Antis were jubilant; Mary Hilliard Hinton happily accepted the framed original presented to her by the 63 signers and assured them that she considered it "one of her most cherished possessions." Suffragists were dismayed. Leaders of the national Democratic Party found the revolt in their ranks annoying and ordered Governor Bickett to act. On August 13 he addressed a joint session of the General Assembly. He reminded legislators that he had opposed woman suffrage in the past but urged them to approve the amendment because it could not be stopped: "Gentlemen, in the words of Grover Cleveland, a condition not a theory confronts us. Woman suffrage is at hand. It is an absolute moral certainty that inside of six months some State will open the door and women will enter the political forum. . . . The very most this General Assembly can do is delay for six months a movement it is powerless to defeat." North Carolina, he concluded, must "accept the inevitable and ratify the Amendment." It was hardly a rousing testimonial. The governor failed to corral wayward Democrats and angered Republicans, who believed that he should have reminded members of his party of their obligation to honor the platform the state convention had adopted in April.[66]

Four days after Bickett's speech, on August 17, the Senate took up the amendment "amid scenes which had not been witnessed since the days of the Civil War." Suffragists and antis packed the galleries and attempted to elbow their way onto the Senate floor. Senator Lindsay Carter Warren of Beaufort County recalled the atmosphere in the chamber that morning: "The heat was simply oppressive, and every exit and window was jammed." The session opened at 10:00 a.m.; discussion on the amendment was scheduled for 11:30. A few minutes before the appointed hour, suffragists "unfurled a large yellow suffrage banner and started a small demonstration." The debate began on time and continued for five hours. On occasion, speakers elicited cheers from their own side or hisses from their opponents. Late in the afternoon, Warren introduced a resolution to postpone action on the amendment until the legislature's next regular session in 1921. It passed 25 to 23, an anticlimactic finale to a day of high drama. Although the House would wait until August 19 to consider, and defeat, a ratification resolution, the Senate vote ended the fight. The Nineteenth Amendment was dead in North Carolina.[67]

Across the border in Tennessee, the Senate's action heartened antis. A crowd in the Hermitage Hotel in Nashville, where many of the state legislators were staying during the special session, applauded and cheered when they heard the news from North Carolina. Their joy was short-lived. The Tennessee Senate had already ratified the amendment, and the next day, August 18, the House followed suit. "The thirty-sixth state is won," Carrie Chapman Catt wired Gertrude Weil.[68]

Weil and other North Carolina suffragists were bitterly disappointed that North Carolina refused to ratify, but they wasted no time grieving. Instead, they encouraged women to exercise their newly acquired right. Leaders of women's voluntary associations had begun urging women to prepare themselves for the ballot soon after Congress approved the Nineteenth Amendment. In August 1919 Lucetta Crum Chase and Gertrude Weil, representing the NCFWC's Civics Department, drafted a letter to clubwomen suggesting that they take the course in American citizenship offered by the University of North Carolina's Extension Bureau. As soon as women were enfranchised, the UDC required that all its members be registered to vote.[69]

The enactment of the Nineteenth Amendment took on special significance for African Americans, who realized that whites would not welcome black women to the polls. In May 1920 W. E. B. DuBois advised readers of the *The Crisis* to be prepared for white attempts to keep black women from voting. "Know the law," he wrote. "Obey the law." He encouraged African Americans to abide by the legal restrictions on voting but to resist extralegal and illegal techniques. He implored southern blacks to resolve "to publish the facts to the civilized world; to choke the courts with case upon case, to appeal, agitate and protest, and to let no threat of poverty, riot or murder turn you from a determination to cast your vote according to law." The Nineteenth Amendment offered African Americans a new weapon in the battle against Jim Crow; DuBois wanted to ensure that they used it.[70]

In North Carolina, Charlotte Hawkins Brown discussed the implications of woman suffrage in a speech before the annual NCFCWC convention in July, and the federation and the NAACP cooperated in a voter registration campaign among African American women. State officials announced that women could register on four consecutive Saturdays in October. Working through local clubs and civic leagues, Brown and NAACP leaders persuaded black women to delay their attempts to register until the last two Saturdays. When large groups of African American women arrived at polling places on October 16, they caught registrars by surprise. Election officials recovered quickly, however, and did what they could to prevent black women from qualifying to vote; Glenda Gilmore estimates that fewer than five hundred African American women were allowed to register. As suffragists had predicted, white supremacy survived the onset of woman suffrage.[71]

While many African American women who wanted to vote were barred from the polls, many white women seemed not to want to vote at all. Throughout the 1920s, officers of white women's organizations fought to overcome apathy among North Carolina's newest voters. The League of Women Voters (LWV) spearheaded the campaign with voter registration drives, civics classes, and a variety of pamphlets and leaflets. In a league publication entitled *Studies in Citizenship for North Carolina Women*, Cornelia Jerman reminded her readers that they had a personal stake in politics. "The food we eat, the clothes we wear, what we shall pay for rent, our health, our schools, our recreations, our finances, are all directly influenced by politics," she wrote. "Hence politics cannot be dismissed with an indifferent shrug." Still, many women continued to shrug off their civic responsibilities. The LWV's newsletter advised local chapters that house-to-house visitation was the most effective means of persuading "reluctant voters" to register and vote. Leaders of other voluntary associations also reminded women of the importance of political participation. In 1928 DAR regent Margaret Overman Gregory decreed, "It is now woman's sacred duty . . . to inform herself in politics." That same year, the president of the NCFWC told delegates to the federation's annual convention that "it should be a duty as sacred as our religion that we promote political education and arouse the women to their responsibilities in the use of the ballot." Despite their efforts, apathy continued to be a problem. "The indifference on the part of our women is staggering," Annie O'Berry lamented.[72]

The LWV conducted educational programs to help women understand the mechanics of government and encouraged women to run for office. For years organized women had insisted that they could make unique contributions in the public sector. Now that women were full-fledged citizens, they should put their skills to use in positions related to education and public welfare. "A few women should be on every school board," declared Annie Foushee, who herself was a member of the Durham board. "I know of no better way in which we can serve our community than to be mothers and housekeepers on a larger scale." Martha Boswell, a Democratic Party activist and frequent contributor to the LWV's monthly newsletter, agreed and added that women were also well qualified to serve on county commissions, "where their experience in social service will be of value to the community," and as juvenile court judges. Although few women sought elective office in the 1920s, some served in appointive positions, and others worked behind the scenes in both political parties.[73]

While individual women increased their involvement in party politics in the 1920s, the major white women's organizations in North Carolina—and the Legislative Council they formed—chose to maintain a nonpartisan stance. The council hoped "to present to the people a united opinion of the women of the State" and believed it could do this more effectively if the council itself and its constituent organizations avoided party affiliations. The council and other women's groups lobbied for a variety of laws and programs that had been of concern to organized women for a long time. They also added new items to their agenda, especially in the areas of electoral reform and women's rights.[74]

Since the early twentieth century, reformers had called on the General Assembly to enact the Australian ballot, a system that regulated the printing and distribution of ballots, required that voters be able to mark their ballots in private, and restricted election officials or other individuals from helping voters make their selections. Lawmakers had repeatedly refused, and by 1923 North Carolina was one of only seven states that had not adopted some version of the Australian ballot. Believing that the system would reduce political corruption and intimidation of voters at the polls, the LWV and the council made the Australian ballot their top legislative priority for 1925. The General Assembly considered an Australian ballot bill, then tabled it. Legislators defeated the proposal again in 1927 and finally passed a modified version of the Australian ballot in 1929. The LWV called it an "entering wedge" and vowed to keep working for a stronger law that met all of its criteria.[75]

The LWV also attempted to improve the legal status of women. Throughout the 1920s it lobbied unsuccessfully for reform of inheritance laws that awarded a wife's entire estate to her husband but entitled a widow to only a portion of her husband's property. Despite their efforts to correct some legal inequities, the North Carolina LWV opposed the federal Equal Rights Amendment, in accordance with national league policy. In 1924 the state convention passed a resolution against the amendment because it might nullify protective labor legislation.[76]

The league's stand on the Equal Rights Amendment reflected the attitude its members shared with other white organized women in the 1920s: they continued to be more concerned with promoting the welfare of others, particularly women and children, than with winning absolute equality with men. White women in voluntary associations, secure in their status as southern ladies, understood that they occupied a privileged position in the South's social and economic structure. Although they believed that they were entitled to the same political rights white men enjoyed, they also felt a strong sense of obligation to help people less fortunate than themselves. They had built a feminine role in the public sphere on an ethos of duty and service, and that ethos continued to shape their approach to public policy after suffrage.

For African American women, on the other hand, the Nineteenth Amendment had different implications. Black organized women had always linked progress for themselves with progress for their race, and after suffrage they, along with many male leaders, continued to see connections between civil rights for women and civil rights for African Americans. They hoped that black women would be able to use their ballots to chisel away at white supremacy. Kelly Miller, writing in the *Baltimore Afro-American* in 1930, argued that woman suffrage was "a greater potential political asset to the race" than black male suffrage because there were more women than men of voting age in the African American population.[77]

Miller and others were doomed to disappointment. Southern whites negated the possibilities of woman suffrage for African Americans by applying the mechanisms of disfranchisement to black women. Jim Crow lived on for nearly half a century after women got the right to vote.

Antisuffragists' predictions that woman suffrage would destroy the racial status quo and inaugurate a revolution in gender relations proved to be nothing more than political hyperbole. But focusing on what did *not* happen after enfranchisement obscures the real impact of woman suffrage. Since the 1880s, North Carolina's organized women had struggled to make a place for themselves in public life. They had emphasized their differences from men in order to demarcate a feminine domain in the public sphere. They argued that they possessed moral authority that was beyond the scope of politics. They did not abandon this argument after enfrancisement; instead, they used the ballot to enhance the power of femininity.

The Nineteenth Amendment established women—white women at first, all women eventually—as permanent fixtures on the political landscape. White southern politicians could not circumvent it in the same way they had subverted the Fifteenth Amendment. Although they succeeded in preventing African American women from exercising the right to vote, they could not bar white women—their wives, mothers, sisters, daughters—from the polls. From 1920 onward women would be a factor, if not a force, in southern politics.

Epilogue

The story of the development of women's organizations in North Carolina between 1880 and 1930 coincided with two other significant chapters in the state's history: the triumph of white supremacy in politics and the growing importance of manufacturing in the economy. These changes affected the lives of all North Carolinians. Some benefited; others suffered. Yet the state's politicians and businessmen—architects of white supremacy and champions of industrialization—stifled criticism of racial discrimination and exploitive labor practices. Busily promoting North Carolina as a model of southern Progressivism, they tried to suppress information that would tarnish the state's image.

It required great courage, therefore, for women—who lacked both political and economic clout—to voice even the gentlest reproach or offer the most tentative suggestion for change in racial policies or labor relations. Many women chose to remain silent; perhaps they were afraid to speak or perhaps they saw nothing to criticize. Some organized women, however, did speak out, especially in the 1920s. When they confronted the problems of race relations and industrial reform, they challenged the economic and political titans of their state. Their experiences demonstrated the ambiguities inherent in the power of femininity.

Most white organized women upheld white supremacy and its corollary, black inferiority. Many of them saw themselves as bearers of "the white woman's burden": a special obligation of white Christian women to care for people of color. As Lula Martin McIver explained, "Let us each remember that to the Southerners of this country, especially the white southern woman, was entrusted the task of training the uncivilized African." Like the kindly mistresses of the plantation legend, white women of the New South would nurture and guide blacks; at the same time, they would defend the system that kept African Americans in a subordinate position. In this spirit, one UDC chapter adopted a resolution "denouncing the presentation of the drama 'Uncle Tom's Cabin' in the South," while another "assisted . . . in the care of some aged slaves."[1]

African American women, on the other hand, condemned the Jim Crow system from its inception. They found segregation in public transportation, which forced them to share smoking cars with the "worst elements of both races," to be especially degrading. In 1896, *Star of Zion* columnist Sarah Dudley Pettey praised black women in Atlanta for holding a mass meeting to protest segregation on the city's trolleys and called on others to follow their example. "Would to God," she implored, "that in every town, village, and hamlet where undue and unjust discrimination is brought to bear upon the race, that we could muster volunteer heroines with sufficient womanhood and unswerving volition to publicly vituperate such unrelenting pusillanimous actions." As Pettey and other African American women understood, every time they spoke out against Jim Crow, they placed themselves and their menfolk at great risk. Challenging segregation required women to demonstrate the moral strength—"sufficient womanhood"—that was the root of feminine power.[2]

The intertwined forces of race and gender shaped the lives of southern women and defined the imperatives of southern womanhood. White and African American organized women shared a sense of feminine obligation, and they responded to racial issues based on their interpretations of the feminine ideal. White women used the lady's fabled benevolence to justify racial oppression and ameliorate its consequences. African American women relied on feminine moral authority to fight against it. The ideology of white supremacy that Democrats crafted to destroy political coalitions between white and African American men in the 1890s undercut possibilities for alliances between white and African American women in the early 1900s.

Sometimes white and African American women overcame conflicting views on racial hierarchy to cooperate on specific projects, and a few white women called for more equitable treatment for blacks. In 1913 the Woman's Missionary Council of the Methodist Episcopal Church, South, outlined a plan to improve race relations and the lives of African Americans. The council urged white women to pressure authorities to improve schools and recreational facilities for black children, enforce sanitation ordinances in black neighborhoods, and prevent mistreatment of black prisoners; to work with African American missionary societies and civic clubs; and to foster among whites "high ideals" in race relations. One African American newspaper called it a "Remarkable Document." It was, indeed, a remarkable departure from southern custom, and many auxiliaries ignored it.[3]

Then the United States entered World War I. The war had a dramatic impact on race relations in two ways. First, it created new opportunities for interracial cooperation. Leaders of the North Carolina Woman's Committee of the Council for National Defense insisted that African Americans be included and recruited black women for Liberty Loan campaigns and the Red Cross. Second, it prompted blacks to intensify their demands for justice. African Americans answered the summons to "make the world safe for democracy" in 1917. When the war ended, they vowed to fight to fulfill the promise of democracy at home.

On January 1, 1919, less than two months after the armistice, African Americans held a mass meeting in Raleigh and adopted "strong resolutions." They demanded their fair share of tax revenues for schools, equal protection under the law, and the right to vote. They called for a boycott of segregated accommodations and an end to lynching. Citing the bravery of African American soldiers in Europe and the loyalty of African American women on the home front, they asked God's blessing "upon our combined efforts to lead ourselves out of this dark maze of oppression."[4]

It was a wake-up call for white North Carolinians, and white supremacists responded quickly. On January 3 the *Raleigh News and Observer* published an editorial denouncing the resolutions, which, according to the newspaper, were misguided and unrealistic. The "mass of the Negroes need steady work and good wages which they now have," the editorial declared; "they need the lessons of self-control and personal character building, they need a cordial and friendly understanding with whites, much more than they need parlor cars." The writer scolded African Americans for being ungrateful to their white benefactors and warned them that citizens must understand their obligations as well as their rights.[5]

No doubt the *News and Observer* hoped to have the last word, but discussion of racial tensions continued, especially among organized women. When the NCFWC's Department of Social Service asked local clubs in 1919, "What is the greatest need of your community?" at least one responded, "Cooperation with the negro [sic]." In May 1920 Charlotte Hawkins Brown addressed the federation's annual convention. She focused on three issues: lynching, a reformatory for African American girls, and woman suffrage. She was pleased with the response. "I have some wonderful things to tell you when I come home about the white women of North Carolina, and the way they have opened their doors to hear the message of my people," she wrote a friend shortly after the meeting.[6]

White women throughout the South were listening to the messages African American women delivered. On October 6 and 7, 1920, ninety-one of them met at a YMCA in Memphis, Tennessee, to discuss the race question. Six white North Carolinians attended the historic conference. Four were affiliated with the Woman's Missionary Society of the Methodist church; another represented the YWCA. The sixth was the field secretary of the Episcopal women's auxiliary, Gabrielle deRosset Waddell. Widow of Alfred Moore Waddell, the white supremacist who led the riot that

Charlotte Hawkins Brown
Educator and president of the North Carolina Federation of Colored
Women's Clubs for more than two decades, Charlotte Hawkins Brown
delivered a riveting address at a women's conference on race relations in
Memphis, Tennessee, in October 1920. Following her speech, white
women voted to form a committee on interracial cooperation.
(Courtesy of North Carolina Division of Archives and History)

terrorized Wilmington's black community in 1898, Gabrielle had always shown more interest in the social register than in social justice. She had devoted her public career to glorifying the past and preserving the established order. She had held statewide offices in the Colonial Dames since 1896, and in 1916 she had begun a nineteen-year stint as the society's president. Just a few months before the interracial conference she had joined antisuffragists in their campaign against the Nineteenth Amendment, a campaign that relied heavily on racist arguments. Her presence at the meeting tantalizes historians, who have combed her diary looking for evidence that it was an act of atonement for her husband's sins. But they have searched in vain; she wrote only of what she did and whom she saw in Memphis.[7]

The North Carolinian who played the most significant role in Memphis was Charlotte Hawkins Brown, one of four African American women to address the conference. She described in vivid detail her experience en route to Tennessee: several young white men forcibly evicted her from a Pullman car while white women, some of them traveling to the same meeting, watched in silence. Brown indicted white women for failing to live up to the code of the southern lady. "The Negro woman of the South lays everything that happens to members of her race at the door of the southern white woman," she declared. Brown called on them to use their moral authority to stop the sexual exploitation of black women and the lynching of black men. She invoked the power of femininity to serve the cause of racial justice and touched the hearts of the delegates. They voted to establish a women's committee on interracial cooperation with branches in every southern state. A year later Brown told another white audience that the Memphis meeting was "the greatest step forward that . . . you [white women] have taken since Emancipation."[8]

Fanny Yarborough Bickett chaired North Carolina's interracial committee. Married to Governor Thomas Bickett, she belonged to most of the major white women's voluntary associations in the state: the Colonial Dames, the DAR, the Raleigh Woman's Club, the WCTU, the YWCA, and the LWV. In 1920 she set out to deliver the message of interracial cooperation, with mixed results. The white federation of women's clubs established a Department of Work Among Colored Women, but its chair received "very few" reports of local work. Jessie Daniel Ames, a leader in the interracial movement, recalled, "Many women were indifferent while others were openly antagonistic."[9]

Most white organized women interpreted "interracial cooperation" to mean they should continue the process of "training the uncivilized African." "The negro is here because we brought him here, not of his own volition," NCFWC president Annie O'Berry reminded white clubwomen in 1928. "He needs the direction of our superior intelligence, and he needs our guidance to free himself of the diseases and handicaps that are a menace to our race as they are to his own, because of the close proximity in which we live." Despite their good intentions, white clubwomen continued to think in the language of benevolent paternalism, a language that precluded partnership between themselves and their African American peers.[10]

White clubwomen embraced only one interracial project with enthusiasm: the campaign for a state-supported home for black delinquent girls. The federation of African American women's clubs started the reformatory at Efland; the white federation and the Legislative Council of North Carolina Women joined with them to urge state officials to assume control. White women's willingness to endorse Efland when they hesitated to cooperate with black clubs on other issues reflected deeply rooted attitudes and racist stereotypes. They could understand the need for an institution to rehabilitate deviant African American girls, but most could not, or would not, identify with the clubwomen who established the home—middle-class African Americans who, like themselves, expected recognition as ladies. The power of femininity could not overcome the tyranny of white supremacy.

Still, the southern feminine ideal energized the women "with sufficient womanhood" to enlist in the crusade for racial justice. If, as Charlotte Hawkins Brown asserted, white southern women bore ultimate responsibility for racial violence, then they and they alone possessed the power to bring about racial harmony. Women like Brown, Sarah Dudley Pettey, and Fanny Bickett exhorted white and African American women to use feminine moral authority to strike down Jim Crow. Their commitment to the interracial movement testifies to their faith in feminine strength.

North Carolina's racial dilemma resulted from centuries of slavery, prejudice, and discrimination. The problems that accompanied industrialization were of more recent vintage, but they proved no easier to solve.

Many North Carolinians, including many organized women, welcomed the factories "whose music," as Mary Speed Mercer observed of Winston-Salem's mills in 1917, "makes glad the great heart of the world." To keep the machines humming, mill owners hired thousands of men, women, and children. White rural southerners, drawn to town in search of economic opportunity, comprised the working class of the New South.[11]

White organized women committed themselves to "the general uplift of the working classes." They established libraries and sponsored clean-up and beautification campaigns in mill villages. They operated night schools, held mothers' meetings, and encouraged mill workers to form their own civic and literary clubs. They opened day nurseries and kindergartens. Years later, some reformers acknowledged the limited value of many of their early attempts at "uplift." In 1964 Gertrude Weil recalled a sewing class she had conducted for factory women: "Looking back on it, I can see that it was a rather superficial thing to do. An uncle of mine told me it would be much more to the point 'if you would go to the board of directors of the mill and tell them to pay those people a decent wage'—but I didn't have the courage."[12]

Weil was not alone. Most of North Carolina's white organized women lacked the courage to face down the men who ran the factories—especially since, in many cases, they would have been confronting their own husbands, fathers, and brothers. Women with the money and leisure to devote to voluntary associations were apt to have some personal connection to North Carolina's business community. They were reluctant to challenge a system that their families perpetuated and that provided them with their livelihood. As Sallie Cotten explained to the North Carolina Conference for Social Service in 1914, clubwomen shied away from industrial reform because "the commercial spirit deters them."[13]

Organized women expressed concern for the plight of women and children in factories, but "the commercial spirit," along with a well-financed and well-organized industrial lobby, forced them to curtail their efforts. Unlike women's associations in other states, which spearheaded campaigns to eliminate child labor and improve working conditions for women, North Carolina women avoided labor issues. When delegates to the NCFWC's fifth convention created a Department of Industrial and Child Labor, they instructed the chair to devote her energies to raising money for a cottage at the reformatory for delinquent white boys. For several years the federation ignored the nondelinquent boys and girls who made up 24% of the labor force in North Carolina textile mills.[14]

When organized women endorsed child labor legislation, they focused on regulation rather than seeking an outright ban. For more than a decade they lobbied unsuccessfully for a law mandating an eight-hour workday for children under sixteen. The General Assembly finally passed the bill in 1927; however, lawmakers amended it so that it applied only to children between fourteen and sixteen who had not completed the fourth grade—a change that, according to the NCFWC's legislative chair, made it "doubtful if any real benefit will accrue to children in industry." For the next several years the Legislative Council of North Carolina Women lobbied to no avail for repeal of "the fourth-grade clause."[15]

With the combined forces of wealth and political power arrayed against them, it is remarkable that organized women accomplished anything at all. Businessmen and politicians forged a formidable alliance. When lawmakers debated proposals to ban or limit child labor, mill owners obligingly provided them with petitions from parents arguing for their children's right to work. For example, when Congress considered a child labor bill in

December 1915 and January 1916, factory owners and managers sent Congressman Edwin Yates Webb several petitions from mill hands who purportedly opposed the measure. One came from J. M. Archer of the Stanley Manufacturing Company. Archer assured Webb that the "boss spinner" circulated the petition "at his own instigation" and that millhands signed voluntarily. Two days later Webb returned the petition. Three of the signers had asked him to support the bill, the Congressman explained; he instructed Archer to "correct" the petition so that he could use it in debate. A staunch ally of factory owners, Webb considered child labor legislation to be a ploy of northern textile interests "who, under the guise of morality and philanthropy, are really aiming to cripple our Southern manufacturers." Clearly, he would not be moved by moral suasion or women's indirect influence.[16]

Webb and men like him opposed woman suffrage because they feared women would use the ballot to enact industrial reform. Many organized women hoped that the vote would increase their influence, and they pursued their agenda more aggressively after the ratification of the Nineteenth Amendment in 1920. By mid-decade they were embroiled in a major conflict with mill owners and politicians, including the governor. It was a novel experience for North Carolina's white female reformers, who as a rule gingerly sidestepped direct confrontation.

The controversy began innocently enough. In 1923 the NCFWC proposed a survey of working conditions of women in North Carolina factories. The Woman's Bureau of the United States Department of Labor, which had undertaken similar studies in other southern states, would conduct the investigation. The YWCA and the LWV also endorsed the proposal.[17]

The state Child Welfare Commission oversaw labor regulations, so in the fall of 1923 a delegation from the federation and the league called on E. F. Carter, the commission's executive secretary. Carter was very gracious. He assured the women that North Carolina factories were inspected regularly and promised to send them reports on working conditions. He then proceeded to dawdle. Organized women waited, but when a year passed and Carter still had not acted, their patience wore thin. They appealed to the Child Welfare Commission, and in January 1926 the commission held a hearing on the matter. Representatives from the NCFWC, the YWCA, and the LWV complained about Carter's lack of cooperation, charged him with lax enforcement of labor laws, and renewed their request for a survey by the Woman's Bureau. Members of the commission concluded that they did not have the authority to invite federal inspectors into the state. They referred the women to the governor.[18]

Organized women knew that the governor, Angus W. McLean, a mill owner himself, was unlikely to be sympathetic in the best of circumstances, and in January and February circumstances went from bad to worse. Carter, angered by the women's criticism, alerted the newspapers that women's associations were seeking federal intervention in the state's factories. It was an inflammatory charge; North Carolinians were firmly committed to states' rights and deeply suspicious of the national government. Women had already alienated manufacturers by asking for the survey; when reporters portrayed it as a states' rights issue, public opinion turned against them as well.[19]

By the spring of 1926 the LWV had taken the lead in the fight for the survey, and league president May Belle McMahon was struggling to fend off the mill owners' relentless campaign to prevent it. An ad hoc committee of Charlotte businessmen summoned her to meet with them; they pressured her to persuade organized women to drop their request. McMahon assured the committee that "no sinister motives or out-of-state influences" were at work; women wanted only to obtain information that could then be used as a basis for regulatory legislation. "Why do employers desire to withhold this information if conditions are good?" she asked. "Is there any objection to the public knowing it?" Although McMahon maintained her composure in public, privately she confessed to Mary Cowper, the LWV's executive secretary, that "I have surely been up a tree to know what to do." Since women had been unable to mollify the mill owners with logic, perhaps they should resort to other methods. "I believe if all the publicity stops that we can smooth these old cudgers with smiles, etc.," she confided, then added, "We can try anyway."[20]

But feminine charm and gentle persuasion proved to be no more effective than reason. To no one's surprise, Governor McLean refused to order the federal study. Instead, he offered a counterproposal: a survey conducted by independent investigators under the supervision of the state Commission on Child Welfare. The women accepted McLean's alternative plan, only to withdraw their support when they learned that E. F. Carter would supervise the "independent" investigation. The governor in turn cancelled the survey, and women's efforts to revive it failed.[21]

In their campaign to prevent the survey, manufacturers applied economic as well as political pressure. Companies and individuals that had formerly donated money to the charities organized women sponsored refused to make further contributions. In Charlotte, businessmen bullied the local YWCA into abandoning industrial reform and backing away from its legislative agenda. "These men are our largest contributors," McMahon told Cowper, "and we have to do what they say." The mill owners did not stop there. Many women's leaders were married to men who worked for or did business with the mills, and high-level executives ordered husbands to restrict their wives' reform activities. Thus some women found themselves involved in disputes at home as well as in public.[22]

May Belle McMahon faced just such a situation. Her husband, Phil, sold factory equipment and worried that his wife's volunteer work would harm his business. He warned her that if the League of Women Voters persisted in its demands, she would have to resign her office. "Our bread and butter comes entirely from the Mills," May Belle McMahon explained to Mary Cowper, "and there are many families in our Company so affected so it's a serious thing for them. It would be better to have a President anyway who is not connected with N. C. Industries, for it is brought back home to them in so many ways." A few months later McMahon did resign, and she promised her husband to "just be a silent member in the ranks."[23]

May Belle McMahon's experience illustrates the dilemmas women faced when they attempted to exercise the power of femininity in the public sphere. Most of North Carolina's organized women had to answer to husbands whom they loved and whose incomes gave them the leisure to participate in voluntary associations. McMahon's work with the LWV jeopardized not only her own family, but also the families of her husband's employees. The imperatives of selflessness and concern for the welfare of others that were so deeply embedded in the southern feminine ideal—the very same imperatives that prompted organized women to call for the survey of working conditions of women in industry—compelled May Belle McMahon to retreat. She could not put so many other people at risk, even for the sake of a good cause.

McMahon's story also underscores the limits of the power of femininity. Motivated by the lady's sense of compassion and obligation and believing in the force of feminine moral authority, North Carolina's white and African American clubwomen tackled the most difficult problems in their state, race relations and labor reform. But men still controlled government, politics, and the economy, and they were willing to use all of the resources at their command to thwart women whose goals conflicted with their own.

Despite the setbacks they met and the defeats they suffered, organized women left an extensive legacy. They made their mark on public policy and, for good or ill, they touched the lives of thousands of North Carolinians: the mill hand who visited the public library after work, the troubled youth who served time in a juvenile reformatory instead of an adult prison, the schoolchild who learned about Confederate heroes and Yankee villains in history class. Long before they could vote or hold office, these "citizen-women" established a feminine presence in town councils, county commissions, and the state legislature. They created a public role for themselves, and they developed a model of ladylike behavior in politics that would endure for years to come.

Abbreviations

Libraries, Archives, and Special Collections

Duke Special Collections Library, Duke University, Durham, North Carolina

NCC North Carolina Collection, Louis Round Wilson Library, University of North Carolina at Chapel Hill

NCDAH North Carolina Division of Archives and History, Raleigh, North Carolina

SHC Southern Historical Collection, Louis Round Wilson Library, University of North Carolina at Chapel Hill

SL Schlesinger Library, Radcliffe College, Cambridge, Massachusetts

TSLA Tennessee State Library and Archives, Nashville, Tennessee

Organizations

AAUW American Association of University Women

AMEZ African Methodist Episcopal Zion Church

DAR Daughters of the American Revolution

DR Daughters of the Revolution

LWV League of Women Voters

NCFCWC North Carolina Federation of Colored Women's Clubs

NCFWC North Carolina Federation of Women's Clubs

RWC Raleigh Woman's Club

UDC United Daughters of the Confederacy

WCTU Woman's Christian Temperance Union

Notes

Introduction

1. The classic work on the ideal of the southern lady is Anne Firor Scott's pioneering study *The Southern Lady: From Pedestal to Politics, 1830–1930* (Chicago: University of Chicago Press, 1970). See also Barbara Welter, "The Cult of True Womanhood: 1820–1860," *American Quarterly* 18 (1966): 151–74.

2. Joel Williamson, *The Crucible of Race: Black-White Relations in the American South Since Emancipation* (New York: Oxford University Press, 1984).

3. Donald G. Mathews and Jane Sherron De Hart, *Sex, Gender, and the Politics of ERA* (New York: Oxford University Press, 1990), 3–27.

4. Evelyn Brooks Higginbotham, *Righteous Discontent: The Women's Movement in the Black Baptist Church, 1880–1920* (Cambridge, Mass.: Harvard University Press, 1993), 185–230. See also Lynda F. Dickson, "Toward a Broader Angle of Vision in Uncovering Women's History: Black Women's Clubs Revisited," in *Black Women's History: Theory and Practice,* ed. Darlene Clark Hine (Brooklyn: Carlson, 1990), vol. 1, 103–20.

5. William L. O'Neill coined the term "social feminist" in his book *Everyone Was Brave: A History of Feminism in America* (Chicago: Quadrangle, 1971). For discussions of maternalism and maternalist politics see Molly Ladd-Taylor, *Mother-Work: Women, Child Welfare and the State, 1890–1930* (Urbana: University of Illinois Press, 1994); and Theda Skocpol, *Protecting Soldiers and Mothers: The Political Origins of Social Policy in the United States* (Cambridge, Mass.: Harvard University Press, Belknap Press, 1992). See Nancy F. Cott, *The Grounding of Modern Feminism* (New Haven: Yale University Press, 1987), for definitions of feminism and Marjorie Spruill Wheeler, *New Women of the New South: The Leaders of the Woman Suffrage Movement in the Southern States* (New York: Oxford University Press, 1993), for a description of the southern version of maternalism.

Chapter 1—"The Foundation for a Sisterhood": Origins of Women's Activism

1. The best description of the antebellum southern feminine ideal is Anne Firor Scott, *The Southern Lady: From Pedestal to Politics, 1830–1930* (Chicago: University of Chicago Press, 1970), 4–21. See also William R. Taylor, *Cavalier and Yankee: The Old South and American National Character* (New York: Harper

and Row, Harper Torchbooks, 1969), 162–76. On the contrast between masculine and feminine roles in the Old South see Bertram Wyatt-Brown, *Southern Honor: Ethics and Behavior in the Old South* (Oxford: Oxford University Press, 1982), 226–53; and Elizabeth Fox-Genovese, *Within the Plantation Household: Black and White Women of the Old South* (Chapel Hill: University of North Carolina Press, 1988), 192–207.

2. Thomas Dew, "Dissertation on the Characteristic Differences Between the Sexes," *Southern Literary Messenger* 1 (May 1835): 493–512, quotation on 496; Scott, *Southern Lady,* 23; Fox-Genovese, *Plantation Household,* 197–98.

3. Fox-Genovese, *Plantation Household,* 197–203.

4. Guion Griffis Johnson, *Ante-Bellum North Carolina: A Social History* (Chapel Hill: University of North Carolina Press, 1937), 247–48. See also George C. Rable, *Civil Wars: Women and the Crisis of Southern Nationalism* (Urbana: University of Illinois Press, 1989), 25–29; and Suzanne Lebsock, *The Free Women of Petersburg: Status and Culture in a Southern Town, 1784–1860* (New York: W. W. Norton, 1984), 146–94.

5. Hamilton Couper to Margaret Couper, August 26, 1856, quoted in Johnson, *Ante-Bellum North Carolina,* 199. See also Johnson, 192–93; and Jane Turner Censer, *North Carolina Planters and Their Children 1800–1860* (Baton Rouge: Louisiana State University Press, 1984), 65–72.

6. Johnson, *Ante-Bellum North Carolina,* 200; Albert Coates, *By Her Own Bootstraps: A Saga of Women in North Carolina* (Chapel Hill: Privately published, 1975), 10–12; Lebsock, *Free Women,* 15–35, 54–86.

7. United States Census Office, *Seventh Census of the United States, 1850. North Carolina* (Washington, 1853), 308, 317. On the education of elite white women see Censer, *North Carolina Planters,* 42–58; and Christie Farnham Pope, "Preparation for Pedestals: North Carolina Antebellum Female Seminaries" (Ph.D. diss., University of Chicago, 1977). In North Carolina, as in the rest of the slaveholding South, only a few women could claim the privileges of the southern lady. The gentry—the wealthiest merchants, manufacturers, doctors, lawyers, and planters—made up only a fraction of the state's population. In 1860 only about 2 percent of free families in North Carolina qualified as "large planters" (owning twenty or more slaves). Most slaveholders, about 72 percent, owned fewer than ten slaves, and two-thirds of the state's free families owned no slaves at all. Wealthy merchants, manufacturers, and professionals were also counted among the gentry, but they represented a small minority. As in other southern states, however, the wealthy few dominated the state's social, economic, and political life. On the social structure of antebellum North Carolina see Johnson, *Ante-Bellum North Carolina,* 55–59; and Paul D. Escott, *Many Excellent People: Power and Privilege in North Carolina, 1850–1900* (Chapel Hill: University of North Carolina Press, 1985), 4–15. On the place of elite white southern women see Rable, *Civil Wars,* 32–49; and Fox-Genovese, *Plantation Household.*

8. Johnson, *Ante-Bellum North Carolina,* 228–29; Rable, *Civil Wars,* 12–15; Jean E. Friedman, *The Enclosed Garden: Women and Community in the Evangelical South, 1830–1900* (Chapel Hill: University of North Carolina Press, 1985), 11–18; Scott, *Southern Lady,* 9–14.

9. Donald G. Mathews, *Religion in the Old South* (Chicago: University of Chicago Press, 1977), 109–10; Ann Douglas, *The Feminization of American Culture* (New York: Alfred A. Knopf, 1977); Rable, *Civil Wars,* 12–15; James L. Leloudis II, "Subversion of the Feminine Ideal: The *Southern Lady's Companion* and White Male Morality in the Antebellum South," in *Women in New Worlds: Historical Perspectives on the Wesleyan Tradition,* vol. 2, ed. Rosemary Skinner Keller, Louise L. Queen, and Hilah F. Thomas (Nashville: Abingdon, 1982), 60–75.

10. Johnson, *Ante-Bellum North Carolina,* 424. See also Johnson, 163, 419–26, 702–3; and Emily Clare Newby Correll, "Woman's Work for Woman: The Methodist and Baptist Women's Missionary Societies in North Carolina, 1878–1930" (M.A. thesis, University of North Carolina at Chapel Hill, 1977), 45. On similar work of other white southern women see Lebsock, *Free Women,* 195–236, 240–43. Although I found no evidence of religious or charitable societies among free black women in antebellum North Carolina, it is quite possible that such societies existed.

11. Quotation is from Johnson, *Ante-Bellum North Carolina,* 425. See also Johnson, 163, 423. Similar organizations existed in other southern towns. For examples see Lebsock, *Free Women,* 196–212; and Barbara L. Bellows, "'My Children, Gentlemen, Are My Own': Poor Women, the Urban Elite, and the Bonds of Obligation in Antebellum Charleston," in *The Web of Southern Social Relations: Women, Family, and Education,* ed. Walter J. Fraser Jr., R. Frank Saunders Jr., and Jon L. Wakelyn (Athens: University of Georgia Press, 1985), 52–71; and Anne Firor Scott, *Natural Allies: Women's Voluntary Associations in America* (Urbana: University of Illinois Press, 1991), chapter 2. As with the church groups, the organizations cited were for white women only. It is possible that free black women formed similar groups.

12. H. M. Wagstaff, ed., *Minutes of the North Carolina Manumission Society, 1816–1834.* James Sprunt Historical Studies, vol. 22 (Chapel Hill: University of North Carolina Press, 1934), 120. See also Wagstaff, 99–187 passim; and John Michael Shay, "The Antislavery Movement in North Carolina" (Ph.D. diss., Princeton University, 1970), 400–403. Despite many references to women in the *Minutes,* information on their activities is scarce. The women's associations appeared for the first time in 1825 and for the last in 1830. Larry E. Tise estimates that there may have been as many as forty female auxiliaries; see Tise, "Confronting the Issue of Slavery," in *The North Carolina Experience: An Interpretive and Documentary History,* ed. Lindley S. Butler and Alan D. Watson (Chapel Hill: University of North Carolina Press, 1984), 198.

13. "How Can Females Assist in Advancing the Temperance Reform?," *North Carolina Temperance Union,* April 9, 1842; *Spirit of the Age,* January 9, 1852; *Constitution, By Laws, and Rules of Order, of Farmington Union, No. 22, Daughters of Temperance of the State of North Carolina* (Raleigh: A. M. Gorman—Spirit of the Age Office, 1852). The national Daughters of Temperance organized in the early 1840s and claimed thirty thousand members by 1848; see Jack S. Blocker Jr., *American Temperance Movements: Cycles of Reform* (Boston: Twayne, 1989), 49–50.

14. Johnson, *Ante-Bellum North Carolina*, 249–50.

15. Elswyth Thane, *Mount Vernon Is Ours: The Story of Its Preservation* (New York: Duell, Sloan and Pearce, 1966). See also Wallace Evan Davies, *Patriotism on Parade: The Story of Veterans' and Hereditary Organizations in America, 1783–1900* (Cambridge, Mass.: Harvard University Press, 1955), 24–27; and Davies, "Ann Pamela Cunningham," in *Notable American Women, 1607–1950: A Biographical Dictionary*, ed. Edward T. James, Janet Wilson James, and Paul S. Boyer (Cambridge, Mass.: Harvard University Press, Belknap Press, 1971), vol. 1, 416–17. The leaders of the Mount Vernon Ladies Association, with the assistance of male advisers, raised and controlled thousands of dollars, a rather unusual situation for an antebellum women's association. Although, as Suzanne Lebsock notes, women in church and charitable organizations frequently raised money, in varying amounts, for their projects, they did not always control the funds they collected. Lebsock found that the larger the sum, the more likely it was to fall under male control. See Lebsock, *Free Women*, 200–201, 223–25.

16. *Mount Vernon Record* 2 (July 1859): 3. The idea that women, especially mothers, were repositories of republican virtue had its roots in the late eighteenth century. See Linda Kerber, *Women of the Republic: Intellect and Ideology in Revolutionary America* (Chapel Hill: University of North Carolina Press, 1980), chapter 9.

17. Davies, *Patriotism on Parade*, 24–27; Davies, "Ann Pamela Cunningham," 417.

18. Quotations are from Davies, *Patriotism on Parade*, 26; and *Mount Vernon Record* 2 (February 1860): 158.

19. Quoted in Johnson, *Ante-Bellum North Carolina*, 249–50. See also Dorothy Ann Gay, "The Tangled Skein of Romanticism and Violence in the Old South: The Southern Response to Abolitionism and Feminism, 1830–1861" (Ph.D. diss., University of North Carolina at Chapel Hill, 1975).

20. Escott, *Many Excellent People*, 32–36, 52–53.

21. Escott, *Many Excellent People*, 37–54; Rable, *Civil Wars*, 113–19; Lucy London Anderson, *North Carolina Women of the Confederacy* (Fayetteville: Privately published, 1926), 14; Drew Gilpin Faust, "Altars of Sacrifice: Confederate Women and the Narratives of War," *Journal of American History* 76 (March 1990): 1213–14.

22. Veritas Saunders, "The History and Accomplishments of the North Carolina Division of the United Daughters of the Confederacy," typescript, 1922, NCC, 2; Anderson, *North Carolina Women*, 14; Escott, *Many Excellent People*, 42.

23. Escott, *Many Excellent People*, 65–67; Rable, *Civil Wars*, 110; Faust, "Altars of Sacrifice," 1225–27; Victoria E. Bynum, *Unruly Women: The Politics of Social and Sexual Control in the Old South* (Chapel Hill: University of North Carolina Press, 1992), 125–29.

24. Faust, "Altars of Sacrifice," 1220–28; Rable, *Civil Wars*, 73–111; Scott, *Southern Lady*, 87–92; Peter Wallenstein, "Rich Man's War, Rich Man's Fight: Civil War and the Transformation of Public Finance in Georgia," *Journal of Southern History* 50 (February 1984): 15–42.

25. C. Vann Woodward, *Origins of the New South, 1877–1913* (Baton Rouge: Louisiana State University Press and the Littlefield Fund for Southern History of the University of Texas, 1951), 167–68; John Carl Ruoff, "Southern Womanhood, 1865–1920: An Intellectual and Cultural Study" (Ph.D. diss., University of Illinois at Urbana-Champaign, 1976). Historians continue to debate the effect of the war on women's status in the South. Some believe the war sounded the death knell of the patriarchy and liberated white women from old constraints. Others argue that defeat reinforced old patterns. For examples that range across the entire spectrum of the debate see Gaines M. Foster, *Ghosts of the Confederacy: Defeat, The Lost Cause, and the Emergence of the New South* (New York: Oxford University Press, 1987), 31–33; Rable, *Civil Wars*, 238–39, 285–88; Lebsock, *Free Women*, 246–49; and Scott, *Southern Lady*, 96–102.

26. *Raleigh Daily Call*, May 10, 1889; [Charlotte Bryan Grimes Williams], *History of the Wake County Ladies Memorial Association, Confederate Monuments in Capitol Square, Memorial Pavilion, the House of Memory, and the Confederate Cemetery* (Raleigh, 1938), 7. See also Confederate Southern Memorial Association, *History of the Confederated Memorial Associations of the South* (New Orleans: Graham, 1904), 227–35; P. F. Pescud Sr., *A Sketch of the Ladies Memorial Association of Raleigh, N. C. Its Origin and History* (n.p., 1882), pamphlet, Ladies Memorial Association folder, Moffitt Papers, SHC; and N. T. Primrose to Elvira E. Moffitt, May 13, 1903, Moffitt Papers, SHC. Pescud cited October 2, 1866, as the date of the association's founding, while the other sources claimed May 23. Two years after the establishment of the Confederate cemetery, in 1869, Henry Mordecai's uncle George Mordecai donated land for the establishment of Oakwood Cemetery. The Confederate cemetery was within Oakwood's boundaries but remained separate, owned and administered by the Ladies Memorial Association. In 1918 the Ladies Memorial Association merged with the local chapter of the UDC and deeded the cemetery to the Daughters. See [Williams], *Wake County Ladies Memorial Association*, 11; and Elizabeth E. Norris, *Historic Oakwood Cemetery* (Raleigh: Edwards and Broughton, 1990).

27. [Williams], *Wake County Ladies Memorial Association*, 7; "Report of Committee Appointed June 2, 1894," 5–7, quotations on 6–7; E. H. Parsley to Mrs. [L. H.] Raines, October 29, 1894 (both in Parsley Papers, SHC.)

28. On the Raleigh association see [Williams], *Wake County Ladies Memorial Association*, 8; *Raleigh Daily Call*, May 10, 1889; Anderson, *North Carolina Women*, 118; and F. A. Olds, "Raleigh's Two Cemeteries," *Raleigh News and Observer*, June 23, 1902. For Warren County women's monument to Anne Lee see Anderson, *North Carolina Women*, 116. On the activities of women in Fayetteville see *Fayetteville Observer*, October 12, 1926, newspaper clipping, Smith Papers, NCDAH. For the work of Wilmington women see "Report of Committee Appointed June 2, 1894," 9–10, Parsley Papers, SHC; and John H. Marshall, John H. Meyer, R. Capps, W. Griffith, B. W. Curtis, F. C. Pettyway, "and Twelve others" to the chairman of Music Committee of the Lee Memorial Association, December 25, 1875, Meares-DeRosset Papers, SHC.

29. "The Great Event," *Raleigh Daily Press*, May 22, 1894; "Unveiled" and "History of Monument," *Raleigh Daily Press*, May 20, 1895; *Raleigh News and Observer*, Woman's Issue, Souvenir Edition, May 20, 1895.

30. Correll, "Woman's Work for Woman," 46–49; Scott, *Southern Lady,* 139–40.

31. Marion Francis Alston Bourne, "Seventy-Five Years of Service," in Diocese of North Carolina, Woman's Auxiliary to the National Council of the Protestant Episcopal Church, *Seventy-Fifth Annual Report and Handbook of Information* (n.p., 1957), 15–19; *A Brief History of the Synodical of North Carolina with Minutes of the First Annual Meeting and the Minutes and Reports of the Second Annual Meeting* (Charlotte: Presbyterian Standard, 1914), 3–14. A national church reorganization in 1920 broadened the scope of the Episcopal Auxiliary's activities and enabled women to elect their own officers.

32. Correll, "Woman's Work for Woman," 3–4.

33. Noreen Dunn Tatum, *A Crown of Service: A Story of Woman's Work in the Methodist Episcopal Church, South, from 1878–1940* (Nashville: Parthenon, 1960), 79–216.

34. Correll, "Woman's Work for Woman," 3.

35. The home mission work of white southern Methodist women has been particularly well documented. See Tatum, *A Crown of Service;* Virginia Shadron, "'Out of Our Homes': The Woman's Rights Movement in the Methodist Episcopal Church, South, 1890–1918" (M.A. thesis, Emory University, 1976); Mary E. Frederickson, "Shaping a New Society: Methodist Women and Industrial Reform in the South," in *Women in New Worlds: Historical Perspectives on the Wesleyan Tradition,* vol. 1, ed. Hilah F. Thomas and Rosemary Skinner Keller, 345–61 (Nashville: Abingdon, 1981); and Anastatia Sims, "Sisterhoods of Service: Women's Clubs and Methodist Women's Missionary Societies in North Carolina, 1890–1930," in *Women in New Worlds,* vol. 2, ed. Rosemary Skinner Keller, Louise L. Queen, and Hilah F. Thomas (Nashville: Abingdon, 1982), 196–210.

36. William J. Walls, *The African Methodist Episcopal Zion Church: Reality of the Black Church* (Charlotte: AME Zion, 1974), 388–90.

37. Rev. J. Harvey Anderson, "Searchlight Scenes. Women and Girls," *Star of Zion,* June 15, 1899; "Missionary Society," *Star of Zion,* June 7, 1900.

38. Katie Hood was the wife of Bishop James W. Hood. Meriah Gion Harris, a graduate of Atlanta University, was married to Bishop Cicero R. Harris, founder of Livingstone College. Victoria Richardson was Bishop Harris's niece and a member of the Livingstone faculty. Marie Clay Clinton was the third wife of Bishop George Wylie Clinton. See Walls, *AMEZ Church,* 404–16.

39. J. A. Whitted, *A History of the Negro Baptists of North Carolina* (Raleigh: Edwards and Broughton, 1908), 112–13, 117–18, quotation on 113.

40. Whitted, *History of Negro Baptists,* 114–19, quotation on 116–17; *Colored Orphan Asylum of North Carolina, Oxford, North Carolina* (Oxford: Public Ledger Print, 1900), pamphlet, NCC.

41. Linda D. Addo and James H. McCallum, *To Be Faithful to Our Heritage: A History of Black United Methodism in North Carolina* (Lake Junaluska: Commission on Archives and History of the North Carolina Conference and Western North Carolina Conference, United Methodist Church, 1980), 60–61.

42. Ruth Bordin, "'A Baptism of Fire and Liberty': The Women's Crusade of 1873–1874," in *Woman's Being, Woman's Place: Female Identity and Vocation in American History,* ed. Mary Kelley (Boston: G. K. Hall, 1977), 283–96. For a gen-

eral discussion of the WCTU and its activities see Ruth Bordin, *Woman and Temperance: The Quest for Power and Liberty, 1873–1900* (Philadelphia: Temple University Press, 1981).

43. Bordin, *Woman and Temperance*, 22–26, 37–38; Blocker, *American Temperance Movements*, 76.

44. Bordin, *Woman and Temperance*, 95–116; Blocker, *American Temperance Movements*, 81–85; Scott, *Natural Allies*, chapter 5.

45. Friedman, *Enclosed Garden*, 118–19; Scott, *Southern Lady*, 144–45.

46. Daniel Jay Whitener, *Prohibition in North Carolina, 1715–1945* (Chapel Hill: University of North Carolina Press, 1945), 61–74, quotation on 67.

47. "Office of State Prohibitory Campaign Com.," *Salisbury Carolina Watchman*, May 26, 1881. See also "Prohibition Convention," *Pittsboro Chatham Record*, May 5, 1881.

48. Quotation is from "Colored Prohibition," *Charlotte Observer*, July 15, 1881; "Woman's Temperance Union," *Pittsboro Chatham Record*, May 5, 1881; "Miscellaneous," *Salisbury Carolina Watchman*, May 26, 1881; "The Ladies Buckling on Armor," *Charlotte Observer*, May 24, 1881; "Prohibition—The Ladies Take Hold," *Tarboro Southerner*, May 26, 1881; *Report of the Twenty-First Annual Session of the Woman's Christian Temperance Union of North Carolina* (Concord: Times Steam Book and Job Printers, 1903) (hereafter cited as WCTU *Minutes* with appropriate year); Whitener, *Prohibition in North Carolina*, 104.

49. Whitener, *Prohibition in North Carolina*, 73; WCTU *Minutes* 1883, 6–8; 1884, 12, 24; 1887, 28. Mississippi was the only other state that lacked a state union in 1873.

50. Travis L. Mathis, "Mary Mendenhall Hobbs," in *Dictionary of North Carolina Biography*, ed. William S. Powell (Chapel Hill: University of North Carolina Press, 1980–1996), vol. 2, 151–52. Seth B. Hinshaw, *The Carolina Quaker Experience* (n.p.: North Carolina Yearly Meeting, North Carolina Friends Historical Society, 1984), 148, 215; Hiram H. Hilty, *New Garden Friends Meeting: The Christian People Called Quakers* (Greensboro: North Carolina Friends Historical Society, North Carolina Yearly Meeting, New Garden Meeting, 1983), 39, 47, 65–66; WCTU *Minutes*, 1885–1911.

51. Olivia Blount Grimes, "Laura Annie Winston," in *Biographical History of North Carolina*, vol. 8, 499–503, quotation on 501; C. Sylvester Green, "Laura Annie Winston," *Dictionary of North Carolina Biography*, vol. 6, 248–49; Otis A. Betts, *The North Carolina School for the Deaf at Morganton, 1894–1944* (Morganton: North Carolina School for the Deaf, 1945), 88–91; WCTU *Minutes*, 1883–1922.

52. Seth B. Hinshaw and Mary Hinshaw, eds., *Carolina Quakers* (Greensboro: North Carolina Yearly Meeting, 1972), 155; Seth Hinshaw, *Carolina Quaker Experience*, 100, 196, 209, 231; Hilty, *New Garden Friends Meeting*, 61–62; Mary Edith Woody Hinshaw, "John Warren Woody," *Dictionary of Carolina Biography*, vol. 6, 266; Hinshaw, "Mary Woody," *Dictionary of North Carolina Biography*, vol. 6, 266–67; WCTU *Minutes* 1885–1917.

53. WCTU *Minutes* 1885, 29; 1886, 63.

54. WCTU *Minutes* 1887, 5, 50–51; 1888, 5, 40–41.

55. Miss E. F. Hooper, "What Our Women Are Doing," *Star of Zion,* August 7, 1890. See also WCTU *Minutes* 1889, 81–82.

56. Quotations are from *Union Signal,* November 27, 1890; WCTU *Minutes* 1890, 18; *Union Signal,* December 10, 1891, 10. For more on the origins of North Carolina's WCTU Number 2 see Glenda Elizabeth Gilmore, "'A Melting Time': Black Women, White Women, and the WCTU in North Carolina, 1880–1900," in *Hidden Histories of Women in the New South,* ed. Virginia Bernhard, Betty Brandon, Elizabeth Fox-Genovese, Theda Perdue, and Elizabeth Hayes Turner (Columbia: University of Missouri Press, 1994), 153–72; and Gilmore, "Gender and Jim Crow: Black Women and the Politics of White Supremacy in North Carolina, 1896–1920" (Ph.D. diss., University of North Carolina, 1992), 103–112.

57. Quotation is from WCTU *Minutes* 1890, 40. On industrialization in North Carolina see Robert F. Durden, "North Carolina in the New South," in Butler and Watson, *North Carolina Experience,* 309–19; Escott, *Many Excellent People,* 136–70; and Dwight B. Billings Jr., *Planters and the Making of a "New South": Class, Politics and Development in North Carolina, 1865–1900* (Chapel Hill: University of North Carolina Press, 1979). On the development of a New South see Woodward, *Origins of the New South;* and David L. Carlton, *Mill and Town in South Carolina, 1880–1920* (Baton Rouge: Louisiana State University Press, 1982).

58. Durden, "North Carolina," 311–14; Samuel Huntington Hobbs Jr., *North Carolina: Economic and Social* (Chapel Hill: University of North Carolina Press, 1930), 132–45; Department of Commerce and Labor, Bureau of the Census, *Manufactures 1905* (Washington: 1907), ccxi; Hugh Talmage Lefler and Albert Ray Newsome, *North Carolina: The History of a Southern State* (Chapel Hill: University of North Carolina Press, 1973), 503–19; Billings, *Planters,* 42, 113–20; Escott, *Many Excellent People,* 196–98.

59. Quotation is from *Thirteenth Annual Convention of the King's Daughters and Sons of the North Carolina Branch, Raleigh, May 13–15, 1902* (n.p., n.d.), 32; Escott, *Many Excellent People,* 174–79; Billings, *Planters,* 72–73; Jacquelyn Dowd Hall et al., *Like a Family: The Making of a Southern Cotton Mill World* (Chapel Hill: University of North Carolina Press, 1987), 3–43.

60. Hall et al., *Like a Family,* 8–9; Escott, *Many Excellent People,* 241–49; Jeffrey J. Crow, "Cracking the Solid South: Populism and the Fusionist Interlude," in Butler and Watson, *North Carolina Experience,* 334–39. See also Helen G. Edmonds, *The Negro and Fusion Politics in North Carolina, 1894–1901* (Chapel Hill: University of North Carolina Press, 1951); and Joseph F. Steelman, "The Progressive Era in North Carolina, 1884–1917" (Ph.D. diss., University of North Carolina, 1955).

61. Edmonds, *Negro and Fusion Politics,* 139–40; Escott, *Many Excellent People,* 248–54; Crow, "Cracking the Solid South," 339–40.

62. WCTU *Minutes* 1896, 40; 1898, 49; 1899, 43. See also Robert C. McMath Jr., *Populist Vanguard: A History of the Southern Farmers' Alliance* (Chapel Hill: University of North Carolina Press, 1975), 55, 67–69; Barton C. Shaw, *Wool-Hat Boys: Georgia's Populist Party* (Baton Rouge: Louisiana State University Press, 1984),

152–53, 176–78; Julie Roy Jeffrey, "Women in the Southern Farmers'Alliance: A Reconsideration of the Role and Status of Women in the Late Nineteenth-Century South," *Feminist Studies* 3 (Fall 1975): 72–91.

63. Quotations are from Sarah Dudley Pettey, "Some of Our Noble Women," *Star of Zion,* November 12, 1896; and W. F. Fonvielle, "Majors and Minors. Women, Old and Young, Maid and Matron," *Star of Zion,* September 7, 1899. See also "Here and There," *Star of Zion,* September 24, 1891; "W.C.T.U. Convention," *Star of Zion,* August 6, 1896; Educational Supplement, *Star of Zion,* April 1, 1897; Monroe Work, ed. *Negro Year Book 1914–15* (Tuskegee, Ala.: Negro Year Book, 1915), 192 (hereafter cited as *Negro Year Book* with appropriate year). *Negro Year Book 1918–19,* 256; Marcus H. Boulware to Mrs. M. J. Bahnson, May 12, 1974, Clipping File—Biography, vol. 91, 725, NCC.

64. A. Elizabeth Taylor, "The Woman Suffrage Movement in North Carolina," *North Carolina Historical Review* 38 (January 1961): 45–46; Coates, *By Her Own Bootstraps,* 64; A. Elizabeth Taylor, "Helen Morris Lewis," *Dictionary of North Carolina Biography,* vol. 4, 58–59.

65. Davies, *Patriotism on Parade,* 57–58; *Minutes of the First Annual Meeting of North Carolina Society of Colonial Dames* (Wilmington: Jackson and Bell, 1895), 5–6 (hereafter cited as Colonial Dames *Minutes* with appropriate year); Jean Dalziel Wood, *A History of the North Carolina Society of the Colonial Dames of America* (n.p., 1935), 11–13. At first the national organization was confined to the former original thirteen colonies. Later it expanded to include women of colonial ancestry all over the United States.

66. North Carolina Society of the Colonial Dames of America, *By-Laws and Directory, 1904–1905* (Wilmington: Wilmington Stamp Works, n.d.), 31; Colonial Dames *Minutes* 1896–97, 16; 1907–8, 61–70. The Colonial Dames' constitution did not explicitly state that membership must be based on male ancestry, but the requirement was implicit in the restrictions. Other patriotic organizations, such as the United Daughters of the Confederacy, allowed women to establish eligibility for membership on the basis of the service of female ancestors. Application procedures were similar for all the patriotic societies; see "Extracts from Constitution and By Laws of Cape Fear Chapter [United Daughters of the Confederacy]" (n.d.), Parsley Papers, SHC.

67. Quotation is from Kate DeRosset Meares to Richard A. Meares, April 19, 1898, Meares-DeRosset Papers, SHC; Wood, *North Carolina Society of the Colonial Dames,* 4, 11.

68. Wood, *North Carolina Society of Colonial Dames,* 14–16, quotation on 14.

69. Wood, *North Carolina Society of Colonial Dames,* 14–15; newspaper clipping, *Wilmington Messenger,* January 21, 1898, Parsley Papers, SHC.

70. Davies, *Patriotism on Parade,* 58–63.

71. Irene Webster, *Seventy-Five Years of Service: History of the National Society Daughters of the American Revolution of North Carolina* (New Bern: Owen G. Dunn, 1975), 17–21; Chalmers E. Davidson, "Edward Dilworth Latta," *Dictionary of North Carolina Biography,* vol. 4, 28; *Eleventh North Carolina State Conference Daughters of the American Revolution* (n.p., 1911), 3, 27 (hereafter cited as DAR *Proceedings* with appropriate year).

72. Quotation is from General Society of the Daughters of the Revolution, *Proceedings of the Twenty-second Annual Meeting* (n.p., [1913]), 40. Davies, *Patriotism on Parade,* 67–69.

73. Elvira Evelyna Moffitt, "Biographical Sketch of Mrs. Spier Whitaker nee Hooper," *North Carolina Booklet* 13 (April 1914): 234–49, quotation on 238.

74. Quotation is from Mrs. E. E. Moffitt, "The N.C. Society Daughters of the Revolution and Its Objects," *North Carolina Booklet* 6 (October 1906): 148; Moffitt, "Biographical Sketch of Mrs. Spier Whitaker nee Hooper," *North Carolina Booklet,* 239–40.

75. Davies, *Patriotism on Parade,* 41–42; Mary B. Poppenheim et al., *The History of the United Daughters of the Confederacy* (Raleigh: Edwards and Broughton, n.d.), 2–9.

76. Lou Rogers, "Eliza Nutt Parsley," *We the People* 3 (November 1945): 17, 21; Saunders, "History and Accomplishments," 3; Eliza Parsley to Mrs. L. H. Raines, October 19, 1894, Parsley Papers, SHC.

77. The WCTU remained the largest. Poppenheim et al., *History of UDC,* 21; *Minutes of the Fifth Annual Convention of the United Daughters of the Confederacy, North Carolina Division* (Raleigh: Capital, 1902), 16 (hereafter cited as UDC *Minutes* with appropriate year). Shortly after affiliating with the UDC, the Wilmington chapter withdrew in a dispute over membership requirements. The UDC's original bylaws decreed that only lineal descendants of Confederate soldiers were eligible to join. Wilmington women objected to this rule because it excluded the mothers, wives, and sisters of soldiers as well as women who had served the Confederacy themselves. The national UDC convention repealed the disputed clause in 1895, and on April 28, 1897, the Cape Fear Chapter was rechartered and authorized to form other chapters in North Carolina. See Saunders, "History and Accomplishments," 3–4.

78. UDC *Minutes* 1899, 47. See also 1907, 12; 1908, 8.

79. Quotations are from Edmonds, *Negro and Fusion Politics,* 141. See also Escott, *Many Excellent People,* 255–58.

80. Joel Williamson, *The Crucible of Race: Black-White Relations in the American South Since Emancipation* (New York: Oxford University Press, 1984), 190–93.

81. Quotation is from Williamson, *Crucible of Race,* 194; see also Josephus Daniels, *Editor in Politics* (Chapel Hill: University of North Carolina Press, 1941), 288–89; "Jim Young Inspecting Apartments in White Blind Institution in Raleigh," *Raleigh News and Observer,* August 19, 1898; Edmonds, *Negro and Fusion Politics,* 141–42. For other examples of Democratic campaign propaganda see "Scrapbook of Newspaper Clippings Dealing with the 1898 Political Campaign in North Carolina," NCC.

82. "Alex Manly on Lynching, 1898," in Butler and Watson, *North Carolina Experience,* 348.

83. "Alex Manly on Lynching, 1898," in Butler and Watson, *North Carolina Experience,* 348–49. For a similar editorial see Ida B. Wells, *Southern Horrors: Lynch Law in all Its Phases* (1812; reprint, New York: Arno Press and the New York Times, 1969).

84. The classic statement of the interaction between race and gender in the South is W. J. Cash, *The Mind of the South* (New York: Vintage, 1941, 1969). See

also Jacquelyn Dowd Hall, *Revolt Against Chivalry: Jessie Daniel Ames and the Women's Campaign Against Lynching* (New York: Columbia University Press, 1979).

85. Jacquelyn Dowd Hall, "'The Mind That Burns in Each Body': Women, Rape, and Racial Violence," in *Powers of Desire: The Politics of Sexuality,* ed. Ann Snitow, Christine Stansell, and Sharon Thompson (New York: Monthly Review, 1983), 334.

86. Quotations are from Daniels, *Editor in Politics,* 286–87; "Negro Supremacy Against White Supremacy in North Carolina," broadside, NCC; Daniels, *Editor in Politics,* 302. See also Edmonds, *Negro and Fusion Politics,* 147–48.

87. Quotations are from Daniels, *Editor in Politics,* 294, 293, 302, 292. See also Edmonds, *Negro and Fusion Politics,* 148–49.

88. *Wilmington Morning Star,* October 16, 1898, 1.

89. *Progressive Farmer,* September 20, 1898; Rebecca Cameron to "My dear Cousin" [Alfred Moore Waddell], October 26, 1898, Waddell Papers, SHC. I wish to thank Lu Ann Jones for bringing Sarah Mitchell's letter to my attention.

90. For accounts of the riot see Edmonds, *Negro and Fusion Politics,* 158–78; Williamson, *Crucible of Race,* 195–201; and Crow, "Cracking the Solid South," 340–41. Casualty estimates ranged from eleven to thirty.

91. Alexander J. McKelway, "The Race Problem in the South—The North Carolina Revolution Justified," *Outlook* 60 (December 31, 1898): 1057–59.

92. Account of race riot in Wilmington, 1898, typescript, 1, 4; manuscript volume, unpaginated, both in Cronly Family Papers, Duke.

93. Steelman, "Progressive Era," 219–21, quotation on 219; Charles Brantley Aycock, "The Keynote of the Amendment Campaign: Speech Accepting the Nomination for Governor (1901)," in *The Life and Speeches of Charles B. Aycock,* ed. R. D. W. Connor and Clarence Poe (Garden City, N.Y.: Doubleday, Page, 1912), 224–25; Wheeler, *New Women of the New South,* 18; "A Woman's Appeal," *Wilmington Morning Star,* July 24, 1900.

94. Lefler and Newsome, *North Carolina,* 550–62; J. Morgan Kousser, *The Shaping of Southern Politics: Suffrage Restriction and the Establishment of the One-Party South* (New Haven: Yale University Press, 1974), 183–95; and Oliver H. Orr Jr., *Charles Brantley Aycock* (Chapel Hill: University of North Carolina Press, 1961), 138–88.

95. On gender, power relationships, and the political process see Joan Wallach Scott, *Gender and the Politics of History* (New York: Columbia University Press, 1988), 28–50. On the impact of white supremacy campaigns on white southern women's quest for the vote see Wheeler, *New Women of the New South,* chapter 1.

96. Quotation is from "Old Fort Meeting," *Raleigh News and Observer,* August 22, 1899. For other examples of Democrats' equating the right to vote with masculinity see Jerry Wayne Cotten, "Negro Disfranchisement in North Carolina: The Politics of Race in a Southern State" (M.A. thesis, University of North Carolina at Greensboro, 1973); and John Timothy Byrd, "The Disfranchisement of Blacks in New Hanover County, North Carolina" (M.A. thesis, University of North Carolina at Chapel Hill, 1976).

97. On African American women's responses to white supremacy campaigns see Glenda Elizabeth Gilmore, "Gender and Jim Crow: Sarah Dudley Pettey's North Carolina, 1896–1900," *North Carolina Historical Review* 68 (July 1991): 261–86.

98.   Hall, "The Mind That Burns in Each Body," 337.

99.   "Mr. Aycock's Speech," newspaper clipping (n.p.), May 20, 1900, in Joseph E. Avent, "Amendment Scrapbook 1900—Literature on the Amendment Proposed to the Constitution of North Carolina by the General Assembly of 1899," NCC.

100.   Hall, "The Mind That Burns in Each Body," 337.

101.   "W.C.T.U. Convention," *Star of Zion*, August 6, 1896. After 1900, African American temperance advocates referred to their organization as the Thurman WCTU, after Lucy Thurman, national Superintendent of Colored Work.

102.   Sallie Southall Cotten Scrapbook, vol. 3, Cotten Family Papers, SHC.

103.   Anne Firor Scott, "Sallie Sims Southall Cotten," in *Notable American Women*, vol. 1, 388–90; Anastatia Sims, "Sallie Southall Cotten and the North Carolina Federation of Women's Clubs" (M.A. thesis, University of North Carolina at Chapel Hill, 1976); William Stephenson, *Sallie Southall Cotten: A Woman's Life in North Carolina* (Greenville, N.C.: Pamlico, 1987).

104.   On the "new men" of the New South see Don H. Doyle, *New Men, New Cities, New South* (Chapel Hill: University of North Carolina Press, 1990); and Carlton, *Mill and Town in South Carolina*. Social scientists have shown that voluntary associations proliferate in times of rapid social change. They provide support for people adapting to new conditions and offer opportunities for people to experiment with new patterns of behavior. See Michael Banton, "Voluntary Associations: Anthropological Aspects," in *International Encyclopedia of the Social Sciences*, ed. David L. Sills (n.p.: Macmillan/Free Press, 1968), vol. 16, 357–62. See also Graham E. Johnson, "Voluntary Associations and Social Change: Some Theoretical Issues," *International Journal of Comparative Sociology* 16 (Winter 1975): 51–63. For the application of general theory in specific American contexts see Richard D. Brown, "The Emergence of Voluntary Associations in Massachusetts, 1760–1830," *Journal of Voluntary Action Research* 2 (April 1973): 64–73; and Don H. Doyle, "The Social Functions of Voluntary Associations in a Nineteenth-Century American Town," *Social Science History* 1 (May 1977): 333–35.

105.   Lou Rogers, *Tar Heel Women* (Raleigh: Warren, 1949), 169–74.

106.   Sallie Southall Cotten, *History of the North Carolina Federation of Women's Clubs, 1901–1925* (Raleigh: Edwards and Broughton, 1925), 15, 41, 196.

107.   Colonial Dames *Minutes* 1896–97, 16, 18; 1907–8, 61–70; 1915, 34; 1929, 35; DAR *Proceedings* 1915, 49; 1920, 55; 1930, 151; UDC *Minutes* 1905, 14; 1910, 202–3; 1915, 38; 1925, 28; 1930, 54.

108.   WCTU *Minutes* 1903, 27; 1906, 33; 1908, vi–ix; 1930, 33; Whitener, *Prohibition in North Carolina*, 100–101. Because of earlier legislation, North Carolina was virtually dry even before it enacted statewide prohibition, which may explain why the union began to lose members even before 1908.

109.   Dorothy F. Ellison, *History of the International Order of the King's Daughters and Sons*, vol. 3 (Oakland, Calif.: Color Art Press for International Order of King's Daughters and Sons, 1970), "Foreword" (unpaginated), 2–6, 201–2; Easdale Shaw, *The History of the North Carolina Branch of the International Order of the King's Daughters and Sons* (Raleigh: Capital, 1929), 2–5; *Twenty-second Annual Convention of the King's Daughters and Sons of the North Carolina Branch Held at Salisbury, North Carolina, June 7–8, 1911* (n.p., n.d.), 35–38 (hereafter cited as

King's Daughters *Convention* with appropriate year). King's Daughters *Convention* 1904, 11. Although men were admitted to the order, men's and women's organizations functioned independently of each other.

110.   Shaw, *History of North Carolina Branch,* 5; "William Hyslop Burgwyn," in *Biographical History of North Carolina,* vol. 8, 73–80; Juanita Ann Sheppard, "William Hyslop Burgwyn," *Dictionary of North Carolina Biography,* vol. 1, 278–79; "Mrs. Burgwyn Dies At Home," newspaper clipping, *Raleigh News and Observer,* January 24, 1941, Clipping File—Biography, vol. 19, 691, NCC; "Florence M. Cooper," *Sky-Land* (September 1914): 642–43; Beth G. Crabtree, "Frederick Augustus Olds," *Dictionary of North Carolina Biography,* vol. 4, 392–93; Charles B. Overman, "William Overman of Salisbury, N.C. 1812–1890, Biography and Genealogy," typescript (n.d.), NCC; UDC *Minutes* 1901, 82; 1902, 16; 1903, 111; 1904, 113; North Carolina Federation of Women's Clubs, *Yearbook 1914–15* (n.p., n.d.), 4.

111.   African American newspapers, such as the *Star of Zion* and *Raleigh Gazette,* carried announcements of the meetings of local circles of the King's Daughters. I have found no record of a state organization, but one may well have existed. On civic and literary clubs for African American women see Cynthia Neverdon-Morton, *Afro-American Women of the South and the Advancement of the Race, 1895–1925* (Knoxville: University of Tennessee Press, 1989), 191–92; Tulia Brown Hamilton, "The National Association of Colored Women, 1896–1920" (Ph.D. diss., Emory University, 1978), 15–22.

112.   Quotation is from Walls, *AMEZ Church,* 416. See also *National Cyclopedia of the Colored Race,* ed. Clement Richards (Montgomery: National, 1919), vol. 1, 272–73, 412; Charles Harris Wesley, *The History of the National Association of Colored Women's Clubs: A Legacy of Service* (Washington, D.C.: National Association of Colored Women's Clubs, 1984), 311, 315.

113.   A. M. Burns III, "Charlotte Hawkins Brown," *Dictionary of North Carolina Biography,* vol. 1, 242–43; Sadie Iola Daniel, *Women Builders* (Washington, D.C.: Associated, 1931), 133–63; Tera Hunter, "The Correct Thing: Charlotte Hawkins Brown and the Palmer Institute," *Southern Exposure* 11 (September–October 1983): 37–43.

114.   "Organization of Equal Suffrage League of North Carolina, Incorporated," Connor Papers, SHC; Taylor, "Woman Suffrage Movement," 48–49, 51; Barbara Elizabeth Lambert, "Anna Forbes Liddell," *Dictionary of North Carolina Biography,* vol. 4, 64–65. Although the organization incorporated as the Equal Suffrage League, suffragists always used the name Equal Suffrage Association on their letterhead and other publications. The number of local branches fluctuated. In February 1920 ESA president Gertrude Weil reported to the convention of the National American Woman Suffrage Association that in the preceding twelve months the number of local groups had increased from ten to twenty-four. See *Handbook of the National American Woman Suffrage Association and Proceedings of the Victory Convention . . . First National Congress League of Women Voters . . . Feb. 12–18, 1920,* ed. Nettie Rogers Shuler (New York: National American Woman Suffrage Association, n.d.): 176–77.

115.   Eliza Skinner McGehee, "Woman's Place Is in Her Home," *Sky-Land Maga-zine* 1 (September 1913): 635–43; Carolyn Murray Happer, "Barbara Bynum Henderson," *Dictionary of North Carolina Biography,* vol. 2, 100–101.

116.   Quotation is from Minutes of Wake County League of Women Voters, November 1926, North Carolina League of Women Voters Papers, NCDAH; "Women Form a League of Women Voters," newspaper clipping, *Henderson Daily Dispatch* (n.d.), encl. Neila W. Allen to Mary O. Cowper, June 3, 1924, Cowper Papers, Duke; Marion Winifred Roydhouse, "The 'Universal Sisterhood of Women': Women and Labor Reform in North Carolina, 1900–1932" (Ph.D. diss., Duke University, 1980), 138, 141.

117.   Sarah Wilkerson-Freeman, "The Emerging Political Consciousness of Gertrude Weil: Education and Women's Clubs, 1879–1914" (M.A. thesis, University of North Carolina at Chapel Hill, 1985); Ellen Fairbanks Diggs Bodman, "Henry Weil," *Dictionary of North Carolina Biography,* vol. 6, 154.

118.   Cotten, *History of NCFWC,* 149; Lyda Gordon Shivers, "The Social Welfare Movement in the South: A Study in Regional Culture and Social Organization," (Ph.D. diss., University of North Carolina, 1935), 125. During the 1920s the Parent-Teacher Association, the Young Women's Christian Association, the state Nurses' Association, and the Woman's Auxiliary of the Episcopal Church also affiliated with the Council.

119.   Rogers, *Tar Heel Women,* 243–50, quotation on 243.

120.   Quotation is from Charlotte Hawkins Brown, "Some Incidents from My Life," reel 1, Brown Papers, SL. See also Lynda F. Dickson, "Toward a Broader Angle of Vision in Uncovering Women's History: Black Women's Clubs Revisited," in *Black Women's History: Theory and Practice,* ed. Darlene Clark Hine (Brooklyn: Carlson, 1990), 103–20; and Higginbotham, *Righteous Discontent.*

121.   Cotten, *History of NCFWC,* 6.

Chapter 2—"The Sword of the Spirit": Crusades for Temperance and Moral Reform

1.   Laura A. Winston, "Duties of North Carolina Women," in *Report of the Twenty-First Annual Session of the Woman's Christian Temperance Union of North Carolina* (Concord: Times Steam Book and Job Printers, 1903), 1884, 17 (hereafter cited as WCTU *Minutes* with appropriate year).

2.   Quotation is from WCTU *Minutes* 1886, 24. For a description and analysis of the development of "female moral authority" and the use of the belief in feminine moral superiority by women's voluntary associations see Peggy Pascoe, *Relations of Rescue: The Search for Female Moral Authority in the American West, 1874–1939* (New York: Oxford University Press, 1990); and Anne Firor Scott, *Natural Allies: Women's Voluntary Associations in America* (Urbana: University of Illinois Press, 1991), 85–110. See also Anne M. Boylan, "Evangelical Womanhood in the Nineteenth Century: The Role of Women in Sunday Schools," *Feminist Studies* 4 (1978): 62–80; Donald G. Mathews, *Religion in the Old South* (Chicago: University of Chicago Press, 1977), 109–10; and Barbara Welter, "The

Feminization of American Religion: 1800–1860," in *Clio's Consciousness Raised: New Perspectives on the History of Women,* ed. Mary Hartman and Lois W. Banner (New York: Harper and Row, Harper Colophon, 1974), 137–57.

3. T. B. McCain, "From the C.N.C. Conference," *Star of Zion,* March 13, 1885.

4. Quotation is from "Colored W.C.T.U. Meeting," *Charlotte Daily Observer,* June 17, 1901; Norman H. Clark, *Deliver Us from Evil: An Interpretation of American Prohibition* (New York: W. W. Norton, 1976), 50–53; Daniel Jay Whitener, *Prohibition in North Carolina, 1715–1945* (Chapel Hill: University of North Carolina Press, 1945), 57–58; Sydney Nathans, *The Quest for Progress: The Way We Lived in North Carolina, 1870–1920* (Chapel Hill: University of North Carolina Press, 1983), 51–52.

5. "Winston Ripples," *Star of Zion,* July 2, 1886, 2; Josephine Silone–Yates, "The National Association of Colored Women," *Voice of the Negro* 1 (July 1904): 283; "The Prohibition Elections," *Star of Zion,* June 11, 1886, 2. See also Glenda Elizabeth Gilmore, "Gender and Jim Crow: Sarah Dudley Pettey's North Carolina, 1896–1900," *North Carolina Historical Review* 68 (July 1991): 261–86; Janette Thomas Greenwood, *Bittersweet Legacy: The Black and White "Better Classes" in Charlotte, 1850–1910* (Chapel Hill: University of North Carolina Press, 1994),88–90; Dorothy Salem, *To Better Our World: Black Women in Organized Reform, 1890–1920* (Brooklyn: Carlson, 1990), 36.

6. "Local Happenings," *Star of Zion,* March 10, 1887, 3; "The Anti-Prohibition Convention," newspaper clipping, *Banner,* June 2, 1881, Scrapbook, 1880–86, box 13, Hunter Papers, Duke; untitled editorial, *Norwich (N.Y.) Union,* January 17, 1929, reel 35, Tuskegee Clipping File. See also Hanes Walton Jr. and James E. Taylor, "Blacks and the Southern Prohibition Movement," *Phylon* 32 (Summer 1971): 247–59.

7. WCTU *Minutes* 1887, 22; Ted Ownby, *Subduing Satan: Religion, Recreation, and Manhood in the Rural South, 1865–1920* (Chapel Hill: University of North Carolina Press, 1990), 172–73; Joel Williamson, *The Crucible of Race: Black-White Relations in the American South Since Emancipation* (New York: Oxford University Press, 1984), 209–10; Whitener, *Prohibition in North Carolina,* 65–71; Glenda Elizabeth Gilmore, "Gender and Jim Crow: Black Women and the Politics of White Supremacy in North Carolina, 1896–1920" (Ph.D. diss., University of North Carolina at Chapel Hill, 1992), 99; Walton and Taylor, "Blacks and the Southern Prohibition Movement," 249, 257–59; Dewey W. Grantham, *Southern Progressivism: The Reconciliation of Progress and Tradition* (Knoxville: University of Tennessee Press, 1983), 176.

8. Gilmore, "Gender and Jim Crow," 94; Barbara Leslie Epstein, *The Politics of Domesticity: Women, Evangelism, and Temperance in Nineteenth Century America* (Middletown, Conn.: Wesleyan University Press, 1981), 100–107; Ruth Bordin, *Woman and Temperance: The Quest for Power and Liberty, 1873–1900* (Philadelphia: Temple University Press, 1981), 7–8; WCTU *Minutes* 1884, 17; 1886, 67–8; 1888, 17; 1900, 20.

9. Gilmore, "Gender and Jim Crow," 111–12. See also Gilmore, "'A Melting Time': Black Women, White Women, and the WCTU in North Carolina, 1880–

1900," in *Hidden Histories of Women in the New South,* ed. Virginia Bernhard, Betty Brandon, Elizabeth Fox–Genovese, Theda Perdue, and Elizabeth Hayes Turner (Columbia: University of Missouri Press, 1994), 153–72.

10. Quotations are from "Salutatory," *North Carolina White Ribbon* 1 (July 1896): 2; WCTU *Minutes* 1888, 24; Bordin, *Woman and Temperance,* 156–62; Epstein, *Politics of Domesticity,* 115–46. See also WCTU *Minutes* 1886, 24; 1890, 30–31, 34; *Union Signal,* December 10, 1891, 10; *North Carolina White Ribbon* 1 (July 1896): 2; Pascoe, *Relations of Rescue.*

11. Gilmore, "Gender and Jim Crow," 95–99. See also Beverly Guy–Sheftall, *Daughters of Sorrow: Attitudes Toward Black Women, 1880–1920* (Brooklyn: Carlson, 1990), 40–50; Elsa Barkley Brown, "Womanist Consciousness: Maggie Lena Walker and the Independent Order of St Luke," *Signs* 14 (Spring 1989): 610–33; Lynda F. Dickson, "Toward A Broader Angle of Vision in Uncovering Women's History: Black Women's Clubs Revisited," in *Black Women's History: Theory and Practice,* ed. Darlene Clark Hine (Brooklyn: Carlson, 1990), vol. 1, 103–20. Black women's clubs also advocated temperance; see Silone–Yates, "The National Association of Colored Women," 283; Beverly Washington Jones, *Quest for Equality: The Life and Writings of Mary Eliza Church Terrell, 1863–1954* (Brooklyn: Carlson, 1990), 28.

12. WCTU *Minutes* 1886, 24; Rev. H. W. Smith, "The Duty of the Church Towards the Saloon," *Star of Zion,* February 1, 1900, 3; "Woman's Work," *Southern Workman* 31 (August 1902): 422.

13. Untitled editorial, *Southern Workman* 28 (October 1899): 370; "Colored W.C.T.U. Meeting," *Charlotte Daily Observer,* June 17, 1901, 8; "The Battle Against Drink," *Charlotte Daily Observer,* June 18, 1901, 4.

14. "Colored W.C.T.U. Meeting," *Charlotte Daily Observer,* June 17, 1901, 8; WCTU *Minutes* 1890, 40.

15. Quotations are from Smith, "The Duty of the Church Towards the Saloon"; WCTU *Minutes* 1888, 17; WCTU *Minutes* 1886, 67–68. See also WCTU *Minutes* 1884, 21. In much of the temperance literature alcohol and the saloon were considered synonymous; indeed, some prohibitionists seemed more concerned with closing saloons than ending drunkenness. Joseph R. Gusfield argues that the attack on saloons was, in fact, an attack on urban, immigrant culture; see Gusfield, *Symbolic Crusade: Status Politics and the American Temperance Movement* (Urbana: University of Illinois Press, 1966), 98–107.

16. Quotations are from Gilmore, "Gender and Jim Crow," 99; WCTU *Minutes* 1887, 21; 1896, 26; 1883, 7; 1893, 58. See also WCTU *Minutes* 1884, 17; 1885, 23–26; 1886, 16; 1888, 32–33; 1889, 34–35; 1893, 58; 1899, 27; 1908, 28; "Local Ripples," *Charlotte Daily Observer,* May 14, 1886, 3; "The W.C.T.U. State Convention," *Star of Zion,* July 23, 1903, 3.

17. WCTU *Minutes* 1892, 66; 1899, 89–90; 1893, 49; 1894, 39; "Livingstone College Notes," *Star of Zion,* February 1, 1900, 3; "City Items," *Star of Zion,* July 19, 1900, 8; "City Items," *Star of Zion,* April 25, 1901, 8; "Colored W.C.T.U.," *Charlotte Observer,* June 20, 1901, 2; "Colored Temperance Union," *Charlotte Observer,* June 24, 1906, 15.

18. WCTU *Minutes* 1885, 35.

19. Bordin, *Woman and Temperance,* 135.

20. Quotations are from WCTU *Minutes* 1884, 22; and 1885, 30–31; WCTU *Minutes* 1884, 8, 14; *Journal of the Senate of North Carolina,* 1885, 28, 244, 363 (hereafter cited as N.C. *Senate Journal* with appropriate year); *Journal of the House of Representatives of North Carolina,* 1885, 192 (hereafter cited as N.C. *House Journal* with appropriate year); *Public Laws of North Carolina,* 1885, c. 174, s. 12 (hereafter cited as N.C. *Public Laws* with appropriate year); Whitener, *Prohibition in North Carolina,* 106.

21. Whitener, *Prohibition in North Carolina,* 106; WCTU *Minutes* 1887, 22, 37–8, quotation on 37. For examples of the petitions see General Assembly Session Records, 1887, box 17, NCDAH. Petitioners were divided into two categories: "Women" and "Voters." Women outnumbered voters on most of the surviving petitions.

22. Quotation is from *Union Signal* (Chicago), December 10, 1891, 10; WCTU *Minutes* 1889, 21; 1891, 59–63; 81–82; *Union Signal,* September 25, 1890, 12; November 20, 1890, 11; March 5, 1891, 1; March 26, 1891, 11; WCTU petitions, General Assembly Session Records, 1891, box 20, NCDAH; N.C. *House Journal,* 1891, 289, 486, 554, 591; N.C. *Senate Journal,* 1891, 537, 585; N.C. *Public Laws,* 1891, c. 169.

23. WCTU *Minutes* 1884, 8. For a discussion of prohibition and moral reform as a precursor to Progressivism see William A. Link, *The Paradox of Southern Progressivism, 1880–1930* (Chapel Hill: University of North Carolina Press, 1992), 50–57.

24. Quotations are from WCTU *Minutes* 1891, 83; and 1892, 101. For efforts to secure enforcement see WCTU *Minutes* 1892, 17, 78, 101; 1893, 86; 1894, 57; 1896, 29; 1898, 106; 1899, 27–28; 1903, 21, 45–48; 1904, 25; 1908, 28; 1909, 11, 30; 1910, 26; 1914, 32; 1915, 27; *North Carolina White Ribbon* 12 (August 1905): 2; 14 (October 1908): 2–3; 15 (October 1909): 5.

25. Quotations are from WCTU *Minutes* 1884, 3; 1889, 21; 1896, 22. See also WCTU *Minutes* 1885, 23–26; 1886, 26–27; 1888, 38; 1889, 37; 1892, 15; "Thurman W.C.T.U. of Asheville," *Star of Zion,* March 18, 1897; "Local Items," *Star of Zion,* August 19, 1897, 3; "Local Items," *Star of Zion,* November 25, 1897; "The Battle Against Drink," *Charlotte Observer,* June 18, 1901, 4; Mrs. W. F. [Rosa] Steele to Col. George Wassom, Nov. 5, 1886, box 1, Hunter Papers, Duke.

26. Quotations are from WCTU *Minutes* 1892, 16; 1885, 6; "A Woman's Work for Her People," *Star of Zion,* July 3, 1890, 1. See also WCTU *Minutes* 1885, 24; 1893, 86; "Thurman W.C.T.U. of Asheville," *Star of Zion,* March 18, 1897, 3; "Local Items," *Star of Zion,* November 25, 1897, 3; "City Items," *Star of Zion,* January 23, 1902, 8; "City Items," *Star of Zion,* October 22, 1903, 8; "Colored Temperance Union," *Charlotte Observer,* June 24, 1906, 15.

27. Quotations are from "Charlotte Goes Wet," *Charlotte Daily Observer,* June 8, 1886, 3; and Greenwood, *Bittersweet Legacy,* 105. See also "The Prohibition War," *Charlotte Daily Observer,* June 1, 1886, 3; "Local Ripples," *Charlotte Daily Observer,* June 5, 1886, 3; "Local Ripples," *Charlotte Daily Observer,* June 7, 1886, 3; Greenwood, *Bittersweet Legacy,* 103–5.

28. Quotation is from Louis Seibold, "Negro Problem of the South Seized on by Prohibitionists for Their First Big Victory," *New York World,* May 13, 1919, reel 11, Tuskegee Clipping File; WCTU *Minutes* 1889, 30.

29. Quotation is from WCTU *Minutes* 1891, 89; WCTU *Minutes* 1892, 17, 101–2; 1893, 80; 1895, 66–67; Whitener, *Prohibition in North Carolina,* 96–99.

30. WCTU *Minutes* 1889, 29; Whitener, *Prohibition in North Carolina,* 133–34; WCTU *Minutes* 1903, 45–48; "The W.C.T.U. Convention," *Star of Zion,* July 23, 1903, 3.

31. Whitener, *Prohibition in North Carolina,* 134–41; WCTU *Minutes* 1903, 25. The African American WCTU may also have endorsed these measures.

32. Quotation is from "North Carolina Woman's Christian Temperance Union," pamphlet [ca. 1908], NCC; Whitener, *Prohibition in North Carolina,* 156–62.

33. Mattie Eaton to Sallie Sue Ellis, March 17, 1908, Peebles Papers, Duke; Whitener, *Prohibition in North Carolina,* 163–64.

34. Whitener, *Prohibition in North Carolina,* 168; WCTU *Minutes* 1908, 22.

35. Anne Firor Scott, "Women's Perspective on the Patriarchy in the 1850s," *Journal of American History* 61 (June 1974): 52–74; James L. Leloudis II, "Subversion of the Feminine Ideal: The *Southern Lady's Companion* and White Male Morality in the Antebellum South, 1847–1854," in *Women in New Worlds,* vol. 2, 60–75.

36. Quotations are from WCTU *Minutes* 1896, 24; WCTU *Minutes* 1887, 15; and 1895, 46. See also WCTU *Minutes* 1891, 50; 1897, 95; 1908, 27; 1909, 30; 1910, 26; 1920, 19; 1926, 23; *North Carolina White Ribbon* 1 (July 1896): 3.

37. "The Colored Man as Seen by One of His Own Race," *Star of Zion,* September 11, 1885, 2; "The White People Do So," newspaper clipping, *Goldsboro Appeal,* April–May 1886, Scrapbook, 1880–1886, box 13, Hunter Papers, Duke; untitled article, *Star of Zion,* July 30, 1891, 2.

38. Quotation is from Nannie H. Burroughs, "Not Color but Character," *Voice of the Negro* 1 (July 1904): 278; Addie Hunton, "Negro Womanhood Defended," *Voice of the Negro* 1 (July 1904): 280–82; Mary Taylor Blauveldt, "The Race Problem as Discussed by Negro Women," *American Journal of Sociology* 6 (March 1901): 664–65; "Federation Grew out of Slur on Women's Virtue," *Baltimore Afro–American,* August 1, 1928, reel 33, Tuskegee Clipping File; Emma L. Fields, "The Woman's Club Movement in the United States" (Master's thesis, Howard University, 1948), 65–68.

39. Deborah Gray White, "The Cost of Club Work, the Price of Black Feminism," in *Visible Women: New Essays on American Activism,* ed. Nancy A. Hewitt and Suzanne Lebsock (Urbana: University of Illinois Press, 1993), 254–55.

40. WCTU *Minutes* 1886, 30; 1889, 23. See also *Annual Report of the Lindley Training School, Asheville, N.C., for The Year Ending March 31, 1900* (n.p., n.d.), 3–4; hereafter cited as *Lindley Report* with appropriate year.

41. Quotations are from WCTU *Minutes* 1887, 15; 1888, 38; 1891, 50; "Petition for the Establishment by the State of an Industrial School for the White Girls of North Carolina," General Assembly Session Records, 1891, box 20, NCDAH. See also WCTU *Minutes* 1893, 44–45; 1903, 60.

42. Quotations are from WCTU *Minutes* 1895, 45–46; King's Daughters *Report* 1913, 23; and 1902, 39–40. See also WCTU *Minutes* 1903, 60; King's Daughters *Report* 1902, 30; 1903, 23, 33–34; 1909, 23; 1911, 25.

43. WCTU *Minutes* 1887, 48; 1891, 50; 1893, 45–46; 1898, 83–84; *Lindley Report* 1897–98, 2; 1900, 6; *North Carolina White Ribbon* 18 (January 1912): 4.

44. WCTU *Minutes* 1887, 24; 1903, 60–62; King's Daughters *Report* 1902, 39–40; 1904, 37–38.

45. WCTU *Minutes* 1885, 31–36; 1886, 44–45; 1887, 22, 48–49; 1895, 45–46; 1903, 60–62; "Minutes of the Second Midwinter Meeting of the Executive Board, North Carolina Federation of Women's Clubs, Feb. 21–22, 1911, Oxford, N.C.," box 68, Weil Papers, NCDAH; Woman's Club of Raleigh *Yearbook, 1914–15* (n.p., n.d.), 9; North Carolina Federation of Women's Clubs, *Yearbook 1925–26* (n.p., n.d.), 110 (hereafter cited as NCFWC *Yearbook* with appropriate year); "Minutes, Wake County League of Women Voters, April 23, 1926," box 21, North Carolina League of Women Voters Papers, NCDAH.

46. David J. Pivar, *Purity Crusade: Sexual Morality and Social Control, 1865–1900* (Westport, Conn.: Greenwood, 1973), 141–43; WCTU *Minutes* 1887, 18; 1888, 17; 1892, 79–80, 17–18; Susan B. Anthony and Ida Husted Harper, *History of Woman Suffrage,* vol. 4 (Rochester: Susan B. Anthony, 1902), 875; WCTU *Minutes* 1895, 14; "Age of Consent," *North Carolina White Ribbon* 7 (May 1903): 4. See also WCTU *Minutes* 1895, 66–67; 1898, 18; 1910, 14, 26.

47. "Age of Consent," 4.

48. "Featureless but Busy Day in Both Houses," *Raleigh News and Observer,* January 28, 1913, 1, 8; "Justice Primary Bill Referred to New Committee," February 7, 1913, 8.

49. "Minutes of the Second Midwinter Meeting of the Executive Board, North Carolina Federation of Women's Clubs, Feb. 21–22, 1911, Oxford, N.C.," box 68, Weil Papers, NCDAH; "Loose Divorce Bills Killed," *Raleigh News and Observer,* February 5, 1913, 1.

50. Quotations are from "Don't Open the Way for Loose Divorces," *Raleigh News and Observer,* February 4, 1913, 1; and "Loose Divorce Bills Killed," *Raleigh News and Observer,* February 5, 1913, 1. See also untitled editorial, *Raleigh News and Observer,* January 21, 1913, 4; "'Patriots' Pass Anti–Trust Bill to 'Aristocrats,'" *Raleigh News and Observer,* January 29, 1913, 1; "Looking to the Senate," *Raleigh News and Observer,* February 4, 1913, 4.

51. "Justice Freight Resolution Passed by Senate," *Raleigh News and Observer,* January 30, 1913, 1; "Loose Divorce Bills Killed."

52. "Loose Divorce Bills Killed." Women's groups continued to oppose reducing the number of years required for divorce on grounds of abandonment; see WCTU *Minutes* 1925, 39.

53. Petition "To the General Assembly of North Carolina," General Assembly Session Records, 1913, box 55, NCDAH.

54. WCTU *Minutes* 1916, 54; WCTU *Minutes* 1897, 85, 95; 1908, 4; 1911, 14; *Annual Report of the Board of Public Charities, 1907* (Raleigh: E. M. Uzzell, 1908), 58; newspaper clipping, *Raleigh News and Observer,* February 3, 1915, Cowper Papers, Duke; WCTU *Minutes* 1916, 54–55; *Biennial Report of the North*

Carolina State Board of Charities and Public Welfare, July 1, 1922 to June 30, 1924 (n.p., n.d.), 58.

55. On the WCTU's objections to newspaper coverage of violent crimes see WCTU *Minutes* 1888, 45; 1908, 27. On objections to immodest dress see WCTU *Minutes* 1913, 27; 1914, 31; 1922, 36. On the Greensboro Woman's Club's objections to Thaw's appearance see "Kirmess Kronikle," February 4, 1914, 2, box 69, Weil Papers, NCDAH. On movie censorship see *North Carolina White Ribbon* 15 (September 1909): 5; WCTU *Minutes* 1908, 27; 1921, 27; NCFWC *Yearbook* 1923–24, 60–61; 1925–26, 57–58; 1927–28, 78–81; Sallie Southall Cotten, *History of the North Carolina Federation of Women's Clubs, 1901–1925* (Raleigh: Edwards and Broughton, 1925), 15, 41, 196. Cotten, *History of NCFWC,* 156–57; quotations from Lida Rodman to Mrs. Eugene Reilley, April 30, 1918, Rodman Papers, NCDAH; and NCFWC *Yearbook* 1919–20, 63.

56. "What About the Negro Girls?" *Star of Zion,* August 3, 1916, 4; Charles N. Hunter to the Rev. C. A. Ashby, May 30, 1919, box 6, Hunter Papers, Duke; "White Man Assaults Negro Woman," newspaper clipping, *Raleigh Independent,* August 25, 1917, scrapbook, 1915–18, box 15, Hunter Papers, Duke; "The Unknown Tragedy of Negro Womanhood," reprinted in *Star of Zion,* October 5, 1922, 1. See also David Bryant Fulton, "A Plea for Social Justice for the Negro Woman" (Yonkers, N.Y.: Negro Society for Historical Research, 1912); "The Plight of Our Colored Womanhood," newspaper clipping, *Amsterdam News,* October 19, 1914, reel 3, Tuskegee Clipping File; "Respect for Our Womanhood a Keynote," newspaper clipping, *Norfolk Journal and Guide,* June 10, 1922, reel 16, Tuskegee Clipping File; Elise Johnson McDougald, "The Task of Negro Womanhood," in *The New Negro,* ed. Alain Locke (1925, reprint, with a preface by Robert Hayden, New York: Atheneum, 1983), 369–84.

57. *Negro Year Book, 1924–25,* ed. Monroe Work (Tuskegee, Ala.: Negro Year Book, 1925), 27; "Where We Are in Race Relations," [1926], Brown Papers, SL; "What About the Negro Girls?"; "Carolina Women's Federation Meets," newspaper clipping (n.p.), [June 1915], reel 4, Tuskegee Clipping File; "Second Biennial Meeting of the Southeastern Federation of Colored Women's Clubs," *Star of Zion,* August 2, 1923, 1; H. Allyene Foster to Kate Burr Johnson, June 23, 1927, box 7, Social Services Department of North Carolina—Commissioner's Office—Subject Files, 1891–1952, NCDAH; Bertha Hampton Miller, "Blacks in Winston-Salem, North Carolina, 1895–1920: Community Development in an Era of Benevolent Paternalism" (Ph.D. diss., Duke University, 1981), 181.

58. WCTU *Minutes* 1917, 36.

59. On age of consent see WCTU *Minutes* 1915, 27; 1916, 40; 1917, 36; 1919, 22; 1920, 19; 1921, 27; 1922, 26–27; Petition "To the Senate and House of Representatives," July 4, 1914, box 51, General Assembly Session Records, 1915, NCDAH; Barbara Henderson to Lida Rodman, January 7, 1915, Rodman Papers, NCDAH; Typescript [1924?] by Mrs. Ida M. Hook about the Legislative Council of North Carolina Women, Cowper Papers, Duke; NCFWC *Yearbook* 1921–22, 74. On prostitution see "Legislative Council of North Carolina Women," *Monthly News* 2 (February 1925); "The Industrial School for Negro Girls," *Monthly News* 5 (February 1927); "How Justice Is Cheated," *Monthly News* 7 (December 1929).

On equal punishment for male and female sex offenders see "Resolutions Adopted at State Convention of North Carolina League of Women Voters, Raleigh, N.C.," *Monthly News* 2 (April 1925); "Program of Work Adopted by Convention," *Monthly News* 4 (April 1926); "Program of Study and Work Adopted by the Convention for 1927–28," *Monthly News* 5 (April 1927). On venereal disease see "Social Hygiene," *Monthly News* 3 (May 1925); Mrs. C. W. Emry, "A Survey of Venereal Disease Work in North Carolina," *Monthly News* 3 (June 1925). For more on women's work for female prisons see chapter 3.

60. Quotations are from "Legislative Program," *Monthly News* 4 (December 1925); and "More Legislative 'Entering Wedges,'" *Monthly News* 7 (April 1929); "Resolutions Passed by the Convention," *Monthly News* 1 (March 1924); "Program of the Legislative Council of North Carolina Women," *Monthly News* 2 (October 1924); Mrs. W. T. Bost, "Notice of Intended Marriage," *Monthly News* 2 (December 1924); "Program of Council," *Monthly News* 2 (January 1925); "Legislative Council of North Carolina Women," *Monthly News* 2 (February 1925); "Summary of Council Work," *Monthly News* 2 (March 1925); "Legislative Forecast," *Monthly News* 5 (September 1926); Bost, "Our Work for Our Legislative Measures," *Monthly News* 5 (October 1926); "The Notice of Marriage Bill," *Monthly News* 5 (January 1927); "The Two Weeks Notice of Marriage," *Monthly News* 5 (March 1927); "Program of Study and Work Adopted by 1928 Convention," *Monthly News* 6 (February 1928); "Legislative Council Meets," *Monthly News* 7 (December 1928); "Our Bills at This Writing," *Monthly News* 7 (March 1929); WCTU *Minutes* 1925, 24; 1929, 37; 1930, 49; "Resolutions Adopted [by the] Fourth Annual Convention of North Carolina League of Women Voters, Durham, March 4–5 [1924]," Cowper Papers, Duke; "Program of the Legislative Council of North Carolina Women For 1927," Cowper Papers, Duke; and "Program of the Legislative Council of North Carolina Women For 1929," Cowper Papers, Duke; NCFWC *Yearbook* 1927–28, 99; 1929–30, 35.

61. WCTU *Minutes* 1923, 28–29; 1924, 25–26; 1926, 21–23; 1927, 22–23; 1929, 21, 25–26; 1930, 25; "Program of Council," *Monthly News* 2 (January 1925); Emry, "A Survey of Venereal Disease"; "The Sedberry Bill," *Monthly News* 5 (March 1927); NCFWC *Yearbook* 1922–23, 49; 1923–24, 24; 1927–28, 138–39.

62. Quotations are from WCTU *Minutes* 1929, 39; and *N.C. Public Laws,* 1929, c. 96; WCTU *Minutes* 1919, 22; 1920, 19; 1927, 38–39; 1928, 11; 1929, 37–39; 1930, 49; *N.C. House Journal,* 1929, 70, 81, 99, 417, 450; *N. C. Senate Journal,* 1929, 90, 104, 141, 179, 194, 279, 297.

63. NCFWC *Yearbook* 1930–31, 7; WCTU *Minutes* 1932, 27; Frances Renfrow Doak, "Why North Carolina Voted Dry" (Raleigh: Capital, 1934), 13.

Chapter 3—"A Power for Good": The Progressive Impulse

1. Postscript from Mina Weil on Eva Rosenthal to Gertrude Weil, March 24, 1899, Weil Papers, NCDAH; "Goldsboro Centennial Celebration, 1847–1947. Official Souvenir Program," 25; Department of the Interior, Census Office, *Report on Population of the United States at the Tenth Census (June 1880)* (Washing-

ton: Government Printing Office, 1883) 1, 284; *Abstract of the Twelfth Census of the United States 1900*, 144, 368; "Address by Judge Frank A. Daniels at the Opening of Wayne County's New Court House, November 30, 1940" (n.p., n.d.), 34. For more on the founding of the Goldsboro Woman's Club see Sarah Wilkerson-Freeman, "The Emerging Political Consciousness of Gertrude Weil: Education and Women's Clubs, 1879–1914" (M.A. thesis, University of North Carolina at Chapel Hill, 1985), 49–52. On the urban spirit in North Carolina towns in this era see Sydney Nathans, *The Quest for Progress: The Way We Lived in North Carolina, 1870–1920* (Chapel Hill: University of North Carolina Press, 1983), 45–53.

    2. Goldsboro Woman's Club, *Constitution and By-laws of the Goldsboro Woman's Club* (Goldsboro, N.C.: Goldsboro Argus Press, 1906); Mina Weil to Gertrude Weil, November 16, 1898, Weil Papers, NCDAH. For similar summaries of the overall goals of female voluntary associations see *Goldsboro Weekly Record*, May 6, 1905, newspaper clipping, and *Keystone*, October 1912, newspaper clipping, both in box 69, Weil Papers, NCDAH; and "First Decade of Growth," Sallie Southall Cotten Scrapbook, vol. 3, Cotten Family Papers, SHC. On the origins of women's clubs in North Carolina see chapter 1. For descriptions of the women's club movement in the United States see Anne Firor Scott, *Natural Allies: Women's Voluntary Associations in America* (Urbana: University of Illinois Press, 1992); Paula Giddings, *When and Where I Enter: The Impact of Black Women on Race and Sex in America* (Toronto: Bantam, 1985); Dorothy Salem, *To Better Our World: Black Women in Organized Reform, 1890–1920* (Brooklyn: Carlson, 1990); and Jane Cunningham Croly, *The History of the Woman's Club Movement in America* (New York: Henry G. Allen, 1898).

    3. Gertrude Weil to Mina Weil, November 20, 1898; Mina Weil to Gertrude Weil [April 10, 1899]; both in Weil Papers, NCDAH.

    4. "Of Service to the State," *Raleigh News and Observer*, May 7, 1913, 4; Kate Burr Johnson, "A Decade of Social Progress in North Carolina," *Journal of Social Forces* 1 (May 1923): 401; Mary Church Terrell, "Progress and Problems of Colored Women," *Boston Transcript*, December 15, 1928, reel 33, Tuskegee Clipping File. See also "Woman's Work," *Southern Workman* 31 (August 1902): 422; "Women Who Serve," *Raleigh News and Observer*, May 29, 1918, 4; newspaper clipping, *Raleigh Times*, November 3, 1915; newspaper clipping (n.p.), June 16, 1923; both in Raleigh Woman's Club folder, Moffitt Papers, SHC; *Everywoman's Magazine* 1 (August 1917): 10.

    5. "Wilson Woman's Club," *Raleigh Farmer and Mechanic*, June 8, 1915, 9.

    6. Paula Baker, "The Domestication of Politics: Women and American Political Society, 1780–1920," *American Historical Review* 89 (June 1984): 640–42; Dewey W. Grantham, *Southern Progressivism: The Reconciliation of Progress and Tradition* (Knoxville: University of Tennessee Press, 1983), xvi–xxii; William A. Link, *The Paradox of Southern Progressivism, 1880–1930* (Chapel Hill: University of North Carolina Press, 1992), xii, 188–89.

    7. Sallie Southall Cotten, *History of the North Carolina Federation of Women's Clubs, 1901–1925* (Raleigh: Edwards and Broughton, 1925) 1–7; King's Daughters *Report* 1913, 42–44; Baker, "Domestication of Politics," 641–42; Carl N. Degler, *At Odds: Women and the Family in America from the Revolution to the*

Present (New York: Oxford University Press, 1980), 319–27; Molly Ladd-Taylor, *Mother-Work: Women, Child Welfare, and the State, 1890–1930* (Urbana: University of Illinois Press, 1994), 3–7; Robyn Muncy, *Creating A Female Dominion in American Reform* (New York: Oxford University Press, 1991), 30–31; Giddings, *When and Where I Enter*, 75–83.

8. Gilmore, "Gender and Jim Crow," 307–54. On the impact of disfranchisement on white women's clubs in North Carolina see chapter 1. For more on black women's clubs and their role in the African American community see Mary Taylor Blauvelt, "The Race Problem as Discussed by Negro Women," *American Journal of Sociology* 6 (March 1901): 662–72; Gerda Lerner, "Early Community Work of Black Club Women," *Journal of Negro History* 59 (1974): 158–67; Jacqueline Ann Rouse, *Lugenia Burns Hope: Black Southern Reformer* (Athens: University of Georgia Press, 1989); Salem, *To Better Our World*; Anne Firor Scott, "Most Invisible of All: Black Women's Voluntary Associations," *Journal of Southern History* 56 (February 1990): 3–20.

9. Gilmore, "Gender and Jim Crow," 319; see also Scott, "Most Invisible of All"; Elvira Moffitt, "Which Name? Village Improvement Association or Municipal Aid League?" August 1902, vol. 18, Moffitt Papers, SHC; NCFWC *Yearbook* 1915–16, 17.

10. Mrs. Al Fairbrother, "About the Women's Clubs of North Carolina," untitled clipping (n.p.), 1910, Sallie Southall Cotten Scrapbook, vol. 3, Cotten Family Papers, SHC; "To Teachers of Institute Held in Raleigh By Prof. Crittenden of Wake Forest—Friday 8th August 1902," Moffitt Papers, SHC.

11. "Report of 10th Annual Meeting, Goldsboro Woman's Club, April 14, 1908," box 69, Weil Papers, NCDAH; King's Daughters *Report* 1902, 30; 1904, 33; 1908, 33; 1909, 37–38; NCFWC *Yearbook* 1902, 9; 1903, 13; 1905, 5, 17; 1906, 11, 15, 28.

12. Quotations are from Nellie Roberson, "The Organized Work of Women in One State," *Journal of Social Forces* 1 (January 1923): 176; and Louis Round Wilson, "Library Development in North Carolina," *Library Journal* 48 (1923): 23. NCFWC *Yearbook* 1911–12, 53–54; 1915–16, 51–52; 1922–23, 78; 1924–25, 73; 1927–28, 74; 1928–29, 84, 90; 1930–31, 80; James S. Jenkins, *Greenville and Pitt County at the Turn of the Century* (Greenville, 1965), 64, 68; "A Live One: The End of the Century Club in Greenville, N.C.," newspaper clipping (n.p., n.d.), Sallie Southall Cotten Scrapbook, vol. 3, Cotten Family Papers, SHC; "Kirmess Kronikle," February 14, 1914, 2, box 69, Weil Papers, NCDAH; *Everywoman's Magazine* 1 (May 1917): 19; UDC *Minutes* 1904, 80; 1920, 65; Ida Sutton to Gertrude Weil, June 10, 1910, Weil Papers, NCDAH; North Carolina Society of the Daughters of the Revolution, Minute Book 1910–19, January 26, 1913, box 2, Daughters of the Revolution Papers, NCDAH (hereafter cited as DR Minute Book). On women's role in the library movement see Scott, *Natural Allies*, 149; Grantham, *Southern Progressivism*, 206; and Willard B. Gatewood, *Aristocrats of Color: The Black Elite, 1880–1920* (Bloomington: Indiana University Press, 1990), 243.

13. Gertrude Weil to Frances Squire Potter, ca. September–October 1912, undated draft attached to Frances Squire Potter to Gertrude Weil, September 28,

1912, Weil Papers, NCDAH; Dee Garrison, "The Tender Technicians: The Feminization of Public Librarianship, 1876–1905," in *Clio's Consciousness Raised: New Perspectives on the History of Women,* ed. Mary Hartman and Lois W. Banner (New York: Harper Colophon, 1974), 158–78, quotation on 161. See also Kathleen D. McCarthy, *Women's Culture: American Philanthropy and Art, 1830–1930* (Chicago: University of Chicago Press, 1991), 3–34; Nancy F. Cott, "Passionlessness: An Interpretation of Victorian Sexual Ideology, 1790–1850," *Signs* 4 (1978): 219–36; Daniel Walker Howe, "Victorian Culture in America," in *Victorian America,* ed. Daniel Walker Howe (Philadelphia: University of Pennsylvania Press, 1976), 26. On the growing separation between high culture and popular culture in the second half of the nineteenth century see Lawrence W. Levine, *Highbrow/Lowbrow: The Emergence of Cultural Hierarchy in America* (Cambridge, Mass.: Harvard University Press, 1988).

14. NCFWC *Yearbook* 1911–12, 55; "Federation of Women's Clubs," *Raleigh Farmer and Mechanic,* February 23, 1915, 16; North Carolina Library Commission, *Handbook of the Citizens' Library Movement* (Charlotte: North Carolina Library Association, 1928), 30 (hereafter cited as NCLC *Handbook*).

15. Louis Round Wilson, "State Libraries, Their Improvement," *North Carolina Review,* supplement to the *Raleigh News and Observer,* January 1, 1911, 2. See also Louis Round Wilson, "The Use of Books and Libraries in North Carolina," *Journal of Social Forces* 1 (January 1923): 78–86. My discussion of Progressives and the promotion of education and culture in the New South is based on Link, *Paradox of Southern Progressivism,* 124–34; James L. Leloudis II, "'A More Certain Means of Grace': Pedagogy, Self, and Society in North Carolina, 1880–1920" (Ph.D. diss., University of North Carolina at Chapel Hill, 1989); and Daniel Joseph Singal, *The War Within: From Victorian to Modernist Thought in the South, 1919–1945* (Chapel Hill: University of North Carolina Press, 1982).

16. NCFWC *Yearbook,* 1917–18, 72. See also "One Need of the Town," *Skyland Magazine* 1 (October 1913): 133–37. The idea of the symbolic value of the library became so firmly entrenched that sixty-seven years later the *News and Observer* editorialized: "A central library provides a cultural focus, just as a courthouse gives law a permanent and visible seat in the county." *Raleigh News and Observer,* May 3, 1984, 4.

17. David Brinkley, *David Brinkley* (New York: Alfred A. Knopf, 1995), 30–31; NCFWC *Yearbook* 1909–10, 21; Mina Weil to Gertrude Weil [April 10, 1899], Weil Papers, NCDAH; Louis Round Wilson, "On the Progress of Our Libraries," *North Carolina Review,* supplement to *Raleigh News and Observer,* September 3, 1911, 7; NCFWC *Yearbook* 1902, 9; 1903, 10; 1906, 8, 11; 1909–10, 21–22; Sallie Southall Cotten, *History of the North Carolina Federation of Women's Clubs,* 28; Gertrude S. Carraway, *Carolina Crusaders: History of the North Carolina Federation of Women's Clubs* (New Bern: Owen G. Dunn for the North Carolina Federation of Women's Clubs, 1941), 28.

18. Wilkerson-Freeman, "Emerging Political Consciousness," 58; Louis Round Wilson, "Library Development in North Carolina," 23; Wilson, "On the Progress of Our Libraries," 7; Cotten, *History of NCFWC,* 44; NCFWC *Yearbook* 1909–10, 20; 1912–13, 45; NCLC *Handbook,* 18; Mary B. Palmer, "What the Library Com-

mission Has Done for North Carolina," *Monthly News* 1 (October 1923); Minutes, North Carolina Society of the Daughters of the Revolution, January 16, 1909, box 2, Daughters of the Revolution Papers, NCDAH (hereafter cited as DR Papers).

19. Quotation is from NCFWC *Yearbook* 1911–12, 55; Wilson, "State Libraries," 2; "Travelling Libraries—The Work of the Women's Clubs," n.d., box 69, Weil Papers, NCDAH; NCFWC *Yearbook* 1909–10, 21.

20. NCFWC *Yearbook* 1922–23, 78; 1923–24, 65; 1925–26, 108; 1928–29, 82–84; 1929–30, 35, 74; William S. Powell, "Citizens' Library Movement in North Carolina," *North Carolina Libraries* 13 (November 1954): 34.

21. Wilson, "Use of Books and Libraries," 79, 84; Wilson, "Library Development in North Carolina," 23; NCLC *Handbook,* 7.

22. "Ex-Mayor A. A. Thompson," newspaper clipping, *Raleigh Gazette,* May 9, 1891, Scrapbook, 1887–1899, box 13, Hunter Papers, Duke; *Negro Year Book 1918–19,* 301; Wilson, "Use of Books and Libraries," 79, 83–84. For a discussion of the work of African American clubwomen for libraries see Willard B. Gatewood, *Aristocrats of Color: The Black Elite, 1880–1920* (Bloomington: Indiana University Press, 1990), 243.

23. Quotation is from NCFWC *Yearbook* 1924–25, 87. On clubwomen's work to promote art see NCFWC *Yearbook* 1911–12, 36; 1913–14, 34; 1922–23, 69–70; 1929–30, 67; 1930–31, 68. On their efforts to promote music see NCFWC *Yearbook* 1909–10, 25; 1915–16, 52–56; 1926–27, 79; 1927–28, 69, 86; 1929–30, 89; "Report of Tenth Annual Meeting, Goldsboro Woman's Club;" King's Daughters *Report,* 1913, 45; Katherine Highsmith Holoman, *Ever Changing, Ever the Same: Seventy-Fifth Anniversary History of the Woman's Club of Raleigh, 1904–1979* (Raleigh: Woman's Club of Raleigh, [1979]), 14; Roberson, "Organized Work of Women in One State," 177; Levine, *Highbrow/Lowbrow,* 200–201.

24. Untitled newspaper clipping, May 5, 1910, Sallie Southall Cotten Scrapbook, vol. 3, Cotten Family Papers, SHC.

25. Elvira Moffitt, "Speech Read at Garner School, April 1903," Moffitt Papers, SHC; Link, *Paradox of Southern Progressivism,* 124–28; Joseph F. Steelman, "The Progressive Era in North Carolina, 1884–1917" (Ph. D. diss., University of North Carolina at Chapel Hill, 1955), 501–4; Leloudis, "A More Certain Means of Grace," 43–63; 136–49.

26. WCTU *Minutes* 1884, 21. See also *Schools vs. Saloons: Governor Jarvis on the Eternal Conflict,* broadside [1908], NCC. For a discussion of the WCTU's campaign for a scientific temperance instruction law see chapter 2.

27. Anne L. Kuhn, *The Role of the Mother in Childhood Education: New England Concepts, 1830–1860* (New Haven: Yale University Press, 1947); Ruth H. Bloch, "American Feminine Ideals in Transition: The Rise of the Moral Mother, 1785–1815," *Feminist Studies* 4 (1978): 101–26; Leloudis, "A More Certain Means of Grace," 122–26, 237–39.

28. Leloudis, "A More Certain Means of Grace," 115–56.

29. Leloudis, "A More Certain Means of Grace," 257–60; quotation is on 258; *The Woman's Association for the Betterment of Public Schoolhouses in North Carolina* (Raleigh: Office of the State Superintendent of Public Instruction, 1908)

pamphlet, NCC, 12–13, quotation on 13. See also *Proceedings of the Eleventh Conference for Education in the South, Memphis, Tenn., April 22–24, 1908* (Nashville: Executive Committee of the Conference, n.d.), 113–16 (hereafter cited as Education Conference *Proceedings* with appropriate year).

30. Education Conference *Proceedings* 1906, 56–60; quotations on 56, 59; "Constitution of the Woman's Association for the Betterment of Public School Houses in North Carolina," in *The Woman's Association for the Betterment of Public Schoolhouses in North Carolina* (Raleigh: Office of the State Superintendent of Public Instruction, 1908. With an Introduction by J. Y. Joyner), 7–8 (hereafter cited as Joyner, *Woman's Association for the Betterment of Public Schoolhouses*). 7–8. See also Leloudis, "A More Certain Means of Grace," 261–62; and Link, *Paradox of Southern Progressivism*, 134–41.

31. Education Conference *Proceedings* 1908, 115.

32. *Twelfth Census of the United States: 1900*, vol. 2, xcv; Steelman, "Progressive Era," 513; *Twelfth Census of the United States: 1900*, vol. 2, ciii, cv; *Twelfth Census of the United States: 1900, Special Reports: Supplementary Analysis and Derivative Tables* (Washington: Government Printing Office, 1906), 345.

33. Quotation is from Charles D. McIver, *Disfranchisement and Education*, for *Southern Workman*, February 1901, pamphlet, NCC; Oliver H. Orr Jr., *Charles Brantley Aycock* (Chapel Hill: University of North Carolina Press, 1961), 180–208; Grantham, *Southern Progressivism*, 260; Leloudis, "A More Certain Means of Grace," 277.

34. Leloudis, "A More Certain Means of Grace," 269; WCTU *Minutes* 1885, 39. For more on the WCTU's efforts at interracial cooperation in the 1880s see chapter 1.

35. "To the Honorable School Committee Raleigh Township, North Carolina," box 2, Hunter Papers, Duke; Wiley Britton Sanders, *Negro Child Welfare in North Carolina* (Chapel Hill: University of North Carolina Press, 1933), 11–12; "Women's Clubs of North Carolina to Build Girls' Home," *New York Age*, May 12, 1923, Tuskegee Clipping File, Reel 19.

36. Quotations are from C. H. Mebane, *The Woman's Association for the Betterment of Public Schoolhouses in North Carolina* (Raleigh: Office of the State Superintendent of Public Instruction, North Carolina Department of Public Instruction, 1908), 40 (hereafter cited as Mebane, *Woman's Association*); and Leloudis, "A More Certain Means of Grace," 278. Descriptions of the schools based on Leloudis, "A More Certain Means of Grace," 277–78, 292; and Link, *Paradox of Southern Progressivism*, 27–28; 126–27; 204–6.

37. "History of Woman's Association for the Betterment of Public School Houses," Wake County (n.d.), folder 48, Moffitt Papers, SHC; McIver to Moffitt, June 20, 1902, Moffitt Papers, SHC.

38. McIver quoted in Leloudis, "A More Certain Means of Grace," 258; J. Y. Joyner, "Introduction," Joyner, *Woman's Association for the Betterment of Public Schoolhouses*, 5; "Address to Patrons and Pupils—Reddick School House" (n.d.), Moffitt Papers, SHC; Education Conference *Proceedings* 1906, 57. See also McIver to Moffitt, June 20, 1902, Moffitt Papers, SHC; untitled newspaper clipping (n.p.), September 14, 1902, vol. 18, Moffitt Papers, SHC; and James L. Leloudis II,

"School Reform in the New South: The Woman's Association for the Betterment of Public School Houses in North Carolina, 1902–1919," *Journal of American History* 69 (March 1983): 895.

39. Education Conference *Proceedings* 1907, 112–13.

40. Lula Martin McIver to Sallie Sue Peebles, September 19, 1906, Peebles Papers, Duke; Joyner, *Woman's Association for the Betterment of Public School-houses,* 18–19, quotation on 18; Mebane, *Woman's Association,* 35–44.

41. McIver to Peebles, September 19, 1906; Joyner, *Woman's Association for the Betterment of Public Schoolhouses,* 19–20, quotation on 19; Minutes of the Executive Board, Raleigh Woman's Club, April 7, 1906, North Carolina Federation of Women's Club Papers, NCDAH (hereafter cited as NCFWC Papers); Leloudis, "A More Certain Means of Grace," 292–93; Link, *Paradox of Southern Progressivism,* 204–7.

42. Quotations are from McIver to Peebles, September 19, 1906; Mebane, *Woman's Association,* 31; Joyner, *Woman's Association for the Betterment of Public Schoolhouses,* 18; Education Conference *Proceedings* 1906, 58. See also Edith Royster, "To the Teachers of Wake County," Moffitt Papers, SHC; "History of the Woman's Association for the Betterment of Public School Houses, Wake County," n.d., folder 48, Moffitt Papers, SHC; Lucy Closs Parker to Mrs. Brodnax, February 3, 1907, Brodnax Papers, Duke; newspaper clipping, *New Bern Sun,* May 8, 1913, Sallie Southall Cotten Scrapbook, vol. 3, Cotten Family Papers, SHC; clipping, *Keystone,* March 1913, box 66, Weil Papers, NCDAH; *Everywoman's Magazine* 4 (April 1920): 7; Education Conference *Proceedings* 1907, 112; 1908, 118; NCFWC *Yearbook* 1911–12, 37; 1912–13, 38; 1917–18, 55; 1926–27, 64; UDC *Minutes* 1908, 80; 1918, 51; 1919, 46; 1920, 40, 64; 1927, 35; 1928, 39–41; 1929, 43.

43. Education Conference *Proceedings* 1906, 58.

44. Education Conference *Proceedings* 1906, 57–59, quotation on 57; Link, *Paradox of Southern Progressivism,* xii, 85–91, 124–42; Leloudis, "'A More Certain Means of Grace,'" 278–80.

45. Quotations are from McIver to Peebles, September 19, 1906; Joyner, *Woman's Association for the Betterment of Public Schoolhouses,* 17–20, "working-bees" mentioned on 17; Mebane, *Woman's Association,* 31–32; NCFWC *Yearbook* 1921–22, 61. See also Education Conference *Proceedings* 1907, 111.

46. Education Conference *Proceedings* 1906, 32; Leloudis, "'A More Certain Means of Grace,'" 270–71; Mebane, *Woman's Association,* 31, 35.

47. Quotations are from Mebane, *Woman's Association,* 36, 35; and Joyner, *Woman's Association for the Betterment of Public Schoolhouses,* 19. See also Mebane, *Woman's Association,* 34–44; Mrs. L. P. Sorrell to Edith Royster, February 3, 1903, Moffitt Papers, SHC; "History of the Woman's Association for the Betterment of Public School Houses, Wake County"; Education Conference *Proceedings* 1906, 58–60; 1907, 111–14; 1908, 117–19; Minutes, December 7 (no year), Minute Book, 1910–19, box 2, DR Papers; *Everywoman's Magazine* 3 (May 1919): 6; Carrie B. Wilson, *History of the North Carolina State Division American Association of University Women 1927–47* (Greensboro: Riser, 1948), 14; NCFWC *Yearbook* 1903–4, 2, 6; 1905, 15; 1909–10, 27; 1912–13, 42; 1925–26, 69; 1927–28, 74,

86; 1928–29, 90; 1929–30, 89; 1930–31, 80–81; Steelman, "Progressive Era," 523–24.

48. Quotations are from Joyner, *Woman's Association for the Betterment of Public Schoolhouses,* 18; NCFWC *Yearbook* 1912–13, 42; 1916–17, 47; 1917–18, 7, 42, 55, 62; 1923–24, 75; 1924–25, 69, 135; 1925–26, 48; 1926–27, 69; WCTU *Minutes* 1919, 22; Roberson, "Organized Work of Women in One State," 53; Link, *Paradox of Southern Progressivism,* 142–54, 206–12; Leloudis, "A More Certain Means of Grace," 292–300.

49. On the demand for music and art classes see NCFWC *Yearbook* 1909–10, 26–27; 1910–11, 41; 1911–12, 37; 1912–13, 47; 1914–15, 30, 42; 1915–16, 40; 1924–25, 57; 1928–29, 27; 1929–30, 88–89. On the WABPS and agricultural education see Leloudis, "A More Certain Means of Grace," 282–88. On vocational training for girls and manual training for boys see NCFWC *Yearbook* 1902, 13; 1903, 14; 1905, 17; 1909–10, 25; 1912–13, 42; 1913–14, 37; 1915–16, 57; 1917–18, 62; 1921–22, 63–64; 1923–24, 45; *Kirmess Kronikle,* February 3, 1914, 2, box 69, Weil Papers, NCDAH; *Everywoman's Magazine* 1 (March 1917): 34; 1 (August 1917): 10; 3 (May 1919): 7; Raleigh Woman's Club, *Yearbook* 1915–16 (Raleigh, 1915), 10 (hereafter cited as RWC *Yearbook* with appropriate year); newspaper clipping (n.p., n.d.), Sallie Southall Cotten Scrapbook, vol. 3, Cotten Family Papers, SHC; Edith Royster to Bessie Bates, 31 May 1911, box 59, NCFWC Papers; Chairman, Department of Education, North Carolina Federation of Women's Clubs, to "Dear Madam," March 29, 1910, Weil Papers, NCDAH.

50. Lucy Closs Parker to Mrs. [Ella] Brodnax, February 3, 1907, John G. Brodnax Papers, Duke; Joyner, "Woman's Association for the Betterment of Public Schoolhouses," 17; Walter Hines Page, *The Southerner: A Novel Being the Autobiography of Nicholas Worth* (New York: Doubleday, Page, 1909), 139.

51. "History of Woman's Association for the Betterment of Public School Houses, Wake County"; Steelman, "Progressive Era," 520–22; *North Carolina White Ribbon* 1 (July 1896): 1, 3; WCTU *Minutes* 1896, 29; "Report of the Sixth Annual North Carolina Federation of Women's Clubs Convention" [1908], box 68, Weil Papers, NCDAH: NCFWC *Yearbook* 1912–13, 42; "For Compulsory Education," *Raleigh News and Observer,* January 12, 1913, 1; "Senate Passes Resolution for an Extra Session," *Raleigh News and Observer,* January 31, 1913, 3; "Under the Dome," *Raleigh News and Observer,* February 4, 1913, 2.

52. Mrs. E. R. Mosher, "Education and the Child in Industry," *Monthly News* 6 (December 1927); Mosher, "Is Our Compulsory Attendance Law Adequate?" *Monthly News* 6 (October 1928). See also "Report of Executive Secretary," *Monthly News* 1 (March 1924); "Board Meeting October 24," *Monthly News* 6 (November 1927); "Program of Study and Work Adopted by 1928 Convention," *Monthly News* 6 (February 1928); "Program for 1930," *Monthly News* 8 (March 1930); Mrs. Bulus B. Swift, "No Idle Children Under Sixteen Years—School or Work; A Popular Measure," *Monthly News* 8 (November 1930); NCFWC *Yearbook* 1913–14, 48; 1917–18, 62.

53. Quotations are from Mrs. Thomas F. O'Berry, "The Attainment Requirement," *Monthly News* 4 (November 1925). See also the following articles in the *Monthly News:* "Resolutions Passed by the Convention," 1 (March 1924); Char-

lotte B. Elliott, "What Should the Committee on Education Work for in This State?" 2 (October 1924); Gertrude Weil, "Why the Public Welfare Department Should Be Supported and Strengthened," 2 (December 1924); "Program of Council," 2 (January 1925); "Department of Public Welfare in Government," 3 (May 1925); "Program of Work Adopted by Convention," 4 (April 1926); "Program of Study and Work Adopted by the Convention for 1927–28," 5 (April 1927); "Board Meeting October 24," 6 (November 1927); "Program of Study and Work Adopted by 1928 Convention," 6 (February 1928); "Legislative Council Minutes," 7 (December 1928); NCFWC *Yearbook* 1921–22, 61; WCTU *Minutes* 1924, 45–46; "Resolutions Adopted Fourth Annual Convention of North Carolina League of Women Voters, Durham, March 4–5 [1924]," and "Report of Legislative Chairman, N.C. League of Women Voters, Charlotte, March 24, 1931," both in Cowper Papers, Duke; Kathryn L. Nasstrom, "'More Was Expected of Us': The North Carolina League of Women Voters and the Feminist Movement in the 1920s" (M.A. thesis, University of North Carolina at Chapel Hill, 1988), 32.

54. Quotations are from "House for Six Months' Term," *Raleigh News and Observer,* February 19, 1913, 1; Steelman, "Progressive Era," 519–20; NCFWC *Yearbook* 1913–14, 36; 1917–18, 62; 1922–23, 73; 1928–29, 35; 1929–30, 35, 73, 75; "Program of the North Carolina Legislative Council of Women," *Monthly News* 2 (October 1924); "Report of the Legislative Chairman, N.C. League of Women Voters Charlotte, March 24, 1931," Cowper Papers, Duke; "Report of Sixth Annual North Carolina Federation of Women's Clubs Convention," box 68, Weil Papers, NCDAH; Samuel Huntington Hobbs Jr., *North Carolina: Economic and Social* (Chapel Hill: University of North Carolina Press, 1930), 251–52.

55. NCFWC *Yearbook* 1912–13, 42; 1913–14, 38, 58; 1915–16, 61–62, 68; 1918–19, 41; 1921–22, 61; 1922–23, 73; 1923–24, 53; 1926–27, 65; "Report of Sixth Annual North Carolina Federation of Women's Clubs Convention"; *Kirmess Kronikle,* February 3, 1914, 2, box 69, Weil Papers, NCDAH; *Everywoman's Magazine* 3 (May 1919): 6; Minute Book, Raleigh Branch, AAUW, January 1916, AAUW Papers, NCDAH; "Program of the North Carolina Legislative Council."

56. Quotation is from Hobbs, *North Carolina,* 253; *Fifteenth Census of the United States: 1930,* vol. 2, table 14, 1104; table 10, 1229; Hobbs, *North Carolina,* 254; Leloudis, "A More Certain Means of Grace," 308.

57. "North Carolina Schools Best of Southern States, Says Crises [sic]," *Topeka (Kansas) Plain Dealer,* April 22, 1927, reel 28, Tuskegee Clipping File; "Negro Child in Public Schools," *Pilot,* [Vass, N.C.?], August 5, 1927, reel 28, Tuskegee Clipping File; Hobbs, *North Carolina,* 262; *Fifteenth Census of the United States,* vol. 2, 1109, table 19.

58. "North Carolina Schools Best of Southern States"; "Negro Child in Public Schools"; Lewis K. McMillan, "North Carolina Has Two $1,000,000 Schools," *Baltimore Afro-American,* November 5, 1927, reel 28, Tuskegee Clipping File.

59. McMillan, "North Carolina Has Two $1,000,000 Schools"; "Supervisor Reports on Cleveland Negro Schools," *Shelby (North Carolina) Star* (n.d.), reel 30, Tuskegee Clipping File; Wiley Britton Sanders, *Negro Child Welfare in North Carolina* (Chapel Hill: University of North Carolina Press, 1933), 10–13. On occasion white clubwomen also assisted black schools; see G. C. Davidson, "The

History of the Roxboro City Schools" (n.p., n.d.), reel 30, Tuskegee Clipping File. For a general discussion of activities of black PTAs see Ladd-Taylor, *Mother-Work*, 55–63.

60. Education Conference *Proceedings* 1907, 114.

61. Quotation is from Josephine Coit to Hope [Summerell] Chamberlain, February 27, 1899, Chamberlain Papers, Duke. On literary and historical programs of women's organizations see "The Ladies Pansy Literary Club," newspaper clipping, *Raleigh Gazette*, November 7, 1891, Scrapbook, 1887–1899, Hunter Papers, Duke; "City Items," *Star of Zion*, July 13, 1899, 8; July 27, 1899, 8; August 3, 1899, 8; September 21, 1899, 8; October 12, 1899, 8; October 26, 1899, 8; November 23, 1899, 8; Jan. 18, 1900, 8; January 25, 1900, 8; March 15, 1900, 8; January 9, 1901, 8; September 5, 1901, 8; NCFWC *Yearbook* 1904–5, 12–15; 1905–6, 11; 1909–10, 29; 1911–12, 50; 1914–15, 26–27; 1915–16, 12; 1917–18, 69; Scott, *Natural Allies*, 111–28; Gatewood, *Aristocrats of Color*, 241. On scholarships see UDC *Minutes* 1900, 94; 1901, 107; 1902, 100; 1907, 65–66; 1908, 68–69; 1910, 25; 1920, 65–66; 1922, 41; 1923, 20; 1927, 44–46; NCFWC *Yearbook* 1909–10, 22–23; 1924–25, 108–11; 1928–29, 115; 1929–30, 104; DAR *Proceedings* 1925, 86; 1926, 59; King's Daughters *Report* 1904, 35; 1912, 50; *Everywoman's Magazine* 4 (April 1920): 7; "Negro Women Seek to Better College Living," *New York City World*, April 23, 1926, reel 26, Tuskegee Clipping File; Fannie Ransom Williams to Mrs. John G. Brodnax, December 17, 1907, and August 8, 1911; Sallie S. Yates Faison to Mrs. John G. Brodnax, January 6, 1908, and August 12, 1908, all four letters in Brodnax Papers, Duke; Carraway, *Carolina Crusaders*, 23–24, 52–54, 58; Carrie B. Wilson, *History of the North Carolina State Division American Association of University Women 1927–1947* (Greensboro: Riser, 1948), 13; Charles Harris Wesley, *The History of the National Association of Colored Women's Clubs: A Legacy of Service* (Washington, D.C.: National Association of Colored Women's Clubs, 1984), 323; Jean Dalziel Wood, *A History of the North Carolina Society of the Colonial Dames of America* (n.p., 1935), 29.

62. "Woman Civilizing Force," newspaper clipping (n.p.), 1913, Sallie Southall Cotten Scrapbook, vol. 3, Cotten Family Papers, SHC; Roberson, "Organized Work of Women in One State," 174; NCFWC *Yearbook* 1928–29, 115.

63. Anna Julia Cooper, *A Voice from the South* (Xenia, Ohio: Aldine, 1892), 79; Mrs. C. C. [Sarah Dudley] Pettey, "Woman's Column," *Star of Zion*, June 27, 1901. See also Miss Tena M. Nichols, "Higher Education for Women," newspaper clipping, *Raleigh Gazette*, May 12, 1892, Scrapbook, 1887–99, box 13, Hunter Papers, Duke; Lucy C. Laney, "The Burden of the Educated Colored Woman," *Southern Workman* 28 (September 1899): 341–44. For more on Pettey and her views see Gilmore, "Gender and Jim Crow," 10–67, 273–75.

64. WCTU *Minutes* 1888, 43–44; 1891, 11–12, 40; 1899, 33–34; NCFWC *Yearbook* 1905, 17; 1906, 11; 1909–10, 29; 1911–12, 50; 1912–13, 3; 1913–14, 40–41; 1914–15, 37–38; 1915–16, 47–49; 1917–18, 67–69; 1921–22, 18, 63–64; 1923–24, 63–64; 1924–25, 82; 1925–26, 48; 1927–28, 61–67; *Union Signal*, March 12, 1891, 14; Minutes of the Executive Board, Raleigh Woman's Club, November 4, 1905, and December 1, 1907, box 1, NCFWC Papers; *North Carolina White Ribbon* 15 (January 1909): 1–3; 18 (January 1912): 1; *By Way of Sug-*

gestion: Summer Reading for the Women's Club, pamphlet attached to Raleigh Woman's Club Minutes, August 21, 1905, vol. 12, Moffitt Papers, SHC; Raleigh Woman's Club, *Yearbook 1914–1915* (Raleigh: n.p., 1914), 10; *Kirmess Kronikle,* February 5, 1914, 2, box 69, Weil Papers, NCDAH; Minute Book, Raleigh Branch, AAUW, AAUW Papers, NCDAH; Roberson, "Organized Work of Women in One State," 52.

65. *Everywoman's Magazine* 1 (January 1917): 36.

66. Quotations are from Sallie Southall Cotten, "Shall We Educate the Girls?" (n.d.), Cotten Family Papers, SHC; "North Carolina Federation Notes," *Greensboro Daily News,* August 1, 1920; NCFWC *Yearbook* 1925–26, 48. On demands for domestic science see NCFWC *Yearbook* 1903, 14; 1905, 17; 1912–13, 42; 1913–14, 37; 1915–16, 57; 1917–18, 62; 1921–22, 63–64; *Kirmess Kronikle,* February 3, 1914, 2, box 69, Weil Papers, NCDAH; *Everywoman's Magazine* 1 (August 1917): 10; 3 (May 1919): 7; RWC *Yearbook* 1915–16, 10; Roberson, "Organized Work of Women in One State," 52.

67. WCTU *Minutes* 1897, 34; 1889, 56–57.

68. WCTU *Minutes* 1888, 43; Orra Langhorne, "Domestic Service in the South," *Southern Workman* 30 (October 1901): 526.

69. Quotations are from Sarah Pettey, "The Up-To-Date Woman," *Star of Zion,* August 13, 1896, 2; and Laney, "Burden of the Educated Colored Woman," 341–42. See also Rev. I. F. Aldridge, "The Race Problem: The Differences Between the Whites North and South," *Star of Zion,* March 2, 1899; Miss Jennie W. Warner, "Domestic Training: The Importance of It Among Our Negro Girls," *Star of Zion,* January 25, 1900, 1; "The Teacher Versus the Housemaid," *Southern Workman* 30 (October 1901): 524–25; Hugh Penn Brinton, "The Negro in Durham: A Study of Adjustment to Town Life" (Ph.D. diss., University of North Carolina, 1930), 401–2; Willie Mae Coleman, "Keeping the Faith and Disturbing the Peace: Black Women From Anti-Slavery to Women's Suffrage" (Ph.D. diss., University of California—Irvine, 1981), 83; Gilmore, "Gender and Jim Crow," 284–85, 330; McMillan, "North Carolina Has Two $1,000,000 Schools."

70. NCFWC *Yearbook* 1911–12, 16; newspaper clipping, *Tarboro Southerner,* January 29 [1913], Sallie Southall Cotten Scrapbook, vol 3, Cotten Family Papers, SHC. See also DAR *Proceedings* 1920, 32.

71. Quotations are from NCFWC *Yearbook* 1917–18, 53–54; and Report to General Meeting, Raleigh Woman's Club [June 9, 1905?], vol. 12, Moffitt Papers, SHC. See also newspaper clippings, *Raleigh News and Observer,* October 15, 1904, November 13, 1904, vol. 12, Moffitt Papers, SHC; "General Report from Oct. 9th 1904 to June 9th 1905"; Minutes, Civic Department, Raleigh Woman's Club, February 21, 1905; "To the Woman's Club of Raleigh"; previous three in Moffitt Papers, SHC; "Women Brave Rain in Plea for Sanitation and Community Beauty," newspaper clipping [1913], Sallie Southall Cotten Scrapbook, vol. 3, Cotten Family Papers, SHC; Minutes, Durham Civic League, April 9, 1919, Southgate Papers; *Everywoman's Magazine* 4 (April 1920): 23; Eloise G. Franks to Mary O. Cowper, October 8, 1924, Cowper Papers, Duke; NCFWC *Yearbook* 1909–10, 24; 1911–12, 37; 1914–15, 32; 1915–16, 42; 1917–18, 54; 1918–19, 64; 1919–20, 42; 1921–22, 58; 1922–23, 25, 70; 1925–26, 75; 1926–27, 46; 1927–28, 72;

1929–30, 63, 70, 90; 1930–31, 72; Carraway, *Carolina Crusaders*, 32; Gilmore, "Gender and Jim Crow," 335–54.

72. Newspaper clipping, *Raleigh Times*, August 19, 1913, Scrapbook, 1908–14, box 14, Hunter Papers, Duke; Charles N. Hunter to Mrs. C. A. [Kate Burr] Johnson, April 3, 1919, box 6, Hunter Papers, Duke; Gilmore, "Gender and Jim Crow," 342–45.

73. WCTU *Minutes* 1885, 31–36; RWC *Yearbook* 1915–16, 11; 1916–17, 11; NCFWC *Yearbook* 1912–13, 42; 1913–14, 39; 1925–26, 61; clipping, *Keystone* (March 1913), box 66, Weil Papers, NCDAH; *Kirmess Kronikle*, February 3, 1914, 2; Roberson, "Organized Work of Women in One State," 53; King's Daughters *Report* 1902, 29; "The Great Negro State Fair," *Search-Light* 4 (October 1914): 33; Gilmore, "Gender and Jim Crow," 351; "Planks That Will Be Presented by the National League of Women Voters," *Monthly News* 2 (June 1924); "Program of Work Adopted by Convention," *Monthly News* 4 (April 1926); "League Notes," *Monthly News* 5 (June 1926); "Infant-Maternity Work in Buncombe County," *Monthly News* 5 (Midsummer 1926); "Program of Study and Work Adopted by the Convention for 1927–28," *Monthly News* 5 (April 1927); "Help for Mothers and Babies," *Monthly News* 6 (November 1927); "Program of Study and Work Adopted by 1928 Convention," *Monthly News* 6 (February 1928); "Maternity and Infancy Work in North Carolina," *Monthly News* 7 (September 1929); "N.C. Needs Maternity-Infancy Funds," *Monthly News* 7 (December 1929); "How Is M. and I. Work in Your County?" *Monthly News* 8 (August–September 1930). For more on the Sheppard-Towner Act see Ladd-Taylor, *Mother-Work*, 167–96; and Theda Skocpol, *Protecting Soldiers and Mothers: The Political Origins of Social Policy in the United States* (Cambridge, Mass.: Harvard University Press, Belknap Press, 1992), 494–524.

74. NCFWC *Yearbook* 1909–10, 29; 1911–12, 49; 1913–14, 35; 1914–15, 36; 1917–18, 54; newspaper clipping, *Wilmington Morning Star,* May 14, 1911, Sallie Southall Cotten Scrapbook, vol. 3, Cotten Family Papers, SHC; Mrs. Charles G. Doak, "In Memoriam," box 8, NCFWC Papers; *Kirmess Kronikle*, February 2, 1914, 2; February 3, 1914, 2; newspaper clipping, November 13, 1904, vol. 12, Moffitt Papers, SHC; Minutes, Civics Department, Raleigh Woman's Club, February 21, 1905, Moffitt Papers, SHC; "Report to the City Planning Committee of the Women's Club" [1912], box 8, NCFWC Papers; Minutes, Durham Civic League, April 9, 1919; NCFWC *Yearbook* 1909–10, 24; Gilmore, "Gender and Jim Crow," 345–50. See also Scott, *Natural Allies*, 141–74; and Martin V. Melosi, *Garbage in the Cities: Refuse, Reform, and the Environment, 1880–1980* (College Station: Texas A & M Press, 1981), 105–33.

75. Quotations are from King's Daughters *Report* 1912, 49; and "Constitution and General Laws of the Royal Knights of King David. Lady Knights Department" (Durham, n.d.), NCC; King's Daughters *Report* 1902, 20–30; 1903, 23; 1904, 34; 1908, 25–35; 1909, 21–43; 1912, 28–49; 1913, 13–33; 1914, 14–35; *Uplift* (January 1917): 6–15; *Uplift* (February 1918): 7–15; Mrs. W. T. Bost, "Activities of Tar Heel Women," newspaper clipping, *Greensboro Daily News,* April 11, 1927, vol. 2, Elsie Riddick Papers, SHC; Greenwood, *Bittersweet Legacy,* 66, 110–12; W. E. B. DuBois, *Some Efforts of American Negroes for Their Own Social Betterment* (At-

lanta: Atlanta University Press, 1898), 13; "City Items," *Star of Zion,* December 11, 1902, 8; Miller, "Blacks in Winston-Salem," 191; Charles Williams Jr. and Hilda J. B. Williams, "Mutual Aid Societies and Economic Development: Survival Efforts," in *African Americans in the South: Issues of Race, Class, and Gender,* ed. Hans A. Baer and Yvonne Jones (Athens: University of Georgia Press, 1992), 28.

76.   King's Daughters *Report* 1909, 33.

77.   King's Daughters *Report* 1912, 40.

78.   Quotation is from *Everywoman's Magazine* 1 (May 1917): 21; King's Daughters *Report* 1912, 36; 1913, 15; *Uplift* (January 1917): 12, 14; *Uplift* (February 1918): 11, 13; NCFWC *Yearbook* 1915–16, 56; 1917–18, 66–67; 1919–20, 45; RWC *Yearbook* 1919–20, 27; Mary Thornton, Carolyn A. Wallace, Guion Griffis Johnson, "Hope Summerell Chamberlain, 1870–1960. A memorial presented to the Historical Society of North Carolina at a meeting held at Meredith College, Raleigh, North Carolina, April 7, 1960," 3, Chamberlain Papers, SHC; clipping, *Keystone,* May 1912, box 66, Weil Papers, NCDAH; Mrs. Sam Berwanger, form letter, November 20, 1917, box 5, NCFWC Papers; *Everywoman's Magazine* 4 (April 1920): 23; Bertha Hampton Miller, "Blacks in Winston-Salem, North Carolina, 1895–1920: Community Development in an Era of Benevolent Paternalism" (Ph.D. diss., Duke University, 1981), 181.

79.   Quotations are from King's Daughters *Report* 1913, 22; and "Negroes Pressing Hospital Campaign," *Henderson Dispatch,* April 12, 1927, reel 28, Tuskegee Clipping File; WCTU *Minutes* 1910, 26–27; NCFWC *Yearbook* 1913–14, 39; 1914–15, 35; 1915–16, 56; 1917–18, 65; 1918–19, 67; 1924–25, 74–75; 1925–26, 75–76; 1927–28, 96; 1928–29, 97, 100; 1929–30, 90; King's Daughters *Report* 1909, 32, 35; 1912, 28–29; 1914, 25, 27; *Uplift* (January 1917): 7, 11; *Uplift* (February 1918): 7, 13; UDC *Minutes* 1919, 69–70; 1920, 77; 1926, 71; 1927, 78; 1928, 21, 40; *Everywoman's Magazine* 4 (April 1920): 21, 23; RWC *Yearbook* 1916–17, 20; Mrs. Sam Berwanger to "Dear Sir," December 5, 1916, and Berwanger, form letter, November 20, 1917, both in box 5, NCFWC Papers; May Belle McMahon to Mary O. Cowper, December 24, 1924, Cowper Papers, Duke; newspaper clipping (n.p., n.d.), Sallie Southall Cotten Scrapbook, vol. 3, Cotten Family Papers, SHC; Carraway, *Carolina Crusaders,* 54; "Negroes Join in White Plague Fight," *Star of Zion,* December 17, 1908.

80.   Quotations are from newspaper clipping, *Tarboro Southerner,* January 29 [1913], Sallie Southall Cotten Scrapbook, vol. 3, Cotten Family Papers, SHC; and NCFWC *Yearbook* 1929–30, 68. See also WCTU *Minutes* 1896, 50–51; newspaper clipping, *Raleigh News and Observer,* October 15, 1904, vol. 12, Moffitt Papers, SHC; RWC *Yearbook* 1904–5, 16; 1911–12, 12; Raleigh Woman's Club Executive Board Minutes, April 8, 1905, box 1, NCFWC Papers; *Kirmess Kronikle,* February 5, 1914, 2; newspaper clipping, *New Bern Sun,* May 7, 1913, Sallie Southall Cotten Scrapbook, vol. 3, Cotten Family Papers, SHC; "Some Suggestions for Committees" (n.d.), Programs and Committees of the Durham Civic Association, 1915–16, James Southgate Papers, Duke; E. D. Mickle to Mrs. Whitted, April 9, 1919, Southgate Papers, Duke; Durham Civic League Minutes, April 9 [1919?], Southgate Papers, Duke; *Everywoman's Magazine* 3 (May 1919):

6; NCFWC *Yearbook* 1906, 18; 1909–10, 24; 1911–12, 16, 37, 41; 1914–15, 31; 1915–16, 42; 1917–18, 54; 1921–22, 60, 64; 1926–27, 46; 1927–28, 72; 1929–30, 63, 68, 70; Paul Boyer, *Urban Masses and Moral Order in America, 1820–1920* (Cambridge, Mass.: Harvard University Press, 1978), 224.

81. Minutes, January 31, 1912, DR Minute Book, 1910–19, 73; DR *Proceedings* 1913, 70; "Some Suggestions for Committees," Southgate Papers, Duke; RWC *Yearbook* 1917–18, 9; NCFWC *Yearbook* 1909–10, 31–32; 1910–11, 34; 1924–25, 13; 1927–28, 27; 1930–31, 29, 70, 73; UDC *Minutes* 1927, 74–77; 1928, 18; 1929, 92–93; Carraway, *Carolina Crusaders*, 32.

82. Quotations are from NCFWC *Yearbook* 1906, 20; and Minutes of the Executive Board, Raleigh Woman's Club, January 7, 1905, box 1, NCFWC Papers. See also NCFWC *Yearbook* 1911–12, 37–40; 1917–18, 55; 1922–23, 25; 1923–24, 75–76; 1926–27, 46; Easdale Shaw, *The History of the North Carolina Branch of the International Order of the King's Daughters and Sons* (Raleigh: Capital, 1929), 6; "The Woman's Club Program, 1904–05," 16, box 6, NCFWC Papers; "Some Suggestions for Committees," Southgate Papers, Duke; *Everywoman's Magazine* 3 (July–August 1919): 27; RWC *Yearbook* 1916–17, 15; 1917–18, 10; Bost, "Activities of Tar Heel Women"; Gilmore, "Gender and Jim Crow," 350.

83. King's Daughters *Report* 1913, 42.

84. NCFWC *Yearbook* 1927–28, 92–93; 1924–25, 25; Rev. J. Harvey Anderson, "Searchlight Scenes," *Star of Zion*, June 15, 1899, 2.

85. Quotations are from King's Daughters *Report* 1909, title page; Shaw, *History of North Carolina Branch*, 5–6; and "City Items," *Star of Zion*, April 25, 1901, 8; King's Daughters *Report*, 1902, 20–25; 1903, 23; 1909, 21–43; 1912, 28–49; 1913, 13–33; 1914, 14–35; *Uplift* (January 1917): 6–15; *Uplift* (February 1918): 7–15; Minutes, February 7, 1891, Whatsoever Circle, Silver Cross Chapter of King's Daughters, Minute Book, 1890–96, Nunn Papers, Duke; "Report of the Silver Cross Chapter King's Daughters," December 14, 1894, Nunn Papers, Duke; handwritten account of founding of St. Luke's Home and King's Daughters in Raleigh (n.d.), Moffitt Papers, SHC; Eulalia Williams, "Report of Activities of Elizabeth Circle, Silver Cross Chapter, King's Daughters" (n.d.), Nunn Papers, Duke; *Union Signal*, February 6, 1890, 11; November 20, 1890, 12; January 8, 1891, 11; WCTU *Minutes* 1885, 33; NCFWC *Yearbook* 1902, 12; 1906, 9; 1921–22, 41; 1922–23, 86, 107–8; 1923–24, 74; 1924–25, 90; 1926–27, 86; 1927–28, 94–96; 1928–29, 101; 1929–30, 78, 90; 1930–31, 95; Minutes of the Executive Board, Raleigh Woman's Club, December 2, 1905, and April 7, 1906, box 1, NCFWC Papers; Mrs. M. R. Adams to Mrs. [John G.] Brodnax, August 6, 1908, Brodnax Papers, Duke; *Everywoman's Magazine* 1 (March 1917): 34–35; 4 (April 1920): 7, 11, 23; *Opening Ceremonies Initiation of Candidates and Initiation of Officers of Subordinate Tents of the Independent Order of J. R. Giddings and Jollifee Union of North Carolina*, pamphlet, NCC; Mrs. Eloise Bibb Thompson, "The Negro Woman in America," *Southern Christian Advocate*, July 2, 1914, reel 3, Tuskegee Clipping File; "Livingstone College Notes," *Star of Zion*, November 22, 1900, 2; "Colored W.C.T.U.," *Charlotte Observer*, June 20, 1901; UDC *Minutes* 1898, 29–30; 1900, 90–101; 1906, 62–112; 1923, 15; 1927, 20; RWC *Yearbook* 1916–17,

20; 1917–18, 15; "Local Leagues," *Monthly News* 1 (March 1924); "About People You Know," *Raleigh Gazette*, January 2, 1897, 3; "Colored Orphan Asylum of North Carolina, Oxford, North Carolina" (Oxford: Public Ledger Print, 1900), NCC; "Dinner to the Old Folks," *Raleigh Gazette*, January 30, 1897, 3; *Annual Report of the Board of Public Charities, 1907*, 63–64; *Annual Report of the Board of Public Charities, 1912* (Raleigh: Edwards and Broughton, 1912), 62–63; *Annual Report of the Board of Public Charities of North Carolina, 1913* (Raleigh: Edwards and Broughton, 1914), 53; William Kenneth Boyd, *The Story of Durham: City of the New South* (Durham: Duke University Press, 1925), 231; Salem, *To Better Our World*, 72, 83.

86. King's Daughter's *Report* 1904, 26; "Constitution and By-Laws of the Associated Charities of Raleigh, N.C. Adopted February 16, 1905," NCC; NCFWC *Yearbook* 1923–24, 74; *Everywoman's Magazine* 1 (March 1917): 34; Grantham, *Southern Progressivism*, 224; Gilmore, "Gender and Jim Crow," 346.

87. Quotations are from Virginia H. Grier, *North Carolina Conference for Social Service, 1912–1962* (Raleigh: North Carolina Conference for Social Service, [1962]), pamphlet, NCC, 1; *Raleigh News and Observer*, January 5, 1913, 1; February 2, 1913, 4; February 13, 1913, 5; Grantham, *Southern Progressivism*, 228–29.

88. Quotation is from NCFWC *Yearbook* 1923–24, 74. See also NCFWC *Yearbook* 1915–16, 61–62; 1918–19, 43; 1921–22, 74; 1922–23, 86; 1923–24, 80, 98; 1924–25, 130; 1926–27, 87, 125; 1927–28, 92–93, 99; 1928–29, 26; "Program of Council," *Monthly News* 2 (January 1923); Gertrude Weil, "Why the Public Welfare Department Should Be Supported and Strengthened," *Monthly News* 2 (December 1924); "Public Welfare Measures," *Monthly News* 2 (March 1925); University of North Carolina Extension Division, University Extension Bulletin, *Public Welfare and the Community As It Relates to the North Carolina Plan of Public Welfare* (Chapel Hill: University of North Carolina Press, [1925]), 44–45; Thornton et al., "Hope Summerell Chamberlain," 6; "Progress in North Carolina," *Survey*, April 15, 1922, reel 16, Tuskegee Clipping File.

89. UDC *Minutes* 1900, 70–71.

90. Quotation is from Rebecca Cameron to Lida Tunstall Rodman, October 30, 1900, Sarah Rebecca Cameron Papers, SHC. On veterans' benefits see UDC *Minutes* 1900, 70; 1901, 79; 1918, 18; 1920, 85; 1921, 51; 1927, 20, 78; "Petition of the North Carolina Division of the United Daughters of the Confederacy for Increased Appropriations for Pensions and the Soldiers Home," January 19, 1901, vol. 20, Moffitt Papers, SHC; *Everywoman's Magazine* 4 (April 1920): 21. On the UDC's contributions to the veterans' home see UDC *Minutes* 1898, 19, 30; 1900, 110; 1901, 46–47; 1902, 33; 1903, 8–9, 24–25, 33–37; 1906, 31; 1907, 70; 1910, 26; 1912, 42–43; 1918, 63–64; 1920, 53–56; 1921, 50–51; 1927, 19–20; 1929, 20; newspaper clipping (n.p.), February 18, 1902, vol. 20, Moffitt Papers, SHC; *Everywoman's Magazine* 4 (April 1920): 7; newspaper clipping, *Fayetteville Observer*, October 12, 1926, Jessica Randolph Smith Papers, NCDAH; Mrs. John S. Henderson to Eliza Parsley, February 21 (no year), Parsley Papers, SHC; Sallie Yates Faison to Rebecca Cameron, September 14, 1909, Sarah Rebecca Cameron Papers, SHC. On petitions to appoint women to the board see UDC

Minutes 1900, 45; 1901, 46, 69–72; 1909, 27; 1910, 62; 1918, 18, 63; 1920, 84–85; 1927, 87; 1928, 20; Rebecca Cameron to Lida Rodman, October 30, 1900, Hinsdale Family Papers, Duke; "Petition of the North Caroliona Division," January 19, 1901.

91. UDC *Minutes* 1908, 21–22; 1909, 28; 1912, 54–55; "Senate Passes Resolution for an Extra Session," *Raleigh News and Observer,* January 31, 1913, 3; "For the Women of the Confederacy Left Dependent," *Raleigh News and Observer,* February 1, 1913, 1; "In a Noble Cause," *Raleigh News and Observer,* February 2, 1913, 4; "Statewide Search and Seizure Law Passed by House," *Raleigh News and Observer,* February 15, 1913, 3; "Many Bills Are Disposed of in Senate and House," *Raleigh News and Observer,* February 16, 1913, 1; "A Noble Philanthropy," *Raleigh News and Observer,* February 18, 1913, 4; "Under the Dome," *Raleigh News and Observer,* February 19, 1913, 2; "Million Dollar Bond Issue Passed by Senate," March 6, 1913, 7; Mrs. E. B. McKethan, "Confederate Woman's Home Opened 1915," *Fayetteville Observer,* March 22, 1958, NCC Clipping File.

92. Quotation is from UDC *Minutes* 1919, 54. See also 1918, 18, 63–64; 1920, 20, 23, 56–57; 1927, 20, 87; 1928, 20, 58–59; 1929, 27; *Everywoman's Magazine* 4 (April 1920): 21; newspaper clipping, *Fayetteville Observer,* October 12, 1926, Smith Papers, NCDAH.

93. WCTU *Minutes* 1896, 18; NCFWC *Yearbook* 1924–25, 78.

94. NCFWC *Yearbook* 1921–22, 41; 1924–25, 130–31; 1926–27, 87, 125; *Public Welfare and the Community,* 50; "Resolutions Adopted at State Convention of North Carolina League of Women Voters, Raleigh, N.C., February 3–4, 1925," *Monthly News* 2 (April 1925).

95. Quotation is from NCFWC *Yearbook* 1924–25, 90. See also WCTU *Minutes* 1885, 33; 1903, 28; King's Daughters *Report* 1902, 22–23; 1903, 24; NCFWC *Yearbook* 1912–13, 40; 1913–14, 46–47, 57; 1916–17, 58–59; 1922–23, 86; 1923–24, 74; 1926–27, 86; 1927–28, 94; 1929–30, 90; "Thurman W.C.T.U. of Asheville," *Star of Zion,* March 18, 1897, 3; W. N. Hartshorn, ed., *An Era of Progress and Promise, 1863–1910* (Boston: Priscilla, 1910), 292; *Kirmess Kronikle,* February 6, 1914, 2; *Everywoman's Magazine* 1 (March 1917): 34–35; Report of Activities of Elizabeth Circle.

96. WCTU *Minutes* 1885, 40; 1886, 16, 26–29; 1887, 14–15, 46; 1888, 16; 1889, 22, 36; 1892, 17, 78; 1894, 58; 1895, 13–14, 66, 82; 1896, 82; 1897, 38, 84; 1898, 26; 1899, 90; 1900, 20; 1903, 10–11, 22, 28; *Union Signal,* September 25, 1890, 12; *North Carolina White Ribbon* 1 (January 1, 1897): 2; S. G. Hawfield, *History of the Stonewall Jackson Manual Training and Industrial School* (Concord: "Published by the Boys of the Printing Department, Stonewall Jackson Manual and Industrial Training School," 1946), 2–13; *Annual Report of the Board of Public Charities,* 1907, 7–8; Shaw, *History of North Carolina Branch,* 6–7.

97. Quotations are from Hawfield, *History of the Stonewall Jackson School,* 4; and WCTU *Minutes* 1889, 36; WCTU *Minutes* 1886, 29; Shaw, *History of North Carolina Branch,* 9.

98. "Woman's World and Work," *Raleigh Morning Post,* June 22, 1902, 3; King's Daughters *Report* 1902, 16; 1903, 6–7, 12–13; 1904, 6–9, 14–19; 1905, 6–9, 29–30; WCTU *Minutes* 1903, 10–11, 22, 28; Hawfield, *History of the Stonewall*

Jackson School, 2–13; Shaw, *History of North Carolina Branch,* 6–7; "Report of
Committee Appointed to prepare account of the steps that led to the formation of
THE WOMAN'S CLUB OF RALEIGH [in 1904]," encl., Edith Royster Judd, 26
July 1916, Moffitt Papers, SHC; Sue V. Hollowell to Elvira Moffitt, June 3, 1904,
Moffitt Papers, SHC; "Address to the Civic and Social Service Department of the
Woman's Club," [1906], Moffitt Papers, SHC; Minutes, Executive Board of the
Raleigh Woman's Club, December 20, 1904, March 4, 1905, December 1, 1907,
box 1, NCFWC Papers; "The Woman's Club Program, 1904–05," box 6, NCFWC
Papers; UDC *Minutes* 1906, 57; 1907, 51, 70; 1908, 70; Lyda Gordon Shivers,
"The Social Welfare Movement in the South: A Study in Regional Culture and
Social Organization" (Ph.D. diss., University of North Carolina, 1935), 112.

99. Shaw, *History of North Carolina Branch,* 7–13, quotation on 9; Hawfield,
History of Stonewall Jackson School, 6–10, 16.

100. Shaw, *History of North Carolina Branch,* 13–14. Shaw also downplayed
the role of other women's organizations.

101. Shaw, *History of North Carolina Branch,* 14–16.

102. Quotation is from WCTU *Minutes* 1908, 28. See also Cotten, *History,* 23;
UDC *Minutes* 1909, 84; NCFWC *Yearbook* 1910–11, 37; 1919–20, 64; 1924–25,
133; 1928–29, 97; 1929–30, 90–91; King's Daughters *Report* 1908, 3–4; 1909,
21–44; 1911, 12–27; 1912, 9–60; 1913, 13–41; 1914, 14–36; *Uplift* (January
1917): 6–15; *Uplift* (February 1918): 7–15; Report of Sixth Annual NCFWC Convention, box 68, Weil Papers, NCDAH; Report of Second Midwinter Meeting of
Executive Board, February 21–22, 1911, box 68, Weil Papers, NCDAH; "Judge
Clark Before Woman's Club Monday," *Raleigh News and Observer,* February 16,
1913, 12; *Public Welfare and the Community,* 23; Shaw, *History of North Carolina
Branch,* 18–22; Carraway, *Carolina Crusaders,* 27.

103. "Things Talked About," *Star of Zion,* September 10, 1896, 2; "Industrial
Reform School," *Star of Zion,* January 3, 1901, 7; "Address of Mrs. Charlotte
Hawkins Brown," Jessie Daniel Ames Papers, Duke; "A Colored Reformatory,"
The Crisis 1 (February 1911): 8; "To Legislature of State of North Carolina," February 25, 1911, box 21, General Assembly Session Records, 1911, NCDAH; "Pe-
tition for Reform School for the Colored Youth of the State" (n.d.), box 21, General
Assembly Session Records, 1911, NCDAH; "Along the Color Line," *The Crisis* 6
(August 1913): 164; "Reform School Will Open," *Star of Zion,* January 21, 1915,
4; "Minutes Woman's Section—North Carolina State Committee on Race Rela-
tions, Raleigh, Oct. 11, 1922," box 5, Social Service—Commissioner's Office—
1891–1952, NCDAH; "Training School for Negroes Now Doing Great Work,"
High Point Enterprise, August 14, 1927, reel 28, Tuskegee Clipping File; Lawrence
A. Oxley, "North Carolina's State-Wide Welfare Program for Negroes," *Survey* 57
(January 15, 1927): 514; Sanders, *Negro Child Welfare in North Carolina,* 8.

104. Quotation is from NCFWC *Yearbook* 1922–23, 108; WCTU *Minutes* 1888,
37–38; 1896, 28; 1915, 16; 1916, 40; NCFWC *Yearbook* 1914–15, 55; 1918–19,
84; 1919–20, 63–64; 1923–24, 81; 1924–25, 92, 130; 1926–27, 86, 124; 1927–
28, 26; 1929–30, 101; 1930–31, 8, 38–39, 94; "To Help Forward to a Clean Life,"
Raleigh News and Observer, February 21, 1913, 8; *Kirmess Kronikle,* February 6,

1914, 2; Thornton et al., "Hope Summerell Chamberlain," 4; *Public Welfare and the Community,* 51; Rev. N. Collin Hughes to Mrs. Clarence Johnson, February 28, 1917, NCFWC Papers; *Everywoman's Magazine* 1 (January 1917): 17; 2 (December 1917): 11; "Resolutions Passed by the Convention," *Monthly News* 1 (March 1924); "The Program," *Monthly News* 2 (December 1924); "Program of Council," "Hearings on Bills," *Monthly News* 2 (February 1925); "Summary of Council Work," *Monthly News* 2 (March 1925); "Social Hygiene," *Monthly News* 3 (May 1925); "Legislative Program," *Monthly News* 4 (December 1925); "Program of Work Adopted by Convention," *Monthly News* 4 (April 1926); "Our Work for Our Legislative Measures," *Monthly News* 5 (October 1926); "The Farm Colony for Women Offenders," *Monthly News* 5 (January 1927); "The Farm Colony for Women Offenders," *Monthly News* 5 (February 1927); "The Farm Colony," *Monthly News* 5 (March 1927); "Legislative Council Meets," *Monthly News* 7 (December 1928); "More Legislative 'Entering Wedges,'" *Monthly News* 7 (April 1929); "Resolutions Adopted Fourth Annual Convention of North Carolina League of Women Voters Durham, March 4–5 [1924]," Cowper Papers, Duke; Shivers, "Social Welfare Movement in the South," 125–26; Rebecca Ragsdale Lallier, "'A Place of Beginning Again': The North Carolina Industrial Farm Colony for Women, 1929–1947" (M.A. thesis, University of North Carolina at Chapel Hill, 1990). For a general discussion of women's prison reform see Estelle B. Freedman, *Their Sisters' Keepers: Women's Prison Reform in America, 1830–1930* (Ann Arbor: University of Michigan Press, 1981).

105. Quotation is from Kate Burr Johnson to Mary O. Cowper, March 24, 1924, Cowper Papers, Duke; *Public Welfare and the Community,* 51; NCFWC *Yearbook* 1912–13, 40; 1923–24, 74; UDC *Minutes* 1919, 70; *Everywoman's Magazine* 2 (December 1917): 11; "Resolutions Passed by the Convention"; "Hearings on Bills"; "Program of Study and Work Adopted by 1928 Convention," *Monthly News* 6 (February 1928); Freedman, *Their Sisters' Keepers,* 59–61, 151–52.

106. Quotations are from NCFWC *Yearbook* 1926–27, 86; and Oxley, "North Carolina's State-Wide Welfare Program for Negroes," 511, 514; "The North Carolina Federation of Colored Women's Clubs," *Baltimore Afro-American,* August 15, 1920, reel 12, Tuskegee Clipping File; "North Carolina Federation of Colored Women's Clubs," *Norfolk Journal and Guide,* June 25, 1921, reel 15, Tuskegee Clipping File; "To Build Home for Delinquent Girls," newspaper clipping (n.p., n.d.), Brown Papers, SL; "Women's Clubs of North Carolina to Build Girls' Home," *New York Age,* May 12, 1923, reel 19, Tuskegee Clipping File; "Inter-Racial Committee Endorses School for N.C. Delinquent Girls," *Norfolk Journal and Guide,* February 28, 1925, reel 24, Tuskegee Clipping File; Charlotte Hawkins Brown to "My dear Co-Worker," March 25, 1925, box 8, Hunter Papers, Duke; "A Call to Negro Women" (n.p.), April 14, 1926, reel 27, Tuskegee Clipping File; "Negro Women to Hold Durham Meet" (n.p.), April 14, 1926, reel 27, Tuskegee Clipping File; untitled newspaper clipping, *Smithfield (North Carolina) Herald,* February 4, 1927, reel 28, Tuskegee Clipping File; Sanders, *Negro Child Welfare in North Carolina,* 9; Constance H. Marteena, *The Lengthening Shadow of a Woman: A Biography of Charlotte Hawkins Brown* (Hicksville, N.Y.: Exposition, 1977), 77.

107. Charlotte Hawkins Brown to James B. Dudley, May 3, 1920, Brown Papers, SL; "Women's Clubs of North Carolina to Build Girls' Home"; "To Build Home for Delinquent Girls"; "North Carolina Federation Women Held 16th Annual Session," *New York Age*, May 30, 1925, reel 24, Tuskegee Clipping File; "Interrace Body Meets in N.C.," *Chicago Defender*, November 20, 1926, reel 26, Tuskegee Clipping File; untitled newspaper clipping, *Smithfield Herald*; "The Program," *Monthly News* 1 (December 1924); "First Council Bill Introduced," *Monthly News* 2 (January 23, 1925); "Reformatory Bill Reported Favorably by House Welfare Committee," *Monthly News* 2 (January 30, 1925); "Summary of Council Work"; "Legislative Program"; "Program of Work Adopted by Convention"; "Legislative Forecast," *Monthly News* 5 (September 1926); Mrs. W. T. Bost, "Our Work for Our Legislative Measures," *Monthly News* 5 (October 1926); "The Industrial School for Colored Girls," *Monthly News* 5 (January 1927); "The Industrial School for Negro Girls," *Monthly News* 5 (February 1927); "The School for Negro Girls," *Monthly News* 5 (March 1927); "Legislative Council Meets"; "Our Bills at This Writing," *Monthly News* 7 (March 1929); "More Legislative 'Entering Wedges'"; Oxley, "North Carolina's State-Wide Welfare Program for Negroes," 514; Sanford, *Negro Child Welfare in North Carolina*, 9; Edwin Mims, *The Advancing South: Stories of Progress and Reaction* (1926; reprint, Washington, N. Y.: Kennikat Press, 1969), 244–45; *Biennial Report of North Carolina State Board of Charities and Public Welfare July 1, 1942 to June 30, 1944* (Raleigh, 1944), 163.

108. Quotation is from "Negro Women to Hold Durham Meet." See also "Women's Clubs of North Carolina to Build Girls' Home."

109. *Public Welfare and the Community*, 6–8.

110. Mrs. Al Fairbrother, "Mrs. Robert R. Cotten," clipping, *Sky-land* [1914], Sallie Southall Cotten Scrapbook, vol. 3, Cotten Family Papers, SHC; Nina Holland Covington, "The Young Woman of the New South," *Everywoman's Magazine* 1 (March 1917): 3.

Chapter 4—"Handmaidens of History": Female Patriots and the Search for a Usable Past

1. DAR *Proceedings* 1903, 67; 1909, 46; 1921, 41. See also DAR *Proceedings* 1902, 21; 1904, 100; 1907, 25, 28; 1913, 23; 1915, 31, 38; 1920, 33; 1921, 41; 1929, 58; "What Our Women May Do for the Development of North Carolina. Address of Clarence Poe at Annual Meeting of North Carolina Federation of Women's Clubs, Goldsboro, May 5, 1915," Poe Papers, NCDAH; Mrs. Clarence Johnson, "To North Carolina Club Women," *Everywoman's Magazine* 2 (December 1917): 3.

2. DAR *Proceedings* 1911, 14, 28; *To the Women of America*, pamphlet, Moffitt Papers, NCDAH; Elvira Evelyna Moffitt, "A Little History of the Peace Movement in North Carolina," typescript, February 26, 1913, NCC. See also UDC *Minutes* 1899, 5; 1900, 140; 1904, 95; 1910, 61; DAR *Proceedings* 1902, 25; 1907, 25, 28; 1909, 46; 1910, 13; 1911, 28; 1913, 23; 1920, 33; 1927, 25; 1929, 40; NCFWC *Yearbook* 1924–25, 59; "General Report from Oct. 9th 1904 to June 9th 1905" [Raleigh Woman's Club], vol. 12, Moffitt Papers, SHC; Colonial Dames *Minutes*

1919, 99; Sallie Southall Cotten, "A National Training School for Girls," *North Carolina Christian Advocate,* April 14, 1897, 2; Mrs. Henry T. Kent et al., *History of the Organization and Work of the National Society Daughters of the Revolution, 1891–1930* (Concord, N.H.: Rumford Press, n.d.), 16; Linda K. Kerber, *Women of the Republic: Intellect and Ideology in Revolutionary America* (1980, reprint New York: W. W. Norton, 1986), 265–88.

3. Kerber, *Women of the Republic,* 185–232, 265–88; Aycock quoted in Marjorie Spruill Wheeler, *New Women of the New South: The Leaders of the Woman Suffrage Movement in the Southern States* (New York: Oxford University Press, 1993), 18.

4. See chapter 1 for a discussion of the origins of the patriotic societies in North Carolina.

5. Quotations are from DAR *Proceedings* 1923, 34, and 1915, 31. See also *Daughters of the Revolution,* circular, May 20, 1895, box 3, DR Papers, NCDAH; DAR *Proceedings* 1903, 75; 1911, 28, 36; "DAR. Greetings," typescript (n.d.), DeRosset Family Papers, SHC; Wallace Evan Davies, *Patriotism on Parade: The Story of Veterans' and Hereditary Organizations in America, 1783–1900* (Cambridge, Mass.: Harvard University Press, 1955), 45–49.

6. DAR *Proceedings* 1912, 24.

7. DAR *Proceedings* 1911, 36. See also DAR *Proceedings* 1902, 22; 1909, 46; 1928, 33–34; UDC *Minutes* 1899, 6; 1903, 21; 1906, 7; 1910, 6. See also DAR *Proceedings* 1902, 22; 1909, 46; newspaper clipping, *Wilmington Messenger,* February 22, 1898, Parsley Papers, SHC; *North Carolina Booklet* 6 (October 1906): 146–47; newspaper clipping, *Wilmington Morning Star,* October 14, 1909, vol. 21, Moffitt Papers, SHC; sketch of history of Johnston Pettigrew Chapter, UDC, Raleigh, N.C., vol. 20, Moffitt Papers, SHC (hereafter cited as Pettigrew Chapter History); Kent et al., *History of the DR,* 18–19, 90.

8. Charles Van Noppen, *The Supineness of the North Carolina Historical Association and the Ignorance of the North Carolina Society of Colonial Dames,* pamphlet (Greensboro, 1912), vol. 7, Waddell Papers, SHC.

9. UDC *Minutes* 1897, 12; 1898, 27–31; 1899, 4, 61–62; 1900, 110–11; 1901, 10, 29, 107; 1902, 93; 1903, 22–23; 1904, 82; 1906, 32, 57–58, 102, 119; 1909, 57; 1910, 80; 1920, 17, 40, 65; 1927, 34–37. Mrs. J. B. Whitaker to Eliza Parsley, December 11, 1898; summary of year's activities, Cape Fear Chapter, Daughters of the Confederacy, January 22, 1901; newspaper clipping, *Wilmington Messenger,* January 21, 1906, all in Parsley Papers, SHC; DR *Proceedings* 1903, 61–62; 1906, 73–74; 1912, 24, 70. "Report from Civic Department, September 8th 1905. Fall Reunion," vol. 12; "Address to Civic and Social Service Department, Raleigh Woman's Club, Spring 1906"; petitions from North Carolina Society, Daughters of the Revolution, to North Carolina General Assembly, requesting construction of a Hall of History, 1906, 1908; Minutes, fall meeting of Raleigh Woman's Club, 1908; Pettigrew Chapter History, all in Moffitt Papers, SHC. Minutes, February 27, 1906, January 5, 1907, DR Minute Book, 1906–7; Minutes, October 25, 1907; July 21, 1908; January 1, 1910, all in DR Minute Book, 1908–10; "Secretary's report for North Carolina Society Daughters of the Revolution," January 24, 1911, inserted between pp. 78 and 79 of Minute Book, 1908–10;

Minutes, January 31, 1912, February 1, 1913, April 5, 1913, June 26, 1913, January 29, 1914, June 30, 1915, all in DR Minute Book, 1910–19; "Some suggestions for Committees," Programs and Committees of Durham Civic Association, 1915–16, Southgate Papers, Duke; Julia Alexander to Lida Rodman, August 18, 1915, Rodman Papers, NCDAH; *Everywoman's Magazine*, 3 (July–August 1919): 29; 4 (April 1920): 7, 14, 15, 17, 21; DAR *Proceedings* 1920, 59–60; 1925, 54–55; 1928, 41; newspaper clipping, *Fayetteville Observer*, October 12, 1926, Smith Papers, NCDAH; Kent et al., *History of the DR*, 91–95; Gertrude S. Carraway, *Carolina Crusaders: History of the North Carolina Federation of Women's Clubs* (New Bern: Owen G. Dunn for the North Carolina Federation of Women's Clubs, 1941), 32.

10. Quotation is from NCFWC *Yearbook* 1921–22, 66. See also UDC *Minutes* 1900, 49, 111; 1902, 19–20; 1927, 34–37; 1928, 38; newspaper clipping (n.p.), May 17, 1903, vol. 20, Moffitt Papers, SHC; newspaper clipping, *Wilmington Messenger*, January 21, 1906, Parsley Papers, SHC; *Everywoman's Magazine* 4 (April 1920): 8.

11. UDC *Minutes* 1904, 95; DAR *Proceedings* 1912, 23.

12. Janet H. W. Randolph to Eliza Parsley, November 30, 1898; summary of year's activities of Cape Fear Chapter, Daughters of the Confederacy, January 22, 1901; newspaper clipping, *Wilmington Messenger*, November 21, 1903, all in Parsley Papers; UDC *Minutes* 1899, 19; 1900, 22, 66; 1901, 9, 31, 76, 107; 1902, 93; 1903, 42–43; 1904, 30; 1906, 15, 34–35, 47; 1907, 52, 67–68; 1908, 16–18, 79; 1909, 26–28; 1918, 19–20; 1920, 76; DAR *Proceedings* 1903, 61; 1912, 71; Bettie (Mrs. H. A.) London to Mrs. Ella Brodnax, February 2, 1905, Brodnax Papers, Duke; Minutes, February 27, 1906, DR Minute Book, 1906–7; Lucy Patterson to Lida Rodman, May 13, 1915; Lida Rodman to Lucy Patterson, May 21, 1915, both in Rodman Papers; DAR *Proceedings* 1917, 59–60; 1925, 55; *Everywoman's Magazine* 2 (December 1917): 28; Kent et al., *History of the DR*, 90–91, 95, 113–16, 130–40; newspaper clipping (n.p.), May 17, 1903; Pettigrew Chapter History, both in vol. 20, Moffitt Papers, SHC. The UDC's choice of subjects sometimes belied its avowed intention of promoting sectional reconciliation. One of the men they chose to honor was Henry Wirz, commander of the notorious Andersonville prison.

13. Quotation is from handwritten notes describing painting of Virginia Dare Baptism, March 1908, Moffitt Papers, SHC; DR *Proceedings* 1903, 61; 1912, 71; Minutes, February 27, 1906, DR Minute Book, 1906–7; Minutes, December 9, 1914, DR Minute Book, 1910–19; "To a Philanthropist" [1908], Moffitt Papers, SHC; Kent et al., *History of the DR*, 91, 95.

14. On the women's committee for the Jamestown Exposition see correspondence files, January–April 1907, box 3, Hunter Papers, Duke. On the attempt to form a literary and historical association see "Fair Bulletin" [1911?], scrapbook, 1908–14, box 14, Hunter Papers, Duke. On the NACW and the Frederick Douglass home see "To Keep Alive Memory of Frederick Douglass," newspaper clipping, *Chicago Defender*, August 16, 1924, reel 22; "Descendant of Fred Douglass Here," newspaper clipping, *Baltimore Afro-American*, July 11, 1928, reel 33; and "Washington Club Women Prepare for Nat'l. Body," newspaper clipping, *New York Age*, July 14, 1928, reel 33, all in Tuskegee Clipping File; Archibald H. Grimke, "Cedar

Hill or the Famous Home of Frederick Douglass," *Voice of the Negro* 2 (November 1905): 759–65, quotation on 764; Dorothy Salem, *To Better Our World: Black Women in Organized Reform, 1890–1920* (Brooklyn: Carlson, 1990), 116–17, 125, 225.

15. "Raise Money for Monuments," newspaper clipping, *Raleigh Times*, December 26, 1912, scrapbook, 1908–14, box 14, Hunter Papers, Duke; R. F. Beasley, "Aycock Statue Unveiled Before Admiring Throng," *Goldsboro News*, March 14, 1924; "Unveil Tablet to Governor Aycock" (n.p.), [1929]; J. Y. Joyner to "Teachers in North Carolina Public Schools," pamphlet [1953], all in NCC Clipping File.

16. Quotation is from DAR *Proceedings* 1911, 36. See also Fanny deBernier Whitaker to Elvira Moffitt, April 4, 1899; petition from Civic Department, Raleigh Woman's Club, to Mayor, Board of Aldermen, and President and Director, State Board of Agriculture, June 9, 1905, vol. 12; "Report from Civic Department. September 8th 1905," vol. 12; Address to Civic and Social Service Department, Raleigh Woman's Club, Spring 1906; Minutes, fall meeting, of Raleigh Woman's Club, 1908; minutes of civic department meeting, November 21 [no year given], vol. 12; all of the above in Moffitt Papers, SHC; Minutes, Executive Board of the Raleigh Woman's Club, January 17, 1906, box 1, NCFWC Papers; DR *Proceedings* 1906, 72; 1912, 69, 71; 1924, 11–12; Minutes, July 12, 1909, January 1, 1910, DR Minute Book, 1908–10; March 27, 1912, June 26, 1913, April 9, 1916, DR Minute Book, 1910–19; Gabrielle deRosset Waddell to Lida Rodman, December 4, 1915, Rodman Papers, NCDAH; Colonial Dames *Minutes* 1921, 15; DAR *Proceedings* 1917, 59–60; 1925, 54; 1926, 51; 1928, 41; Kent et al., *History of the DR*, 94–95.

17. For examples see UDC *Minutes* 1898, 29; 1899, 63; 1900, 111; 1902, 93; 1904, 31, 65, 72, 73, 83, 92, 97; 1906, 15, 47; 1908, 17, 20; 1909, 26–27; 1920, 39–41, 82; summary of year's activities of Cape Fear Chapter, Daughters of the Confederacy, January 22, 1901; invitation to unveiling of monument to Rowan County Confederate Soldiers, May 10, 1909; invitation to unveiling of statue of George Davis, April 20, 1911; manuscript history of George Davis memorial, untitled (n.d.); all in Parsley Papers, SHC; *Everywoman's Magazine* 4 (April 1920): 8; newspaper clipping, *Fayetteville Observer*, October 12, 1926, Jessica Randolph Smith Papers, NCDAH. For more information on the construction of Confederate monuments in the South during this period see Gaines M. Foster, *Ghosts of the Confederacy: Defeat, the Lost Cause, and the Emergence of the New South* (New York: Oxford University Press, 1987), 128–31.

18. Foster, *Ghosts of the Confederacy*, 116–26; Paul D. Escott, *Many Excellent People: Power and Privilege in North Carolina, 1850–1900* (Chapel Hill: University of North Carolina Press, 1985), 52–53.

19. UDC *Minutes* 1908, 10.

20. *Confederate Veteran* 3 (October 1895): 302; UDC *Minutes* 1900, 140; 1906, 7; 1907, 10; 1910, 8. See also John Thompson to Sarah Rebecca Cameron, May 19, 1909, Sarah Rebecca Cameron Papers, SHC.

21. Walter Hines Page, *The Southerner, a Novel; Being the Autobiography of Nicholas Worth* (New York: Doubleday, Page, 1909), 160; Foster, *Ghosts of the Confederacy*, 116, 180–82.

22. UDC *Minutes* 1905, 4–5.

23. Quotations are from UDC *Minutes* 1908, 10; and Lucy London Anderson, *North Carolina Women of the Confederacy* (Fayetteville: privately published, 1926), 77. See also newspaper clipping, *Wilmington Messenger,* February 22, 1898, Parsley Papers, SHC; Rebecca Cameron to UDC chapter historians, September 8, 1903, Sarah Rebecca Cameron Papers.

24. DAR *Proceedings* 1904, 98; 1907, 27; 1912, 40; 1915, 38. See also 1905, 3.

25. Quotation is from Maud Turner Finger to Mrs. John G. Brodnax, November 3, 1909, Brodnax Papers, Duke. See also UDC *Minutes* 1900, 138; 1901, 12–14; 1903, 4; 1906, 7–8; 1907, 9; 1909, 7; 1910, 8; DAR *Proceedings* 1904, 100; 1905, 5; 1912, 38.

26. Quotations are from Ida Clyde Clarke, *Uncle Sam Needs a Wife* (Philadelphia: John C. Winston, 1925), 115; DAR *Proceedings* 1912, 40; 1926, 50; Anderson, *North Carolina Women of the Confederacy,* 7. See also DAR *Proceedings* 1905, 3; UDC *Minutes* 1897, 12; 1901, 11; 1903, 22–23; Minutes, October 25, 1906, DR Minute Book, 1906–7; Minutes, May 1, 1915, January 1, 1916, DR Minute Book, 1910–16, Bloomsbury Chapter, Daughters of the Revolution, box 3, DR Papers; Elvira Evelyna Moffitt, "The N.C. Society D.R. and Its Objects," *North Carolina Booklet* 6 (October 1906): 148.

27. *To the Women of America.*

28. Quotations are from "The Memorial Virginia Dare Desk," typescript (n.d.); and Elizabeth Henderson Cotten to Dr. Christopher Crittenden, April 17, 1950, both in Cotten Family Papers, SHC. See also "Virginia Dare Desk," *Carolina Comments* 1 (March 1953); "Additional Facts Regarding the Virginia Dare Desk," *Carolina Comments* 2 (July 1953).

29. Quotations are from *To the Women of America* and newspaper clipping, *Atlanta Constitution,* November 3, 1895, Sallie Southall Cotten Scrapbook, vol. 1. See also Sallie Southall Cotten, "A National Training School for Women, *North Carolina Christian Advocate,* April 14, 1897, 2; newspaper clipping, *Omaha World-Herald* [October 1898], Sallie Southall Cotten Scrapbook, vol. 2, Cotten Family Papers, SHC; Elvira Moffitt to "Mrs. Sprunt," March 22, 1908, Moffitt Papers, SHC; DR *Proceedings* 1907, 5; William S. Powell, *Paradise Preserved* (Chapel Hill: University of North Carolina Press, 1965), 55–57. For more on organized women's work for domestic education see chapter 3.

30. *To the Women of America.*

31. Sallie Southall Cotten, *The White Doe: The Fate of Virginia Dare* (Philadelphia: J. B. Lippincott, 1901); Powell, *Paradise Preserved,* 62. For more on Cotten see chapter 1.

32. Sallie Southall Cotten to Elvira Moffitt, March 24, 1894, Moffitt Papers, SHC. On the popular fascination with parliamentary procedure in the late 1800s see Don H. Doyle, "Rules of Order: Henry Martyn Robert and the Popularization of American Parliamentary Law," *American Quarterly* 32 (Spring 1980): 3–18.

33. Cotten to Moffitt, March 24, 1894.

34. Quotations are from Moffitt, "The N.C. Society D.R.," 149; and Fanny deBernier Whitaker to Elvira Evelyna Moffitt, December 12, 1903, Moffitt Papers, SHC. See also Eunice B. Haywood to Fanny deBerniere Whitaker, March

20, 1901, Moffitt Papers, SHC; newspaper clipping (n.p.) January 6, 1903, vol. 10, Moffitt Papers, SHC; Helen DeBerniere Wills, "Address to the D.A.R.," October 25, 1906, DR Minute Book, 1906–7; DR *Proceedings* 1903, 62; 1907, 61–62; DAR *Proceedings* 1907, 27; Kent et al., *History of the DR,* 93. On the Edenton Tea Party see Kerber, *Women of the Republic,* 41; and Don Higginbotham, "Decision for Revolution," in *The North Carolina Experience: An Interpretive and Documentary History,* ed. Lindley S. Butler and Alan D. Watson (Chapel Hill: University of North Carolina Press, 1984), 128, 136–37. Historians disagree on the exact number of women who signed the boycott agreement. See F. S. Iredell to Fanny deBernier Whitaker, October 10, 1905; "Letter No. 1 from Dr. Dillard," [1905]; and "From Dr. Dillard—No. 2," February 6, 1906, all in Moffitt Papers, SHC.

35. Quotations are from Whitaker to Moffitt, December 12, 1903; and Kent et al., *History of the DR,* 93. See also DR *Proceedings* 1903, 62; 1907, 61–62; 1909, 59; "D.A.R. in Henderson 120th Anniversary Edenton Tea Party," newspaper clipping (n.p.), October 26, 1906, Minutes, October 25, 1906, February 27, 1907, all in DR Minute Book, 1906–7; "Summary of the Minutes of the Penelope Barker Chapter of the Daughters of the Revolution, May 23, 1907," DR Minute Book, 1908; DAR *Proceedings* 1907, 27; 1911, 25; Moffitt, "N.C. Society D.R.," 147–49; Adeline Cleveland Blair to Lida Rodman, March 9, 1915, Rodman Papers, NCDAH; Wills, "Address to the D.A.R."

36. Quotation is from UDC *Minutes* 1906, 7–8. See also "Monument to Southern Women," *Confederate Veteran* 3 (January 1895): 22; Foster, *Ghosts of the Confederacy,* 175.

37. Quotation is from UDC *Minutes* 1906, 123–24. See also UDC *Minutes* 1899, 19; Foster, *Ghosts of the Confederacy,* 175.

38. Quotations are from Foster, *Ghosts of the Confederacy,* 177; UDC *Minutes* 1911, 15; and Mrs. Geo. H. Tichenor, "To the Editor of the Times-Democrat," May 10, 1911, broadside, Sarah Rebecca Cameron Papers, SHC. See also "Monument to Women of Arkansas," *Confederate Veteran* 21 (June 1913): 28.

39. Quotation is from UDC *Minutes* 1911, 15. See also UDC *Minutes* 1906, 123–24; 1907, 52; 1910, 58–59; 1920, 77; Escott, *Many Excellent People,* 52–58. I am grateful to Professor Alan Downs for the statistics on Confederate dead.

40. Quotation is from "Monument to North Carolina Women," *Confederate Veteran* 22 (August 1914): 340. See also Minutes, February 27, 1912, July 24, 1912, February 3, 1914, Horne Committee of the Memorial to North Carolina Women of the Confederacy, NCDAH; UDC *Minutes* 1912, 14–15; "North Carolina Woman's Monument," *Confederate Veteran* 20 (September 1912): 412; "Addresses at the Unveiling of the Monument to North Carolina Women of the Confederacy," NCC. The committee was chaired by J. A. Long and included J. Bryan Grimes, Henry A. London, W. H. S. Burgwyn, and R. D. W. Connor.

41. Minutes, July 24, 1912, Horne Committee Papers, NCDAH.

42. Quotations are from Horne Committee Minutes, July 24, 1912; and DAR *Proceedings* 1923, 33. See also DAR *Proceedings* 1903, 67–68; 1904, 103; 1907, 25; 1911, 36; 1912, 24; 1921, 41; 1924, 26–27; 1927, 25; 1929, 41, 58; UDC *Minutes* 1901, 77; 1920, 64; 1927, 34–37; 1929, 43; NCFWC *Yearbook* 1910–11, 39.

43. Newspaper clipping, *Raleigh News and Observer,* October 16, 1903, vol. 20, Moffitt Papers, SHC; UDC *Minutes* 1908, 8. See also UDC *Minutes* 1899, 4; 1900, 113, 140; 1907, 12, 68; 1910, 8, 11; 1929, 43; Mrs. James Kenan to Lida Rodman, March 21, 1916, Rodman Papers, NCDAH.

44. The exact figure she gave was 112,487. The number is much higher than that reported for either of the two following years (1928: 47,888; 1929: 38,000). See UDC *Minutes* 1927, 35; 1928, 36; 1929, 43. See also UDC *Minutes* 1898, 27; 1900, 7, 113; 1901, 77; 1907, 53; 1908, 8, 79–80; 1909, 24; 1920, 64.

45. Helen DeBerniere Wills and Mrs. Fred A. Olds to J. Y. Joyner [1904], vol. 20, Moffitt Papers, SHC; Lucy Closs Parker to Mrs. John G. Brodnax, February 7, 1907, Brodnax Papers, Duke.

46. Helen DeBerniere Wills and Mrs. Fred A. Olds to J. Y. Joyner [1904]; J. Y. Joyner to Mrs. Helen DeBerniere Wills, March 3, 1904, both in vol. 20, Moffitt Papers, SHC; UDC *Minutes* 1901, 45; 1904, 45; 1906, 31–34; 1920, 19, 40–42; 1922, 17, 47–48. See also Davies, *Patriotism on Parade,* 235–36.

47. UDC *Minutes* 1920, 19, 40–42, quotation on 42.

48. See Frances FitzGerald, *America Revised: History Schoolbooks in the Twentieth Century* (Boston: Little, Brown, 1979); and Foster, *Ghosts of the Confederacy,* 180–91.

49. Quotation is from Minutes, October 1908, DR Minute Book 1908, 67. See also Elvira E. Moffitt, "A Little History of the Peace Movement in North Carolina," typescript, February 26, 1913, NCC; Minutes, June 28, 1907, DR Minute Book 1906–7; WCTU *Minutes* 1908, 28; 1913, 27; DR *Proceedings* 1909, 59; Cora Rogers Bleakley to Mary Hilliard Hinton, August 12, 1914, box 1, DR Papers; Minutes, December 9, 1914, DR Minute Book, 117.

50. Katie R. Beckwith to Mattie (Southgate) Jones, November 23, 1917, Southgate Papers, Duke.

51. Laura Holmes Reilley, Chairman, Woman's Committee, North Carolina Council of National Defense, *First Annual Report June 1917–July 1918* (Charlotte: Observer Printing House, 1918), box 56, Weil Papers, NCDAH.

52. For the names of the members of the North Carolina Woman's Committee see *Everywoman's Magazine* 1 (June–July 1917): 45–46; Reilley, *First Annual Report;* and William J. Breen, "Southern Women in the War: The North Carolina Woman's Committee, 1917–1919," *North Carolina Historical Review* 55 (1978): 251–83. Several of these women were members of more than one voluntary association. Gertrude Weil, for example, held office in the Equal Suffrage Association as well as the NCFWC, and Lucy Robertson and Fanny Bickett were active in the WCTU. The names of the county chairmen are included on a list attached to a letter dated March 16, 1917, in the Connor Papers, SHC.

53. Reilley, *First Annual Report,* 5; William J. Breen, "Black Women and the Great War: Mobilization and Reform in the South," *Journal of Southern History* 44 (August 1978): 421–40. See also "Southern White Women's Interest in the South's Problems," *Norfolk (Virginia) Journal and Guide,* March 27, 1919, reel 10, Tuskegee Clipping File.

54. Quotations are from *Proceedings of the Fourth Annual Convention of the Equal Suffrage Association of North Carolina,* 1917, 6 (hereafter cited as ESA *Proceedings,* with appropriate year); and "Women Will Put Ban on Goods of Ger-

man Make," *Raleigh News and Observer,* May 29, 1918; *Everywoman's Magazine* 2 (December 1917): 23, 25; 3 (May 1919): 6–7; 3 (July–August 1919): 27; DAR *Proceedings* 1917, 45; NCFWC *Yearbook* 1918–19, 40, 62–63; WCTU *Minutes* 1917, 36; 1918, 31; Reilley, *First Annual Report,* 4; "Report of Work Done by Committees on Food Conservation" [March 1918?]; Lida Rodman to Mrs. Eugene Reilley, April 30, 1918, both in Rodman Papers, NCDAH; "Negroes Adopt Strong Resolutions on Emancipation Day," *Raleigh Independent,* January 11, 1919, Tuskegee Clipping File; Bertha Hampton Miller, "Blacks in Winston-Salem, North Carolina, 1895–1902: Community Development in an Era of Paternalism" (Ph.D. diss., Duke University, 1981), 193.

55. DAR *Proceedings* 1917, 46.

56. Quotations are from Reilley, *First Annual Report,* 4, 8. See also WCTU *Minutes,* 1917, 36; 1918, 29; *Everywoman's Magazine* 1 (June–July 1917): 17.

57. Quotations are from Reilley, *First Annual Report,* 4; and NCFWC *Yearbook* 1918–19, 67. See also NCFWC *Yearbook* 1917–18, 79; 1919–20, 44; DAR *Proceedings* 1917, 16–18, 56–58, 60; 1919 (18th convention), 30–33. Because of the influenza epidemic in the fall of 1918 the DAR postponed its annual convention; thus both the eighteenth and nineteenth conventions were held in 1919. UDC *Minutes* 1918, 17, 52–99; WCTU *Minutes* 1918, 29–31; Minutes, October 26, November 24, 1917, Minute Book, Raleigh Branch, AAUW, AAUW Papers, NCDAH; *Everywoman's Magazine* 2 (December 1917): 5, 28; 3 (May 1919): 6; 3 (July–August 1919): 11–14, 27; Reilley, *First Annual Report,* 6; Lida Rodman to Mrs. Eugene Reilley, April 30, 1918, Rodman Papers, NCDAH; "Negroes Adopt Strong Resolutions on Emancipation Day," *Raleigh Independent,* January 11, 1919, reel 10, Tuskegee Clipping File; Miller, "Blacks in Winston-Salem," 191–92; Carrie B. Wilson, *History of the North Carolina State Division American Association of University Women, 1927–47* (Greensboro: Riser, 1948), 54; Wood, *History of Colonial Dames,* 22, 29, 48; Carraway, *Carolina Crusaders,* 49.

58. Mrs. Ernest Clark to Lida Rodman, October 5, 1918, Rodman Papers, NCDAH.

59. Mamie Brown Latham to Lida Rodman, October 16, 1918, Rodman Papers, NCDAH; Lida Rodman to Mrs. Eugene Reilley, April 30, 1918, Rodman Papers, NCDAH; "Women Will Put Ban on Goods of German Make," *Raleigh News and Observer,* May 29, 1918, 1; NCFWC *Yearbook* 1918–19, 17. See also NCFWC *Yearbook* 1918–19, 67; DAR *Proceedings* 1917, 16–17; 1919 (18th convention), 31, 33; UDC *Minutes* 1918, 17, 57; Raleigh Woman's Club, *Yearbook* 1918–19, 20; Minutes, October 26, 1917, Minute Book, Raleigh Branch, AAUW, AAUW Papers, NCDAH; "Negroes Adopt Strong Resolutions"; Carraway, *Carolina Crusaders,* 49.

60. Latham to Rodman, October 16, 1918.

Chapter 5—"The Many Public Duties": Woman Suffrage and White Supremacy

1. W. T. Bost, "Repudiation of Suffrage Pledges by Both Parties," *Greensboro Daily News,* August 9, 1920. See also A. Elizabeth Taylor, "The Woman Suffrage Movement in North Carolina," *North Carolina Historical Review* 38 (January 1961):

47–48; and *The History of Woman Suffrage,* vol. 6, ed. Ida Husted Harper (New York: National American Woman Suffrage Association, 1922), 500.

2.   On the political campaigns of the 1890s see chapter 1. See also Marjorie Spruill Wheeler, *New Women of the New South: The Leaders of the Woman Suffrage Movement in the Southern States* (New York: Oxford University Press, 1993), 18–19, 112–25; and Edward L. Ayres, *Promise of the New South: Life After Reconstruction* (New York: Oxford University Press, 1992), 317.

3.   Quotation is from "Old Fort Meeting," *Raleigh News and Observer,* August 22, 1899. See also Donald G. Mathews and Jane Sherron De Hart, *Sex, Gender, and the Politics of ERA* (New York: Oxford University Press, 1990), 6–8.

4.   UDC *Minutes* 1899, 5; DAR *Proceedings* 1903, 67; "Read at Garner School April 1903 by Mrs. E. E. Moffitt," Moffitt Papers, SHC; newspaper clipping, *Raleigh News and Observer,* October 15, 1904, vol. 12, Moffitt Papers, SHC.

5.   "About People You Know," *Raleigh Gazette,* November 21, 1896; "A Banquet Given Complimentary to Hon. James H. Young," *Raleigh Gazette,* December 5, 1896; "A Reception and Banquet Given on Friday Evening of Last Week," *Raleigh Gazette,* February 6, 1897; Anna Julia Cooper, *A Voice from the South* (Xenia, Ohio: Aldine, 1892), 139.

6.   "To Make Raleigh Beautiful: Progressive Women Organize for Aid in Improving Raleigh," newspaper clipping, *Raleigh News and Observer,* November 13, 1904; untitled address about city improvement department, Raleigh Woman's Club (n.d); speech, October 9, 1904; all in vol. 12, Moffitt Papers, SHC. See also Anne Firor Scott, *Natural Allies: Women's Voluntary Associations in America* (Urbana: University of Illinois Press, 1992).

7.   Minutes, Guilford Battle Chapter DAR, Greensboro, N.C., June 17, 1902, John G. Brodnax Papers, Duke. If members of the Guilford Battle chapter pursued their inquiry, they discovered that while the General Federation of Women's Clubs was for whites only, patriotic societies such as theirs were ineligible to affiliate.

8.   Hollinger F. Barnard, ed., *Outside the Magic Circle: The Autobiography of Virginia Foster Durr* (New York: Simon and Schuster, Touchstone, 1987); Mrs. Al Fairbrother, "About the Women's Clubs of North Carolina," clipping (n.p.), [1910], Sallie Southall Cotten Scrapbook, vol. 3, Cotten Family Papers, SHC. A few years later, Mrs. Fairbrother changed her mind and became an active proponent of woman suffrage.

9.   Elizabeth Cady Stanton, Susan B. Anthony, Matilda Joslyn Gage, *History of Woman Suffrage,* vol. 3 (Rochester: Susan B. Anthony, 1886), 825; Susan B. Anthony and Ida Husted Harper, *History of Woman Suffrage,* vol. 4 (Rochester: Susan B. Anthony, 1902), 874; *North Carolina White Ribbon* 12 (August 1905), 2; WCTU *Minutes* 1910, 27; James L. Leloudis II, "School Reform in the New South: The Woman's Association for the Betterment of Public School Houses in North Carolina, 1902–1919," *Journal of American History* 69 (1983): 893–94; Ada V. Womble, "Women Can Now Serve on the School Boards," newspaper clipping (n.p.), [1913], Sallie Southall Cotten Scrapbook, vol. 3, Cotten Family Papers, SHC; newspaper clipping, *Wilmington Morning Star,* May 14, 1911, Sallie Southall Cotten scrapbook, vol. 3, Cotten Family Papers, SHC; Zebulon Judd, "Judd's Rea-

sons for Naming Women," *Raleigh News and Observer,* February 28, 1913, 10. Cotten's other major goal was establishing an endowment fund for the federation.

10. Sallie S. Cotten, "A Line a Day Book. A Condensed, Comparative Record for Five Years, 1908–1912," May 5, 1912, NCC.

11. For descriptions and analyses of this form of feminine power see "Feminine Versus Feminist. By the Author of 'An Englishwoman's Home,'" *Living Age,* 11th series, 54 (1912): 587–92; Estelle Freedman, "Separatism as Strategy: Female Institution Building and American Feminism, 1870–1930," *Feminist Studies* 5 (Fall 1979): 512–29; Jean Bethke Elshtain, *Power Trips and Other Journeys: Essays in Feminism and Civic Discourse* (Madison: University of Wisconsin Press, 1990), 24–41.

12. Sallie Southall Cotten, *History of the North Carolina Federation of Women's Clubs, 1901–1925* (Raleigh: Edwards and Broughton, 1925), 50; Cotten to Walter Clark, November 19, 1912, *The Papers of Walter Clark,* vol. 2, ed. Aubrey Lee Brooks and Hugh Talmage Lefler (Chapel Hill: University of North Carolina Press, 1950), 180–81; "Aycock Memorial As Women's Clubs Would Arrange It," newspaper clipping, *Raleigh News and Observer,* May 9, 1912, Sallie Southall Cotten Scrapbook, vol. 3, Cotten Family Papers, SHC. Cotten's letter to Clark demonstrated her political acumen. She was aware of the obstacles the bill would face ("Naturally it would involve the color question," she wrote), but she adopted the deferential tone of a helpless, naive woman: "If I am impertinent or intrusive, pardon me, and I withdraw my questions, but believing you to be woman's real friend I may become too bold. If you are busy, reply at your leisure."

13. "Under the Dome," *Raleigh News and Observer,* January 26, 1913, 15; Cotten to Clark, November 19, 1912. At the same time that he introduced this bill, Bryant proposed two other bills of interest to women, one to give married women control over their own wages and the right to sue for damages and wages, and another to eliminate private examinations of married women in property transactions.

14. "Judd's Reasons for Naming Women," *Raleigh News and Observer,* February 28, 1913, 10.

15. "Judd's Reasons"; "Women To Be on School Boards," *Raleigh News and Observer,* February 20, 1913; "School Needs the Women," *Raleigh News and Observer,* February 8, 1913, 4; Cotten to Clark, November 19, 1912; Sallie Southall Cotten to Elvira Moffitt, February 13, 1913, Moffitt Papers, SHC; untitled editorial, *Raleigh News and Observer,* February 18, 1913, 4. Articles endorsing the Bryant bill and praising women for their contributions to education appeared frequently in the *Raleigh News and Observer* during the campaign. See "A Plea for a Constitutional Convention," January 5, 1913, 7; "Women Help Progress," January 18, 1913, 2; untitled editorial, February 9, 1913, 4; "We Need the Women," February 20, 1913, 4; "Wanted: A Few Sensible Women," February 27, 1913, 4; untitled editorial, March 7, 1913, 8; "Need of Women's Influence," March 11, 1913, 4.

16. "Judd's Reasons"; Sallie Southall Cotten to Bruce Cotten, March 30, 1913, Cotten Family Papers, SHC; Cotten, *History of the NCFWC,* 61; "Women To Be on School Boards," *Raleigh News and Observer,* February 20, 1913, 5. See also Ada V. Womble, "Women Can Now Serve on School Boards," newspaper clipping

(n.p.), March 16, 1913, box 69, Weil Papers, NCDAH. Only one of the petitions survives—"Petition of the Friday Afternoon Book Club of Greensboro relative to the service of women on school boards," General Assembly Session Records, 1913, box 22. However, the *Raleigh News and Observer* frequently mentioned the presentation of petitions in its daily accounts of legislative proceedings. For examples see "Featureless but Busy Day in Both Houses," January 28, 1913, 1; "Justice Freight Resolution Passed by Senate," January 30, 1913, 1; "Senate Passes Resolution for an Extra Session," January 31, 1913, 3; "House Has Passed Bills for Twenty Judicial Districts," February 2, 1913, 1; "Senate Defers Action on Bill For 20 Judges," February 4, 1913, 8; "Little Talk, Much Work Monday in the Legislature," February 11, 1913, 3; "Primary Bill Is Killed on Second Reading in House," February 21, 1913, 3.

17.   Cotten to Moffitt, February 13, 1913; "Four Hundred in Social Service First Congress," *Raleigh News and Observer,* February 13, 1913, 5.

18.   Sallie Southall Cotten to Bruce Cotten, March 30, 1913, Cotten Family Papers, SHC; "Women to Be on School Boards" and "Million Dollar Bond Issue Passed by Senate," *Raleigh News and Observer,* March 6, 1913, 1; "Senate Votes for Women to Serve on School Boards," *Raleigh News and Observer,* March 11, 1913, 1; "Justice Corrupt Practices Act Is Passed by Senate," *Raleigh News and Observer,* March 12, 1913, 1; Cotten, *History of the NCFWC,* 61–62.

19.   Womble, "Women Can Now Serve on School Boards." See also "Senate Votes for Women to Serve on School Boards," *Raleigh News and Observer,* March 11, 1913, 1; "Justice Corrupt Practices Act Passed in Senate," *Raleigh News and Observer,* March 12, 1913, 1, 3.

20.   Sallie Cotten to Bruce Cotten, March 30, 1913; "Under the Dome," *Raleigh News and Observer,* January 26, 1913, 15; "Featureless but Busy Day"; "Justice Freight Resolution Passed by Senate"; "House Has Passed Bill for Twenty Judicial Districts"; "House in Night Session Passes Score of Bills," *Raleigh News and Observer,* February 8, 1913, 5. For more information on the 1913 legislative session see Joseph F. Steelman, "The Progressive Era in North Carolina, 1884–1917" (Ph.D. diss., University of North Carolina, 1955), chapter 9.

21.   See chapter 2 for a discussion of age of consent laws and divorce reform. On the bill to eliminate the "privy examination" see "Featureless but Busy Day"; "House in Night Session"; "Under the Dome," *Raleigh News and Observer,* January 26, 1913, 15; and "Under the Dome," February 5, 1913, 4. Married women in North Carolina had been given control over their real and personal property in 1868. A married woman's property could not be seized by her husband's creditors, and she could bequeath her property to whomever she chose. In order to sell her property, however, a married woman had to obtain her husband's written consent and undergo a private examination. See Albert Coates, *By Her Own Bootstraps: A Saga of Women in North Carolina* (n.p., 1975), 11–14. On the municipal suffrage bill and woman suffrage referendum see "Woman Suffrage Bill Introduced," *Raleigh News and Observer,* January 18, 1913, 3; "Revenue Bill Is Passed by Senate in Night Session," *Raleigh News and Observer,* March 8, 1913, 2; and Steelman, "Progressive Era," chapter 9.

22. The gentlemen of the General Assembly apparently harbored an inordinate fear of "petticoat government." Joseph Steelman reported that when the Senate was considering a resolution to invite William Jennings Bryan, Robert LaFollette, and Woodrow Wilson to address a joint session, one senator predicted that "if it passed a 'calvacade' of women would appear before the legislature to tell its members how to run the state." Steelman, "Progressive Era," 365.

23. Quotations are from Walter Clark to E. Yates Webb, March 19, 1914, *Papers of Walter Clark,* vol. 2, 240–41. See also Steelman, "Progressive Era," 337; Clark "To Various Women Leaders," *Papers of Walter Clark,* vol. 2, 179–80; Cotten to Clark, November 19, 1912; Clark to Henry Watterson, April 12, 1919, *Papers of Walter Clark,* vol. 2, 395–96; Wheeler, *New Women of the New South,* 12, 22.

24. "Raleigh Women Not in Politics," *Raleigh News and Observer,* February 19, 1913, 4; Walter Clark to Kate Gordon, July 29, 1913, *Papers of Walter Clark,* vol. 2, 208. See also *Raleigh News and Observer,* January 5, 1913, 7; January 19, 1913, 4. Later that year Clark told the annual NCFWC convention, "It is quite certain that the majority of women in North Carolina do not yet desire what is known as equal suffrage." Clark attempted to change that. See *The Legal Status of Women in North Carolina. Paper Presented to the State Federation of Women's Clubs by Walter Clark, Jr., and J. Melville Broughton, Jr.* (Raleigh: 1914), 12–23, pamphlet, box 69, Weil Papers, NCDAH.

25. Cotten to Clark, November 19, 1912; William M. Wilson to Walter Clark, October 24, 1913, *Papers of Walter Clark,* vol. 2, 225; Steelman, "Progressive Era," 472–74; *History of Woman Suffrage,* vol. 6, 490–91. The other male advisors were industrialist Julian S. Carr, University of North Carolina professor Archibald Henderson, UNC president Edward Kidder Graham, and *Charlotte Observer* editor Wade Hampton Harris.

26. Quotations are from *History of Woman Suffrage,* vol. 6, 491; and *Proceedings of the Second Annual Convention of the Equal Suffrage Association of North Carolina* (Henderson: Jones-Stone, 1916), 11. See also Mrs. Archibald Henderson, "Suffrage in North Carolina," in Ida Clyde Clarke, *Suffrage in the Southern States* (n.p., [1914?]), 62; Eliza Skinner McGehee, "Woman's Place Is in the Home," *Sky-land Magazine* 1 (September 1913): 640–41; and "North Carolina Suffragists to Meet at Greensboro in 1916," newspaper clipping, *Asheville Citizen,* October 30, 1915, clippings, Cowper Papers, Duke. On the Congressional Union in North Carolina and the South see Taylor, "Woman Suffrage Movement," 175–76; Sidney R. Bland, "Mad Women of the Cause: The National Woman's Party in the South," *Furman Studies* 26 (December 1980): 82–91; Christine A. Lundarini, *From Equal Suffrage to Equal Rights: Alice Paul and the National Woman's Party, 1910–1928* (New York: New York University Press, 1986); and Wheeler, *New Women of the New South,* 76–78; 170–71.

27. DAR *Proceedings* 1914, 20; Edwin Yates Webb to Mrs. R. S. Reinhardt, January 25, 1915, Webb Papers, SHC; Mrs. E. B. Cline to "Mrs. Palmer" [Miss Mary Palmer], October 14, 1914, box 55, Rodman Papers, NCDAH. On the origins and development of antisuffrage ideology in the South and elsewhere see Jane Jerome Camhi, "Women Against Women: American Antisuffragism, 1880–

1920" (Ph.D. diss., Tufts University, 1973); Elna C. Green, "Those Opposed: Southern Antisuffragism, 1890–1920" (Ph.D. diss., Tulane University, 1992); Aileen S. Kraditor, *The Ideas of the Woman Suffrage Movement, 1890–1920* (1965, New York: W. W. Norton, 1981), 14–42, 163–218; Susan E. Marshall, "In Defense of Separate Spheres: Class and Status Politics in the Antisuffrage Movement," *Social Forces* 65 (December 1986): 327–51; Mathews and De Hart, *Sex, Gender,* 8–27; Anastatia Sims, "Beyond the Ballot: The Radical Vision of the Antisuffragists," in *VOTES FOR WOMEN! The Woman Suffrage Movement in Tennessee, The South, and The Nation,* ed. Marjorie Spruill Wheeler (Knoxville: University of Tennessee Press, 1995), 105–28; Manuela Thurner, "'Better Citizens Without the Ballot': American Antisuffrage Women and Their Rationale in the Progressive Era," *Journal of Women's History* 5 (Spring 1993): 33–60; Wheeler, *New Women of the New South,* chapter 1.

28. Mrs. E. B. Cline to "Mrs. Palmer," October 14, 1914; Lida Rodman to Barbara Henderson, October 6, 1915, Rodman Papers, NCDAH; newspaper clipping, *Goldsboro Argus News,* December 6, 1964, box 96, Weil Papers, NCDAH. See also Mrs. J. S. Cuningham, "The Spirit of Democracy Makes One Happy," *Everywoman's Magazine* 3 (July–August 1919): 10.

29. J. G. de Roulhac Hamilton, "A Plea for a Constitutional Convention, Part IV," *Raleigh News and Observer,* January 5, 1913, 7; "Do They Want It?" *Raleigh News and Observer,* January 19, 1913, 4.

30. Quotations are from Jessie Vanpel Bicknell to "My dear Miss Palmer" [Mary Palmer, Charlotte, N.C.], March 12, 1914; and Lida Rodman to Barbara Henderson, May 8, 1915, both in box 55, Rodman Papers, NCDAH. See also McGehee, "Woman's Place Is in the Home," 638; ESA *Proceedings* 1915, 4–5; Lida Rodman to Barbara Henderson, January 21, 1915; and J. T. Taylor to Lida Rodman, November 1, 1915, both in box 55, Rodman Papers, NCDAH.

31. ESA *Proceedings* 1915, 8. See also *History of Woman Suffrage,* vol. 6, 491–92; Taylor, "Woman Suffrage Movement," 55.

32. F. P. Hobgood introduced the amendment in the Senate; Gallatin Roberts presented it in the House. ESA *Proceedings* 1915, 8, 17, 6.

33. "Addresses Delivered Yesterday by Equal Suffrage Leaders," *Raleigh News and Observer,* February 3, 1915; ESA *Proceedings* 1915, 9; *History of Woman Suffrage,* vol. 6, 491–92; Taylor, "Woman Suffrage Movement," 56. Lingle was elected NCFWC president in May 1915.

34. "Addresses Delivered Yesterday."

35. "Addresses Delivered Yesterday."

36. "Addresses Delivered Yesterday."

37. "Addresses Delivered Yesterday."

38. Mathews and DeHart, *Sex, Gender,* 9; Wheeler, *New Women of the New South,* 90–99; William A. Link, *The Paradox of Southern Progressivism, 1880–1930* (Chapel Hill: University of North Carolina Press, 1992) 193; and LeeAnn Whites, "Rebecca Latimer Felton and the Problem of 'Protection' in the New South," in *Visible Women: New Essays on American Activism,* ed. Nancy A. Hewitt and Suzanne Lebsock (Urbana: University of Illinois Press, 1993), 41–61.

39. "Addresses Delivered Yesterday."

40. Quotations are from Walter Clark to Lalyce Duffy Buford, February 6, 1915, *Papers of Walter Clark*, vol. 2, 271; and ESA *Proceedings* 1915, 9. See also *History of Woman Suffrage*, vol. 6, 500; Taylor, "Woman Suffrage Movement," 57–59; Steelman, "Progressive Era," 474–75.

41. Quotations are from ESA *Proceedings* 1919, 6; and Lindsay C. Warren, "Observations on the Suffrage Amendment (19th Amendment) in N.C., 1919–1920," folder 127, Warren Papers, SHC. See also Steelman, "Progressive Era," 475–77; Taylor, "Woman Suffrage Movement," 173–81; *History of Woman Suffrage*, vol. 6, 500.

42. Quotations are from "A Gain for Suffrage," *Raleigh News and Observer*, May 31, 1918; and WCTU *Minutes* 1919, 39. See also W. T. Bost, "Suffrage Camps Have Appeared in Raleigh," newspaper clipping [*Greensboro Daily News*, August 1920], box 56, Weil Papers, NCDAH.

43. "A Gain for Suffrage"; *History of Woman Suffrage*, vol. 6, 493; Cotten, *History of the NCFWC*, 127.

44. "A Gain for Suffrage"; Margaret C. Robinson, "Woman Suffrage: A Menace to Social Reform" (n.p.: Women's Anti-Suffrage Association of Massachusetts, n.d.; reprinted from *Cambridge Chronicle*, October 16, 1915), box 1, folder 3, Pearson Papers, TSLA. See also Freedman, "Separatism as Strategy"; Paula Baker, "The Domestication of Politics: Women and American Political Society, 1780–1920," *American Historical Review* 89 (June 1984), 620–47; Ellen DuBois, "The Radicalism of the Woman Suffrage Movement: Notes Toward the Reconstruction of Nineteenth Century Feminism," *Feminist Studies* 3 (Fall 1975): 63–71.

45. Katie R. Beckwith to Mattie (Southgate) Jones, November 23, 1917, Southgate Papers, Duke; NCFWC *Yearbook* 1918–19, 37, 44–45; "Women's Clubs Ask for Suffrage in Final Session," *Raleigh News and Observer*, May 31, 1918, 1; ESA *Proceedings* 1918, 9. See also "A Gain for Suffrage"; Cotten, *History of the NCFWC*, 127; and Wheeler, *New Women of the New South*, 96–99.

46. "Women's Clubs Ask for Suffrage in Final Session."

47. Hallett S. Ward to Walter Clark, September 27, 1917, *Papers of Walter Clark*, vol. 2, 359; E. C. Branson to B. G. Crisp, December 5, 1919, folder 19, Branson Papers, SHC. See also Gertrude Weil to Walter Clark, April 12, 1919, *Papers of Walter Clark*, vol. 2, 395.

48. Wheeler, *New Women of the New South*, 29–30; Eleanor Flexner, *Century of Struggle: The Women's Rights Movement in the United States* (1959, New York: Atheneum, 1974), 306–20; *History of Woman Suffrage*, vol. 6, 493; Carrie Chapman Catt and Nettie Rogers Shuler, *Woman Suffrage and Politics: The Inner Story of the Suffrage Movement* (1923, Seattle: University of Washington Press, 1969), 422.

49. *History of Woman Suffrage*, vol. 6, 493–95; Harriet Morehead Berry to Clara B. Byrd, April 9, 1920, Berry Papers, SHC; Pamela Dean, "Learning to be New Women: Campus Culture at North Carolina Normal and Industrial College," *North Carolina Historical Review* 68 (July 1991): 286–306; ESA *Proceedings* 1918, 7; Catt and Shuler, *Woman Suffrage and Politics*, 476–77; "Raleigh

Suffragists Plan for Legislature," newspaper clipping (n.p.), [1920], vol. 2, Riddick Papers, SHC. See also A. L. Brooks to Walter Clark, November 17, 1916, *Papers of Walter Clark,* vol. 2, 321; and Mathews and DeHart, *Sex, Gender,* 12.

50.   *History of Woman Suffrage,* vol. 6, 493; ESA *Proceedings* 1918, 8; Wheeler, *New Women of the New South,* 30–31; Glenda Elizabeth Gilmore, "Gender and Jim Crow: Black Women and the Politics of White Supremacy in North Carolina, 1896–1920" (Ph.D. diss., University of North Caroina, 1992), 432–33; Mathews and DeHart, *Sex, Gender,* 11–12; David Morgan, *Suffragists and Democrats: The Politics of Woman Suffrage in America* (East Lansing: Michigan State University Press, 1972), 176.

51.   Quotations are from Warren, "Observations on the Suffrage Amendment"; Catt and Shuler, *Woman Suffrage and Politics,* 477; Walter Clark to Carrie Chapman Catt, April 9, 1920, *Papers of Walter Clark,* vol. 2, 409; *History of Woman Suffrage,* vol. 6, 495–96; Mathews and DeHart, *Sex, Gender,* 12–14.

52.   Quotations are from Warren, "Observations on the Suffrage Amendment"; *History of Woman Suffrage,* vol. 6, 496; and *Suffragist* 8 (August 1920): 179. Catt and Shuler, *Woman Suffrage and Politics,* 477–78; Mathews and DeHart, *Sex, Gender,* 12.

53.   "North Carolina to Join Suffrage States," newspaper clipping (n.p., n.d.), box 2, folder 8, Catt Papers, TSLA; "As to North Carolina"; Carrie Chapman Catt to Mrs. Guilford Dudley, box 1, folder 6, Catt Papers, Tennessee State Library and Archives.

54.   Mathews and DeHart, *Sex, Gender,* 21–22; Green, "Those Opposed," 322–24; Taylor, "Woman Suffrage Movement," 183–84; Marjorie Spruill, "White Supremacy and the Southern Ideal of Woman: A Study of the Woman Suffrage Movement in North Carolina" (Senior Honors Essay, Curriculum in American Studies, University of North Carolina, 1973), 40; newspaper clipping (n.p.), July 23 [1920?], vol. 7, Waddell Papers, SHC. W. T. Bost, a reporter for the *Greensboro Daily News,* claimed that 75 percent of the advisory board of the Southern Women's Rejection League was Episcopalian and that all were "old-line Democrats." He also reported that at least three of the women on the board—Mrs. W. W. Kitchin, Mrs. Bennehan Cameron, and Mrs. George Pell—were married to men who favored woman suffrage. See Bost, "Suffrage Camps Have Appeared in Raleigh," newspaper clipping, [*Greensboro Daily News,* 1920], box 56, Weil Papers, NCDAH.

55.   "An Appeal to the People of North Carolina," *Raleigh News and Observer,* August 5, 1920, 11, and *Greensboro Daily News,* August 6, 1920, 7; *The State's Defense,* pamphlet published by Southern Rejection League and State's Rights Defense League (Raleigh: 1920), 1, in Equal Suffrage Amendment Collection, NCDAH; *America When Feminized,* broadside, Equal Suffrage Amendment Collection, NCDAH; "Letters on Woman Suffrage," *Raleigh News and Observer,* July 18, 1920, 9. For other examples of antisuffrage literature see the Equal Suffrage Amendment Collection and Bennehan Cameron Papers, SHC.

56.   *We plead in the Name of Virginia Dare that North Carolina Remain White,* broadside, box 55, Weil Papers, NCDAH; Hinton quoted in Kemp Plummer Battle, "Mary Hilliard Hinton," in *Biographical History of North Carolina,* ed. Samuel A'Court Ashe, Stephen B. Weeks, and Charles L. Van Noppen (Greensboro: Charles

L. Van Noppen, 1927), vol. 8, 242; Henry Groves Connor Jr., "Shall This General Assembly of North Carolina Ratify the 19th Amendment?" *North Carolina Booklet* 19 (April–July 1920): 121–32.

57. Antisuffrage broadsides, Oversize Papers, Bennehan Cameron Papers, SHC. See also *The State's Defense*.

58. Gilmore, "Gender and Jim Crow," 430–39; Green, "Those Opposed," 315, 324–25.

59. For more on the antisuffragists' concern for the preservation of traditional gender roles see Gertrude Weil to Walter Clark, April 12, 1919, *Papers of Walter Clark*, vol. 2, 394–95; Sims, "Beyond the Ballot"; and Mathews and DeHart, *Sex, Gender*, 18–21. On the relationship of race and gender in the New South see Jacquelyn Dowd Hall, *Revolt Against Chivalry: Jessie Daniel Ames and the Women's Campaign Against Lynching* (New York: Columbia University Press, 1979). On southern suffragists and white supremacy see Wheeler, *New Women of the New South*, 100–32.

60. [Gertrude Weil], form letter, August 4, 1920, box 55, Weil Papers, NCDAH; *Woman Suffrage Amendment Raises No Race Issue* and *Woman Suffrage and White Supremacy in the South*, broadsides, Equal Suffrage Association of North Carolina, NCC. See also Susan Franks Iden, "Some Suffragists I Have Known," *Everywoman's Magazine*, Special Session Edition, 4 (July–August 1920): 11–12; Cuningham, "The Spirit of Democracy"; "Suffragists Believe in State's Rights, Too," *Raleigh News and Observer*, August 7, 1920, 3; Gilmore, "Gender and Jim Crow," 437–38; Ann D. Gordon, "Woman Suffrage (Not Universal Suffrage) by Federal Amendment," in Wheeler, *VOTES FOR WOMEN!*, 3–24.

61. Carrie Chapman Catt to Mrs. John M. Kenny, June 29, 1920, Catt Papers, TSLA; Pattie D. R. Freeman to the Editor, *Raleigh News and Observer*, August 2, 1920, 4; Wheeler, *New Women of the New South*, 125–32; Gilmore, "Gender and Jim Crow," 436–39.

62. Blackwell quoted in Beverly Guy-Sheftall, *Daughters of Sorrow: Attitudes Toward Black Women, 1880–1920* (Brooklyn: Carlson, 1990), 114; "Votes for Women," *The Crisis* (August 1914): 180; "Woman Suffrage," *The Crisis* (April 1915): 285; Martha Gruening, "Two Suffrage Movements," *The Crisis* (September 1912): 247. See also "The Suffrage," *The Crisis* (November 1914): 18–19; "Votes for Women: A Symposium by Leading Thinkers of Colored America," *The Crisis* (August 1915): 178–92; "Woman Suffrage," *The Crisis* (November 1915): 29–30; Kelly Miller, "The Risk of Woman Suffrage," *The Crisis* (November 1915): 37–38; "The Colored Vote," *The Crisis* (December 1915): 71–72; "Votes for Women," *The Crisis* (November 1917): 8; "A Great Meeting," *Wilberforce (Ohio) Bee*, August 15, 1914, reel 3, Tuskegee Clipping File; Gilmore, "Gender and Jim Crow," 439–45; Rosalyn M. Terborg-Penn, "Afro-Americans and the Struggle for Woman Suffrage" (Ph.D. diss., Howard University, 1977); Paula Giddings, *When and Where I Enter: The Impact of Black Women on Race and Sex in America* (Toronto: Bantam, 1984), 119–31; Gordon, "Woman Suffrage (Not Universal Suffrage) by Federal Amendment."

63. Charlotte Hawkins Brown to James B. Dudley, May 3, 1920, and typescript (n.d.), both in Brown Papers, SL; Gilmore, "Gender and Jim Crow," 443–47.

64. Quotations are from Green, "Those Opposed," 324; "Suffragists Open Booth in the Yarborough Hotel Lobby," *Raleigh News and Observer,* August 11, 1920, 3; and "Suffragists to Maintain Lobby," *Charlotte Observer,* July 10, 1920, 7. See also W. T. Bost, "Question of Suffrage Looms Large on the Legislative Horizon," *Greensboro Daily News,* August 6, 1920, 1; Taylor, "Woman Suffrage Movement," 176; and Mathews and DeHart, *Sex, Gender,* 16–17.

65. Theodore Tiller, "Anthony Amendment Has Little Chance in State of Tennessee," *Greensboro Daily News,* August 2, 1920, 1; "Special Session Will Open Today at Eleven O'Clock," *Raleigh News and Observer,* August 10, 1920, 1.

66. Quotations are from *Telegram to the Tennessee Legislature and the Sixty-Three Members of the House Who Signed It,* broadside, NCC; Warren, "Observations on the Suffrage Amendment"; Catt and Shuler, *Woman Suffrage and Politics,* 479. See also "Majority Members of House Sign Anti Wire to Tennessee," *Raleigh News and Observer,* August 12, 1920, 1; "North Carolina Legislators Send Protest to Tennessee," newspaper clipping (n.p., n.d.), box 2, folder 7, Catt Papers, TSLA; *History of Woman Suffrage,* vol. 6, 498; Mathews and DeHart, *Sex, Gender,* 22–23; Green, "Those Opposed," 327–28.

67. Quotations are from Catt and Shuler, *Woman Suffrage and Politics,* 480; and Warren, "Observations on the Suffrage Amendment." See also *History of Woman Suffrage,* vol. 6, 499–500; Taylor, "Woman Suffrage Movement," 184–88; Mathews and DeHart, *Sex, Gender,* 24–25.

68. "The People Against the Politicians," *Lookout: A Journal of Southern Society* 25 (August 21, 1920), Pearson Papers, TSLA; telegram, Carrie Chapman Catt to Gertrude Weil, box 3, folder 4, Catt Papers, TSLA.

69. Mrs. H. W. Chase and Gertrude Weil, "To the Clubwomen of North Carolina (or Dear Club President?)," August 6, 1919, box 69; Weil Papers, NCDAH; UDC *Minutes* 1920, 6; 1927, 6.

70. W. E. B. DuBois, "Get Ready," *The Crisis* 20 (May 1920): 5.

71. Fannie Latta Hargrave, "The North Carolina Federation of Women's Clubs," *Afro-American,* August 15, 1920, reel 12, Tuskegee Clipping File; Gilmore, "Gender and Jim Crow," 442–62.

72. Quotations are from Mrs. Palmer Jerman, "The Growing Importance of Popular Education in Politics," in *Studies in Citizenship for North Carolina Women,* ed. Mrs. Phil McMahon (Charlotte: News Printing House for North Carolina League of Women Voters, 1926), 5; DAR *Proceedings* 1928, 38; NCFWC *Yearbook* 1928–29, 26; NCFWC *Yearbook* 1927–28, 60. See also RWC *Yearbook* 1919–20, 22; NCFWC *Yearbook* 1921–22, 18; NCFWC *Yearbook* 1923–24, 58–59; NCFWC *Yearbook,* 1930–31, 63–64; *Monthly News* 1 (November 1923); *Monthly News* 1 (March 1924); WCTU *Minutes* 1921, 27; 1923, 28–29; DAR *Proceedings* 1926, 88; 1929, 59; Gertrude Weil, "Annual Report of Acting President—Durham—March 5, 1924," Cowper Papers, Duke; Gertrude Weil to NCFWC local presidents and LWV local presidents, May 29, 1924, Cowper Papers, Duke; Gertrude Weil, "Suggestions to Women's Clubs. Citizenship Division, Civics Department, N.C.F.W.C." (n.d.), Weil Papers, NCDAH, Cowper Papers, Duke; Kathryn L. Nasstrom, "'More Was Expected of Us': The North Carolina League of Women Voters and the Feminist Movement in the 1920s," *North Carolina Historical Review* 68 (July 1991): 310.

73. Quotations are from Annie W. Foushee, "Women on School Boards," *Monthly News* 1 (September 1923); and Martha Boswell, "Women in Office," *Monthly News* 4 (November 1925). See also "Gertrude Weil's Recommendations on Citizenship to the NCFWC," *Monthly News* 1 (November 1923); and Sarah Wilkerson-Freeman, "From Clubs to Parties: North Carolina Women in the Advancement of the New Deal," *North Carolina Historical Review* 68 (July 1991): 320–39.

74. Ida M. Hooks, untitled typescript about the Legislative Council of North Carolina Women [1924?], Cowper Papers, Duke.

75. Quotation is from "More Legislative Entering Wedges," *Monthly News* 7 (April 1929). See also "The Australian Ballot," *Monthly News* 1 (July 1923); "Australian Ballot Bill Introduced," *Monthly News* 2 (February 1925); "Summary of Council Work," *Monthly News* 2 (March 1925); "Rise, Stand, and Be Counted," *Monthly News* 2 (April 1925); "Report of Board Meeting," *Monthly News* 4 (October 1926); "Australian Ballot Bill First," *Monthly News* 5 (January 1927); "The Australian Ballot," *Monthly News* 5 (March 1927). The Australian ballot was a frequent topic in the pages of the *Monthly News*; see vols. 1–8 (1923–1930). For the history of the movement for the Australian ballot up to 1917 in North Carolina see Steelman, "Progressive Era," 469–71.

76. "Report of Board Meeting," *Monthly News* 4 (October 1926); "Program of Study and Work Adopted by the Convention for 1927–28," *Monthly News* 5 (April 1927); "Board Meeting, October 24," *Monthly News* 6 (November 1927); "Dower-Curtesy Equalization," *Monthly News* 7 (July–August 1929); "Program for 1930," *Monthly News* 8 (March 1930); "Resolutions Passed by the Convention," *Monthly News* 1 (March 1924); Nasstrom, "More Was Expected of Us," 318–19.

77. Kelly Miller, "Colored Women Show Little Interest in Politics," *Baltimore Afro-American*, October 18, 1930, reel 37, Tuskegee Clipping File; Gilmore, "Gender and Jim Crow," 462–63.

Epilogue

1. Lula Martin McIver to Charlotte Hawkins Brown, April 6, 1920, reel 2, Brown Papers, SL; Anne Alexander Cameron to Lida Rodman, September 19, 1902, Rodman Papers, NCDAH; UDC *Minutes* 1906, 102.

2. "Separate Car Agitation," *Star of Zion*, July 16, 1891, 2; Sarah Dudley Pettey, "Reflections," *Star of Zion*, October 8, 1896, 3. See also G. F. Richings, *Evidence of Progress Among Colored People* (Philadelphia: Geo. S. Ferguson, 1902), 425–26; *Minutes of the Eighth Biennial Convention of the National Association of Colored Women, July 23–27, 1912* (n.p., n.d.), 39–40, 58; Charlotte Hawkins Brown, "Some Incidents from My Life," reel 1, Brown Papers, SL; and Glenda Elizabeth Gilmore, "Gender and Jim Crow: Women and the Politics of White Supremacy in North Carolina, 1896–1920" (Ph.D. diss., University of North Carolina, 1992)

3. "Women of South Plead for Justice to Negro," *Birmingham Reporter*, April 19, 1913, reel 2, Tuskegee Clipping File.

4. "Negroes Adopt Strong Resolutions on Emancipation Day," *Raleigh Independent*, January 11, 1919, reel 10, Tuskegee Clipping File.

5. "Negroes Adopt Strong Resolutions on Emancipation Day."

6. NCFWC *Yearbook* 1919–20, 64; Charlotte Hawkins Brown to Miss [Louise] Brooks, May 13, 1920, reel 2, Brown Papers, SL.

7. History of Woman's Division, Commission on Interracial Cooperation, Ames Papers, Duke; *Southern Women and Race Co-operation: A Story of the Memphis Conference, October Sixth and Seventh, 1920,* pamphlet, NCC; Jacquelyn Dowd Hall, *Revolt Against Chivalry: Jessie Daniel Ames and the Women's Campaign Against Lynching* (New York: Columbia University Press, 1979), 90–95; Gilmore, "Gender and Jim Crow," 414.

8. Quotations are from Address of Charlotte Hawkins Brown, Memphis meeting, October 7, 1920; and Address of Charlotte Hawkins Brown, Atlanta, October 1921, both in Ames Papers, Duke. See also Brown, "Some Incidents"; Hall, *Revolt Against Chivalry,* 93–94; and Gilmore, "Gender and Jim Crow," 413–14.

9. NCFWC *Yearbook* 1923–24, 89; History of Woman's Division, Ames Papers, Duke.

10. NCFWC *Yearbook* 1928–29, 26.

11. DAR *Proceedings* 1917, 34. On the origins of factory workers see Jacquelyn Dowd Hall et al., *Like a Family: The Making of a Southern Cotton Mill World* (Chapel Hill: University of North Carolina Press, 1987).

12. Mrs. Al Fairbrother, "About the Women's Clubs of North Carolina," untitled clipping (n.p.), 1910, Sallie Southall Cotten Scrapbook, vol. 3, Cotten Family Papers, SHC; newspaper clipping, *Goldsboro Argus News,* December 6, 1964, Gertrude Weil folder, box 96, Weil Papers, NCDAH.

13. Sallie Southall Cotten, "Address to Social Service Conference," February 13, 1914, Cotten Family Papers, SHC.

14. NCFWC *Yearbook* 1909–10, 28; 1910–11, 36–37; Hugh Talmage Lefler and Albert Ray Newsome, *North Carolina: The History of a Southern State* (Chapel Hill: University of North Carolina Press, 1973), 509; C. Vann Woodward, *Origins of the New South, 1877–1913* (Baton Rouge: Louisiana State University Press, 1951), 416.

15. Untitled report of sixth annual NCFWC convention, box 68, Weil Papers, NCDAH; WCTU *Minutes* 1910, 27; NCFWC *Yearbook,* 1913–14, 48; Gertrude Weil to Mary Hinton Fearing, June 17, 1928, vol. 2, Mary Hinton Fearing Scrapbooks, Duke; "Program of the Legislative Council of North Carolina Women 1929"; "Report of the Legislative Chairman, N.C. League of Women Voters, Charlotte, March 24, 1931," both in Cowper Papers, Duke; NCFWC *Yearbook* 1930–31, 8.

16. J. M. Archer to E. Y. Webb, December 27, 1915; E. Y. Webb to J. M. Archer, December 29, 1915; E. Y. Webb to L. F. Groves, February 20, 1915, all in Webb Papers, SHC. See also John P. Yount to E. Y. Webb, January 11, 1916; and Samuel Turner to E. Y. Webb, January 15, 1916, both in Webb Papers, SHC.

17. NCFWC *Yearbook,* 1923–24, 80, 129; Nell Battle Lewis, "Bucking the North Carolina Mill Owners," typescript, box 30, Lewis Papers, NCDAH; Mrs. J. Henry Highsmith, "Explains Why Survey of Women in State Industry Was Dropped," *Raleigh News and Observer,* December 1, 1929, 3. For a detailed account of the survey controversy see Marion Winifred Roydhouse, "The 'Universal

Sisterhood of Women': Women and Labor Reform in North Carolina, 1900–1932" (Ph.D. diss., Duke University, 1980), 306–25.

18.   Mary O. Cowper to Carl Taylor, April 1, 1926, Cowper Papers, Duke; Roydhouse, "Universal Sisterhood," 307–12.

19.   Roydhouse, "Universal Sisterhood," 312.

20.   May Belle McMahon to H. L. McClaren, March 1, 1926; May Belle McMahon to Mary O. Cowper, March 1, 1926, both in Cowper Papers, Duke.

21.   Lewis, "Bucking the North Carolina Mill Owners;" Highsmith, "Explains Why Survey of Women in State Industry Was Dropped;" Angus W. McLean to Mrs. E. L. McKee, July 20, 1926, encl. in McLean to Gertrude Weil, July 24, 1926, Weil Papers, NCDAH; Roydhouse, "Universal Sisterhood," 315–25.

22.   May Belle McMahon to Mary O. Cowper, September 1, 1926, Cowper Papers.

23.   May Belle McMahon to Mary O. Cowper, "Friday evening, the 25th"; McMahon to Cowper, September 1, 1926, both in Cowper Papers, Duke.

Bibliography

Manuscript Collections

Cambridge, Massachusetts. Radcliffe College. Arthur and Elizabeth Schlesinger Library.

Charlotte Hawkins Brown Papers.

Chapel Hill, North Carolina. University of North Carolina. Louis Round Wilson Library. North Carolina Collection.

Avent, Joseph E. "Amendment Scrapbook 1900—Literature on the Amendment Proposed to the Constitution of North Carolina by the General Assembly of 1899."

Cotten, Sallie Southall. "A Line A Day Book. A Condensed, Comparative Record for Five Years, 1908–1912."

———. "Journal from Chicago Exposition, 1893."

O'Neil, Mrs. Maurice. "The History and Accomplishments of the North Carolina Division United Daughters of the Confederacy" (typescript). N.d.

Saunders, Miss Veritas. "The History and Accomplishments of The North Carolina Division of The United Daughters of The Confederacy." 1922.

Chapel Hill, North Carolina. University of North Carolina. Louis Round Wilson Library. Southern Historical Collection.

Harriet Morehead Berry Papers.
Eugene Cunningham Branson Papers.
Bennehan Cameron Papers.
Sarah Rebecca Cameron Papers.
Hope Summerell Chamberlain Papers.
Otelia Carrington (Cuningham) Connor Papers.
Cotten Family Papers.
DeRosset Family Papers.
Meares-DeRosset Papers.
Elvira Evelyna Moffitt Papers.
Eliza Hall (Nutt) Parsley Papers.
Elsie Riddick Papers.
Salisbury Book Club Minutes.
Alfred Moore Waddell Papers.
Lindsay Carter Warren Papers.
Edwin Yates Webb Papers.

Durham, North Carolina. Duke University. Special Collections Library.

Jessie Daniel Ames Papers.
John G. Brodnax Papers.
G. Hope (Summerell) Chamberlain Papers.
Mary Octavine (Thompson) Cowper Papers.
Cronly Family Papers.
Mary Hinton Fearing Scrapbooks.
Hinsdale Family Papers.
Charles N. Hunter Papers.
Romulus Armistead Nunn Papers.
Sallie Sue (Ellis) Peebles Papers.
James Southgate Papers.

Nashville, Tennessee. Tennessee State Library and Archives.

Carrie Chapman Catt Papers.
Josephine Anderson Pearson Papers.

Raleigh, North Carolina. North Carolina Division of Archives and History.

American Association of University Women, Raleigh Branch, Papers.
Daughters of the Revolution Papers.
Equal Suffrage Amendment Collection.
General Assembly Session Records.
Horne Committee on the Memorial to North Carolina Women of the Confederacy Papers.
Nell Battle Lewis Papers.
Elvira Worth Moffitt Papers.
North Carolina Federation of Women's Clubs–Raleigh Woman's Club Papers.
North Carolina League of Women Voters Papers.
Clarence Poe Papers.
Rodman Papers.
Jessica Randolph Smith Papers.
Social Services Department of North Carolina. Commissioner's Office. Subject Files, 1891–1952.
Gertrude Weil Papers.

Books and Articles

Addo, Linda D. and James H. McCallum. *To Be Faithful to Our Heritage: A History of Black United Methodism in North Carolina*. Lake Junaluska: Commission on Archives and History of the North Carolina Conference and Western North Carolina Conference, United Methodist Church, 1980.

Agnew, Theodore L. "Reflections on The Woman's Foreign Missionary Movement in Late Nineteenth Century American Methodism." *Methodist History* 1 (January 1968): 3–16.

Ayres, Edward L. *The Promise of the New South: Life After Reconstruction*. New York: Oxford University Press, 1992.

Baer, Hans A. and Yvonne Jones, eds. *African Americans in the South: Issues of Race, Class, and Gender*. Athens: University of Georgia Press, 1992.

Baker, Paula. "The Domestication of American Politics: Women and American Political Society, 1780–1920." *American Historical Review*. 89 (June 1984): 620–47.

Banton, Michael. "Voluntary Associations: Anthropological Aspects". In *International Encyclopedia of the Social Sciences*. edited by David L. Sills. New York: Macmillan Company and the Free Press, 1968. Vol. 16, 357–62.

Berg, Barbara J. *The Remembered Gate: Origins of American Feminism, The Woman and the City 1800–1860*. New York: Oxford University Press, 1978.

Betts, Otis A. *The North Carolina School for the Deaf at Morganton, 1894–1944*. Morganton: North Carolina School for the Deaf, 1945.

Billings, Dwight B., Jr. *Planters and The Making of a "New South": Class, Politics and Development in North Carolina, 1865–1900*. Chapel Hill: University of North Carolina Press, 1979.

Blair, Karen J. *The Clubwoman as Feminist: True Womanhood Redefined, 1868–1914*. New York: Holmes and Meier, 1980.

Bland, Sidney R. "Mad Women of the Cause: The National Woman's Party in the South." *Furman Studies* 26 (December 1980): 82–91.

Bloch, Ruth H. "American Feminine Ideals in Transition: The Rise of the Moral "Mother." *Feminist Studies* 4 (June 1978): 101–26.

Blocker, Jack S., Jr. *American Temperance Movements: Cycles of Reform*. Boston: Twayne, 1989.

Bordin, Ruth. "'A Baptism of Fire and Liberty': The Women's Crusade of 1873–1874." In *Woman's Being, Woman's Place: Female Identity and Vocation in American History*, edited by Mary Kelley. Boston: G. K. Hall, 1977.

———. *Woman and Temperance: The Quest for Power And Liberty, 1873–1900*. Philadelphia: Temple University Press, 1981.

Bourne, Marion Frances Alston. "Seventy-five Years of Service." In Diocese of North Carolina, Woman's Auxiliary to the National Council of the Protestant Episcopal Church, *Seventy-Fifth Annual Report and Handbook of Information*. N.p.: 1957.

Boyer, Paul. *Urban Masses and Moral Order in America, 1820–1920*. Cambridge: Harvard University Press, 1978.

Boylan, Anne M. "Evangelical Womanhood in the Nineteenth Century: The Role of Women in Sunday Schools." *Feminist Studies* 4 (June 1978): 62–80.

Breen, William J. "Black Women and the Great War: Mobilization and Reform in the South." *Journal of Southern History* 44 (August 1978): 421–40.

———. "Southern Women in the War: The North Carolina Woman's Committee, 1917–1919." *North Carolina Historical Review* 55 (July 1978): 251–83.

Brinkley, David. *David Brinkley: 11 Presidents, 4 Wars, 22 Political Conventions, 1 Moon Landing, 3 Assassinations, 2,000 Weeks of News and Other Stuff on Television and 18 Years of Growing Up in North Carolina*. New York: Alfred A. Knopf, 1995.

Brooks, Aubrey Lee and Hugh Talmage Lefler, eds. *The Papers of Walter Clark*. 3 vols. Chapel Hill: University of North Carolina Press, 1950.

Brown, Elsa Barkley. "Womanist Consciousness: Maggie Lena Walker and the Independent Order of St. Luke." *Signs* 14 (Spring 1989): 610–33.

Brown, Richard D. "The Emergence of Voluntary Associations in Massachusetts, 1760–1830." *Journal of Voluntary Action Research* 2 (April 1973): 64–73.

Butler, Lindley S. and Alan D. Watson, eds. *The North Carolina Experience: An Interpretive and Documentary History.* Chapel Hill: University of North Carolina Press, 1984.

Bynum, Victoria E. *Unruly Women: The Politics of Social and Sexual Control in the Old South.* Chapel Hill: University of North Carolina Press, 1992.

Carlton, David L. *Mill and Town in South Carolina, 1880–1920.* Baton Rouge: Louisiana State University Press, 1982.

Carraway, Gertrude S. *Carolina Crusaders: History of North Carolina Federation of Women's Clubs.* New Bern: Owen G. Dunn for the North Carolina Federation of Women's Clubs, 1941.

Cash, Wilbur J. *The Mind of the South.* New York: Vintage Books, 1941.

Censer, Jane Turner. *North Carolina Planters and Their Children 1800–1860.* Baton Rouge: Louisiana State University Press, 1984.

Chafe, William H. *Women and Equality: Changing Patterns in American Culture.* New York: Oxford University Press, 1977.

Clark, Norman H. *Deliver Us From Evil: An Interpretation of American Prohibition.* New York: W. W. Norton and Company, Inc., 1976.

Coates, Albert. *By Her Own Bootstraps: A Saga of Women in North Carolina.* Chapel Hill: Privately published, 1975.

———. *Citizens in Action: Women's Clubs, Civic Clubs, Community Chests—Flying Buttresses to Governmental Units.* Chapel Hill: Privately published, 1976.

Conway, Jill. "Women Reformers and American Culture, 1870–1930." *Journal of Social History* 5 (Winter 1971–72): 164–77.

Cott, Nancy F. *The Bonds of Womanhood: "Woman's Sphere" in New England, 1780–1835.* New Haven: Yale University Press, 1977.

———. *The Grounding of Modern Feminism.* New Haven: Yale University Press, 1987.

———. "Passionlessness: An Interpretation of Victorian Sexual Ideology, 1790–1850." *Signs* 4 (Winter 1978): 219–36.

Davies, Wallace Evan. *Patriotism on Parade: The Story of Veterans' and Hereditary Organizations in America, 1783–1900.* Cambridge: Harvard University Press, 1955.

Dean, Pamela. "Learning to be New Women: Campus Culture at North Carolina Normal and Industrial College." *North Carolina Historical Review* 68 (July 1991): 286–306.

Degler, Carl N. *At Odds: Women and The American Family from The Revolution to The Present.* New York: Oxford University Press, 1980.

Dickson, Lynda F. "Toward a Broader Angle of Vision in Uncovering Women's History: Black Women's Clubs Revisited." In *Black Women's History: Theory and Practice,* edited by Darlene Clark Hine, vol. 1, 103–20. Brooklyn: Carlson, 1990.

Doak, Frances R. *Toward New Frontiers. A History of the North Carolina Federation of Women's Clubs, 1942–1962.* N.p., n.d.

Douglas, Ann. *The Feminization of American Culture*. New York: Alfred A. Knopf, 1977.

Doyle, Don H. *New Men, New Cities, New South*. Chapel Hill: University of North Carolina Press, 1990.

———. "Rules of Order: Henry Martyn Robert and the Popularization of American Parliamentary Law." *American Quarterly* 32 (Spring 1980): 3–18.

———."The Social Functions of Voluntary Associations in a Nineteenth-Century American Town." *Social Science History* 1 (May 1977): 333–55.

DuBois, Ellen. "The Radicalism of the Woman Suffrage Movement: Notes Toward the Reconstruction of Nineteenth Century Feminism." *Feminist Studies* 3 (Fall 1975): 63–71.

Edmonds, Helen G. *The Negro and Fusion Politics in North Carolina, 1894–1901*. Chapel Hill: University of North Carolina Press, 1951.

Ellison, Dorothy F. *History of the International Order of the King's Daughters and Sons*. Vol. 3. Oakland, Calif.: Color Art Press for International Order of King's Daughters and Sons, 1970.

Elshtain, Jean Bethke. *Power Trips and Other Journeys: Essays in Feminism and Civic Discourse*. Madison: University of Wisconsin Press, 1990.

Epstein, Barbara Leslie. *The Politics of Domesticity: Women, Evangelism and Temperance in Nineteenth Century America*. Middletown, Conn.: Wesleyan University Press, 1981.

Escott, Paul D. *Many Excellent People: Power and Privilege in North Carolina, 1850–1900*. Chapel Hill: University of North Carolina Press, 1985.

Faust, Drew Gilpin. "Altars of Sacrifice: Confederate Women and the Narratives of War." *Journal of American History* 76 (March 1990): 1200–28.

Filene, Peter Gabriel. *Him/Her/Self: Sex Roles in Modern America*. New York: Harcourt Brace Jovanovich, 1974.

FitzGerald, Frances. *America Revised: History Schoolbooks in the Twentieth Century*. Boston: Little, Brown and Company, 1979.

Flexner, Eleanor. *Century of Struggle: The Woman's Rights Movement in the United States*. 1959. Reprint, New York: Atheneum, 1974.

Foster, Gaines M. *Ghosts of the Confederacy: Defeat, the Lost Cause, and the Emergence of the New South*. New York: Oxford University Press, 1987.

Fox-Genovese, Elizabeth. *Within the Plantation Household: Black and White Women of the Old South*. Chapel Hill: University of North Carolina Press, 1988.

Frankel, Noralee and Nancy S. Dye, eds. *Gender, Class, Race and Reform in the Progressive Era*. Lexington: University Press of Kentucky, 1991.

Fraser, Walter J., Jr., R. Frank Saunders, Jr., and Jon L. Wakelyn. Eds. *The Web of Southern Social Relations*. Athens: University of Georgia Press, 1985.

Frederickson, Mary E. "Shaping a New Society: Methodist Women and Industrial Reform in the South." In *Women in New Worlds: Historical Perspectives on the Wesleyan Tradition*, edited by Hilah F. Thomas and Rosemary Skinner Keller, vol. 1, 345–61. Nashville: Abingdon, 1981.

Freedman, Estelle B. "Separatism as Strategy: Female Institution Building and American Feminism, 1870–1930. *Feminist Studies* 9 (Fall 1979): 512–29.

———. *Their Sisters' Keepers: Women's Prison Reform in America, 1830–1930*. Ann Arbor: University of Michigan Press, 1981.

Friedman, Jean E. *The Enclosed Garden: Women and Community in the Evangelical South, 1830–1930.* Chapel Hill: University of North Carolina Press, 1985.

Gatewood, Willard. *Aristocrats of Color: The Black Elite, 1880–1920.* Bloomington: Indiana University Press, 1990.

Giddings, Paula. *When and Where I Enter: The Impact of Black Women on Race and Sex in America.* Toronto: Bantam, 1984.

Gilmore, Glenda Elizabeth. "'A Melting Time': Black Women, White Women, and the WCTU in North Carolina, 1880–1900." In *Hidden Histories of Women in the New South,* edited by Virginia Bernhard, Betty Brandon, Elizabeth Fox-Genovese, Theda Perdue, and Elizabeth Hayes Turner, 153–72. Columbia: University of Missouri Press, 1994.

Grantham, Dewey W. *Southern Progressivism: The Reconciliation of Progress and Tradition.* Knoxville: University of Tennessee Press, 1983.

Greenwood, Janette Thomas. *Bittersweet Legacy: The Black and White "Better Classes" in Charlotte, 1850–1910.* Chapel Hill: University of North Carolina Press, 1994.

Grimes, Alan P. *The Puritan Ethic and Woman Suffrage.* New York: Oxford University Press, 1967.

Gusfield, Joseph R. *Symbolic Crusade: Status Politics and the American Temperance Movement.* Urbana: University of Illinois Press, 1966.

Guy-Sheftall, Beverly. *Daughters of Sorrow: Attitudes Toward Black Women, 1880–1920.* Brooklyn: Carlson, 1990.

Hall, Jacquelyn Dowd, et al. *Like A Family: The Making of a Southern Cotton Mill World.* Chapel Hill: University of North Carolina Press, 1987.

Hall, Jacquelyn Dowd. "'The Mind That Burns in Each Body': Women, Rape, and Racial Violence." In *Powers of Desire: The Politics of Sexuality,* edited by Ann Snitow, Christine Stansell, and Sharon Thompson. New York: Monthly Review, 1983.

———. *Revolt Against Chivalry: Jessie Daniel Ames and the Women's Campaign Against Lynching.* New York: Columbia University Press, 1979.

Hartman, Mary and Lois W. Banner, eds. *Clio's Consciousness Raised: New Perspectives on the History of Women.* New York: Harper Colophon, 1974.

Haskell, Thomas L. *The Emergence of Professional Social Science: The American Social Science Association and the Nineteenth–Century Crisis of Authority.* Urbana: University of Illinois Press, 1977.

Hewitt, Nancy A. "Beyond the Search for Sisterhood: American Women's History in the 1980s." *Social History* 10 (October 1985): 299–321.

———. *Women's Activism and Social Change: Rochester, New York, 1822–1872.* Ithaca: Cornell University Press, 1984.

——— and Suzanne Lebsock, eds. *Visible Women: New Essays on American Activism.* Urbana: University of Illinois Press, 1993.

Higginbotham, Evelyn Brooks. *Righteous Discontent: The Woman's Movement in the Black Baptist Church, 1880–1920.* Cambridge, Mass.: Harvard University Press, 1993.

Higham, John. "Hanging Together: Divergent Unities in American History." *Journal of American History* 61 (June 1974): 5–28.

Hilty, Hiram H. *New Garden Friends Meeting: The Christian People Called Quakers.* Greensboro: North Carolina Friends Historical Society, 1983.

Hine, Darlene Clark, ed. *Black Women's History: Theory and Practice.* 2 vols. Brooklyn: Carlson, 1990.

———. *Hine Sight: Black Women and the Re-Construction of American History.* Brooklyn: Carlson, 1994.

Hinshaw, Seth B. *The Carolina Quaker Experience.* N. p.: North Carolina Friends Historical Society, 1984.

Holoman, Kathleen Highsmith. *Ever Changing, Ever the Same: Seventy-Fifth Anniversary of the Women's Club of Raleigh, 1904–1979.* Raleigh: Woman's Club of Raleigh, Inc., 1979.

Howe, Daniel Walker. "Victorian Culture in America," in *Victorian America,* edited by Daniel Walker Howe. Philadelphia: University of Pennsylvania Press, 1976.

Howell, Gertrude Jenkins. *The Woman's Auxiliary of The Synod of North Carolina, 1912–1937.* Wilmington: Wilmington Stamp and Printing, 1938.

Hunter, Tera. "The Correct Thing: Charlotte Hawkins Brown and the Palmer Institute." *Southern Exposure* 11 (September–October 1983): 37–43.

James, Edward T., Janet Wilson James, and Paul S. Boyer. *Notable American Women, 1607–1950: A Biographical Dictionary.* 3 vols. Cambridge, Mass.: Harvard University Press, 1971.

Janeway, Elizabeth. *Man's World, Woman's Place: A Study in Social Mythology.* New York: Dell, 1971.

Jeffrey, Julie Roy. "Women in the Southern Farmers' Alliance: A Reconstruction of the Role and Status of Women in the Late Nineteenth–Century South." *Feminist Studies* 3 (Fall 1975): 72–91.

Jenkins, James S. *Greenville and Pitt County at the Turn of the Century.* Greenville, N.C., 1965.

Jensen, Richard. "Family, Career, and Reform: Women Leaders of the Progressive Era." In *The American Family in Social-Historical Perspective,* edited by Michael Gordon. New York: St. Martin's Press, 1973.

Johnson, Graham E. "Voluntary Associations and Social Change: Some Theoretical Issues." *International Journal of Comparative Sociology* 16 (Winter 1975): 51–63.

Johnson, Guion Griffis. *Ante-Bellum North Carolina: A Social History.* Chapel Hill: University of North Carolina Press, 1937.

———. "The Changing Status of the Southern Woman." In John C. McKinney and Edgar T. Thompson, eds., *The South in Continuity and Change.* Durham: Duke University Press, 1965.

Jones, Beverly Washington. *Quest for Equality: The Life and Writings of Mary Church Terrell, 1863–1954.* Brooklyn: Carlson, 1990.

Katzman, David M. *Seven Days a Week: Women and Domestic Service in Industrializing America.* New York: Oxford University Press, 1978.

Keller, Rosemary Skinner, Louise L. Queen, and Hilah F. Thomas, eds. *Women in New Worlds: Historical Perspectives on the Wesleyan Tradition.* Vol. 2. Nashville: Abingdon, 1982.

Kerber, Linda. "The Republican Mother: Women and the Enlightenment—An American Perspective." *American Quarterly* 28 (Summer 1976): 187–205.

———. *Women of the Republic: Intellect and Ideology in Revolutionary America.* Chapel Hill: University of North Carolina Press, 1980; New York: W. W. Norton, 1986.

Kousser, J. Morgan. *The Shaping of Southern Politics: Suffrage Restriction and the Establishment of the One–Party South.* New Haven: Yale University Press, 1974.

Kondert, Nancy. "The Romance and Reality of Defeat: Southern Women in 1865." *Journal of Mississippi History* 35 (May 1973): 141–52.

Kraditor, Aileen S. *The Ideas of the Woman Suffrage Movement, 1890–1920.* Garden City, New York: Doubleday, Anchor Books, 1971.

Kuhn, Anne L. *The Mother's Role in Childhood Education: New England Concepts, 1830–1860.* New Haven: Yale University Press, 1947.

Ladd-Taylor, Molly. *Mother–Work: Women, Child Welfare, and the State, 1890–1930.* Urbana: University of Illinois Press, 1994.

Lebsock, Suzanne. *The Free Women of Petersburg: Status and Culture in a Southern Town, 1784–1860.* New York: W. W. Norton 1984.

Lefler, Hugh Talmage and Albert Ray Newsome. *North Carolina: The History of a Southern State.* Chapel Hill: University of North Carolina Press, 1973.

Leloudis, James L., II. *Schooling the New South.* Chapel Hill: University of North Carolina Press, 1996.

———. "School Reform in The New South: The Woman's Association for the Betterment of Public School Houses in North Carolina, 1902–1919." *Journal of American History* 69 (March 1983): 886–909.

———. "Subversion of the Feminine Ideal: The *Southern Lady's Companion* and White Male Morality in the Antebellum South." In *Women in New Worlds: Historical Perspectives on the Wesleyan Tradition,* edited by Rosemary Skinner Keller, Louise L. Queen, and Hilah F. Thomas, vol. 2, 60–75. Nashville: Abingdon, 1982.

Lemons, J. Stanley. *The Woman Citizen: Social Feminism in the 1920s.* Urbana, Chicago, London: University of Illinois Press, 1973.

Lerner, Gerda. "Community Work of Black Club Women." *Journal of Negro History* 59 (Spring 1974): 158–67.

———. "New Approaches to the Study of Women in American History." *Journal of Social History* 3 (Fall 1969): 53–62.

———. "Placing Women in History: A 1975 Perspective." In Berenice A. Carroll, ed., *Liberating Women's History: Theoretical and Critical Essays.* Urbana, Chicago, London: University of Illinois Press, 1976.

Levine, Lawrence W. *Highbrow/Lowbrow: The Emergence of Cultural Hierarchy in America.* Cambridge, Mass.: Harvard University Press, 1988.

Link, William A. *The Paradox of Southern Progressivism, 1880–1930.* Chapel Hill: University of North Carolina Press, 1992.

Marshall, Susan E. "In Defense of Separate Spheres: Class and Status Politics in the Antisuffrage Movement." *Social Forces* 65 (December 1986): 327–51.

Marteena, Constance H. *The Lengthening Shadow of a Woman: A Biography of Charlotte Hawkins Brown.* Hicksville, N. Y.: Exposition, 1977.

Martin, Theodora Penny. *The Sound of Our Own Voices: Women's Study Clubs,
    1860–1910.* Boston: Beacon Press, 1987.
Mathews, Donald G. *Religion in the Old South.* Chicago: University of Chicago
    Press, 1977.
—— and Jane Sherron DeHart. *Sex, Gender, and the Politics of ERA: A State
    and the Nation.* New York: Oxford University Press, 1990.
McCarthy, Kathleen D. *Women's Culture: American Philanthropy and Art, 1830–
    1930.* Chicago: University of Chicago Press, 1991.
McGovern, James R. "The American Woman's Pre–World War I Freedom in Man-
    ners and Morals." *Journal of American History* 55 (September 1968): 315–33.
McMath, Robert C., Jr. *Populist Vanguard: A History of the Southern Farmers' Alli-
    ance.* Chapel Hill: University of North Carolina Press, 1975.
Melder, Keith. *Beginnings of Sisterhood: The American Woman's Rights Movement,
    1800–1850.* New York: Schocken Books, 1977.
——. "Ladies Bountiful: Organized Women's Benevolence in Early Nineteenth
    Century America." *New York History* 48 (July 1967): 231–54.
Melosi, Martin V. *Garbage in the Cities: Refuse, Reform, and the Environment,
    1880–1980.* College Station: Texas A & M Press, 1981.
Morgan, David. *Suffragists and Democrats: The Politics of Woman Suffrage in
    America.* East Lansing: Michigan State University Press, 1972.
Mueller, Marnie W. "Economic Determinants of Volunteer Work by Women." *Signs*
    1 (Winter 1975): 325–38.
Muncy, Robyn. *Creating A Feminine Dominion in American Reform.* New York:
    Oxford University Press, 1991.
Nathans, Sydney. *The Quest for Progress: The Way We Lived in North Carolina,
    1870–1920.* Chapel Hill: University of North Carolina Press, 1983.
Neverdon-Morton, Cynthia. *Afro-American Women of the South and the Advance-
    ment of the Race, 1895–1925.* Knoxville: University of Tennessee Press, 1989.
O'Neill, William L. *Everyone was Brave: A History of Feminism in America.* Chi-
    cago: Quadrangle, 1971.
Orr, Oliver H., Jr. *Charles Brantley Aycock.* Chapel Hill: University of North Caro-
    lina Press, 1961.
Ownby, Ted. *Subduing Satan: Religion, Recreation, and Manhood in the Rural
    South, 1865–1920.* Chapel Hill: University of North Carolina Press, 1990.
Pascoe, Peggy. *Relations of Rescue: The Search for Female Moral Authority in the
    American West, 1874–1939.* New York: Oxford University Press, 1990.
Pivar, David J. *Purity Crusade: Sexual Morality and Social Control, 1865–1900.*
    Westport, Conn.: Greenwood, 1973.
Powell, William S. "Citizens' Library Movement." *North Carolina Libraries* 13
    (November 1954): 33–39.
——, ed. *Dictionary of North Carolina Biography.* 6 vols. Chapel Hill: University
    of North Carolina Press, 1980–1996.
——. *Paradise Preserved.* Chapel Hill: University of North Carolina Press, 1965.
Rable, George C. *Civil Wars: Women and the Crisis of Southern Nationalism.* Ur-
    bana: University of Illinois Press, 1989.
Rogers, Lou. "Eliza Nutt Parsley." *We The People* 3 (November 1945): 17, 21.
——. *Tar Heel Women.* Raleigh: Warren, 1949.

Rosaldo, Michele Zimbalist. "Women, Culture, and Society: A Theoretical Overview." *Woman, Culture, and Society,* edited by Michele Zimbalist Rosaldo and Louise Lamphere. Stanford: Stanford University Press, 1974.

Roth, Darlene. "Feminine Marks on the Landscape: An Atlanta Inventory." *Journal of American Culture* 3 (Winter 1980): 673–85.

Rothman, Sheila M. *Woman's Proper Place: A History of Changing Ideals and Practices, 1870 to the Present.* New York: Basic Books, Inc., 1978.

Rouse, Jacqueline Ann. *Lugenia Burns Hope: Black Southern Reformer.* Athens: University of Georgia Press, 1989.

Ryan, Mary P. *Cradle of the Middle Class: The Family in Oneida County, New York, 1790–1865.* Cambridge: Cambridge University Press, 1981.

———. "The Power of Women's Networks: A Case Study of Female Moral Reform in Antebellum America." *Feminist Studies* 5 (Spring 1979): 66–86.

———. *Women in Public: Between Banners and Ballots, 1825–1880.* Baltimore: The Johns Hopkins University Press, 1990.

Salem, Dorothy. *To Better Our World: Black Women in Organized Reform, 1890–1920.* Brooklyn: Carlson, 1990.

Schaffer, Ronald. "The Problem of Consciousness in the Woman Suffrage Movement: A California Perspective." *Pacific Historical Review* 45 (Fall 1976): 469–93.

Schlesinger, Arthur M., Sr. "Biography of a Nation of Joiners." *American Historical Review* 50 (September 1944): 1–25.

Scott, Anne Firor. "After Suffrage: Southern Women in the Twenties." *Journal of Southern History* 30 (August 1964): 298–318.

———. "Most Invisible of All: Black Women's Voluntary Associations." *Journal of Southern History* 56 (February 1990): 3–20.

———. *Natural Allies: Women's Voluntary Associations in America.* Urbana: University of Illinois Press, 1991.

———. *The Southern Lady: From Pedestal to Politics, 1830–1930.* Chicago: University of Chicago Press, 1970.

———. "Women's Perspective on the Patriarchy in the 1850s." *Journal of American History* 61 (June 1974, 52–74.

Scott, Joan Wallach. *Gender and the Politics of History.* New York: Columbia University Press, 1988.

Sims, Anastatia. "Sisterhoods of Service: Women's Clubs and Methodist Women's Missionary Societies in North Carolina, 1890–1930." In *Women in New Worlds: Historical Perspectives on the Wesleyan Tradition,* edited by Rosemary Skinner Keller, Louise L. Queen, and Hilah F. Thomas, vol. 2, 196–210. Nashville: Abingdon, 1982.

———. "'The Sword of the Spirit': The WCTU and Moral Reform in North Carolina, 1883–1933." *North Carolina Historical Review* 64 (October 1987): 394–415.

Singal, Daniel Joseph. *The War Within: From Victorian to Modernist Thought in the South, 1919–1945.* Chapel Hill: University of North Carolina Press, 1982.

Skocpol, Theda. *Protecting Soldiers and Mothers: The Political Origins of Social Policy in the United States.* Cambridge, Mass.: Harvard University Press, Belknap Press, 1992.

Smith-Rosenberg, Carroll. "Beauty, the Beast, and the Militant Woman: A Case Study in Sex Roles and Social Stress in Jacksonian America." *American Quarterly* 23 (Winter 1971): 562–84.

———. "The Female World of Love and Ritual: Relations Between Women in Nineteenth-Century America." *Signs* 1 (Spring 1975): 1–29.

Stein, Allen. "That Civilizing Spirit." *Southern Exposure* 4 (December 1977): 65–69.

Stephenson, William. "Part-Way from Pedestal to Politics." In *Awakenings: Writings and Recollections of Eastern North Carolina Women,* edited by Sally Brett. Greenville, N.C.: Pamlico, 1978.

———. *Sallie Southall Cotten: A Woman's Life in North Carolina.* Greenville, N. C.: Pamlico, 1987.

Tatum, Noreen Dunn. *A Crown of Service: A Story of Woman's Work in the Methodist Episcopal Church, South, From 1878–1940.* Nashville: Parthenon, 1960.

Taylor, A. Elizabeth. "The Woman Suffrage Movement in North Carolina." *North Carolina Historical Review* 38 (January 1961): 45–62; (June 1961): 173–89.

Taylor, William R. *Cavalier and Yankee: The Old South and American National Character.* New York: Harper and Row, Harper Torchbooks, 1969.

Thane, Elswyth. *Mount Vernon is Ours: The Story of Its Preservation.* New York: Duell, Sloan, and Pearce, 1966.

Thomas, Hilah F. and Keller, Rosemary Skinner, eds. *Women in New Worlds: Historical Perspectives on the Wesleyan Tradition.* Vol. 1. Nashville: Abingdon, 1981.

Thurner, Manuela. "Better Citizens Without the Ballot": American Antisuffrage Women and Their Rationale in the Progressive Era." *Journal of Women's History* 5 (Spring 1993): 33–70.

Tindall, George B. *The Emergence of the New South, 1913–1945.* Baton Rouge: Louisiana State University Press and the Littlefield Fund for Southern History of the University of Texas, 1967.

Wallenstein, Peter. "Rich Man's War, Rich Man's Fight: Civil War and the Transformation of Public Finance in Georgia." *Journal of Southern History* 50 (February 1984): 15–42.

Walls, William J. *The African Methodist Episcopal Zion Church: Reality of the Black Church.* Charlotte: AME Zion Publishing House, 1974.

Walton, Haynes, Jr. and James E. Taylor. "Blacks and the Southern Prohibition Movement." *Phylon* 32 (Summer 1971): 247–59.

Webster, Irene. *Seventy-five Years of Service: History of the National Society Daughters of the American Revolution of North Carolina.* New Bern: Owen G. Dunn, 1975.

Weddell, Marsha. *Elite Women and the Reform Impulse in Memphis: 1875–1915.* Knoxville: University of Tennessee Press, 1991.

Welter, Barbara. "The Cult of True Womanhood: 1820–1860." *American Quarterly* 18 (Summer 1966): 151–74.

Wesley, Charles Harris. *The History of the National Association of Colored Women's Clubs: A Legacy of Service.* Washington, D. C.: National Association of Colored Women's Clubs, 1984.

Wheeler, Marjorie Spruill. *New Women of the New South: The Leaders of the Woman Suffrage Movement in the Southern States.* New York: Oxford University Press, 1993.

———. *VOTES FOR WOMEN! The Woman Suffrage Movement in Tennessee, the South, and the Nation.* Knoxville: University of Tennessee Press, 1995.

Whitener, Daniel Jay. *Prohibition in North Carolina, 1715–1945.* Chapel Hill: University of North Carolina Press, 1945.

Wiebe, Robert. *The Search For Order: 1877–1920.* New York: Hill and Wang, 1967.

Wilkerson-Freeman, Sarah. "From Clubs to Parties: North Carolina Women in the Advancement of the New Deal." *North Carolina Historical Review* 68 (July 1991): 320–39.

Williamson, Joel. *The Crucible of Race: Black-White Relations in the American South Since Emancipation.* New York: Oxford University Press, 1984.

Wilson, Carrie B. *History of the North Carolina State Division American Association of University Women, 1927–1947.* Greensboro: Riser, 1948.

Wilson, John. *Introduction to Social Movements.* New York: Basic, 1973.

Wood, Jean Dalziel. *A History of the North Carolina Society of the Colonial Dames of America.* N. p., 1935.

Woodward, C. Vann. *Origins of the New South, 1877–1913.* Baton Rouge: Louisiana State University Press and the Littlefield Fund for Southern History of The University of Texas, 1951.

Wyatt-Brown, Bertram. *Southern Honor: Ethics and Behavior in the Old South.* Oxford: Oxford University Press, 1982.

Contemporary Books and Articles

Anderson, Lucy London. *North Carolina Women of the Confederacy.* Fayetteville: Privately published, 1926.

Ashe, Samuel A'Court, Stephen B. Weeks, and Charles L. Van Noppen, eds. *Biographical History of North Carolina. From Colonial Times to the Present.* Old North State Edition. 8 vols. Greensboro, N. C.: Charles L. Van Noppen, 1905–1917.

"As To Women's Clubs." *Atlantic Monthly* 103 (January 1909): 135–36.

Blauveldt, Mary Taylor. "The Race Problem as Discussed by Negro Women." *American Journal of Sociology* 6 (March 1901): 664–65.

Bowden, A. O. "The Woman's Club Movement: An Appraisal and A Prophecy." *Journal of Education* 111 (1930): 257–60.

Breckinridge, Sophonisba P. *Women in the Twentieth Century.* New York: McGraw-Hill Book Co., Inc., 1933.

A Brief History of the Synodical of North Carolina with Minutes of the First Annual Meeting and the Minutes and Reports of the Second Annual Meeting. Charlotte: Presbyterian Standard, 1914.

Burroughs, Nannie H. "Not Color But Character." *Voice of the Negro* 1 (July 1904): 277–79.

Catt, Carrie Chapman and Nettie Rogers Shuler. *Woman Suffrage and Politics: The Inner Story of the Suffrage Movement*. 1923. Reprint, Seattle: University of Washington Press, 1969.

Confederated Southern Memorial Association. *History of the Confederated Memorial Associations of the South*. New Orleans: Graham, 1904.

Connor, R. D. W. and Clarence Poe, eds. *The Life and Speeches of Charles B. Aycock*. Garden City: Doubleday, Page, 1912.

Cotten, Bruce. *As We Were: A Personal Sketch of Family Life*. Baltimore: "Privately printed for the family only," 1935.

Cooper, Anna Julia. *A Voice from the South*. Xenia, Ohio: Aldine, 1892.

Cotten, Sallie Southall. *History of the North Carolina Federation of Women's Clubs, 1901–1925*. Raleigh: Edwards and Broughton, 1925.

Croly, Jane Cunningham. *The History of the Woman's Club Movement in America*. New York: Henry G. Allen, 1898.

Daniel, Sadie Iola. *Women Builders*. Washington, D. C.: Associated, 1931.

Daniels, Josephus. *Editor in Politics*. Chapel Hill: University of North Carolina Press, 1941.

Decker, Sarah S. Platt. "Meaning of the Woman's Club Movement." *Annals of American Academy of Political and Social Science* 28 (September 1906): 1–6.

Deland, Margaret. "The Change in the Feminine Ideal." *Atlantic Monthly* 105 (March 1910): 289–302.

Dew, Thomas. "Dissertation on the Characteristic Differences Between the Sexes." *Southern Literary Messenger* 1 (May 1835): 493–512.

"Feminine vs. Feminist. By the Author of 'An Englishwoman's Home.'" *Living Age*, 11th Series, 54 (1912): 587–92.

Fulton, David Bryant. "A Plea for Social Justice for the Negro Woman." Yonkers, N.Y.: Negro Society for Historical Research, 1912.

Granger, Mrs. A. O. "The Effect of Club Work." *Annals of American Academy of Political and Social Science* 28 (Sept. 1906): 50–58.

Harrison, Mrs. Burton. "Home Life as a Profession." In *Women and Womanhood in America*, edited by Ronald W. Hogeland. Lexington, Mass.: D. C. Heath and Company, 1973.

Hartshorn, W. N., ed. *An Era of Progress and Promise, 1863–1910*. Boston: Priscilla, 1910.

Henry, Josephine K. "The New Woman of the New South." *Arena* 11 (February 1895): 353–62.

Hobbs, Samuel Huntington, Jr. *North Carolina: Economic and Social*. Chapel Hill: University of North Carolina Press, 1930.

Hunton, Addie. "Negro Womanhood Defended." *Voice of the Negro* 1 (July 1904): 280–82.

Johnson, Guion Griffis. "Feminism and Economic Development of Women." *Journal of Social Forces* 3 (May 4, 1925): 612–16.

Kent, Mrs. Henry T. et al. *History of the Organization and Work of the National Society Daughters of the Revolution, 1891–1930*. Concord, N. H.: Rumford Press, n.d.

Lewis, Nell Battle. "History of the Woman Movement." *Raleigh News and Observer*, April 19, 26, May 3, 10, 17, 1925.

Mayo, A. D. "The Woman's Movement in the South." *New England Magazine* 5 (October 1894): 249–60.

McDougald, Elise Johnson. "The Task of Negro Womanhood." In *The New Negro*, edited by Alain Locke. 1925. Reprint, New York: Atheneum, 1983. With a preface by Robert Hayden.

McGehee, Eliza Skinner. "Woman's Place is in Her Home," *Sky-land Magazine* 1 (September 1913): 635–43.

McIver, Mrs. Charles D. "The Betterment of Public School Houses in North Carolina." *State Normal Magazine* 7 (October 1902): 56–60.

McKelway, Alexander J. "The Race Problem in the South—the North Carolina Revolution Justified." *Outlook* 60 (December 31, 1898): 1057–59.

Mendenhall, Marjorie Stratford. "Southern Women of A 'Lost Generation.'" *South Atlantic Quarterly* 33 (October 1934): 334–53.

Mims, Edwin. *The Advancing South: Stories of Progress and Reaction*. 1926. Reprint, Washington, N. Y.: Kennikat Press, 1969.

———. "The Southern Woman: Past and Present." Lynchburg, Va.: Bulletin of Randolph-Macon Woman's College 1 (July 1915).

Moffitt, Elvira Evelyna. "Biographical Sketch of Mrs. Spier Whitaker nee Hooper." *North Carolina Booklet* 13 (April 1914): 234–49.

———. "The N. C. Society Daughters of the Revolution and Its Objects." *North Carolina Booklet* 6 (October 1906): 148.

North Carolina Historical Commission. *Literary and Historical Activities in North Carolina, 1900–1905*. Raleigh: E. M. Uzzell, 1907.

North Carolina Library Commission. *The Handbook of the Citizens' Library Movement*. Charlotte: North Carolina Library Association, 1928.

Page, Walter Hines. *The Southerner: A Novel, Being the Autobiography of Nicholas Worth*. New York: Doubleday, Page, 1909.

Poppenheim, Mary B., et al. *The History of The United Daughters of The Confederacy*. Raleigh: Edwards and Broughton, n.d.

Richards, Clement, ed. *National Cyclopedia of the Colored Race*. Montgomery: National, 1919.

Roberson, Nellie. "The Organized Work of Women in One State." *Journal of Social Forces* 1 (November 1922): 50–55, (January 1923): 173–77, (September 1923): 613–15.

Sanders, Wiley Britton. *Negro Child Welfare in North Carolina*. Chapel Hill: University of North Carolina Press, 1933.

Shaw, Easdale. *History of the North Carolina Branch of the International Order of the King's Daughters and Sons*. Raleigh: Capital, 1929.

Silone-Yates, Josephine. "The National Association of Colored Women." *Voice of the Negro* 1 (July 1904): 283.

Stanton, Elizabeth Cady, Susan B. Anthony, and Ida Husted Harper, eds. *History of Woman Suffrage*. 6 vols. Rochester, N. Y.: 1881–1922.

White, Martha E. D. "The Work of the Woman's Club." *Atlantic Monthly* 93 (May 1904): 614–623.

Whitted, J. A. *A History of the Negro Baptists of North Carolina*. Raleigh: Edwards and Broughton, 1908

Wilson, Louis Round. "Library Development in North Carolina." *Library Journal* 48 (1923): 21–25.

———. "On The Progress of Our Libraries." *North Carolina Review* September 3, 1911, 7.

———. "State Libraries, Their Improvement." *North Carolina Review* January 1, 1911, 1–3.

Winslow, Helen M. "Story of the Woman's Club Movement." *New England Magazine* 38 (July 1908): 543–57; 39 (October 1908): 214–22, (November 1908): 301–10.

Wood, Mary I. *The History of the General Federation of Women's Clubs*. New York: Norwood, 1912.

———. "The Woman's Club Movement." *The Chautauquan* 59 (June 1910): 13–64.

Pamphlets

Chapel Hill, North Carolina. University of North Carolina. Louis Round Wilson Library. North Carolina Collection.

Brooks, E. C. *Women Improving School Houses; The Story of a Little Group of College Students Who Formed an Organization of 1,000 Women Who Have Revolutionized the School Buildings and School Grounds of a Whole State*. Extract from *World's Work*, September 1906.

Clark, Walter. *Legal Status of Women in North Carolina, Past, Present, and Prospective. Address before the Federation of Women's Clubs, New Bern, N. C. 8 May 1913*. N.p., 1913

Colored Orphan Asylum of North Carolina, Oxford, North Carolina. Oxford: Public Ledger Print, 1900.

Constitution, By-laws, and Rules of Order, of Farmington Union, No. 22, Daughters of Temperance of the State of North Carolina. Raleigh: A. M. Gorman—*Spirit of the Age* Office, 1852.

Cotten, Sallie Southall. *To the Women of North Carolina*. Raleigh, n. d.

Doak, Frances Renfrow. *Why North Carolina Voted Dry*. Raleigh: Capital, 1934.

Goldsboro Centennial Celebration, 1847–1947. Official Souvenir Program. Goldsboro: The Gate City of Eastern North Carolina.

McIver, Charles D. *Disfranchisement and Education*. Hampton, Va.: *Southern Workman*, 1901.

Mebane, C. H. *The Woman's Association for the Betterment of Public Schoolhouses in North Carolina*, Raleigh: Office of the State Superintendent of Public Instruction, North Carolina Department of Public Instruction, 1908.

Negro Supremacy Against White Supremacy in North Carolina. (Broadside).

Norris, Elizabeth E. *Historic Oakwood Cemetery*. Raleigh: Edwards and Broughton, 1990.

Southern Women and Race Cooperation: A Story of the Memphis Meeting, October Sixth and Seventh, 1920. N.p.

[Williams, Charlotte Bryan Grimes.] *History of the Wake County Ladies Memorial Association, Confederate Monuments in Capitol Square, Memorial Pavilion, the House of Memory, and the Confederate Cemetery.* Raleigh, 1938.

Woman's Association for the Betterment of Public Schoolhouses in North Carolina: A Bit of History. N.p., 1905.

Woman's Association for the Betterment of Public Schoolhouses in North Carolina. *Constitution and By-laws.* Greensboro, 1902.

Woman's Association for the Betterment of Public School Houses in North Carolina. Raleigh: Office of the Superintendent of Public Instruction, 1908.

Woman's Association for the Betterment of Public Schoolhouses in North Carolina. Introduction by J. Y. Joyner. Raleigh: Office of State Superintendent of Public Instruction, 1908.

Woman's Christian Temperance Union. *North Carolina Woman's Christian Temperance Union.* N.p., 1908.

Newspapers and Periodicals

Anchor
Charlotte Daily Observer
Charlotte Observer
The Crisis
Everywoman's Magazine
Monthly News (League of Women Voters, Durham, N. C.)
Mount Vernon Record
North Carolina Christian Advocate
North Carolina Temperance Union
North Carolina White Ribbon
(Pittsboro) Chatham Record
Raleigh Daily Call
Raleigh Daily Press
Raleigh News and Observer
(Salisbury) Carolina Watchman
Southern Workman
Spirit of the Age
Star of Zion
Tarboro Southerner
Tuskegee Institute News Clipping File. Microfilm Edition.
Union Signal
Wilmington Morning Star

Theses and Dissertations

Brinton, Hugh Penn. "The Negro in Durham: A Study of Adjustment to Town Life." Ph.D. Dissertation, University of North Carolina, 1930.

Byrd, John Timothy. "The Disfranchisement of Blacks in New Hanover County, North Carolina." M.A. Thesis, University of North Carolina at Chapel Hill, 1976.

Camhi, Jane Jerome. "Woman Against Woman: American Antisuffragism, 1880–1920." Ph.D. Dissertation, Tufts University, 1992.

Coleman, Willie Mae. "Keeping the Faith and Disturbing the Peace: Black Women From Anti–Slavery to Women's Suffrage." Ph.D. Dissertation, University of California–Irvine, 1981.

Correll, Emily Clare Newby. "Woman's Work for Woman: The Methodist and Baptist Woman's Missionary Societies in North Carolina, 1878–1930." M.A. Thesis, University of North Carolina at Chapel Hill, 1977.

Cotten, Jerry Wayne. "Negro Disfranchisement in North Carolina: The Politics of Race in a Southern State." M.A. Thesis, University of North Carolina at Greensboro, 1973.

Fields, Emma L. "The Women's Club Movement in the United States." M.A. Thesis, Howard University, 1948.

Gay, Dorothy Ann. "The Tangled Skein of Romanticism and Violence in the Old South: The Southern Response to Abolitionism and Feminism, 1830–1861." Ph.D. Dissertation, University of North Carolina at Chapel Hill, 1975.

Gilmore, Glenda Elizabeth. "Gender and Jim Crow: Black Women and the Politics of White Supremacy in North Carolina, 1896–1920." Ph.D. Dissertation, University of North Carolina at Chapel Hill, 1992.

Green, Elna C. "Those Opposed: Southern Antisuffragism, 1890–1920." Ph.D. Dissertation, Tulane University, 1992.

Hamilton, Tulia Brown. "The National Association of Colored Women, 1896–1920." Ph.D. Dissertation, Emory University, 1978.

Lallier, Rebecca Ragsdale. "'A Place of Beginning Again': The North Carolina Industrial Farm Colony for Women, 1929–1947." M.A. Thesis, University of North Carolina at Chapel Hill, 1990.

Leloudis, James L., II. "'A More Certain Means of Grace': Pedagogy, Self, and Society in North Carolina, 1880–1920." Ph.D. Dissertation, University of North Carolina at Chapel Hill, 1989.

MacMillan, Genevieve. "History of Higher Education of Women in the South." M.A. Thesis, University of North Carolina, 1923.

Miller, Bertha Hampton. "Blacks in Winston–Salem, North Carolina, 1895–1920: Community Development in an Era of Benevolent Paternalism." Ph.D. Dissertation, Duke University, 1981.

Nasstrom, Kathryn L. "'More Was Expected of Us': The North Carolina League of Women Voters and the Feminist Movement in the 1920s." M.A. Thesis, University of North Carolina at Chapel Hill, 1988.

Perry, Margaret K. "A Study of Social and Legal Changes of Status of Women Following the Civil War." M.A. Thesis, University of North Carolina, 1937.

Pope, Christie Farnham. "Preparation for Pedestals: North Carolina Antebellum Female Seminaries." Ph.D. Dissertation, University of Chicago, 1977.

Price, Margaret Nell. "The Development of Leadership By Southern Women Through Clubs and Organizations." M.A. Thesis, University of North Carolina, 1945.

Rankin, Richard, "Benevolence and Progress: Motives for Leadership of North Carolina's Evangelical United Front, 1814–1837." Ph.D. Dissertation, University of North Carolina at Chapel Hill, 1985.

Roth, Darlene Rebecca. "Matronage: Patterns in Women's Organizations, Atlanta, Georgia, 1890–1940." Ph.D. Dissertation, George Washington University, 1978.

Roydhouse, Marion Winifred. "The 'Universal Sisterhood of Women:' Women and Labor Reform in North Carolina, 1900–1932." Ph.D. Dissertation, Duke University, 1980.

Ruoff, John Carl. "Southern Womanhood, 1865–1920: An Intellectual and Cultural Study." Ph.D. Dissertation, University of Illinois at Urbana-Champaign, 1976.

Shadron, Virginia. "Out of Our Homes: The Woman's Rights Movement in The Methodist Episcopal Church, South, 1890–1918." M.A. Thesis, Emory University, 1976.

Shay, John Michael. "The Antislavery Movement in North Carolina." Ph.D. Dissertation, Princeton University, 1970.

Shivers, Lyda Gordon. "The Social Welfare Movement in the South: A Study in Regional Culture and Social Organization." Ph.D. Dissertation, University of North Carolina, 1935.

Spruill, Marjorie J. "White Supremacy and the Southern Ideal of Woman: A Study of the Woman Suffrage Movement in North Carolina." Honors Essay, Curriculum in American Studies, University of North Carolina, 1973.

Steelman, Joseph F. "The Progressive Era in North Carolina, 1884–1917." Ph.D. Dissertation, University of North Carolina, 1955.

Terborg-Penn, Rosalyn M. "Afro-American Women and the Struggle for Woman Suffrage." Ph.D. Dissertation, Howard University, 1977.

Wheeler, Marjorie Spruill. "New Women of the New South: Leaders of the Woman Suffrage Movement in the Southern States." Ph.D. Dissertation, University of Virginia, 1990.

Wilkerson-Freeman, Sarah. "The Emerging Political Consciousness of Gertrude Weil: Education and Women's Clubs, 1879–1914." M.A. Thesis, University of North Carolina at Chapel Hill, 1986.

———. "Women and the Transformation of American Politics: North Carolina, 1898–1940." Ph.D. Dissertation, University of North Carolina at Chapel Hill, 1995.

Published Minutes, Reports, Yearbooks, and Directories

Annual Report of the Board of Public Charities, 1907. Raleigh: E. M. Uzzell, 1908.

Annual Report of the Board of Public Charities of North Carolina, 1912. Raleigh: Edwards and Broughton, 1912.

Annual Report of the Board of Public Charities of North Carolina, 1913. Raleigh: Edwards and Broughton, 1914.

Annual Report of the Lindley Training School, Asheville, N. C., For the Year Ending March 31, 1900. N.p., n.d.

Biennial Report of the North Carolina State Board of Charities and Public Welfare, July 1, 1922 to June 30, 1924. N. p., n.d.

Biennial Report of North Carolina State Board of Charities and Public Welfare July 1, 1941 to June 30, 1944. Raleigh, 1944.

Daughters of the American Revolution of North Carolina. *Proceedings of the Annual State Conference.* 1901–1931. Publisher varies.

Daughters of the Revolution. *Proceedings of the Annual Meeting.* 1903–1930. Publisher varies.

Equal Suffrage Association of North Carolina. *Proceedings of the Annual Convention.* 1914–1920. Publisher varies.

King's Daughters and Sons of North Carolina. *Annual Convention.* 1902–1912

North Carolina Federation of Women's Clubs. *Yearbook.* 1902–1931. Publisher varies.

North Carolina Society of the Colonial Dames of America. *By-Laws and Directory,* 1904–1905. Wilmington: Wilmington Stamp Works, n.d.

North Carolina Society of the Colonial Dames of America. *Minutes of the Annual Meeting.* 1895–1930. Publisher varies.

Proceedings of the Ninth Conference for Education in the South. 1906. Richmond, 1906.

Proceedings of the Tenth Conference for Education in the South, 1907. Richmond, 1907.

Proceedings of the Eleventh Conference for Education in the South, 1908. Nashville, 1908.

Shuler, Nettie Rogers, ed. *Handbook of the National American Woman Suffrage Association and Proceedings of the Victory Convention . . . First National Congress League of Women Voters . . . Feb. 12–18, 1920.* New York: National American Woman Suffrage Association, n. d.

United Daughters of the Confederacy. North Carolina Division. *Minutes of the Annual Convention.* 1897–1931. Publisher varies.

Wagstaff, H. M., ed. *Minutes of the North Carolina Manumission Society, 1816–1834.* James Sprunt Historical Studies. Vol. 22. Chapel Hill: University of North Carolina Press, 1984.

Woman's Christian Temperance Union of North Carolina. *Minutes of the Annual Meeting.* 1883–1931. Publisher varies.

Work, Monroe, ed. *Negro Year Book.* 1913–1930. Tuskegee, Ala.: Negro Year Book.

Government Documents

Department of Commerce and Labor. Bureau of the Census. *Manufactures, 1905.* Washington: 1907.

Journal of the House of Representatives of North Carolina. 1885; 1929.

Journal of the Senate of North Carolina. 1885; 1929.

Public Laws of North Carolina. 1885; 1929.

United States Census Office. *Seventh Census of the United States, 1850. North Carolina.* Washington, 1853.

Index